Sacramental Theology

Herbert Vorgrimler

Translated by
Linda M. Maloney

A Liturgical Press Book

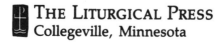
THE LITURGICAL PRESS
Collegeville, Minnesota

Cover design by Greg Becker.

Sacramental Theology was originally published by Patmos Verlag GmbH under the title: Herbert Vorgrimler *Sakramententheologie.* © 1987 Patmos Verlag. Third edition © 1992.

10

Library of Congress Cataloging-in-Publication Data

Vorgrimler, Herbert.
    [Sacramenten Theologie. English]
    Sacramental theology / Herbert Vorgrimler ; translated by Linda M. Maloney.
       p.   cm.
    Translation of: Sacramenten Theologie.
    Includes bibliographical references and index.
    ISBN 0-8146-1994-0
    1. Sacraments—Catholic Church. 2. Catholic Church—Doctrines.
3. Catholic Church—Liturgy. I. Title.
BX2200.V67 1992
234'16—dc20   92-12399
                                                 CIP

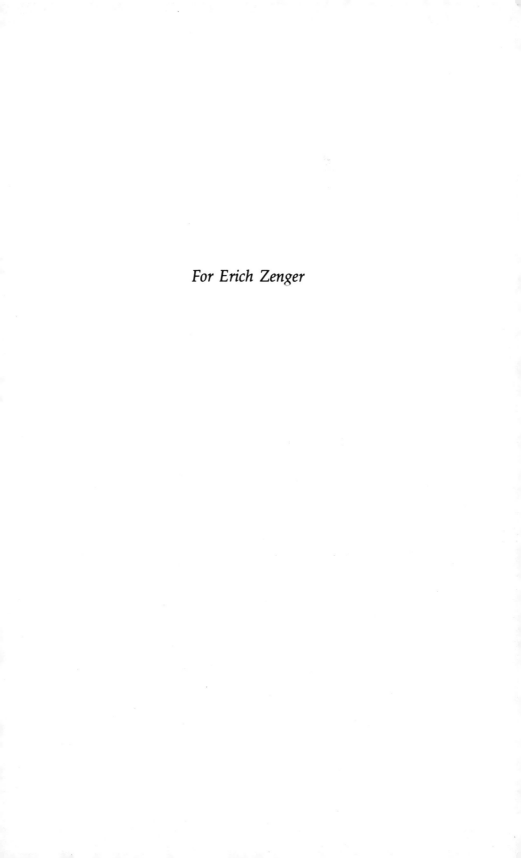

For Erich Zenger

Contents

Abbreviations xi

Introduction 1

1   *Theological Preconditions for Sacramental Theology* 5
1.1   Experience of God and God's Revelation 5
1.2   Images and Symbols of God 8
1.3   The "Sacramental Principle" in Jewish-Christian
      Tradition 12
1.4   Christian Theology, "Old Testament Sacraments,"
      and "Natural Sacraments" 15
1.5   Christological, Pneumatological, and Trinitarian
      Presuppositions 16

2   *Determining the Place of the Sacraments* 20
2.1   The Sacraments as the Church's Liturgy 20
2.2   The Subject of the Church's Liturgy 23
2.3   The Presence of Jesus Christ in the Liturgy 24

3   *The Sacramental Economy of Salvation* 27
3.1   Creation and Election as Sacrament 28
3.2   Jesus Christ as the Primordial Sacrament 30

3.3   Church as Fundamental Sacrament 32
3.4   Individual Sacraments as Actualizations of the
        Fundamental Sacrament 40

4   *The Sacraments in General* 43
4.1   The General Concept of a Sacrament................... 43
4.2   History of General Sacramental Theology 46
4.2.1   New Testament 46
4.2.2   The Church Fathers............................... 49
4.2.3   Middle Ages 50
4.2.4   The Sacramental Theology of the Reformers 55
4.2.5   The Church's Official Sacramental Teaching 57
4.2.6   The Development of Sacramental Theology
          after Trent 62
4.3   Limits and Structure of General Sacramental Theology
        and Doctrine of the Individual Sacraments 66

5   *Fundamentals of General Sacramental Theology* 68
5.1   Symbolic Liturgical Actions as Mediation of the
        Presence of God..................................... 68
5.1.1   Effective Symbolic Event 68
5.1.2   Jesus Christ as Author of the Sacraments 73
5.1.3   The Number Seven and the Inequality of the
          Sacraments....................................... 75
5.2   Sacrament—Event of the Word of God 76
5.3   Sacrament, Prayer, and Discipleship 79
5.4   Sacraments of Faith................................. 82
5.5   Sacraments as Mediation of Divine Grace 86
5.6   Sacrament and History............................... 89
5.7   Sacraments of the Church........................... 90

        Bibliography 1 94
        Bibliography 2 100

6   *Baptism* 102
6.1   Biblical Foundations 102
6.2   The Rite of Initiation............................... 107
6.3   Historical Decisions................................ 109
6.4   Baptism of Children 113

6.5	Ecumenical Perspectives	116
6.6	Summary	117
	Bibliography 3	119
	Bibliography 4	120
7	***Confirmation***	122
7.1	Biblical Foundations	122
7.2	Historical Decisions	125
7.3	Summary	129
	Bibliography 5	131
8	***Eucharist***	132
8.1	Introduction	132
8.2	Biblical Foundations	137
8.2.1	The Last Supper Accounts	137
8.2.2	Other New Testament Texts	143
8.2.3	Summary and Problems	144
8.3	Concept and Basic Form of the Eucharist	148
8.3.1	The Fundamental Liturgical Form	148
8.3.2	The Concept of Eucharist	152
8.4	Historical Stages and Decisions	153
8.4.1	The Development of a Eucharistic Theology	153
8.4.2	Concentration on the Real Presence	156
8.4.3	Scholastic Theology of the Eucharist	160
8.4.4	Reformation Teaching on the Lord's Supper	164
8.4.5	The Real Presence	166
8.4.6	The Sacrifice of the Mass	172
8.4.7	The Eucharist and the Office of Priesthood	180
8.4.8	Vatican Council II	184
8.4.9	Communion	187
8.5	The Renewal of Eucharistic Theology	191
	Bibliography 6	195
9	***The Sacrament of Reconciliation***	200
9.1	Preliminary Theological Questions	200
9.2	Forms of Forgiveness	203

9.3	Biblical Foundations	205
9.4	The History of the Sacrament of Reconciliation	207
9.5	Ecclesial Decisions	211
9.6	Summary	219
9.7	Indulgences	220

Bibliography 7 223

10	*Anointing of the Sick*	226
10.1	Biblical Foundations	226
10.2	The History of Anointing of the Sick	228
10.3	Ecclesial Decisions	230
10.4	Summary	234

Bibliography 8 236

11	*The Sacrament of Orders*	237
11.1	Introduction	237
11.2	The Origins of Office in the Church	242
11.2.1	Biblical Findings	242
11.2.2	Postbiblical Developments	248
11.3	The Development of Teaching about the Sacrament of Orders	253
11.3.1	From Antiquity to the Scholastics	253
11.3.2	Historical Decisions	255
11.3.3	Vatican Council II and the New Code of Canon Law	260
11.4	The Sacrament of Orders: Systematic Aspects	266
11.4.1	Bishop	266
11.4.2	Priest	268
11.4.3	Deacon	270
11.4.4	The Ordination of Women	270
11.5	Ecumenical Dialogue	274
11.5.1	The Perspective of the Eastern Churches	274
11.5.2	A Minimal Consensus	276
11.5.3	Questions Still Outstanding	277

Bibliography 9 278

12   *The Sacrament of Marriage* 283

12.1   Introduction 283

12.2   Biblical Foundations 286

12.2.1   Old Testament 286

12.2.2   Jesus and the Jesus Traditions 288

12.2.3   Paul and the Letter to the Ephesians 289

12.2.4   Additional Statements 290

12.3   Historical Decisions 291

12.3.1   The Development of a Theology, Liturgy, and Law of
Marriage 291

12.3.2   Statements of Earlier Church Teaching 296

12.3.3   Vatican Council II and the New Code of
Canon Law 301

12.4   Theology of Marriage: Summary 308

Bibliography 10 311

13   *The Sacramentals* 314

Bibliography 11 319

Additional Bibliography 320

Index 324

Abbreviations

AAS   *Acta Apostolicae Sedis* (Official teachings of the Pope and the Vatican congregations)

COD   *Conciliorum Oecumenicorum Decreta,* ed. G. Alberigo and others (Barcelona: 1962 and later editions)

DS   H. Denzinger and A. Schönmetzer, *Enchiridion symbolorum, definitionum et declarationum de rebus fidei et morum* 35th ed. (Barcelona: 1973). Citations are according to the numbers in the text.

EKL   *Evangelisches Kirchenlexikon,* ed. E. Fahlbusch and others, 3d rev. ed. (Göttingen: 1986ff.)

J. Finkenzeller I and II
       J. Finkenzeller, *Die Lehre von den Sakramenten im allgemeinen. Von der Schrift bis zur Scholastik* (Freiburg: 1980): (= J. Finkenzeller I); idem, *Die Lehre von den Sakramenten im allgemeinen. Von der Reformation bis zur Gegenwart* (Freiburg: 1982): (= J. Finkenzeller II)

HKR   *Handbuch des katholischen Kirchenrechts,* eds. J. Listl, H. Müller, and H. Schmitz (Regensburg: 1983)

LThK   *Lexikon für Theologie und Kirche,* 2d ed., eds. J. Höfer and K. Rahner (Freiburg: 1957–1965)

MySal *Mysterium Salutis, Grundriß heilsgeschichtlicher Dogmatik,* eds. J. Feiner and M. Löhrer (Einsiedeln, Zürich, and Cologne: 1965–1981)

NHthG *Neues Handbuch theologischer Grundbegriffe,* ed. P. Eicher (Munich: 1984–1985)

NR J. Neuner and H. Roos, *Der Glaube der Kirche in den Urkunden der Lehrverkündigung,* newly edited by K. Rahner and K.-H Weger 11th ed. (Regensburg: 1983). Cited according to the numbers in the text.

Schriften K. Rahner, *Schriften zur Theologie* (Einsiedeln, Zürich, and Cologne: 1954–1984)

ThWNT *Theologisches Wörterbuch zum Neuen Testament,* eds. G. Kittel and G. Friedrich (Stuttgart: 1933–1973)

TRE *Theologische Realenzyklopädie,* eds. G. Krause and G. Müller (Berlin and New York: 1976ff.)

The documents of the Second Vatican Council are denoted by the initial letters of the title, e.g., SC = Sacrosanctum Concilium; cf. *Kleines Konzilskompendium* (Freiburg: 1966 and later editions) 7–10.

For the abbreviation of the writings of classical theologians (Augustine, Thomas, etc.), see the lists in the corresponding articles of the theological dictionaries.

Introduction

From current theological discussions and from published materials devoted to the sacraments, we might often suppose that at the present time neither the mood nor the direction of thinking is favorable to the sacraments. The focus of many people on that which is scientifically demonstrable and technically possible, and the "strangeness of all that belongs to religion" in this world are given as reasons why sacramental actions are and will remain alienating. This kind of resistance occurs not only in the narrower forum of the sacraments themselves, but extends even beyond the ecclesial realm to affect Christian faith as a whole. But it should not be overlooked that many Christians also have only minimal interest in the sacraments. Sacraments are—quite rightly—considered to be symbols, and some Christians regard symbolic actions as an alibi, a convenient substitute for more difficult Christian praxis. It is quite often said that inhabiting this special, inner-churchly world focussed on the sacraments is a way of withdrawing from a Christianity expressed in deeds and in credible witness to the world at large. The restriction of the sacraments within prescribed courses of action makes impossible any of the spontaneous, creative expression for which so many people today are longing; the impression of constant, mechanical repetition contrasts sharply with hoped-for but always unexpected adventures in faith. In this way, a good part

1

of the critique directed at the Church today becomes a critique of the sacraments. In many places, under the influence of theological education, a historical-critical consciousness has arisen which in turn is used to exercise a rigorous critique of the origins and practice of the sacraments. In speaking, as we must, of the historical Jesus, we are conscious that an "institution" or establishment of sacraments by him is quite improbable. The practical shape of some sacraments reveals strong ecclesial interests that are not always religious in nature. It is often but a short step from the insight that something is "historically conditioned" to the judgment that it is "unimportant."

But other evidence contrasts with the reports of these and similar difficulties in bringing together present-day human experience and the Church's sacramental faith. A quest for that which is strange, which is at odds with the world of hi-tech, which is even religious is expressed in the flood of esoteric literature. There are any number of initiatives toward the realization of human encounter and community, and these include a new kind of ritual gestures.[1] Communication within the field of religion has become more lively; it is in search of new means of expression and is reviewing the possibilities contained in the older ones. Symbols are capturing the attention of more and more scholarly disciplines, and there is an increasing body of research on symbols.[2]

Theology is increasingly concerned with the "perimeter" where there are indications of new possibilities for understanding the sacraments. For example, there is an effort being made to construct anthropological approaches to the meaning of symbolic actions.[3] Theology is paying attention to the structures of external and internal apprehension and communication of knowledge, and concentrating on the indispensable function of human bodiliness in every form of communication. It is locating the sacraments within a context that is accessible to other scholarly disciplines as well, in terms of such phenomena as language-event and symbolic reality (in particular the notion of real

1. Cf. F.-J. Nocke, *Wort und Geste* (Munich: 1985) 11–58; U. Kühn, *Sakramente* (Gütersloh: 1985) 197ff.

2. E.g., depth psychology, psychoanalysis, religious studies, cultural anthropology, behavioral research, communications theory, computer science, etc. See also 5.1 below.

3. Successful examples are the approaches to sacramental theology of T. Schneider, "Die dogmatische Begründung" (see Bibliography 1) and F.-J. Nocke, *Wort und Geste*.

symbols). The ecumenical dialogue of the (still) separated Churches is at the present time concerned primarily with questions connected with the sacraments and has already discovered a number of common ideas (for example, on the relationship of word and sacrament).

These two contrasting realities, resistance to and renewed inclination toward the field of the sacraments, cannot be described in a single overview. I do not wish to tarry in the "foreground," making the sacraments acceptable on the basis of structures and experiences that occur elsewhere in the human context as well. But at the same time, the sacraments should not be viewed, in a kind of "legal positivism," as isolated institutions from God through Jesus Christ that stand out like foreign bodies within the remaining content of faith and theology. Instead, I want to proceed on the assumption that God's relationship to human beings cannot be other than "sacramental." Sacramental structures and events characterize the history of God with human beings from the beginning, i.e., as long as humans have existed, and therefore they are formative for all areas of theology, since theology is constructed in the form of "salvation history." But such a sacramental view of things is not a matter of course; it only becomes apparent when we take as our key the reality we call "revelation." In other words: faith is one of the indispensable preconditions for a sacramental theology. And faith, in turn, in its ecclesial shape and in its liturgical expression, is dialogically structured.

Therefore I would like first to demonstrate the preconditions of faith on which sacramental theology rests, and what is its place within the whole of theology. This will be followed by brief presentations of the concept of sacraments and the history of that idea, the teachings of Church tradition on sacraments in general, and the basic features of a sacramental theology. Next will come the theological explanations of the seven sacraments of the Catholic Church, including related topics such as indulgences and sacramentals.

I would like to conclude this introduction with some personal remarks. I had no assistance in the development of this sacramental theology, since an unusual burden of work, including the exercise of two professorates at one time and, in the third year, the duties of dean of the faculty, fully occupied the time of my assistants with other tasks. Therefore the bibliographies contain literature I have seen, but they make no claim to completeness. I am sure, however, that those who are interested in pursuing a single question in more depth can make a beginning on the basis of these overviews of the literature. I was very anxious to keep as much contact as possible with theology outside Germany, and I consider it anything but an advantage of the most recent German-language works in sacramental theology that they take no notice of foreign literature.

A graduate seminar held in cooperation with the Lutheran New Testament scholar Martin Rese on the subject of the Lima document, despite its friendly and collegial atmosphere, confronted the Catholic members continually and inexorably with the question: how can you protect your notion of sacraments from succumbing to the idea that you have control over divine grace? That question remains continually present in this book. If I myself were to describe this sacramental theology, I would say that it is ecumenical and also open to and ready for dialogue with Judaism, that it is liturgical-*theological* in nature, and that it seeks its foundation in Jesus-mysticism.

I dedicate the book to my friend and colleague Erich Zenger. I owe him gratitude for many reasons: because he is a master of the art of expounding the Old Testament as a book of life; because he is a tireless engine of Jewish-Christian dialogue, and because I have received from him some very concrete and inestimable assistance.

Münster, January 1987   Herbert Vorgrimler

1

Theological Preconditions
for Sacramental Theology

1.1 *Experience of God and God's Revelation*

The sacraments are a particular part of the relationship between God and human beings. This rather banal statement is intended to point out that reflection on the sacraments presumes a prior reflection on God's relationship with humans. God, as perceived in Jewish-Christian tradition, remains the great, impenetrable, and incomprehensible mystery. God is, in his inmost being, so different from human beings that groping thought cannot comprehend God, nor can human language fully and accurately describe him.[1] Of course, this is true in the other direction as well: immediate communication between God and the human person seems to be impossible, because of the total disparity between the two "partners."

But Jewish-Christian tradition, in contrast, for example, to Greek ideas of the divine, says that God was and is involved with the ut-

1. See the brief remarks and bibliography in H. Vorgrimler, *Theologische Gottes-lehre* (Düsseldorf: 1985) 21-37.

most concern in his creation, that God wanted and still wants to communicate with and be in touch with human beings. It understands the creation of the universe and of humanity as the work of the overflowing goodness of God, and human beings as the partners whom God seeks for intimate association. Because of the impossibility of entering into immediate communication, God's self-revelation to human beings requires a mediation that lies within their receptive capacity. Jewish faith-understanding conceived the idea that God, while remaining always within and present to himself, could reveal himself in a twofold way: through the divine word, and through spiritual indwelling.[2] To the extent that we can say anything by way of analysis about the processes by which God allows himself to be known ("reveals" himself), it is that people receive an internal insight, or are carried along by an impulse that they cannot trace to their own normal experiences, but in which, instead, they feel themselves carried outside themselves (they go beyond or transcend themselves). Since such experiences contain something that terrifies human beings, that runs contrary to their ordinary desires, they cannot be wishful dreams or projections. It is true that they can be called "experiences of the self," but with the distinction that the self here grows beyond its own dimensions, by aid of a dynamic that is not produced from within, but is given by another. Experiences like these, which transcend the human, always require interpretation. Interpretation is already taking place when someone organizes his or her own experiences conceptually, and it is certainly occurring when the individual attempts to explain them (the interpreted experiences) to others. No one is forced to believe that God's own dynamic has been communicated to the human person, that God has personally spoken a word within the human heart. To put it another way: God's self-testimonies toward human beings are not so compelling that a person cannot freely deny them. Human acceptance and acquiescence should take place on the basis of faith, and not on the basis of evidence (i.e., certainty founded on proof). If a person is convinced that God has revealed himself to her or him, and if that person accepts this utterance of God, the dialogical character of the process, expressly recognized or not, becomes evident. A "yes," no matter what form it takes, to God's leading, is prayer.

2. This is evident from Jewish concepts of the divine *logos* and of God's *shekinah*, ideas that were, in any event, possible within the boundaries of orthodox Judaism.

Jewish and Christian theology calls the process just described "revelation." According to the testimonies of faith, it takes place primarily within the human person, at the place where the person is not yet divided between intellectual insight and the impulse of the will, but is still the original unity: in the person's "conscience," as tradition says, in his or her "heart." "God is more interior to me than I am to myself," in Augustine's words.[3] But revelation happens not only within individuals (who, in fact, are not isolated units by the very fact of being oriented to and dependent on language). It can also find entry through human exchange of experiences and information. God can be apprehended from outside one's own self, in the way God has communicated himself and continues to communicate in other people or in events, in human deeds or in happenings (actions) that also involve the non-human sphere of the created universe. When people exchange these experiences of God, and allow their acknowledgment of a common conviction, common memory, and shared prayer to grow out of that exchange, communities of faith arise, communities we call Church.

To this point we have spoken of the way in which God's revelation takes place, but not of its content. We have not addressed the question of the kind of God whom God has communicated and is communicating. The God who, according to Jewish and Christian faith, has desired to begin a common history with human beings and to carry that history to a successful end, is inclined in love to human beings and intends all-encompassing goodness (*shalom*) for them. This God, as the love that overflows itself, seeks to be close to people. When God allows himself to be known in the intimate depths of a human person, God's very self is there. When God's word and God's glory (*shekinah*) are present to human beings, they do not "represent" an absent God; instead, they present the manner in which God is most intimately present within the human person. "Human beings" here refers to everyone, since the saving will of God excludes no one from divine love. But that does not yet fulfill the purpose of this God who has come so close to us. God's love is concrete, and has a concrete goal. It is embedded in a humanity that is always resistant to it. In the face of this resistance, it seeks to change humanity in such a radical way that, as a community of just, reconciled, peaceful people, it is prepared to accept God's unrestricted rule forever. According to the

---

3. "Interior intimis meis," *In Ps.* 118, 22, 6 (German translation from E. Przywara).

faith of Jews and Christians, God is continually at work in making himself available, creating a hearing and a response to himself, in order to achieve God's final purpose in creation. One of the true mysteries of a religious view of history is the question of how far human beings can succeed in preventing God (whom the believer regards as all-powerful) from achieving his ends. It is, at any rate, a matter of experience that a great many people have refused to acknowledge God's closeness and have refused to practice God's revealed will. This indicates a dependence of God on human beings, which of course does not mean that God lets himself be manipulated by humans. But the ways in which God is present are always vulnerable: people can be blind to them or misinterpret them. That changes nothing in the reality of God's presence, but it can hinder its effectiveness. We do not mean to say that experiences of the absence of God are only subjective self-deceptions. The faith demanded of Jews and Christians is not merely a blindly optimistic trust in a "loving God." It is subject to darknesses that cannot be traced simply to human guilt, but it is called upon to hold fast to God's desire for a continuing, effective presence, and to the demonstration of God's power within history, if only at that history's end.

Having stated these basic preconditions of faith[4] for an understanding of the sacraments, we turn to a discussion of their more immediate theological presuppositions.

1.2 *Image and Symbols of God*

A more precise beginning point for a theology of sacraments is the faith-conviction just mentioned, that God's revelation, the knowledge of God, God's communication of the divine will and God's presence are given to us humans only through mediation, and are not immediate to us. But how shall we understand this mediation more precisely? God's presence and will are communicated through persons and/or events. This communication is not "news about," "information," "tidings"—it is God's very self. God is internal to human persons or

4. These are more fully discussed in various special areas of theology. Therefore, for a deepening of understanding, one should turn to treatments of the philosophy of religion and fundamental theology (especially the ways of knowing God and of divine revelation), and dogmatic works on the theology of creation and of grace.

events in order to approach people in love, to change them, to impel them to further action, to move them to advance together with creation on the way home to God. At the same time, human beings do not cease to be human, and the events remain human accomplishments: in both, God is present and active, without destroying their uniqueness. That is the "sacramental structure" or "sacramental principle" that penetrates the whole history of God and humanity, and that also shapes every individual human life, whether that person knows it or not.

Since the word *sacrament*, from which the adjective *sacramental* is derived, is a term appropriated by technical ecclesial language, and since an explanation of it would indeed constitute an entire sacramental theology, we should ask at this point whether there are other concepts with which we can more precisely explain "sacramental structure" or "sacramental principle."

An honorable tradition of culture holds that an *image* or picture can make the subject (especially a holy person, an angel, even God) present. This has been a powerful conviction in Christianity, not only because of the influence of Platonic philosophy (in which the subject, the archetype, is present in the image), but because it is validated especially by the New Testament theology of the image. It finds even today a concrete expression in the theology and veneration of icons in the Eastern Churches. Incense and candles before the icon are presented to the one or ones who are believed to be spiritually and mystically present in the image. In Western terms we could certainly call an icon of the Trinity or of Christ "sacramental": mysterious divine presence in a visible form. If the possibility of understanding "sacrament" on the basis of the theology of images is not pursued here, it is because the image can only be a limited and static part of the sacrament, since it lacks the living element that is present either in persons (including their interpretive and responsive speech) or in events. Still, the pictorial or imaging element must always be mentioned in any discussion of the sacraments.

In the language of theology and of the Church, another concept has been applied to the sacraments since ancient times: they are called "symbols."[5] "Symbol," which originated in antiquity to describe a

---

5. This usage goes back to Augustine's (d. 430) theory of signs. By way of Gratian's *Decretum* (ca. 1142) it reached the Council of Trent which, in 1551, described a sacra-

sign of recognition, can, like the word "sign," refer simply to an indicator, in the sense of a signpost or signal for something distant or absent. In that sense it cannot describe the "sacramental structure." Karl Rahner (d. 1984) pointed out in a fundamental essay[6] that in the strict and proper sense a symbol is never a mere pointer, but is always a "real symbol." This is based on the philosophical consideration that all being[7] necessarily creates its own "expression," in order to come to itself, to discover its own being. That means that all being is necessarily "symbolic." A being realizes itself by expressing itself. To put it another way: a symbol is effective because it brings a being to reality. That is what is meant by "real symbol": a genuine symbol does what it symbolizes. Rahner's favorite example is the human body: the human being is only "real" in the fundamental symbol of his/her body; the human spirit "expresses" and realizes itself in its bodiliness. External bodiliness "means" the human spirit acting within it. A further exploration of this line of thought about symbols belongs to theological anthropology.[8] Anyone who has understood the essential character of symbolism cannot play off the "merely symbolic" against the "real."

If all human reality is symbolic reality, this is certainly true of the relationship God has willed to establish with human beings, and that decisively shapes human reality from beginning to end. If God desires to be present to human beings, God's presence must create a symbolic expression for itself in order that it can be "real" for human beings, since the complete disparity between God and the human makes an unmediated presence and communication of God impossible. Thus in this case "symbolic expression" means that God, in order to reach human beings, to be given or uttered to them, is present in a created medium that retains its created uniqueness, but is transparent to an interpretive recognition of God. A turning toward this medium does not imply ordinary growth in knowledge or information; instead, it

ment as "symbolum rei sacrae" (DS 1639), translated by Neuner/Roos as "sensible sign of a sacred reality [sinnfälliges Zeichen einer heiligen Sache]" (NR 571). See also M. Schmidt, ed., *Typus, Symbol, Allegorie bei den östlichen Vätern und ihre Parallelen im Mittelalter* (Regensburg, 1982).

6. "On the Theology of Symbols" (1959), in *Schriften zur Theologie* IV, 275–311.

7. German: "alles Seiende."

8. Still valid is the essay by F. P. Fiorenza and J. B. Metz, "Der Mensch als Einheit von Leib und Seele," in *MySal* II (1967) 584–632.

is a self-opening of the human person for God's self-communication, an opening that is not the autonomous work of the human person, but is caused by the prevenient grace of God. Thus it is *in* the turn to this medium that the person becomes conscious of the most intimate nearness of God; it is here that revelation occurs.

A theology that pursues these ideas systematically will conclude that the whole reality we humans encounter is imbued with symbolic or sacramental possibilities. The life that is given to us, the people we encounter, the beloved one, the companions who live in solidarity with us, our work and its products, those events in life that really touch and shake us (and above all, death itself), experiences of liberation, justice, and reconciliation, true works of art, God's creation that makes up the world with us and around us: all these can be so transparent to God that they reveal God's true presence. In this way, our whole life can be understood as the fundamental sacrament,[9] to the extent that our understanding of life and our interpretations take account of this transparency and do not remain on the banal surface of things.

In terms of the history of theology, this idea was always present from the time Israel began to reflect on God's self-revelation. In the course of the Reformation there arose a great degree of doubt about whether creation and human life could be understood sacramentally in this way. If human beings are fundamentally deformed, of themselves they can only obscure God even more. It would seem that only God's own word (but how can we recognize it as God's?) and the signs given uniquely by God can provide security. Jews and Catholics, in contrast, have insisted on the transparency of creation—until Auschwitz. This word representative of the radical threat to humanity and creation shows how much sacramental thinking is dependent on faith, a faith that is endangered by the deepest darkness. It lives out of memory and out of hope for the fulfillment of the promises of God.

9. On this, see A. Schmied, *Perspektiven* (see Bibliography 1), section VI: ''Sakramente und 'Gottesdienst des Lebens.' '' The approaches in L. Boff's *Kleinen Sakramentenlehre* go more deeply into these reflections. This recognition is key to insights into the types of faith and the possibilities for salvation of non-Christian people, as discussed by K. Rahner under the term ''anonymous Christianity.'' We cannot discuss this subject further at this point. Cf. E. Klinger, ed., *Christentum innerhalb und außerhalb der Kirche* (Freiburg: 1976); N. Schwerdtfeger, *Gnade und Welt. Zum Grundgefüge von Karl Rahners Theorie der 'anonymen Christen'* (Freiburg: 1982).

1.3   The "Sacramental Principle" in Jewish-Christian Tradition

The common life of faith communities is based on agreement on experiences of God that are acknowledged by the community as authentic and binding. Since human experiences of God always have a sacramental structure, it follows that there are two basic kinds of sacraments or symbols: those that tend to have only individual validity and are determined by the particular situation, and can happen to anyone at all times; and those that are recognized within a faith tradition as the special places or events in which the presence of God is to be found. We will speak first of this second kind.

In the Jewish and Christian tradition, a privileged place in which God is present is called: the human being. "And God said: let us make humankind in our image, according to our likeness . . . So God created humankind in his image, in the image of God he created them, male and female he created them" (Gen 1:26-27, New RSV). The way in which Genesis (here the Priestly writer) speaks of human beings as the image of God has a threefold meaning. The second and third parts have to do with the protection and careful upbuilding of creation. But the first element is explained by Erich Zenger in this way:

> From the meaning of the Hebrew word *saelaem*, human beings are to be a kind of living picture or statue of God in the world. In the mind of the ancient Orient and early Egypt, an image of a god represents the god who is depicted and is the vehicle of the god's power. It is, so to speak, the place from which the divinity extends its effectiveness. The image of the god signalizes the where and how of the divine life and activity. Images of the gods were therefore treated as though they were living things. They are like a body into which the living god enters, in order to be present and active within the world through that body. Against this background of interpretation, the human beings, as living images and statues of the creator God, are to be the media of the power of divine life on earth.[10]

---

10. E. Zenger, "Das Geheimnis der Schöpfung als ethische Vor-Gabe an Juden und Christen," *Damit die Erde menschlich bleibt*, eds. W. Breuning and H. Heinz (Freiburg: 1985) 36–60, at p. 44. The more precise exegetical foundation is in E. Zenger, *Gottes Bogen in den Wolken. Untersuchungen zu Komposition und Theologie der priesterschriftlichen Urgeschichte* (Stuttgart: 1983) 84–96 (with discussion of other translations and interpretations). On page 87 of that book, Zenger refers to E. Otto: "It thus makes no sense to seek a special characteristic in the human beings that makes them the image of God. The human being as such *is* that image. Moreover, if the meaning of the Egyptian attribution of power to images is that the king as

This notion of the human being makes clear why, according to the will of the creator God, it is possible to encounter God in encountering other human beings, to love God in loving other humans, and to honor God in honoring other human persons. Here the sacramental principle emerges: the representation of God does not mean the substitution for one who is absent (or, still more, a replacement), but indicates the real, and not only the imaginary or the intellectual, making present of the one who in and of himself cannot be visible in our human dimension. It is also clear how much sacrament/symbol can be threatened by misunderstanding and misuse. It can happen that people are not honored and respected as the images of God who make God present, but are disgraced and reviled; they can also dishonor themselves and thus make their symbolic nature a lie.

Hans Urs von Balthasar (b. 1905) developed an essential aspect of this Jewish and Christian idea of the human being as sacrament/symbol in his reflections on the human being as word of God:[11] since the human person has received from God an essence that finds an expression of itself through speech, human beings themselves are capable of becoming the word of God. This quality of the human essence is fully realized in the incarnation of the Word of God, in whom at the same time a human response to God's word is accomplished.

The faith statement concerning human beings as image/sacrament of God certainly does not rest on the Genesis passage alone, though this has been highly influential in the tradition. It is found throughout the entire Jewish and Christian idea of the human,[12] an idea that has remained effective until the present day. From the Christian point of view it is found, for example, in Karl Rahner's thesis of the unity of human love and the love of God.[13] Among Jews, it is the basis both

'image' is the representative of God on earth, then the divinity appears where the king appears. Israel's tradition regarding the human being corresponds to this: where the human being is, there is God."

11. H. U. von Balthasar, "Gott redet als Mensch," in his *Verbum Caro* (Einsiedeln: 1960) 73–99.

12. Translator's note: in light of current discussion on the existence or non-existence of a cultural synthesis that can accurately be described as "Jewish/Christian" or "Judaeo-Christian," I have consistently rendered this expression in the text as "Jewish and Christian."

13. This is extensively described, with its sources and implications, in A. Tafferner, *Die Einheit von Gottes- und Nächstenliebe in der Theologie Karl Rahners* (Diss. Liz., Munich: 1986), with bibliography.

of the dialogical philosophy of Martin Buber and of Emmanuel Lévinas' reflections on the Other as the inviting access to transcendence. Against the background of the Old Testament's sensibility toward strangers, widows, and orphans, Lévinas understands the experience of God as a "search for [divine] traces in the countenance of the other."[14]

The presence of God is also realized, according to the "sacramental principle," in historical events and dimensions. The best event that can be cited from the Jewish tradition is the Exodus of the people from their slavery in Egypt.[15] Here we can clearly recognize the difference between a banal and superficial understanding and an interpretation in faith that looks beneath the surface. What appears to a hasty glance as the fortunate escape of a tiny group of slaves through the border defenses is in reality a breaking out and growing beyond the human dimension that cannot be explained on the basis of human strength alone, combined with the recognition that God's will aims at justice and freedom. God wishes to participate in the festive memorial of liberation, "so that the *whole nation* may see the glory of the Exodus God who is present in its midst, and welcome this God in praise and gratitude."[16]

Israel, as people of God, is, from more than one point of view, a historical, sacramental/symbolic entity. When the people are gathered to a festal celebration, when they hold services of atonement and thanksgiving at the sanctuary, the God who calls together the liberated community appears in glory.[17]

This sacramentality is valid in the first instance for Israel itself. But Israel is called and assembled for the sake of the other nations as well. In the common festival "of free human beings" (and to speak in more modern terms, we should say "free and equal") God's command is fulfilled, "by the example of their lives to show what, in the last analysis, are the goal and meaning of the created universe given by the creator God to all peoples."[18]

14. Cf. J. Becker, *Im Angesicht des Anderen—Gott erfahren* (Frankfurt: 1981).
15. E. Zenger, *Das Buch Exodus* 2d ed. (Düsseldorf, 1982): *Concilium* 23 (1987) no. 1.
16. E. Zenger, *Das Geheimnis der Schöpfung*, 54.
17. Ibid.
18. Ibid.

1.4 *Christian Theology, "Old Testament Sacraments," and "Natural Sacraments"*

The preceding discussion of the "sacramental structure" has employed the words *sacramental* and *sacrament* in a broad, not specifically theological sense. Classical theology of the sacraments also recognized, in the history of God with humanity *before* Jesus Christ, the existence of sacraments in the narrower sense and called them "natural sacraments" or "Old Testament sacraments." In identifying sacraments in Israel before Jesus Christ, Christian theology concentrated narrowly on institutionalized rites and objects. Special attention was given to circumcision as a mark of the covenant and sign of salvation. Thomas Aquinas (d. 1274) mentions a great number of "Old Testament sacraments,"[19] including especially the Paschal lamb. Circumcision and the Paschal lamb, the signs of salvation that played a role in the life of Jesus the Jew, must obviously be acknowledged. In a process of thought that began as early as Paul and his disciples, the sacraments of the old covenant were regarded as true signs of divine favor which, however, had lost their effectiveness when the new covenant came into force (Col 2:11). In the eyes of Christians, they were only "shadows" of good things to come (Heb 10:1). This corresponds to a concept of salvation history that is still widely held, namely that the old covenant was dissolved by the new, and that the Church as the new Israel had replaced the old. This took no account of the fact that God's gracious promises and call could not be revoked (Rom 11:29), and that God had never abrogated either the covenant with the Jews or that with the people before Israel (the Noachic covenant). It is to be hoped that Christian theology will arrive at a more nuanced concept. A theology of incarnation based on the will of God to enter into God's own creation and, in the human Jesus of Nazareth, both to pledge God's own self to humanity and to effect the acceptance of that pledge, can certainly make clear that everything is to be understood in relationship to Jesus Christ (Col 1:15ff.). A "typological" interpretation of the Bible as we see it developing within the New Testament, which, for example, sees Moses or the Paschal lamb as a "type" (anticipatory image) of Jesus Christ, must not devalue the type: it can accept it in its unique validity. Paul's

19. Cf. K. Rahner, "Sakramente, alttestamentliche," in *LThK* IX, 239–240.

statement "that our ancestors . . . all drank the same supernatural drink, for they drank from the supernatural Rock which followed them, and the Rock was Christ" (1 Cor 10:1-4) has no necessary connection with the subsequent statement that "with most of them God was not pleased."

Under the concept of "natural sacraments," sacramental theology discusses the question whether there were and are (a) in human history *before* the Jewish-Christian revelation or (b) in non-Christian, non-Jewish humanity up to the present day symbols—primarily cultic ones—of divine presence and activity ("embodiments of the general saving will of God," as Otto Semmelroth wrote).[20] If, as here, we are speaking in a broader and not institutionally fixed sense of sacraments/symbols, an affirmative answer must of course be given to both questions. Undoubtedly there are events in individual and community life that disturb and fascinate us (such things as being born, common meals, sexuality, death) and therefore incline people to surround them with rites, and in this way to pay attention to the deeper dimensions of their being and to give heed to the presence of God. In the face of the fundamental (even though often endangered or obscured) symbolism of human life and human history it is probably superfluous to seek for legally definable divine institution or particular, individual symbols in connection with this subject. Beginning with the supposition that God's will to save is directed to *all* human beings, and that God alone knows all God's effective means of salvation, Christian faith must take account of God's saving presence in all places and at all times, without needing to pass a nervous judgment on non-Christian symbols.

1.5 *Christological, Pneumatological, and Trinitarian Presuppositions*

Among the necessary preconditions for understanding sacramental theology, the faith conviction that in Jesus of Nazareth, God's self-communication to human beings has occurred in an ultimate and unique fashion is essential. The biblical witnesses to the "historical Jesus" are not sufficient. Their "implicit Christology" is, of course, indispensable for sacramental theology. That Jesus knew himself to

20. Cf. O. Semmelroth, "Natursakramente," in *LThK* VII, 829–830. On the classical theology of the pre-Christian sacraments, see J. Finkenzeller I, 66–68 (preScholastic), 90–93, 99–100 (early Scholasticism), 148–157 (high Scholasticism).

be sent by God; that he constantly and fully turned to God in prayer and action; that his praxis of helping, liberating, and reconciling human beings was inextricably bound up with this relationship to God; that Jesus knew himself to be the authentic revealer of God's will; that he addressed himself to human senses and opened them to a deeper dimension; that, despite his prophetic criticisms of the cult, he had a positive relationship to the symbolic actions of his people: these characteristic features of the person and work of Jesus are basic to sacramental theology. But they could only arise from meditation in faith on the Easter events. From that meditation grew[21] the thematic Christological and soteriological interpretation of the person and work of Jesus, leading ultimately to the dogma of Chalcedon, the statement of the unity of divinity and humanity, without separation or mixture, in Jesus of Nazareth. The resurrection of Jesus shed new light on his life and death. It became clear—in faith—that this life was and is the transparent shape and form of the presence and activity of God. The possibility of being "sacrament," which in principle applies to every human being, a possibility so often obscured and blocked, was realized to its ultimate here, in this person who made no resistance to God, who was sinless because he was completely possessed by God.

In Jesus, as seen in the light of Christological dogma, it is evident how the God who comes to us in the greatest intimacy, who desires to communicate God's very self—God in that which can be expressed about God, i.e., God as "Logos"—needed a created form, a human expression, in order to be recognizable to human beings. In Jesus we can recognize how the most intimate nearness of God does not reduce or destroy the uniqueness and autonomy of our createdness, but instead liberates it to be itself. According to Christological dogma, the unseparated and unmixed unity of divinity and humanity penetrates the whole life of Jesus from its earliest beginnings to its fulfillment in God. That means that not only the "official" high points of this life (birth and death) are realization and expression of the presence of God, God's love and God's salvation, but that God is also "expressed" in the tiniest and most humdrum parts of life. From this follow two important preconditions for sacramental theology. First, a separation of reality into sacred and profane realms is impossible within Christian faith. A sacred realm (i.e., related to the "sacrum," the "holy") would

21. Cf. H. Vorgrimler, *Theologische Gotteslehre* (see n. 1) 62–68.

absorb people and things that are removed from the "profane" and are ordered exclusively to God, reserved to God, and close to God alone. In contrast, the incarnation of God in Jesus of Nazareth affirms that the realm in which God comes to human beings, communicating God's own self and remaining with them, is not removed from the world, no matter how depraved that world may seem to us to be. Christian separation from the evil in this world thus does not express itself in the creation of a sacred space, and the religious realization of Christianity cannot consist in sacred actions. The second point is that even the unique presence of God in Jesus, in order to be recognized as such, required the "eyes of faith" and interpretation; it was not evident in and of itself and it was only accepted where people did not close themselves against the insight offered by God. Thus God's revelation, even in Jesus, does not exclude a genuine hiddenness of God, but includes it. God's nearness is not only concealed in the modest humility of a human life (creaturely disguise), but is obscured also in the terrible death of the cross (culpable disguise). The "message about the cross" (1 Cor 1:18-30) is an abiding guide for sacramental theology.

Among the preconditions in faith for an understanding of the sacraments is the conviction that God did not abandon to death this Jesus whom God had sent, but accepted him into the divine dimension. According to the witnesses of faith, God accomplished the rescue of all that is human and mortal in Jesus through the divine Spirit, who is able to give to all that is earthly and passing away a new, imperishable being. The humanity, the bodiliness of Jesus is, from this point on, filled and enlivened by the Spirit; it is spiritual (pneumatic) and thus freed from the limitations of time and space.

The same divine Spirit is, after Jesus' passage to God, the way in which God remains present to human beings, communicating God, making Jesus present to them and animating them to enter into the mission of Jesus.[22] The Spirit gives them—us—the ability to understand the life and work of Jesus within the divine mystery and thus to understand its deeper dimensions, which must remain concealed from those who are mere historians. What the Church is in its inmost being, what makes the sacraments to be what they are, simply cannot be understood apart from the divine Spirit. The Spirit not only effects a per-

---

22. On this point, see the pneumatologies in Y. Congar, *Der Heilige Geist* (Freiburg: 1982), and C. Schütz, *Einführung in die Pneumatologie* (Darmstadt: 1985).

sonal, individual understanding of Jesus and his mission, but also prepares believers to receive Jesus from the Church, whose insights into Jesus' reality are always more comprehensive than any private image of him. That has very concrete consequences for our approach to the New Testament in the matter of Church and sacraments; it includes the willingness to accept the ongoing, Spirit-driven unity of the exalted Jesus with the Church that we call the "body of Christ"; it means accepting as authentic the theological developments that go beyond the Synoptics and are connected with the names of Paul and John; it also leads us to acknowledge as legitimate work of the Spirit the sacramental testimonies in the New Testament that, as research has revealed, are certainly community creations from the early days of the Church. It is the Spirit of God who, as animator of the Church, drives it forward in history; it is this Spirit who seeks to teach the Church the right way of witnessing to its faith, wishing to preserve it from stagnation and from looking only backward; and it is this Spirit who seeks to illuminate the obscuring of its presence caused by human guilt. Acknowledging the Spirit therefore requires that we accept the necessity of changes and reforms, in the sacramental realm as well.

The Spirit keeps humanity in motion—the humanity that from the very beginning is and has been Church,[23] and the institutionally constituted Church that has grown from Israel, its vanguard[24]—keeps it on the way that began in the eternal, incomprehensible mystery of God and will find its end there as well. Trinitarian theology calls this divine ground of all that is and will be by the name with which Jesus addressed God: "Father." This is the self-overflowing love from whom proceeded, in different ways, Word, Spirit, and humanity, in order that creation and humanity may be prepared as the realm of God's glory. Sacramental theology, concentrating on the field of symbols, considers the twofold direction of this movement, from God to humanity in the sending of the Son and the Spirit, and from humanity, together with the Son and the Spirit, to the glory of God the Father.

---

23. Still important on this subject: Y. Congar, "Ecclesia ab Abel," *Abhandlungen über Theologie und Kirche*, ed. R. Reding (Düsseldorf: 1952) 79–108.

24. Cf. J. Daniélou and H. Vorgrimler, eds., *Sentire Ecclesiam*. Festschrift for Hugo Rahner (Freiburg: 1961).

2

Determining the Place of the Sacraments

2.1 *The Sacraments as the Church's Liturgy*

Now it is possible to determine the more precise theological place of the sacraments: the sacraments are an essential part of the Church's liturgy. This needs some further explanation.

In the course of the renewal of reflection on the Church that has occurred during this century, there have been repeated attempts to summarize the Church's tasks in a few significant concepts. Certainly, a formula like this has achieved a certain ecumenical consensus: the Church seeks to follow Jesus through divine worship, proclamation, service to others and to society[1] or, in other words, *leitourgia, martyria, diakonia.* Such a description of the fundamental tasks of the Church is certainly less problematic than Vatican Council II's reference to the derivative concepts of the offices of priest, teacher, and shepherd (much in need of clarification), which belong to Jesus Christ and to the Church (the hierarchy and all other members) as a whole.[2] But there is always

1. See H. Häring, "Kirche/Ekklesiologie," *NHthG* II (1984) 310. The article offers a good systematic overview (309–323) of the problems of ecclesiology.
2. Cf. L. Schick, *Das dreifache Amt Christi und der Kirche* (Frankfurt and Bern: 1982). See also n. 11 below.

a temptation to give a one-sided emphasis to one of these tasks, namely the liturgy, and to devalue the other two by comparison. If the Church is not a purely human, sociologically definable grouping, but the body of Christ that lives only with and from its head, so that *all* successful actions of the Church are, and necessarily must be, the result of the initiative and aid of the divine Spirit, it must remain for God to decide which of the concrete tasks of the Church is preeminent. The liturgy, of which the sacraments are an essential component, cannot be regarded from the outset as the highest form of the Church's realization. That was always clear to the great theologians: God has not "chained" divine grace to the sacraments.[3]

These considerations should be kept in mind when we ask what liturgy really is, or how to define it. Emil Joseph Lengeling (1916-1986), summarizing official Catholic tradition, formulated it as follows: "Liturgy is the actualization of the new covenant, carried out by the church community through Christ, the mediator between God and humanity, in the Holy Spirit, under effective signs and according to proper order."[4] But a problem emerges here: "covenant" is a designation for the relationship to God that can be used only with qualifications;[5] in employing the notion of a "new covenant" we should be careful that it is not misused so as to devalue the "old covenant;" the proper relationship, willed by God, is also realized in the Church through "martyria" and "diakonia." These, too, are "sacramental" in a wider sense to the extent that they are tangible and visible evidence of God's real presence. With these exceptions, the definition is well adapted to sacramental theology. In what follows, the expressions of Vatican Council II will always form part of the basis of our discussion. This council was not only heir to the liturgical movement of this century, but itself developed a notable liturgical theology.[6]

3. Aquinas, *S. th.* III, q. 64, ad 7c.

4. *NHthG* III (1985) 29. Lengeling's whole article, "Liturgie/Liturgiewissenschaft" (26–53) is very informative.

5. Old Testament research has shown that in the final redaction of Deuteronomy the notion that God is related to his people Israel by means of a kind of contract between lord and vassal was abandoned: YHWH is a faithful God whose indescribable fidelity is not connected with human fulfillment of a contract. The concept of covenant has a juristic coloring and does not, of itself, include the ideas of love and graciousness.

6. Cf. F. Eisenbach, *Die Gegenwart Jesu Christi im Gottesdienst. Systematische Studien zur Liturgiekonstitution des Zweiten Vatikanischen Konzils* (Mainz: 1982).

Of essential importance is the insight, consequent on the theology of grace that has been presupposed, that liturgy is made possible and empowered by God; it is God who incorporates those who entrust themselves to God in the liturgy into the great homeward movement to God. It is true that liturgists like to speak of two aspects or components of liturgy,[7] and they are right to do so. The "descending" or "katabatic" aspect refers to God's sanctifying "descent" in the Holy Spirit; the "ascending" or "anabatic" aspect describes the glorifying of God the Father, which is worship or cult in the narrower sense. But the two components should not be thought of as if only the first were the work of God, and the second purely human activity. And God's "coming" may of course not be interpreted to mean that God had not been present "before." Human beings are only able to give praise to God through the divine Spirit who dwells within them (Rom 8:26; 5:5). In this connection we should keep in mind that Jesus Christ and the Church may never be identified with one another (contrary to the common 19th-century notion that the Church is "the continuation of Christ's life" on earth), but that there is one and the same divine Spirit in the head and members of the body of Christ.[8]

The "actualization of the new covenant" in the definition of liturgy refers to the covenant terminology in the Last Supper accounts (especially 1 Cor 11:25; Luke 22:20). The "new covenant" means the whole of the saving actions of Jesus Christ, his work of redemption (to employ the common theological shorthand for that which Jesus was and did for us). In the liturgical constitution of Vatican II the "work of redemption" (SC 2; 5) is also called "work of salvation" (SC 6) or "mystery of Christ" (SC 35; 102). It encompasses his whole life until his coming at the parousia (SC 102), with its highpoint the "paschal mystery" (SC 5). By "actualization of the new covenant," the definition of liturgy, which, as we have said, incorporates a whole ecclesial tradition, means the salvific making-present of this whole reality of the saving works of Jesus. But since those works are not separable from the person of Jesus, and since faith presumes that Jesus and his saving works are living in God's presence, and that neither, through any

---

7. E. J. Lengeling, (see n. 4 above) 30ff. Vatican Council II calls these two components "sanctification" and "glorification" (SC 7).

8. H. Mühlen, *Una mystica persona* 3d ed. (Munich and Paderborn: 1966) 359–598 (on the pneumatic ecclesiology of Vatican II).

human power, can be truly made present or brought into an existential moment of time, it is Jesus Christ himself who creates this presence in the Holy Spirit (as the definition says: "carried out . . . through Christ . . . in the Holy Spirit"). This brings up an ancient topic: especially with reference to the Eucharist, there has existed for many centuries a question about how a past event can be really present, and how the presence of Jesus Christ can be more precisely understood.[9]

For our subject, sacramental theology, it is important to understand at this point *who*, in the conviction of the Catholic Church and its theology, is the subject (the active agent) of the liturgy and *how* the presence of Jesus Christ in the liturgy should be regarded.

2.2 The Subject of the Church's Liturgy

The theological position of Vatican II on the subject of liturgy can be summarized as follows:[10] Jesus Christ is not simply an object of memory, or a constant basis or origin of the liturgy; Jesus Christ is, rather, the present, really active subject of all liturgical actions that are relevant to the salvation of human beings. He thus joins to himself the Church, which is only a secondary subject of the liturgy, since it is always dependent upon and turned toward him.

That Jesus Christ is the primary subject of the liturgy, its active agent and principal actor, is an idea that may be traced to the theology of the Fathers of the Church and their meditation on the sacramental texts of Paul, John, and particularly the Letter to the Hebrews; Augustine deserves particular mention. The basis of these reflections is, of course, the faith conviction that Jesus was raised from the dead, exalted, and lives forever with God, and that he wills to act in order to fulfill his task of gathering all humanity and bringing it to the Father.

Dependent on Jesus Christ, and not acting on its own, the Church is the secondary subject of the liturgy. Vatican Council II made a num-

9. The topic is of great ecumenical importance. The most promising perspectives rest on reflections initiated by Odo Casel, which have been repeatedly taken up and clarified, and that have also attracted considerable respect among Lutherans and others. Cf. F. Eisenbach (n. 6 above); A. Schilson, *Theologie als Sakramententheologie. Die Mysterientheologie Odo Casels* (Mainz: 1982). See also 8.5 below.

10. I am dependent here, though with my own emphases, on F. Eisenbach (see n. 6 above), 217–218. The principal texts are SC 7 and 47.

ber of efforts to strengthen awareness of the fact that *all* believers are the Church. Among these are the emphases on the people of God (LG 9–16) as the primary body that includes clerics and laity, and the statements about the *common* priesthood of all believers (SC 14; 48; LG 9; 10; 26; 34). The fact that the council regarded it as necessary, at the same time, to give repeated emphasis to hierarchical distinctions and competencies does not alter the fundamental concept that all members of the Church are active agents of the liturgy.[11]

This kind of talk about "the Church" can seem too abstract. Who, concretely, is the Church that, in its service to Jesus Christ, is the secondary agent of the liturgy? According to a constant teaching witnessed by many of the Fathers of the Church and reappropriated by Vatican II, the Church in its concreteness is the assembled community, no matter how small. The concrete secondary subject of the liturgy is the community assembled for worship. What Church is and what its core is (its essence, its mystery) relative to human salvation is both realized in the liturgical assembly, even the tiniest one, and thereby proclaimed as such to the outside world. And it is precisely in this that Jesus Christ is made present.[12]

2.3 *The Presence of Jesus Christ in the Liturgy*

The praxis of the liturgy, and thus of the sacraments, is based on the faith conviction that Jesus, in whom divinity and humanity were and are united, desires to be and is able to be really present, as the living and exalted one, to those who believe in him and have oriented their lives to him. This faith conviction, in turn, is founded on experiences of the presence of Jesus risen from the dead: "Where two

11. Cf. H. Vorgrimler, "Liturgie als Thema der Dogmatik," in K. Richter, ed., *Liturgie—ein vergessenes Thema der Theologie?* (Freiburg: 1986) 113–127, especially 125ff., with cautions against a liturgy exclusively "from above."

12. K. Rahner, "Über die Gigenwart Christi in der Diasporagemeinde nach der Lehre des Zweiten Vatikanischen Konzils," *Schriften* VIII 409–425. A genuine action of the Church takes place when members of the Church, empowered and supported only by the grace of God, address their prayer to God. As K. Rahner has shown (despite the objections of J. Pascher), no authorization from ecclesial authorities is necessary for a prayer "in the name of the Church." On this, see F. Eisenbach (n. 6 above), 273–274. The new Code of Canon Law of 1983 has, accordingly, abandoned the distinction between private and church blessings; see 13 below.

or three are gathered in my name, I am there among them'' (Matt 18:20).

The idea of the presence of God in the assembled community is part of the fund of convictions common to Judaism and Christianity. The assembly of Israel (*qahal*, which appears in the Greek translation of the Old Testament as *ecclesia*, those who are called out →Church) lives consciously in the presence of God. As the mysterious, glory-filled *shekinah*, God dwells with or in human beings. "When two sit together and words of Torah are between them, the *shekinah* abides with them," says the Mishnah (Sayings of the Fathers III 2). That the assembled community *causes* the presence of God is not the Christian conception of divine worship, nor is it the Catholic notion of liturgy. The community as (dependent) subject of the liturgy is oriented, in faith, hope, and love, to the coming of God and can only pray for that coming. This prayer trusts in the promises of the Risen One.

But what does "presence" mean in this connection? Karl Rahner developed the idea[13] that presence, for human beings, is always mediated presence. It always requires a "medium" that is humanly perceptible. This is true also of the presence of God as soon as this presence, passing beyond its silent, abiding being-there within creation, makes a breakthrough within the human heart, and reaches the level of human consciousness. From a theological point of view there is only *one* presence of God, namely, God's self-communication to what is not God. But this presence is experienced and consciously perceived in different *types* of presence, in which God's presence as grace affects human beings dynamically. This effect may always have different levels of intensity. The goal, however, is always the same: genuine, grace-filled, personal communication between human beings and God.

The foregoing thoughts on the mediated presence of God require further precision with regard to the liturgy. In terms of Trinitarian theology we may say that the presence of God promised in the liturgical assembly is not simply that eternal, ineffable divine mystery that Jesus addressed as his Father and ours. It would be wrong to think that the liturgy makes God the Father present. Instead, it is *we* (also) who in and by means of the liturgy are made present to God the Father, are brought before his face: *through* his Son Jesus *in* the Holy Spirit. The

13. K. Rahner, "Die Gegenwart des Herrn in der christlichen Kultgemeinde," *Schriften* VIII, 395–408.

divine Spirit who is the common possession of Jesus and of the community is, in the liturgy, the medium of the presence of Jesus,[14] his person and the whole of his life and fate. The precise ways in which this medium—the Spirit of God—is active in the liturgy, bringing about the presence of Jesus in his person and actions, are the symbolic actions of the church (or "effective signs"—preeminently the sacraments—as the definition of liturgy cited above expresses it), in which Jesus is the real actor, the Word whose voice is heard when it is proclaimed, read or meditated as the word of God, as also in the prayer and song of the assembled community (SC 7).

It should be clear from what has been said that God's becoming present through Jesus in the Holy Spirit is effected through the initiative of the divine Spirit, and that initiative is also the author of the faith of the Church, which is celebrating the liturgy. But this making-present of God reaches its *goal* only when the means of mediation, especially the liturgy, are consciously and emotionally brought into awareness. Self-surrender to the liturgy, whose basis and bearer is always Jesus Christ, means in every case (and thus in every sacrament) remembering Jesus. Participation in the liturgy is a celebration of the memory of Jesus, and its intensity depends on the Jesus-mysticism of the human being who is taking part. That participation is always a self-surrender to the will of God revealed in Jesus, and thus its intensity is also measured by one's willingness to engage in a praxis of life that accords with that of Jesus.

14. Ibid., 398.

3

The Sacramental Economy of Salvation

"Sacramental thinking" is a way of understanding. The word "sacramental" in this sentence is broadly conceived. It refers to the faith experience that tells us that a reality perceptible to the senses, an external object or event, is "more than," "deeper than" the surface reveals at first glance. The word "sacramental" was consciously chosen, in reference to a point of view proper to Christian faith, because the deeper, interior reality that makes use of the external as its mediator is the reality of the transcendent God. The word "sacramental" is more precise in this context than the word "symbolic," since everything sacramental is symbolic (in the sense of real symbols), but not everything symbolic is sacramental, since not every (real) symbol mediates the presence of God.

In a specifically Catholic conception, the history of God with humanity has a sacramental structure, in the sense that the movement proceeding from God and, through the whole course of human history, returning home to God, is continually taking on more precise sacramental characteristics. For our understanding of faith, "more precise" here means that these sacramental characteristics do not rest merely on human understanding and human interpretation, but are connected with the express promise and effective guarantee of God.

It is true that this point of view goes back to the concept of God's Christocentric historical saving activity, founded on New Testament theology and most pregnantly expressed in the *Symbolum*, the creed. This historical saving activity of God, the *oikonomia*, certainly takes place in a theo-logical framework: it originates in the overflowing love of the Father and, in glorifying him, leads back to him, in order that he may be ''all in all'' (1 Cor 15:28). ''In between,'' however, everything is concentrated on the historical expression of that in God which can be expressed, the radical self-communication of God to what is not God, the coming of God in human flesh. ''The whole *oikonomia* is Christ-event. It is not that Christ communicates himself to the Spirit, but that the whole belongs to him (as objective-historical work, described in the Symbolum), and thus it all belongs to the Spirit, which is of Christ—as that which he is to make his own.''[1]

The event that begins with creation is Christ-event and thus sacramental in a non-institutional sense. On the other hand, the taking possession of creation that proceeds from the Spirit of Jesus Christ is sacramental in an institutional sense. This corresponds to a simple division of the sacramental economy of salvation: creation and election as sacrament—Jesus Christ as primordial sacrament—Church as fundamental sacrament—the individual sacraments as actualizing fulfillments of the fundamental sacrament.

3.1   *Creation and Election as Sacrament*

Our faith in creation tells us that the eternal and uncreated God, in sovereign freedom, brings into existence that which is utterly different and, by affirming it, keeps it in being. God's relationship to human beings, which is a fixed component of Jewish and Christian faith, is something different from what is affirmed in this brief description

---

1. A. Grillmeier, ''Christologie,'' in *LThK* II, 1156–1166, at 1161. The whole article is very enlightening for the relationship between *theologia* and *oikonomia* in Christian tradition. See also the good overview of the rediscovery of and research on the sacramental economy of salvation in the twentieth century by C. E. O'Neill in *Bilanz der Theologie im 20. Jahrhundert* III, eds. H. Vorgrimler and R. Vander Gucht (Freiburg: 1970), 252–261.

of creation faith. First of all: God wishes to be present to the consciousness of human beings, to come to an understanding with them, to open
up to them the meaning and goal of their lives. This happens in that
God reveals Godself, by means of created reality, as one who is Father,
one who is interested in human beings. Humans cannot be aware of
this utterly different God, this spiritual reality living in a different
dimension, except by some sensible mediation. When these created
realities are transparent to God, and when human beings give a religious interpretation to their experiences of those realities, a fundamental faith results. It does not consist in a human idea that they can take
control of that supernatural power—which would be magic—but instead, it is the recognition of one's complete, creaturely dependence
on God, and a humble assent to the goal proposed by God. Human
beings can give a physical expression to this faith in visible signs or
symbolic actions, and in so doing can reproduce situations in which
God is recognized. Who would deny that God, whom no one seeks
without already having found him, can use such occasions to create
a gracious encounter with Godself? These are what classical theology
called "natural sacraments."

The Jewish faith tradition proclaims additional experiences: that
God, in choosing one people, desired to communicate God's concrete
will to all humanity, to abide permanently among men and women
who desired to unite love of God and love of humanity in such a way
as to create the right conditions for the whole human world to become
the reign of God. Although the fundamental difference between God
and human beings means that God's encounter with God's chosen
ones must still be mediated, two outstanding "sacramental structures"
exist for that mediation: the communication of God's word in human
words, and the assembly of those who remember, give thanks, praise
God, and make reparation. Of course, both these structures are dialogical in character, and are combined with responsive and petitionary prayer. It is especially in the liturgical assembly of the children of
Israel that, to look at it from a Christian theological point of view, we
find the "Old Testament sacraments."

Later Christian fixation on isolated rites as representing the "Old
Testament sacraments" was conditioned by schematic ideas about the
"matter" of a sacrament. It ought to be evident that a ritual act like
circumcision, which was rooted both in national and in hygienic interests, cannot claim the same status as a worshipping assembly of the

chosen people. The example shows how problematic it is for Christians to make judgments "from outside" about those non-Christian signs and symbolic actions in which an encounter with God may take place. We should simply remark at this point, regarding other non-Christian religions, that there is no evident reason why there should not be "extra-Christian sacraments" in those religions as well.

But the sacraments of Israel are something different: not only because the Jews remain the chosen people of God, whose gifts are never taken away, but also because the word of God given to human beings in and through Israel retains its validity for the Church, and because the liturgical assembly of Israel that calls on God's presence in its prayer remains, from more than one point of view, connected with the Church's liturgy.

3.2 *Jesus Christ as the Primordial Sacrament*

The faith conviction that Jesus is the sacrament of God is deeply rooted in the New Testament. The witnesses to the events of his life, his dealings with human beings, show how much he was, in his very person, a "sign," a making-visible of the presence of God. (This life also reveals the dangers to which a sacrament is subject: e.g., temptation, fear.) His whole life, but especially its high points or the great moments, and his death, are real symbols of the concrete presence of God. In addition, we have the interpretation given them by Jesus himself: the word-event that took place in him also had sacramental character, the ability to make God present.[2]

The later understanding of Christ reflected in the New Testament gave the first emphasis to this sacramentality of Jesus. Without losing his personal character, says Augustin Schmied, Jesus as the Christ attracted to himself the power of primal human symbols (light, wellspring, shepherd, door, bread).[3] He could be called the icon, the image of God pure and simple (2 Cor 4:4; Col 1:15),[4] the visible epiphany

---

2. On this, see the indications listed by A. Schmied, "Perspektiven" (see Bibliography 1).

3. Ibid., 19.

4. C. von Schönborn, *L'Icône du Christ* 2d ed. (Fribourg, Switzerland: 1978) shows that there is a genuine salvation-historical-typological and Trinitarian-Christological theology of original and image that is not Platonic in origin.

of the invisible essence of God (Heb 1:1-2; 1 John 1:1; also John 14:9). The Christological dogma of Chalcedon, from 451 (NR 178/DS 301) gave additional depth to this sacramental understanding of Jesus. It is precisely when God's intention regarding humanity is evident, in the fact that God desired to communicate his own self, utter himself in humanity, that it is clear that God only arrived at this goal, free from interruption or danger, when his communication and affirmation received full acceptance from the human side. The most intimate closeness of God (God's essence, uncreated grace) and receptive human nature as its real symbol (effective sign) are present in Jesus, unseparated and without confusion. Of course, this formula also makes evident the limits of Christological dogma: the event-character of this unsurpassed union of God and humanity, its dynamic nature, is at most implicit in the rather static statement about two united natures.

The *description* of Jesus Christ as sacrament rests on New Testament theology of the *mysterion*.[5] In the Letters to the Ephesians and the Colossians, *mysterion* does not refer to something secret, but to God's saving intent as revealed and realized in the course of the divine *oikonomia*. Its complete revelation and first realization happened in Jesus Christ (Eph 1:9-10; 2:11-3:13; Col 1:20, 26-27; 2:2; cf. also Rom 16:25-26). Therefore many Church Fathers, including the influential Augustine, call him the *mysterium Dei*. Since, in the old Latin translations of the Bible, the word *mysterium* was given as *sacramentum* (see 4.1), it was natural to call Jesus Christ the *sacramentum Dei*. Thomas Aquinas understood Jesus Christ to be "the fundamental sacrament, insofar as his human nature, as the instrument of divinity, effects salvation" (Wolfgang Beinert).[6] Martin Luther was probably referring to Augustine[7] when he said: "Sacred Scripture knows but a single sacrament, and that is Christ the Lord himself."[8] When the great nineteenth-century renewal of ecclesiology (see 3.3) occasioned a more penetrating reflection on the sacramentality of the Church and its relationship to the sacramentality of Jesus Christ, he was first referred to as "the great

5. Still basic is the article by G. Bornkamm, "mysterion," *TDNT* IV (1942; engl. 1967) 802-828.
6. *Summa Contra Gentiles* IV a. 41. W. Beinert, "Die Sakramentalität der Kirche im theologischen Gespräch," *Theologische Berichte* 9 (Zürich: 1980), 13–66, at 17–18.
7. "Non est enim aliud dei mysterium nisi Christus" (Ep. 187, 9, 34; CSEL 57/4, 113).
8. *Disp. de Fide infusa et acquisita* (WA 6, 86, 5ff.).

sacrament."[9] It appears that Carl Feckes (d. 1958) was the first person in the twentieth century who, in reviving these ideas, called Jesus Christ the "primordial sacrament [Ursakrament]" on whom rest the "sacramental world" of the Church and the individual sacraments (1934).[10] In the spirit of renewed Thomism and under the influence of an existential philosophy of encounter (experience of the Other), Edward Schillebeeckx (b. 1914) described Jesus Christ as sacrament of the encounter with God.[11] More precisely, he saw the humanity of Jesus Christ as the primordial sacrament, since it was in his humanity that there occurs the twofold movement consisting of the inbreaking of grace "from above," and the cultus of love of God "from below." In Karl Rahner's Christology—also developed before the council—Jesus Christ is understood as "the real presence in history of the victorious eschatological mercy of God in the world," or as "the sacramental primordial Word of God in the history of the one humanity."[12] The Second Vatican Council expressed the sacramentality of Jesus Christ, following the Christology of Chalcedon and that of Thomas Aquinas, without using the words "sacrament" or "primordial sacrament." In more recent Catholic theology, as far as I know, the interpretation of Jesus Christ as the primordial sacrament is universally accepted.

3.3   *Church as Fundamental Sacrament*

If Jesus Christ is the Living One, and if, in the Holy Spirit, he continues his mission of reshaping humanity until creation is perfected, to the glory of God the Father, all this presumes an effective work of the Risen One within humanity. The ecclesiology of the New Testament conceives the Church, from the beginning, as the community

9. W. Beinert, "Sakramentalität der Kirche," 22.

10. Ibid., 23. In ibid., 17, we find the note that the Lutheran canon lawyer Rudolf Sohm (d. 1917), in a research report first published in 1918, wrote: "The primal sacrament, for the old Catholic Church, is Christ himself."

11. E. Schillebeeckx, *Christ the Sacrament of the Encounter with God* (New York: Sheed and Ward, 1960). This is an abbreviated version of the second volume of his sacramental theology in the spirit of Thomas and in the light of current sacramental questions. The first volume was published originally at Antwerp under the title *De sacramentele heilseconomie,* and exists only in Dutch; it contains valuable material on the Church traditions relating to the whole of this third chapter.

12. K. Rahner, *Kirche und Sakramente* (Freiburg: 1960) 99.

of disciples who, filled and guided by the divine Spirit, continue the mission of Jesus Christ. This continuation of the saving work of Jesus Christ is never conceived in the New Testament in such a way that the Church takes over the task given to Jesus, becoming the representative of someone who is absent and attempting to replace him. Instead, the very earliest self-concept of the Church affirms that it recognizes its complete dependence on Jesus Christ, as it is being formed by the Holy Spirit into a useful instrument of the continuing presence of Jesus Christ. The description of the local church as the body of Christ made up of many members united by the divine Spirit, as described in Romans and 1 Corinthians, with Jesus Christ as its head (Ephesians, Philippians), is more than merely an image; we may add to it the figures of the Church throughout the New Testament, all of which acknowledge the complete dependence of the Church on its true, not merely human, shepherd, bridegroom, vinedresser, builder, etc.[13] It was precisely because of this subordination and dependence that the earliest Church was conscious of being able and required to render true service, as the instrument of God, for the salvation of human beings, a service through word and sacrament (as the later expression has it), in which, as the Church fulfills itself or is actualized (to use a later expression), Jesus Christ is present as the one who really speaks and acts.

The New Testament also tells us that even the earliest Church carried out its service in very imperfect fashion. Christians failed in many ways, and their sins damaged the Church itself (which, in its penitential practice, sought to restore the form God willed for it). The Church was threatened, from the beginning, by the temptation to make of itself an independent organization, to become the object of its own proclamation, not to act according to the pattern of God's will revealed in Jesus, but instead to react in the manner of "this world," not to entrust itself to the movement initiated by the divine Spirit, but to be fixated on its own traditions.

The Church's place in the history of God with humanity, in the *oikonomia*, was characterized from the beginning by its relative and

---

13. These images are collected in *Lumen Gentium* 6–7. In this connection, attention should be given to the ecclesiology of Miguel M. Graijo Guembe, whose publication was, at this writing, planned for 1988. For a Lutheran viewpoint, see U. Kühn, *Kirche* (Gütersloh: 1980).

provisional position (and it is precisely these features that marked and mark its radical difference from Jesus Christ): its service is directed ultimately to the honor of God, but in the first instance it is for the sake of human beings and their union with God; the Church's task was and is only to mediate what has been given to it; it was not and is not intended by God to be the final form of humanity, since it will be surpassed in the reign of God.

This brief description of the theological components of the Church makes clear that here we find a continuation of that sacramental structure that was discussed earlier. As a community of believing human beings who desire to follow Jesus, the Church has an external, visible dimension that points to something deeper. Its inner dimension is constituted by the fact that Jesus Christ, in the Holy Spirit, makes it his sign and instrument, which he uses in order to carry out his work of renewing and reshaping humanity, to the glory of his Father. The external dimension is thus like an historically and communally structured sign that does not point to a foreign, absent entity, but to one who is present, one who is the real agent of the whole. The human community that constitutes the external reality cannot even hope and pray, on its own initiative, to be fit for this service, unless hope and prayer are given to it by the divine Spirit. The external dimension is always threatened by misuse and thus in danger of obscuring and damaging the internal, gracious reality.

In view of this sacramental structure of the Church it was inescapable that the Church itself be called a sacrament. This meant applying the broader concept of sacrament to the Church, at a time when the narrower, "technical" concept of sacraments did not even exist.

We must be content at this point with some sketchy remarks on the *history* of this designation.[14] The sacramentality of the Church was expressed by the Fathers in an even greater variety of images than is found in the New Testament. Hugo Rahner (d. 1968) summarized some

14. More detail can be found in W. Beinert, "Sakramentalität der Kirche"; J.-M. R. Tillard, in *Initiation à la pratique de la théologie* II (Paris: 1983) 387–391 (on the sacramentality of the Church); W. Kasper, "Die Kirche als universales Sakrament des Heils," *Glaube im Prozeß*, eds. E. Klinger and K. Wittstadt (Freiburg: 1984) 221–239 (with bibliography); T. Schneider, "Die dogmatische Begründung der Ekklesiologie nach dem Zweiten Vatikanischen Konzil. Dargestellt am Beispiel der Rede von der Kirche als dem Sakrament des Heils für die Welt," *Renovatio et reformatio*, eds. M. Gerwing and G. Ruppert (Münster: 1985) 80–116 (with bibliography).

of them: "The Church is on pilgrimage and yet already at home. Her heavenly earthiness, so to speak, is part of her indispensable twofoldness. She is, as the most recent theology again emphasizes and as the Fathers of ancient times already knew, the great sacrament directed toward the reign of God, the mother who dies in giving life, the moon who decreases as it approaches Christ the sun, the ark from which the rescued family of God goes forth when it reaches shore in the kingdom of peace."[15] The sacramental concept is applied to the Church by way of the *mysterion* (Ephesians), while in the East the first witness of this application is the *Didache* (Syrio-Palestine, first half of the second century), which calls the Church a "cosmic mystery." Cyprian (d. 258), the first Western witness, refers to the Church as "*sacramentum unitatis.*"[16] Important Church Fathers, including Augustine, referred to the sacrament (or *mysterium*) of the Church in the context of a description of the entire sacramental economy of salvation.[17] A fifth-century prayer (oration) that is still part of the liturgy, and was cited by Vatican II (SC 5), implores God to look graciously on "the wondrous sacrament of your whole Church."

In the wake of the development of a more narrow and technical concept of sacrament in the middle of the twelfth century, this sacramental view of the Church withdrew into the background (in contrast to Christology; cf. 3.2). The external, institutional dimension of the Church was overemphasized in reaction to all types of reform movements "from below."[18] With the rise of a renewed ecclesiology in the nineteenth century, the concept of "sacrament" as a designation for the Church in its deeper dimension was rediscovered, and not only in the romanticism of the first half-century, but also among the neo-Scholastics of the second half. Special mention is due to the theologians Johann E. Kuhn (d. 1887),[19] Johann H. Oswald (d. 1903),[20] and Matthias

---

15. H. Rahner, *Symbole der Kirche. Die Ekklesiologie der Väter* (Salzburg: 1964) 653.
16. Patristic references in W. Beinert, "Sakramentalität der Kirche," 15–17.
17. Ibid., 16–17.
18. Ibid., 18. Beinert points to Louis de Thomassin (d. 1695), the first modern theologian who again took up the theme of the sacramentality of the Church, in the context of the economy of salvation in which he views first humanity itself, then Adam and Jesus Christ as sacramental.
19. On his sacramental ecclesiology, see J. Finkenzeller II, 139–143.
20. Ibid., 145–148.

J. Scheeben (d. 1888).[21] After an interruption lasting until the 1930s, we see the development of the ecclesiology that became normative through Vatican II and continuing to the present.

In neo-Scholasticism there were occasional attempts to make clear conceptual distinctions between Jesus Christ, the Church, and the Church's individual sacraments. If Jesus Christ is called the "primordial sacrament," the Church is now the "higher sacrament."[22] Erich Przywara called it the "whole sacrament."[23] In an attempt to renew ecclesiology in the spirit of the Fathers of the Church, the French theologians Yves Congar (1937) and Henri de Lubac (1938) reapplied the perspective of the sacramental economy of salvation and the understanding of the Church as "sacrament."[24] The designation "primordial sacrament" was applied to the Church by Otto Semmelroth and Karl Rahner after the war.[25] To avoid the terminological confusion occasioned by simultaneously calling Jesus Christ the "primordial sacrament," and in order to highlight the enduring, qualitative difference between Jesus Christ and the Church, Semmelroth later referred to the Church as the "root sacrament,"[26] while Rahner called it the "fundamental sacrament."[27]

The Second Vatican Council took up the word "sacrament" as a designation for the Church.[28] Walter Kasper summarizes well the content and intention of the statement: "When this term is used by the

21. Ibid., 148–153.

22. This expression was used by C. Feckes, a scholar of great influence in ecclesiology, in 1934. W. Beinert, "Sakramentalität der Kirche," 23–24.

23. This was in a text from 1942: E. Przywara, *Ignatianisch* (Frankfurt: 1956) 98.

24. W. Beinert, "Sakramentalität der Kirche," 24–25. H. U. von Balthasar also understood the Church as sacrament; cf. most recently his *Theodramatik* II/2 (Einsiedeln: 1978).

25. W. Beinert, "Sakramentalität der Kirche," 25–29; on K. Rahner, see also J. Herberg, *Kirchliche Heilsvermittlung. Ein Gespräch zwischen Karl Barth und Karl Rahner* (Frankfurt: 1978).

26. *MySal* IV/1 (1972) 318–348.

27. *Grundkurs des Glaubens* (Freiburg: 1976) 396; E. Jüngel and K. Rahner, *Was ist ein Sakrament?* (Freiburg: 1971) 75.

28. The most important instances are: LG 1, 9, 48; GS 42, 45; AG 1, 5; see also the citations from the Church Fathers in SC 5, 26. For a more precise interpretation, see W. Kasper, "Die Kirche." Kasper points out that *veluti* ("also a sacrament") was inserted to satisfy those who were concerned about the sacraments as seven in number; "sacrament" is not used in the technical theological sense.

Second Vatican Council to refer to the Church, it is one conceptual method among others used to overcome ecclesiological triumphalism, clericalism and juridicism, and to represent the mystery of the Church that is concealed in its visible form and only evident through faith; to express and emphasize that the Church, on the one hand, proceeds totally from Christ and is always turned toward him, and on the other hand is completely a sign and instrument for service to human beings and to the world. The concept is especially well suited for relating and differentiating, in a nuanced way, the visible structure and spiritual essence of the Church.''[29] The council's sacramental ecclesiology thus fully intends to view the Church relatively, i.e., in relationship to the one, true author of salvation, Jesus Christ in the Holy Spirit according to the will of the Father. The council's unwillingness to locate the foundation of human salvation in the Church is the reason for its avoidance of a conscious application of the term "primordial sacrament" to the Church. Instead, it pointed to the simple analogy, that is, similarity in a still greater difference, between the mystery of Jesus Christ and the mystery of the Church, between the humanity of Jesus and the visible form of the Church (LG 8), in order to direct attention to the limits of a sacramental ecclesiology. The sacrament, "Church," according to Vatican II, exists in service to the salvation of all humanity. The council, in its most expressly theological documents, described this service more precisely: as *martyria* or service to the Word of God (Constitution on Divine Revelation; Decree on Missions), as *leitourgia* (Constitution on the Liturgy), as *diakonia* (Pastoral Constitution). The council declared in emphatic phrases that the Church will not complete this service; instead, the Church itself is preliminary and, together with its sacraments, will disappear (LG 48). God alone remains both the author of salvation and the one who will accomplish it to the full.

In addition, the council frequently acknowledged that the Church remains subject to sin. It is part of the Church's sacramentality that the Church is not identical with the saving reality contained within it, that it can fulfill its task of service as sign and instrument only in an imperfect way, and that in doing so, it often obstructs its own action. Therefore the council had to admit also that, while all human beings belong within the sacramental economy of salvation, and thus are in principle intended to follow the way that is willed by God and that

29. W. Kasper, ''Die Kirche,'' 228-229.

calls upon the service of the Church, still the possibility of salvation is also open to those who are not members of the Church (LG 12–16). The understanding of the Church as sacrament is of great ecumenical significance. The statement of the Church's sacramentality is an especially important approach to the position of the Eastern Churches.[30] They have preserved a manner of thinking from the heritage of the Fathers of the Church that is able to speak of the cosmos as the universal sacrament and interprets all ecclesiology in a Eucharistic-sacramental manner. The theology of the Churches stemming from the Reformation responds in different ways to the teaching about the sacramentality of the Church.[31] The great concern of Lutheran and Protestant theology is to maintain the difference between God's speaking and acting on the one side, and the speaking and acting of the Church on the other.[32]

In Karl Rahner's theology the great opportunities as well as the limitations of the idea of a sacramental economy of salvation are evident.[33] If God's creation is directed not only to bringing human beings into existence (thus as creating a kind of partnership with God), but aims from the very beginning at divine self-communication, so that that self-communication is understood radically as God's own coming into what is not God, then all reality is and always has been directed toward Jesus Christ, in whom the very self-communication of the triune God, in truth and love, should occur and has occurred. This central saving event, this "incarnation," is then the meaning of the whole creation and of human history as a whole. The central saving event was not

30. W. Beinert, "Sakramentalität der Kirche," 41–44, and especially R. Hotz, *Sakramente* (see Bibliography 1).

31. W. Beinert, "Sakramentalität der Kirche," 44–49 notes sympathy in, for example, P. Tillich, K. Barth, W. Pannenberg, H. Ott; rejection on the part of, for example, R. Bultmann, E. Käsemann, Pl. Brunner. Cf. also H. Döring, *Grundriß der Ekklesiologie* (Darmstadt: 1986), therein "Die sakramentale Struktur der Kirche," 100–106 (also from an ecumenical perspective), with bibliography on pp. 324–327.

32. U. Kühn, *Sakramente* (see Bibliography 1) 213; also, pp. 208–211, the description of the ecclesiological interpretation of sacraments, with Lutheran critique of that interpretation, pp. 211–212.

33. Cf. especially K. Rahner, "Überlegungen zum personalen Vollzug des sakramentalen Geschehens," *Schriften* X, 405–429, a very important article written after the council, in which Rahner also explains why the sacraments can "still" accomplish what they "already" signify. Cf. W. Kasper's agreement, "Die Kirche," 236–237.

annulled by human sin and did not come about for the removal of sin (as redemptive reparation). This opinion of Rahner's is within a great Christian tradition beginning with the Letters to the Ephesians and Colossians and extending through the theology of pedagogy, ascent, and divinization in the work of the Greek theologians and the thought of Augustine to the great Franciscan theology of the Middle Ages (Scotism). Although Rahner was not aware of it, it has its roots in the optimistic view of creation characteristic of Jewish Wisdom literature.

In this perspective, the Church and the individual sacraments (for more on the latter, see 3.4 below) are not to be viewed as medicinal interventions of God from outside, but as manifestations of what the world and human history already are, in their internal truth, because of the divine self-communication. They are manifestations of the "liturgy of the world," real symbols of God's successful intention, saving events for the world. Thus, as Rahner himself (who speaks of a "Copernican shift" in our understanding of sacraments)[34] says, the movement is not one of effects proceeding from the sacraments into the world, but it is a "spiritual movement" *from the world* to the sacrament.

Nevertheless, two cautions should be kept in mind. We must take quite seriously the Protestant and Lutheran concern that the fundamental difference between God and the Church not be obliterated, and that God's absolute sovereignty not be obscured by a new kind of ecclesial-sacramental triumphalism. In Rahner's work, God and Church are sometimes brought dangerously close to one another, as is evident from the following statements: "God, Jesus and the Church—all three considered, in a sense, as *one* acting subject—present a sign, a gesture, that not only expresses the grace-filled relationship of the human being receiving this gesture to God, but also brings about that grace-filled relationship,"[35] and "The Church is the great, unique gesture of God and the gesture of receptive humanity, in which divine love, reconciliation and divine self-communication are eternally announced and bestowed."[36]

---

34. K. Rahner, *Schriften* X, 405.

35. K. Rahner, "Fragen der Sakramententheologie," *Schriften* XVI, 398–405, at 398. Cf. also my objection to a too-triumphalist view of the Church in Rahner's work, in *Schriften* XIV, 60–61.

36. K. Rahner, *Schriften* XVI, 401.

The second caution is most effectively formulated in the questions that, for example, Johann Baptist Metz directed at Rahner's optimistic, salvation-historical point of view—the questions regarding the "apocalyptic thorn." Metz can also call upon a great biblical and Christian tradition, that of apocalyptic literature. It is true that Rahner is correct to the extent that, by common Jewish and Christian conviction, God will be vindicated in the end. But the threat to human history—posed by evil even from within (the "negative existential," in Rahner's words) is a threat not only in areas outside the Church, but is also a threat to the Church and its sacramentality.

3.4   *Individual Sacraments as Actualizations of the Fundamental Sacrament*

If, as Vatican II says, the Church is the universal saving sacrament of Jesus Christ, the question remains how this being-a-sacrament (being-a-symbol, a sign, or an instrument) is to be realized. It must be realized, because the statement, "the Church is sacrament" is too abstract; in the concrete, it could receive a false content. Church must exist as concretely as sacraments must concretely perform their function as signs and instruments. The realization occurs in *martyria, leitourgia,* and *diakonia,* since in all three forms of the Church's service the effective saving will of God must be made apparent. The outstanding form in which the Church's liturgy is actualized is the praxis of the individual sacraments in concrete liturgical assemblies (no matter how small).

This notion of the individual sacraments as perfection, actualization, or unfolding of the fundamental sacrament that is Church, always to be understood, of course, in the Holy Spirit and based on the primordial sacrament, Jesus Christ, was introduced into Catholic theology shortly before Vatican II—prepared for by renewed reflection on the sacramental economy of salvation. At first, those involved were not aware that the Eastern Churches had always regarded the celebration of the Eucharist as the pre-eminent concrete realization of the Church.

Two theologians deserve special mention because of the influence of their ideas. Edward Schillebeeckx, in the sacramental theology he developed from 1952 on, interpreted the individual sacraments as "ecclesial manifestation of Christ's divine love for humanity (gift of grace) and human love for God (cult),"[37] thus grounding sacraments both Christologically and ecclesiologically. Karl Rahner, in an essay that first appeared in 1955,[38] treated the different "degrees of actuality" and "self-realizations" of the Church; here the individual sacraments were seen as self-realizations of the Church at the highest level of actuality, that of "official-historically described publicness." Thus he could also call the individual sacraments "the essential, fundamental realizations of the Church itself,"[39] situated at the critical moments in the salvation history of each individual human being.

The decisive theological question introduced by this way of looking at things was that of the mediation of God's grace by the Church. Catholic theology, with which Rahner essentially agreed, emphasizes the complete dependence of the Church's activity on the divine Spirit who unites Jesus Christ, the head, with the human members of his body.[40] The importance of nuances of language in this sensitive area is evident in the work of Ulrich Kühn: while he, as a Lutheran theologian, has no difficulty in saying that "sacraments are actions, or better, realizations of the life of the Church,"[41] he wishes to avoid the concept of the Church's *self*-realization, since that expression is liable to obscure the meaning of the sacraments "as events of divine saving graciousness, prior to anything human."[42]

Rahner's preferred ordering of the individual sacraments to the all-encompassing sacrament of the Church sheds light on problems that will be discussed individually below. This point of view permitted dog-

---

37. E. Schillebeeckx, *Christus, Sakrament der Gottesbegegnung* [*Christ the Sacrament of the Encounter with God*] (Mainz: 1959) 74. Also very influential was his "Sakramente als Organe der Gottbegegnung," in J. Feiner, J. Trütsch, and F. Böckle, eds., *Fragen der Theologie heute* (Einsiedeln: 1957) 379–401. On this, see C. E. O'Neill, in *Bilanz der Theologie im 20. Jahrhundert* III, 256–259 (good summary); J. Ambaum, *Glaubenszeichen. Schillebeeckx' Auffassung von den Sakramenten* (Regensburg: 1980), and H. Häring's remarks in *Theol. Revue* 78 (1982) 221–223.

38. As a book: K. Rahner, *Kirche und Sakramente* (Freiburg: 1960).

39. Ibid., 21.

40. Cf. R. Schulte, "Einzelsakramente als Ausgliederung des Wurzelsakraments," *MySal* IV/2, 45–155; H. Denis, "Les sacrements font l'Eglise-sacrement," *La Maison Dieu* 152 (1982) 7–35 (the Christological and pneumatological principle of sacramental theology).

41. U. Kühn, *Sakramente*, 197.

42. Ibid., 212.

matic theology to understand sacraments (again) as liturgy and not as juridical acts. Such concepts as "accomplish," "actualize," or even "celebrate" stand in the way of a notion of sacraments as fixed objects that were all bestowed on the Church by God at the same time. The words "accomplishment" or "fulfillment" encompass without qualification the activity of all who take part in the liturgical assembly, the community of the baptized; they permit the infelicitous division of those celebrating into "ministers" and "recipients" to recede into the background. The question why God, according to Catholic thinking, willed exactly seven individual sacraments, neither one more nor one less, is blunted when the institutional-sacramental aspect is embedded in the matrix of the general-sacramental economy of salvation. The number seven can be understood symbolically, and there is no compulsion to give proofs for it. The attempt to trace the individual sacraments to the historical Jesus is shown to be a mistaken route into which theology was drawn by Martin Luther's insistence on the institution of visible signs by Jesus himself. New Testament pneumatology and Johannine theology of the origins of the Church and its sacraments from the wound in the side of the Crucified have pointed the way and the opportunity for the Church to view the shape of the sacraments and the fixing of their number in a positive light, without placing the grace of Jesus, the One who is really at work in the liturgy and sacraments, through his Spirit, at the disposal of the Church.

4

The Sacraments in General

4.1 The General Concept of a Sacrament

There is no satisfactory general concept of "sacrament," because there is no general sacrament: there are only concrete individual sacraments. But there have been attempts to summarize what is common to all the individual sacraments in *one* concept, and these attempts, with all their inadequacies, have nevertheless contributed something to our understanding of the relationship between God and human beings. We may begin by addressing some of the important stages in the attempt to form such a concept.[1]

As regards the communities described in the New Testament, we can proceed on a twofold basis. On the one hand, we find witnesses of a manifold liturgical and ritual praxis, although with different layers of meaning: baptism and Eucharist were primary, but we also find mention of penitential practice, the imposition of hands, and anointing. There is no single unified term for these different practices in the New

---

1. On this history, cf. J. Finkenzeller I and II, and his "Sakrament," in *LThK* IX, 220–225, with bibliography.

Testament (and, of course, no common theology). On the other hand, we find the concept of *mysterion*, which, as indicated above (3.2) denotes the realization and revelation of God's plan of salvation. This plan had been decided by God from all eternity, was at work in the history of Jesus Christ and was revealed in him. For the authors of Ephesians (ch. 3) and Colossians (ch. 1), the Church is the form in which this divine plan of salvation is to be further realized and made known. The goal of this *mysterion* is the complete unity of all human beings with God and with one another, the fulfillment of what has been begun in Jesus Christ, the creation of a just and reconciled humanity in which divisive differences are abolished—that very thing that in the preaching of Jesus is called the "reign of God." Thus this concept of the *mysterion* encompasses the sacramental economy of salvation, to the extent that it contains Jesus Christ, the Church, and the totality of their life.

In the Old Latin Scriptures, *mysterion* was translated either with the imitative word *mysterium* (Itala, Vulgate) or with *sacramentum* (African versions). The word *sacramentum* is connected to *sacrare* and *sacrum*. *Sacrare* in Roman pagan religion meant the legal transfer of a person or thing to the realm of the *sacrum*, the holy, i.e., its removal from the secular world and placement in a special realm in which special rights and duties imposed by the gods were in force. *Sacramentum*, in this context, designated the vow of a recruit ("flag oath"), accepted by a public authority, by which the recruit was incorporated in the "sacred army" (*sacra militia*) and through which he obligated himself to corresponding ethical conduct. *Sacramentum* could also designate a sum of money that had to be deposited in the temple by parties to a lawsuit; the loser's share went to the temple and was used for cultic purposes. Again the element of religious-ethical self-commitment is present.

The transfer of *sacramentum* to ecclesial-theological vocabulary was accomplished by the African theologians Tertullian (d. after 220), Cyprian (d. 258) and Augustine (d. 430). In their interpretations of *mysterion* in Ephesians and Colossians, the realization of the plan of salvation, Jesus Christ, the incarnation (*sacramentum incarnationis*), the Church (Cyprian: *sacramentum unitatis*), faith, and the creed are all called *sacramentum*. Tertullian, so far as we know, was the first to refer to baptism and Eucharist as *sacramenta*. In the case of baptism he pointed to its similarity to the religious-ethical self-obligation in the recruit's oath. In general, we can say that the widest possible variety of rites are referred to as *sacramenta* in the writings of the Fathers.

It was Augustine who first developed a theory of sacraments, in the context of his interpretation of the New Testament in light of Neoplatonic philosophical thought.[2] He placed the *sacramentum* in the category of *signa*, visible signs that represent an invisible reality. A *sacramentum* is a *sacrum signum*, that is, a sign designated by God to point to a divine reality (*res divina*) and containing that reality within itself (see further at 4.2.2).

Augustine's influence on Western theology was and remained over-mastering. His thought survived the collapse of the ancient world and penetrated the new cultures (West Gothic, Anglo-Saxon, Frankish, etc.). In his spirit, important pre-Scholastic theologians[3] understood *sacramentum* to refer to the visible form of invisible grace (*invisibilis gratiae visibilis forma*), a description that was accurate to a large degree, but was not a real definition.

Attempts to define a general concept of "sacrament" that would apply to all the sacraments of the Church were taken up in the Scholastic period. We will describe the two most important of these.[4]

Hugh of St. Victor (d. 1141) defined sacrament as a bodily or material element that is used in an external, sensible manner and, through a certain similarity, makes present an invisible and spiritual grace, indicates that grace because of its institution (by Jesus Christ) and contains what is salvific (for human beings). Several parts of this definition indicate the difficulties involved: it ties the "sacrament" to the presence of a bodily or material element and to an institution (*institutio*) by Jesus Christ; it can say nothing specific about grace, and it offers no indication of *how* this grace can be "contained" in the sign. The fact that a theology that was essentially fashioned by and for monks omitted any reference to the world at large—a reference still contained in the biblical "mysterion"—contributed to the development of a special sacramental world alongside "normal" life. It is less understandable that no attempt was made, in the liturgy- and prayer-soaked world of the cloisters and cathedral schools, to fashion a definition of sacraments that located them within liturgy and prayer.

2. J. Finkenzeller I, 38–61.
3. See the summary in J. Finkenzeller I, 62–64.
4. See ibid., 84–88, for a description of these attempts in early Scholasticism, and 127–137 for the high Scholastic period.

The bishop of Paris, Peter Lombard (d. 1160), defined "sacrament" as the sign of God's grace and the form of invisible grace, in such a way that it is both the image and the cause (*causa*) of that grace. Here the bodily element (as well as institution by Jesus Christ) were omitted and instead, with a certain dependence on Augustine, the sacrament is understood as *signum* (sign and image). Here, for the first time, it is said that the sacrament is the cause or reason for divine grace. Since Peter Lombard's "Sentences" were *the* textbook for university theology from the thirteenth century well into the sixteenth, the Lombard's contribution to the understanding of sacraments was highly influential.[5] However, even in the period of Scholasticism there were voices raised, questioning whether a definition of sacraments was possible at all, since too many different things would have to be comprehended within it.[6] In fact, the suggested definitions of sacrament remained so broad that we cannot speak of an exact concept, for example, when Thomas Aquinas defined sacrament as a "sign of a sacred reality, to the extent that it sanctifies human beings."[7] Often enough people abstained from an attempt at definition and offered, instead, some explanations of a summary nature.

4.2   *History of General Sacramental Theology*

What is important in this brief overview is to indicate the essential *theological* themes of a general doctrine of sacraments, without describing them in detail.

4.2.1   *New Testament*

The *mysterion* theology of the late New Testament writings is not a reflection on Church life and thus is not about the seven sacraments, although it is not difficult to discern that the divine plan of salvation contains everything by means of which the gracious event of God

5. On the acceptance of his formula by important theologians of high Scholasticism, including Bonaventure, Albert the Great, and Thomas Aquinas, see ibid., 131–132.
6. Ibid., 127.
7. *S. Th.* III, q. 60, a. 2.

through Jesus Christ in the Holy Spirit is effective and perceptible to the senses.

For the later seven sacraments of the Catholic Church, the New Testament offers some basic theological elements, as will be shown later in detail. In the case of baptism and Eucharist these are more than the mere fundamentals; the imposition of hands may have some relationship to the communication of the Holy Spirit; at an anointing of the sick, both the forgiveness of sins and healing are mentioned; the religious sign-value of marriage is emphasized; and with regard to penitential practice it is clear that the relationship of the sinner to the Church community affects his or her religious situation before God. Jewish points of view were and remained formative in the development of the basic elements of sacramental theology in the New Testament. The following are the two most important insights.[8]

Corresponding to and rooted in Jewish thought is the notion that, in *memory* (Hbr. *zkr*), a past event can be brought into the present and be made effective, so that it even provides the impulse for action. This memory is a real making-present, not a backward-looking memorial. Jewish memorial feasts, when the community called on the name of YHWH, were more than simply looking back at the past. Everyone who took part in the Pesach feast shared, in the present moment, in the liberating and redeeming event of the Exodus. Both the great Christian memorial feasts that are theologically depicted in the New Testament, the Eucharist (1 Cor 10:14-22, 11:26-29) and baptism (1 Cor 6:11; Rom 6:2-11) combine ritual and word-event, and thus make present the death of Jesus as saving event (Eucharist: 1 Cor 11:26; baptism: Rom 6:3). The fact that these memorial feasts praise the mighty deeds of God, who wakened Jesus from the dead and sent the Holy Spirit, is clear from the whole literary context. In the same way, we cannot overlook the fact that in baptism and the Eucharist, believers received a gift, which had to have immediate and concrete religious-ethical consequences in their lives.

Jewish thought is also the source of the idea of the "corporate" (or "collective") person: an individual person is really identified with the community to whom she or he belongs; the action of one person has concrete consequences for the community; what one person receives

8. On this, see B. van Iersel, "Einige biblische Voraussetzungen des Sakraments," *Concilium* 4 (1968) 2–9.

from YHWH has a value for the community. We find this conviction active also in the case of the principal New Testament sacraments, baptism and Eucharist. The baptized person belongs to, that is, he or she is really integrated into the corporate Christ-person (Rom 6:3-8) and simultaneously into the corporate person to which Jesus Christ belongs, the person of Abraham (Gal 3:26-29; cf. Col 2:11ff.). Pauline pneumatological body of Christ theology is very closely connected to this notion (1 Cor 12:12-31, cf. especially vv. 12, 13, and 27; cf. also 1 Cor 10, where Paul speaks of baptism and Eucharist together in an indirect typology), as is the important idea that the death of Jesus was for the benefit of others (cf. the background in Jewish tales of martyrdom and the theme of the suffering servant of God).

This Jewish thinking shaped the origins of the Church's sacramental life; it interprets the sacraments as present saving event, through the making-present of Jesus Christ in the Holy Spirit within the praise of the Father's mighty deeds; it shows the constitutive connection between Church and sacramental praxis as well as the concrete ethical and social consequences of the sacraments.

In its own partly suggestive, partly symbolic language, the Fourth Gospel certainly speaks of baptism and Eucharist in the sense of sacraments, i.e., in such a way that through them, after the sending of the Holy Spirit, the unique saving action of Jesus is present and effective within the Church.[9] The most important texts are about baptism (John 3) and Eucharist (John 6:52-58), the origin of both sacraments and their saving effectiveness from Jesus' death on the cross (John 19:34 with 1 John 5:6-8), and the forgiveness of sins through the power of the Holy Spirit who has been given to the Church (John 20:22-23). This sacramental theology, probably shaped under increasing Hellenistic influence, is so strongly interested in the continuing union of the believers with Jesus Christ and the consequent "eternal life," that it, more than the theologies mentioned earlier, is subject to being misunderstood in terms of otherworldliness and personal salvation.

---

9. J. Finkenzeller I, 14–16, with bibliography and an overview of controversial minimalist, cultic, and "middle" positions. Further information on New Testament sacramental theology (theses of the school of the history of religions, mystery theology) can be found in summary in R. Schnackenburg's article in *LThK* IX, 218–220; see also R. Tragan, ed., *Fede e sacramenti negli scritti giovannei* (Rome: 1985).

4.2.2 The Church Fathers

The attitude of the Fathers of the Church before Augustine was quite similar to that of the New Testament authors. They spoke of the individual actions of the Church, with great emphasis on baptism and Eucharist, and stressing the making-present of the saving event in Jesus Christ and the fruits of salvation that flow from it. They vigorously opposed pagan worship, but they did not develop a "general theology of sacraments." The concepts of *mysterion/mysteria* conveyed to them a wide variety of ideas: truths of faith, saving events or institutions of the Old Testament in their typological meaning, promises and their fulfillment through Jesus Christ, and also the liturgical-sacramental aspect of the Church. From the time of Tertullian, Latin theology used the concept of *sacramentum* in a similarly broad manner.[10]

The highly influential sacramental theology of Augustine is woven together on the basis of several strands of reasoning. It is not a general theology of sacraments, but rather is based on the examples of baptism and Eucharist, even though Augustine also knew of other rites that had sacramental effects, e.g., penitential practice.

The starting point is the location of sacraments within the genre of signs, or more precisely, of those visible signs that in and of themselves, that is, of their very nature, and not by convention (based on general agreement) lead us to perceive something other than what their external appearance at first reveals, and thus facilitate direct inferences, as, for example, from smoke to fire. This "something other" is an invisible reality (*res*, an important concept of later sacramental theology). The most dignified of all signs is the word, for through it the invisible reality itself can be perceived. Augustine then applied this philosophy of the connectedness of different entities to the field of things. Material goods are signs of higher, spiritual realities; the visible world is a sign of the eternal universe. Human beings are called to apply themselves to the task of discerning the deeper realities and of practicing a proper relationship with things, i.e., merely to use material things, but to enjoy those that are spiritual. In his theological interpretation, Augustine determined that Adam had perverted the relationship to signs and things that God had planned, but God, in the divine plan of salvation, had begun to restore the right order. Within this plan is

10. There is a good overview in J. Finkenzeller I, 16–37.

the gift of the *sacramenta*, the sacred signs that indicate and contain the divine. Thus their external side has a similarity to their sacred content, so that the sacraments are not conventional, but "natural" signs, whose meaning is inherent in themselves. The *sacramenta* signs are composed of an element, perceptible to the senses, and an interpretive word. But since the word is the most dignified, it is first of all the word that makes the element to be a sacrament; thus the sacrament can also be called a "visible word" (*visibile verbum*). This word that effects the sacrament is the Church's word of faith. The invisible reality that is indicated and is present in the sacrament is not simply grace, it is *Christus totus*, the whole Christ composed of head and members in the Holy Spirit, who as the real and active agent in the sacraments causes grace, but in such a manner that the sacraments are always actions of the Church. But since Jesus Christ is the one who is really acting in the sacraments, their inner, sacred reality and effect cannot be damaged by unworthy ministers.[11]

4.2.3   *Middle Ages*

The influence of Augustinian sacramental theology in the Western Church can be traced throughout the whole medieval period, through the modern era, and into the present. Its principal ideas were repeated throughout the Middle Ages, until the twelfth century, without essential expansion. The early Middle Ages were a period without a theology,[12] and yet sacramental theology passed several decisive forks in its road during those centuries. There was a general effort to establish the proper rite for administering the sacraments. Because of the superior authority of the apostle Peter, the bearer of the keys of the kingdom of heaven, the Roman liturgy was seen to be the locus of that appropriate rite, and efforts were made to introduce and imitate the Roman liturgy wherever possible in the new cultures that were replac-

11. See n. 2; W. Simonis, *Ecclesia visibilis et invisibilis. Untersuchungen zur Ekklesiologie und Sakramentenlehre in der afrikanischen Tradition von Cyprian bis Augustinus* (Frankfurt: 1970) 103–109: "Christus als der eigentliche Taufspender bei Augustinus."

12. A. Angenendt, "Bonifatius und das Sacramentum initiationis. Zugleich ein Beitrag zur Geschichte der Firmung," *Römische Quartalschrift* 72 (1977) 133–183, especially 159–169; idem, "Religiosität und Theologie. Ein spannungsreiches Verhältnis im Mittelalter," *Archiv für Liturgiewissenschaft* 20–21 (1978-79) 28–55.

ing those of the ancient world. But the broad, generous Roman spirit was not appropriated along with the rites! While in Rome attention was concentrated on the symbolism of the means of grace, in other places (as witnessed, for example, in Milan by Ambrose in the fourth century) the sacraments were regarded as consecrated matter. This was the source of the conviction of early Scholasticism that grace was contained in the sacrament like medicine in a bottle.[13]

Whereas, in the Roman (and Eastern) liturgy, the minister and recipient of the sacraments were joined in a dialogue, now the consecration of the elements (bread, wine, water, oil) was seen as the real, constitutive action in the sacrament's coming-to-be. While earlier the elements were only "symbolizing" factors in the transmission of grace, now they themselves were the means of grace and worthy of veneration.[14] In the early Middle Ages the idea of the existence of sacred, blessed objects achieved wide acceptance. The original liturgical celebration of the sacraments was "emptied, becoming only the distribution of sacred matter prepared beforehand."[15]

Particularly important for early medieval theology, in addition, were questions about the qualifications of the persons doing the consecrating, and about the correct utterance of the holy sacramental words given by the Son of God himself.[16] "Only a literally correct expression guaranteed validity."[17] Even though in many areas high Scholasticism recovered a broader perspective, legalistic and ritualized notions continued to dominate sacramental theology.

Among the other questions that were discussed, a notable variation in the numbering of the sacraments is of particular interest. At first there was a tendency to expand the number of the sacraments, and with it the Church's competence. Thus Peter Damian (d. 1072) counted twelve sacraments, including marriage and the consecration of kings. As a consequence of the investiture struggle, Church and world were more sharply separated, and the Church more strongly clericalized (so that the consecration of hermits, nuns, and kings were no longer counted among the sacraments), and the realm of the sacraments became even more markedly a world unto itself.

13. A. Angenendt, "Bonifatius," 159–160.
14. Ibid., 160–161.
15. Ibid., 161, with further reference to J. Ratzinger.
16. Ibid., 163.
17. Ibid., 164.

In the mid-twelfth century, under the normative influence of Peter Lombard, the tally of seven sacraments achieved acceptance, not least because it was seen as desirable, finally, to make a precise distinction between the sacraments of the new covenant and the broad "sacramental realm" of natural sacraments, Old Testament sacraments, consecrations resembling sacraments, and blessings. A superior dignity and certainty of effect were now definitively attributed to the New Testament sacraments. In this connection, the teachings about the *opus operatum*, about intention, and—in the case of baptism, confirmation, and orders—about the "sacramental character" were developed.

Opus operatum (the work worked; *ex opere operato* = by the power of the completed rite) has designated, since the twelfth century, the objective effectiveness of a sacrament, which is considered the work of God with regard to the "minister" and "recipient." *Opus operantis* (earlier *operans*), the work of the one working, then means the human, subjective action in carrying out a sacrament. The source of grace is exclusively the *opus operatum*; the *opus operantis* is only the condition that permits the grace to be present. The discussion of this point was always affected by the thought of unworthy officiants. In order to guarantee the effectiveness of the sacraments, in addition to the teaching about *opus operatum*, further minimal conditions were discussed: the minister's possession of power, and the existence of an intention to do what, in this particular sacrament, the Church does. The teaching about a "sacramental character" was based on the ideas of Augustine, starting with the consideration that the effects of some sacraments (especially baptism) cannot be restricted to the brief moment of the sacramental action, but instead must be an inextinguishable, long-term effectiveness, implying a seal imprinted on the soul. (Augustine, in order to illustrate the endurance of the effects of baptism even in sinners and apostates, had made a comparison with the brand or "character" imprinted on Roman legionaries.) This insight was accompanied by the development of the teaching that, precisely because of this imprinted and enduring effect, certain sacraments cannot be repeated. (See further remarks in section 4.3.)

General sacramental theology was greatly broadened due to the influence of newly-rediscovered Aristotelian ideas in the thirteenth century. The hylomorphic doctrine, that everything physical and perceptible by the senses is a union of the changeable (matter) and the principle (form) that gave structure and definition, was applied to the sacraments from the beginning of the thirteenth century onward. This effort to achieve intellectual clarity on the problem of what the *signum* (sign) really means in the case of sacraments resulted in the schematization of all sacraments. In all of them, there must be some kind of matter, i.e., a visible, changeable, and determinable element,[18] and form, the interpretive and determinative words of the "minister."

As a necessary result of all this, interest in the liturgical context declined. Concentration on the "essentials" of a sacrament led inevitably to a search for the minimum conditions under which it could come about. These could be fulfilled even in an emergency rite. This kind of security-minded thinking evoked a series of further questions: what is it exactly that effects the sacrament? At what precise point does the effect take place? Who is it, precisely, who can bring it about?

High Scholastic theology tried to answer these questions on the basis of Christology, and therefore concentrated on the influence of Jesus Christ on the sacraments. Their "institution" by Jesus Christ was important, as was his bestowal of power over the sacraments on the apostles, to whom Jesus Christ could also have communicated the knowledge that he had instituted a sacrament, even if no words of institution from his own lips have been retained.

The doctrine, first evident in the work of Peter Lombard, that the sacrament is the cause (*causa*) of grace, was now considered in detail, especially by Thomas Aquinas. The high Scholastic theologians were quite aware that a direct connection between the production of the cause (the sacrament) by the Church and the resulting effect (divine grace) would mean that human beings had God's grace at their disposal. God, who in the "institution" of the sacraments by Jesus Christ had promised that they would bestow grace, and thus had personally guaranteed their effectiveness, is and remains the principal cause (*causa principalis*) of divine grace; the sacraments entrusted to the Church by

18. In high Scholasticism there was still a more precise distinction made between the purely material element and the gesture that was carried out by means of or in connection with that element. Where the purely material element was lacking, as in reconciliation, the ritual action in company with the word could suffice. (There was also talk of quasi-matter.) In connection with the development of the various units of doctrine in the Middle Ages, let me again refer to J. Finkenzeller's treatment. On the theme of "matter and form," see his work at I, 138–142. For further clarification, of course, one must have recourse to extensive studies of the history of devotion and works of social history, such as those by Arnold Angenendt.

Jesus Christ are instrumental causes (*causa instrumentalis*), in God's hand, of that grace.[19]

A threefold distinction was important: the external sign, consist-ing of matter and form, is only a sign and is not yet its content. It is called *sacramentum* or external sacrament. The content, the ultimate ef-fect of the sacrament, that is, the grace of God, is not, for its own part, a sign. It is called the *res sacramenti*. Finally, there is a middle term be-tween the two: it is brought into the visible realm by the first, external sign, and it immediately produces the second, grace. This middle is called *res et sacramentum*, or internal sacrament.[20]

Finally, we should mention Thomas' attempt to found the sacra-ments as seven in number on the fact that in that very number they reflect the individual and social nature of humanity, and indicate through this double imagery that all of human life will be incorporated into the life of God. The most important moments in human develop-ment—birth, becoming adult, and receiving nourishment—are sancti-fied and made whole through baptism, confirmation, and Eucharist; the things that threaten people and make them ill are also transformed into healing through reconciliation and the anointing of the sick; human social existence is made fruitful before God through holy orders and marriage.

The Scholastic contributions to sacramental theology have left a deci-sive mark on it to this day. The fact that they themselves were shaped by a particular philosophy has bound their fate to the fate of that phi-losophy. Obviously, the precision of their questions and the attempts at answers corresponded to a still greater legalization and clericaliza-tion, trends that in any case were at work in the Church's develop-ment at that period. The extraction and isolation of the sacraments from their liturgical context is also expressed in the fact that the sacramen-tal prayers (by which the Holy Spirit is invoked) were replaced by in-dicative formulas. The sacraments were transformed from symbolic liturgical actions and life-events to extremely brief, punctual gestures.

19. For more detail, see J. Finkenzeller I, 203–207, including a discussion of the development of the doctrine by Thomas himself. At pp. 199–203, there is a descrip-tion of the differing views of the Franciscan theologians, who rejected the idea of grace being "contained in" the sacraments and said that the sacraments only prepared for the reception of grace directly given by God.

20. J. Finkenzeller I, 142–144.

In this shortened form it was no longer possible to accommodate any expressions of self-obligation to service and witnessing in the world. The objections of the Reformers to the Church's sacraments can be explained to a great extent by the practical consequences of these developments.

4.2.4 *The Sacramental Theology of the Reformers*

There is no attempt, either in the works of Martin Luther or in Lutheran confessional documents, to develop a general concept of sacraments.[21] Luther expressed himself on the subject of "the sacrament" in connection with his discussions of concrete sacraments (baptism and the Lord's Supper). His theological reflections on this subject are thoroughly imbued with Christology, proceeding from Jesus Christ as the only sacrament to which the Bible testifies, and from the sacrament of his cross. In Luther's view of the Church's sacramental symbolic actions, the highest significance belongs to the promise of God, who can neither lie nor deceive; in the word spoken in the sacrament God's saving action in Jesus reaches and touches human beings. If the person is a believer, that is, if she or he accepts the word of Christ as foundation and fastness and gives him- or herself freely without trusting in human works, the faith proclaimed in the sacrament effects salvation. Thus the connection between promise, word, and faith is decisive. (Here we can recognize essential elements of Augustine's theology of the word.) Despite this pre-eminence, the Church's sacramental sign is indispensable, because of God's will and decree. If those are followed, the sacrament even exists in the absence of faith, though it does not produce a saving effect. Luther understood the *opus operatum* as a merit-work of the human being, and therefore rejected the concept. Concerning the number of the sacraments, Luther viewed the decisive criterion as the connection of a word of promise from Jesus Christ with a visible sign. These he saw as certainly evident only in baptism and the Lord's Supper, and he wavered on the subject of absolution: it is only the biblical witnesses to Jesus, and these probably

21. On Luther and the Lutheran confessional documents (especially the *Confessio Augustana*) there is a summary with bibliography in J. Finkenzeller II, 2-25; for more detail, see U. Kühn, *Sakramente*.

without the human traditions of the Church, that guarantee the sure connection and thus the sacrament.

The Lutheran confessional statements understand the sacraments as signs (*signa*, as well as *ritus* or *ceremonia*) that, because they were instituted by God and Jesus Christ and not by human beings, are real signs of grace, visible witnesses to God's saving will toward human beings, and not mere marks of Christian profession. When, as a result of the institution (*institutio*), God's command and promise (*mandatum* and *promissio*) are given and the promise is believed, a sacrament infallibly conveys divine grace. Following Augustine, the sign is seen as composed of word and element, both of which are essential, although the word has priority. The recipient, but not the minister, must have faith, trusting in the promise. Sacraments in the strict sense are only those rites that were instituted by divine command and are connected with a promise of grace; three such can certainly be discerned, while the rest, to which the Catholic Church clings, are not *certain* signs of grace.

Calvin, who also supported his view of sacraments on the authority of Augustine, understood a sacrament to be an external, visible sign or symbol indicating a sacred gift although it is not mingled with it; in this sign God acts on us by strengthening our faith and sealing his promises. A natural element or *signum* becomes a sacrament, when God, by instituting it, has bound his promise to this sign. The sacrament is the promise made visible and, because it comes from God, has an objective value independent of faith.

According to Calvin, referring to Augustine's statement in relation to the wound in Christ's side, there are two sacraments (even if the Old Testament sacraments were genuine sacraments and were effective through faith in God's promises). In faith, the sacraments, through the action of the Holy Spirit, become means or instruments of grace that effect what they signify. (In contrast, Zwingli said that the sacraments were only memorials and marks of Christian profession.) Their function can be seen in the fact that they incorporate us into Jesus Christ and the mysteries of his life; the power of the Holy Spirit overcomes the distance between him and us. In accord with his teaching on predestination, Calvin said that the sacraments are only effective in those who are positively predestined; they are necessary not for the conferral of grace, but because of the physical character of human nature and the weakness of human faith.

The view of sacraments in the Reformed confessional documents is entirely governed by their theology of the word of God. Through the proclamation of the word of God the real, living presence of Jesus Christ is activated in the community and in individual believers; the sacrament, as "visible word," is part of the word proclaimed. It can also be called an "external sign of God's grace" or "sealing in the Holy Spirit." It effects what it signifies; the real agent and true minister of the sacrament is its founder, Jesus Christ. The saving content of word and sacrament is identical, and is distinguished only in regard to the way in which it is apprehended and to the manner by which it produces its effects: the word seeks to awaken faith in itself, while the sacrament is intended to strengthen the already awakened faith in the word. Thus the sacrament exists primarily for the sake of those who are weak in faith; one may not despise it, but it is possible to dispense with it.

4.2.5 The Church's Official Sacramental Teaching

The first official Church positions adopted toward the questions of general sacramental theology defend the teaching, upheld since Augustine, that the validity and effectiveness of a sacrament are not dependent on the worthiness of the minister (Pope Innocent III [1208]: NR 498/DS 793; Council of Constance [1415 and 1418]: NR 499-500; DS 1154, 1262). The Council of Florence produced a more detailed exposition of the general doctrine of sacraments. At the time of the (brief) reunion of the Armenian and Coptic Churches with the Roman Church, representatives of those Eastern Churches had to subscribe to decrees that included, among other things, the Roman Catholic view of the sacraments. The Eastern Churches did not succeed in having their priceless heritage, the incorporation of the sacraments within the liturgy, together with the prayer for the coming and action of the Holy Spirit, included in the conciliar texts. The more extensive text for the Armenians ([1439]: NR 501-504/DS 1310-1313) was largely drawn from Thomas Aquinas' brief essay *De articulis fidei et Ecclesiae sacramentis*. It thus witnesses to the high regard accorded to him as a theologian and reflects the language of Scholastic sacramental theology:

> We here set out the true doctrine of the sacraments of the Church in a brief formula which will facilitate the instruction of the Armenians, both now and in the future. There are *seven* sacraments of the New Law,

namely, baptism, confirmation, the Eucharist, penance, extreme unction, Order and matrimony; and they differ greatly from the *sacraments of the Old Law*. For these did not cause grace but were only a figure of the grace that was to be given through the passion of Christ; but our sacraments both *contain grace* and confer it on those who receive them worthily.

The first five of these are ordained to the *interior spiritual perfection* of the person himself; the last two are ordained to the *government and increase of the whole Church*. For by baptism we are spiritually reborn and by confirmation we grow in grace and are strengthened in the faith; being reborn and strengthened, we are nourished with the divine food of the Eucharist. If by sin we become sick in soul, we are healed spiritually by penance; we are also healed in spirit, and in body insofar as it is good for the soul, by extreme unction. Through Order the Church is governed and receives spiritual growth; through matrimony she receives bodily growth.

All these sacraments are constituted by *three elements*: by things as the *matter*, by words as the *form*, and by the person of the *minister* conferring the sacrament with the intention of doing what the Church does. And if any one of these three is lacking, the sacrament is not effected.

Among these sacraments there are three, baptism, confirmation and Order, which imprint on the soul an *indelible character*, that is a certain spiritual *sign* distinguishing (the recipient) from others. Hence, these are not repeated for the same person. The other four, however, do not imprint a character and may be repeated.[22]

The Council of Trent felt it necessary to react to the Reformers' statements on the praxis and theology of the sacraments and to strengthen the Church's teaching in opposition to them. The sacraments in general were treated in the seventh session, in 1547. The decrees of Florence served as guidelines, but it was agreed that Scholastic technical terms should be avoided, that the decrees should be limited to essentials, and that the Reformers' teaching on the number of the sacraments and their effectiveness should be rejected only on the basis of faith, without condemning the Reformers by name. The participants also agreed not to take a position on contradictory opinions among Scholas-

22. J. Neuner, S.J., and J. Dupuis, S.J., eds., *The Christian Faith in the Doctrinal Documents of the Catholic Church*, rev. ed. (New York: Alba House, 1982) 369–370. See also the decree for the "Jacobites," or Copts (1442): DS 1348. The decrees for the Armenians and for the Jacobites have not been accepted as defined doctrine.

tic theologians that did not endanger the faith. The *Decree on the Sacraments* of 1547, which was approved by all the members of the council who were present, was restricted as far as the general doctrine of sacraments was concerned to a foreword and thirteen doctrinal statements (NR 505–518/DS 1600–1613):

Foreword

In order to bring to completion the salutary doctrine of justification promulgated with the unanimous consent of the Fathers in the session immediately preceding, it seemed fitting to deal with the holy sacraments of the Church. For all true justification either begins through the sacraments, or, once begun, increases through them, or when lost is regained through them. Therefore, in order to do away with errors and to root out heresies which in our age are directed against the holy sacraments partly inspired by heresies already condemned in the past by our Fathers and partly newly devised—and which are doing great harm to the purity of the Catholic Church and to the salvation of souls, the most holy, ecumenical and general Council of Trent, . . . adhering to the teaching of the Holy Scriptures, to the apostolic traditions and to the consensus of the Fathers and of the other Councils, has thought that the present canons should be drawn up and decreed. . . .

Canons on the Sacraments in General

1. If anyone says that the sacraments of the New Law were not all instituted by Jesus Christ our Lord; or that there are more or fewer than seven, that is: baptism, confirmation, the Eucharist, penance, extreme unction, Order and matrimony; or that any one of these is not truly and properly a sacrament, *anathema sit.*

2. If anyone says that these same sacraments of the New Law do not differ from the sacraments of the Old Law, except that the ceremonies and external rites are different, *anathema sit.*

3. If anyone says that these sacraments are so equal to one another that one is not in any way of greater worth than another, *anathema sit.*

4. If anyone says that the sacraments of the New Law are not necessary for salvation, but that they are superfluous; and that without the sacraments or the desire of them [human persons] obtain from God the grace of justification through faith alone, although it is true that not all the sacraments are necessary for each person, *anathema sit.*

5. If anyone says that these sacraments are instituted only for the sake of nourishing faith, *anathema sit.*

6. If anyone says that the sacraments of the New Law do not contain the grace which they signify or that they do not confer that grace on those who do not place an obstacle in the way, as if they were only external signs of the grace or justice received through faith and a kind of marks of the Christian profession by which among [human beings] the faithful are distinguished from the unbelievers, *anathema sit*.

7. If anyone says that, as far as God's part is concerned, grace is not given through these sacraments always and to all, even if they receive them rightly, but only sometimes and to some, *anathema sit*.

8. If anyone says that through the sacraments of the New Law grace is not conferred by the performance of the rite itself (*ex opere operato*) but that faith alone in the divine promise is sufficient to obtain grace, *anathema sit*.

9. If anyone says that in three sacraments, namely, baptism, confirmation and Order, a character is not imprinted on the soul, that is, a kind of indelible spiritual sign by reason of which these sacraments cannot be repeated, *anathema sit*.

10. If anyone says that all Christians have the power (to preach) the word and to administer all the sacraments, *anathema sit*.

11. If anyone says that the intention, at least of doing what the Church does, is not required in the ministers when they are performing and conferring the sacraments, *anathema sit*.

12. If anyone says that a minister in the state of mortal sin, though he observes all the essentials that belong to the performing and conferring of the sacrament, does not perform or confer the sacrament, *anathema sit*.

13. If anyone says that the accepted and approved rites of the Catholic Church which are customarily used in the solemn administration of the sacraments may be despised or omitted without sin by the ministers as they please, or that they may be changed to other new rites by any pastor in the Church, *anathema sit*.[23]

Very little is said in a positive vein. A number of earlier doctrinal decisions are repeated (the number seven, the teaching that grace is contained in the sacrament, the intention of the minister and the non-necessity of personal worthiness on the minister's part, the sacramental character). No definition of sacrament or description of the essence of sacraments is offered; in its Eucharistic teaching of 1551, the council

23. English in Neuner and Dupuis, *The Christian Faith*, 371–373.

says of a sacrament in general that it is a "symbol of a sacred thing and a visible form of invisible grace" (NR 571/DS 1639). The counter-position to that of the Reformers is made unmistakably clear: regarding the number of the sacraments[24] (can. 1), their relationship to faith (can. 4, 5, 8), the *opus operatum* (can. 8), the necessary authority (can. 10), the intention of the minister (can. 11). A thesis of Scholastic theology, rejected by the Reformers, was accepted by the council: that on the part of the recipient it was sufficient precondition (*dispositio*) for the reception of grace that the recipient place no obstacle (*obex*) to it (can. 6). The council did not wish to demand more personal preparation, so as not to endanger the practice of infant baptism, which was here made the norm for the schema of sacraments in general. A result of this minimal condition was that the liturgical context of the sacraments was, from this point on, left totally out of consideration. A recipient of a sacrament who is not conscious of it—as in the case of infants—is not capable of participation in liturgy.

The council made no attempt to give a positive value to the opinions of the Reformers, and this was particularly true with regard to the subject of grace. Problems that were already seen at the time remained unresolved because the council could not settle them and did not wish to: for example, what exactly was to be understood as "institution" by Jesus Christ (though the council did take a position on this with respect to several individual sacraments), what the "desire" (*votum*) for a sacrament might be (can. 4), or what was to be understood by the term "sacramental character" and what were the grounds for that concept.

Much of what is lacking in the spirit of the exposition here was stated by the Second Vatican Council, four hundred years after the Council of Trent, in an impressive theological and spiritual synthesis. Vatican II described the sacramental life of the Church as the work of the Holy Spirit, who joins believers in the body of Christ in which "through the sacraments, [they] are united in a hidden and real way" to Christ (LG 7). It interpreted the sacraments as means by which the nature and structure of the Church are brought into operation (LG 11), and as "sacraments of faith" (LG 21). It saw the sacraments within the

24. On the number of the sacraments, see M. Seybold, "Die Siebenzahl der Sakramente (Conc. Trid. sessio VII, can. 1)," *Münchener Theol. Zeitschrift* 27 (1976) 113–138; on the number seven in the Eastern Churches, J. Finkenzeller II, 166–172.

whole context of the liturgy (SC 6, 7, 27). It devoted an important document to the word of God (Constitution on Divine Revelation), repeatedly emphasized the privileged importance of its proclamation and
stressed the action of the Holy Spirit "through the faithful preaching
of the gospel . . . [and] administration of the sacraments" (UR 2; on
the word of God UR 21). It recognized essential common convictions
among the separated Churches with regard to the sacraments (UR 15,
22). It avoided the philosophically one-sided language of Scholasticism
and showed itself to be extremely open to images and symbols. Not
least, it repeatedly indicated the close connection between sacramental life and secular praxis.

4.2.6   *The Development of Sacramental Theology after Trent*

This one-sided, scholastically colored sacramental theology endured
in the Catholic Church from the Council of Trent until well into the
twentieth century. It was very attached to theoretical speculation, and
the author who writes that "post-Tridentine theology made no substantial productive contributions to the doctrine of the sacraments"
did it no injustice.[25] Nor is it unjust to say that its theories about the
intention of the sacraments and the manner of their effectiveness are
of merely historical interest. As a result of the teaching on minimal
preconditions and requirements as practiced by Trent and increasingly
expanded after the council, sacramental theology fell under the sway
of canon law, and gradually ceased to be theology at all.

The twentieth-century renewal movements (liturgical, ecumenical,
scriptural, and new approaches to tradition, especially in patristics)
gave sacramental theology a new lease on life.[26] Since we will be dis-
cussing current issues in section 5 (necessarily in brief form), a few
summary remarks on the larger topics should suffice at this point.

1. The most important movements in the field of sacramental theology between the two world wars were mystery theology and the re-

25. J. Finkenzeller in *LThK* IX, 224.
26. C. E. O'Neill in *Bilanz der Theologie im 20. Jahrhundert* III (1970) 244–294, with
a bibliography that still offers a valuable overview of the literature; C. Schütz in
MySal Ergänzungsband (1981) 347–353; A. Schilson, *Sakrament als Symbol* (see Bibliography 1) 122–150; A. Schmied, "Perspektiven."

newal of the idea of the Church as the body of Christ.[27] Regarding the first of these, we may cite Colman E. O'Neill's summary:

> From the suggestion of a relationship between the pagan mystery cults and the Christian sacraments (in which, as became clear in the controversy with his opponents, the pagan mysteries offered him only a formal, and not a causal analogy), Odo Casel (1886–1948) came to the conclusion that the cult represented a mysterious way leading to entrance into the saving mysteries of Christ. The essential idea to which he gave a renewed life was this: in order to participate in redemption, the human being must be conformed to Christ by participating in his saving mysteries. In order for this to be possible, the liturgy must make Christ's saving actions really present to us. The fundamental intention evidently agrees with Paul and the authentic tradition. . . . According to Casel's insight, Christ's saving actions themselves are present in the cultic symbolic actions of the Church—the saving action itself, not in its original historical conditions, but "sacramentally." For, since in a saving event God acts in history to effect salvation, this event transcends time and is able to be present in the sacraments according to a new way of being. This presence in mystery is hidden under the signs, and yet it is through the signs that an objective presence occurs. It is, in the first place, the presence of the death of Christ, and therefore also of the whole Paschal mystery and of the whole work of salvation from Incarnation to Parousia.[28]

Through the intuitive impulse of this theology—which, of course, left many questions open and was of more significance for baptism and Eucharist than for the sacraments in general—the sense of mystery in the liturgy was reawakened, Jesus-mysticism was encouraged (as well as by the biblical movement), and thus the canonistic narrowing and minimalizing of sacramental theology was overcome. In the Constitution on the Liturgy of Vatican Council II at least some elements of mystery theology are still evident. The insistence on the presence of Jesus Christ in *all* liturgical actions (SC 7) offers a good basis for understanding the sacraments in a systematic manner on the basis of their unique character as liturgy.

2. On the renewal of ecclesiology and the rediscovery of the sacramental economy of salvation, see above at 2.1 and 3.

27. C. E. O'Neill, *Bilanz der Theologie*, 248.

3. On the rediscovery of the sacraments as word-event, see below at 5.2.

4. Since Helmut Peukert's groundbreaking effort to explore events of communication and interaction as fundamental theological categories,[29] the sacraments have repeatedly been described as "communicative actions," either in a general sense as a space within which the reality of God and of humanity can be communicated,[30] or in the more circumscribed context of communications theory.[31] Christian Schütz correctly points out that these interpretations appear artificial, because they do not ask themselves "whether and to what extent the model of communication among human persons and the consequences for communications theory that are drawn from that model can be applied to the relationship of God and human beings."[32] This relationship seems to be described in a much too technical fashion when Alexandre Ganoczy writes of Church as the "collective communication of God among humans,"[33] and defines sacraments as "systems of verbal and nonverbal communication, through which people called to faith in Christ enter into the movement of exchange within a particular, concrete community, take part in it and thus, supported by God's self-communication in Christ and by his Spirit, advance along the way to becoming themselves."[34] In these proposals, the description of the com-

---

28. Ibid., 250–251. Cf. the extensive scholarly description and evaluation of mystery theology and the discussion of it in A. Schilson, *Theologie als Sakramententheologie* (see Bibliography 1); cf. also T. Maas-Ewerd, "Odo Casel OSB und Karl Rahner SJ," *Archiv für Liturgiewissenschaft* 28 (1986) 193–234 (with additional literature).

29. H. Peukert, *Wissenschaftstheorie—Handlungstheorie—Fundamentale Theologie* (Düsseldorf: 1976); on the history of Peukert's influence, see H. U. von Brachel and N. Mette, eds., *Kommunikation und Solidarität* (Fribourg and Münster: 1985).

30. L. Lies, "Sakramente als Kommunikationsmittel," in G. Koch and others, *Gegenwärtig in Wort und Sakrament* (Freiburg: 1976) 110–148.

31. P. Hünermann, "Sakrament—Figur des Lebens," in R. Schaeffler and P. Hünermann, *Ankunft Gottes und Handeln des Menschen* (Freiburg: 1977) 51–87; A. Ganoczy, *Einführung in die katholische Sakramentenlehre* (Darmstadt, 1979) 106–135. For a critical evaluation, see C. Schütz's article in *MySal* Ergänzungsband, 349ff.; U. Kühn, *Sakramente*, 220–221, with bibliography; A. Schilson, "Sakrament als Symbol," 137.

32. C. Schütz in *MySal* Ergänzungsband, 351.

33. A. Ganoczy, *Einführung*, 114.

34. Ibid., 116; there is an explicit rejection of the idea of the sacraments as "the Church's self-fulfillment," since this Church can scarcely be discovered empiri-

munication of divine grace takes place in an ambiguous manner and is subject to misunderstanding, either because it is said that "the human actors" "enter into discipleship of the one who has uttered the creative pronouncement" and "repeat the words of God,"[35] or because "a repetition of the beginning," of the constitution of the Church in the life, death, and resurrection of Jesus[36] is thought to be possible.

5. Two contrasting positions interpret the sacraments on the basis of the cultic realm. Their primary weakness lies in the fact that "cult" appears as a onesidedly human activity in contrast to the theologically rich concept of liturgy. Thus while it is true that an important aspect of the sacraments appears when they are considered as human interpretations of being [Dasein][37] or when, quite rightly, they are viewed as imperatives of social transformation and anticipations of a reconciled life (also, and especially, in the "material" realm).[38] But in these discussions, the Christological and Trinitarian theological bases of the sacraments are not brought into the picture.

6. Finally, we should mention here the various "approaches" that attempt to expound the sacraments on the basis of anthropological considerations. When Karl Rahner interpreted the individual sacraments as God's promise of salvation to individual human beings, spoken by the Church in absolute commitment, and taking place in decisive situations in the salvation history of each individual, he was proposing a new formulation of Thomas Aquinas' interpretation of the total of seven sacraments on the basis of the development of human life, both individual and collective.[39] This point of view was taken up in pastoral

cally. See also statements like: a Christian "moves from one stage of communication to another"; the practice of the sacraments should occur in the manner "of a progressive 'strategy of the future' " (ibid., 127); not the Scholastic notion of causality, but rather "images drawn from cybernetics" should be applied to the sacramental event (ibid.); ministers of the sacraments are to be seen as "catalysts in service of interactive relations," and the sacramental sign "as reality-laden information intrinsically related to the addressee" (ibid., 134).

35. Ibid., 121.
36. P. Hünermann, "Sakramente—Figur des Lebens," 76.
37. R. Schaeffler, "Kultisches Handeln," Ankundt Gottes, 9–50.
38. F. Schupp, Glaube—Kultus—Symbol. Versuch einer kritischen Theorie sakramentaler Praxis (Düsseldorf: 1974). On this, see C. Schütz in MySal Ergänzungsband, 353ff.; U. Kühn, Sakramente, 227.
39. K. Rahner, Kirche und Sakramente, 37–67.

publications, sometimes in a simplified form. For example, the Würz-burg synod of the German bishops said: "In the individual sacraments, the sacramental nature of the Church unfolds itself in the concrete situa-tions of human life."[40] Some people now say that "critical points" in the corporal-spiritual existence of the human being have become sym-bols of humanity's direction toward transcendence.[41] In such discus-sions it seems to be easier to rediscover the creative sacramentality of human nature, and its character as image and real symbol of God, than to say anything about the individual sacraments of the Church. For even when the fundamental, biological situations of human life are in-terpreted religiously, and in fact, even when this results in an expressly Christological conclusion, that in Jesus Christ a human life becomes the highest form of expression of God, still the theologies of grace and of the Trinity, which are also essential to sacramental theology, have not yet been touched on.

4.3 Limits and Structure of General Sacramental Theology and Doctrine of the Individual Sacraments

Sacramental theology as a division of theology or "treatise"[42] is a part of dogmatics (dogma of faith) and thus of systematic theology, but it has strong ties to practical theology, as well. Of course, when the study of liturgy is regarded as a discipline of theology, and there-fore as neither a purely historical nor purely practical science, it can also bring sacramental theology under its umbrella. Sacramental the-ology exercises a critical function with respect to official Church teach-ing and practice. It "certainly includes a warning not to make of the sacraments simply the primary and adequate guide for a description of the whole of Christian life. The Church is neither a purely sacramen-tal Church; nor does the sacramental life of Christians encompass their

---

40. "Schwerpunkte heutiger Sakramentenpastoral," *Gemeinsame Synode der Bistümer in der Bundesrepublik Deutschland. Offizielle Gesamtausgabe* (Freiburg: 1976) 1:245–257.

41. See, for example, the bibliographic references to W. Kasper and J. Ratzinger in A. Schilson, "Sakrament," 134. It is not possible here to discuss the extensive literature on the sacraments in the fields of catechesis, religious education, and pastoral liturgy.

42. Still valid on this is K. Rahner, "Sakramententheologie," in *LThK* IX, 240–243.

whole existence; nor did God make divine grace totally dependent on the sacraments."[43] Sacramental theology most definitely has this critical function toward canon law and its normative demands.

Karl Rahner made the suggestion, based on his insight about the sacramental structure of all created reality and the developing clarification of sacramentality in salvation history, that the individual sacraments should not simply be treated one after another, but instead, each should be described in its appropriate setting in an anthropology of believing human beings living in the Church.[44] This suggestion was followed by *Mysterium Salutis* and *Initiation à la pratique de la théologie*. Still, there is still some practical sense in making a special overview of the sacraments in the traditional order.

In the same context, Rahner determined that the proper place for general sacramental theology is ecclesiology, the theological teaching on the Church.[45]

Thus it still makes sense, on the basis of the theological insight into the sacramental structure of the Church and its liturgy, to speak summarily of the sacraments in general and in doing so to cover all the essential contents of traditional sacramental theology, so long as we avoid a procedure by which, at a later stage, all sacraments would be uniformly pressed into a single, identical schema.

When the individual sacraments are described singly, Catholic tradition has followed a certain order (which is, certainly, not obligatory): baptism, confirmation, Eucharist, reconciliation, anointing of the sick, orders, marriage (cf. Council of Trent, NR 501/DS 1310, and Vatican Council II, LG 11). Here the first five correspond to the individual, the last two to the collective life-situation, a division that was familiar to Thomas Aquinas. The beginning of the series with baptism, confirmation, and Eucharist reflects the sequence of solemn initiation in the old Roman Church,[46] and thus carries a special weight of tradition. The connection between the two "major sacraments" of baptism and Eucharist is not really interrupted by confirmation, which belongs to baptism. In this book, therefore, the individual sacraments will be discussed in the traditional order.

43. Thomas Aquinas, *S. Th.* III, q. 64, ad 7c, quoted in Rahner, "Sakramenten-theologie," 242.
44. *Schriften*, I, 28, 42, 44–47.
45. Ibid., 42; *LThK* IX, 241ff.
46. A. Angenendt, "Bonifatius" (see n. 12 above).

5

Fundamentals of
General Sacramental Theology

5.1 Symbolic Liturgical Actions as Mediation of the Presence of God

5.1.1 Effective Symbolic Event

As long as there has been reflection on sacramental theology, sacraments have been thought of as "signs" (see above, 4.1 and 4.2.2). But this understanding of sacraments is imprecise and in need of clarification. There are signs that are mere pointers to something distant, to someone or something that is absent. There are conventional, agreed-upon signs, signals, etc. Therefore the concept of "symbol" seemed better suited as a more precise term. The Greek word "symbol," stemmed from *symballein*, meaning "to throw together," and therefore describes the bringing together of two parts that originally belonged together, for the purpose of recognition: therefore a symbol is a "sign of recognition." (And thus it is understandable that the Christian creed was known very early as a *symbolum*.) Symbol, therefore, is essentially connected with recognition, understanding, and communication. Still, there is no single concept of symbol that is agreed upon by the various groups and fields of scholarship that concern themselves with symbols at the present time.[1] It is the indisputable right of theology to insist on its own understanding of symbols; but in order for there to be communication about the things that pertain to faith, it is important that we seek common points in Christian and non-religious views of symbols.

There are such points of commonality, and they consist, principally, in the following:

Symbols are not simply images or fixed, static signs, representations of something that is absent. Instead, they are "relational events," they create relationships and belong within an "intentional field," i.e., they lead to an understanding of reality that is relational, dynamic, and process-oriented.[2] Thus they have the characteristics of conscious event, of action, and they overcome divisions of time—among other things, they make present what is past and thus are not dissipated in pure actualism. The recognition, understanding and communication that happen in the symbolic event are unthinkable without language and its critical function. Thus symbol and language can agree in two quite essential aspects: (1) a reality "expresses" itself in a dramatic, eventful "representation"; this "representation" is composed of materials drawn from our world of experience, so that it does not immediately arise from its inner reality and yet is intimately connected with it; (2) the inner reality that is intended is itself "there" in the eventful representation and dramatically "unfolds" itself out of that representation.

If a reality expresses itself *in the realm of symbols* as actually present in the event, the symbol is called a "real symbol." If a reality expresses

1. The most important of these are depth psychology (symbols as expressions of the psychic unconscious), philosophy of language, cultural anthropology and ethnology (rituals), social psychology, and sociology (construction or promotion of identity through symbolic interaction). Principal works are: E. Ortigues, *Le Discours et le Symbole* (Paris: 1962); T. Todorov, *Théories due symbole* (Paris: 1977); L.-M. Chauvet, *Du symbolique au symbole* (Paris: 1979)—this last in dialogue with the structuralists, Heidegger, and Rahner. See also *Neue Zeitschrift für Systematische Theologie und Religionsphilosophie* 27 (1985) no. 2 (a special issue on modern theories of symbol).

2. D. Zadra, "Symbol und Sakrament," in *Christlicher Glaube in moderner Gesellschaft* 28 (Freiburg: 1982) 88–121, at 94–95.

itself *in the realm of language* in an eventful representation, this process is called "myth."[3] Considered from the point of view that the intended reality itself is present in the language event (that is, that the language does more than simply inform), that event is called "performative utterance."[4] Precisely these characteristics illustrate the extraordinary agreement between religious and non-religious concepts of symbol. First, we should mention the efforts of scholars in the field of religious studies in regard to symbols. If these symbols tend to represent a making-present of some transcendence that still remains rather indefinite, Christianity can, nonetheless, recognize therein authentic values from which it need not make violent efforts to distance itself. Gerard van der Leeuw's remarks are worthy of notice: "Some ancient symbols reappear again and again. They constitute the bridges existing within human nature itself between the two worlds in which human beings participate. The symbols are the borders where the two realities meet. They are not the imaginative creations of the human mind; they are given." He also writes: "Every event can be an instance of the holy. If it is, we speak of a 'symbol.' "[5] Here also, of course, we witness the relationship of symbolism, poetry, and especially myth.[6]

3. This presumes, within the context of the extensive discussion of myth (cf. the literature listed in n. 6 below), that a reality *can* express itself in a symbol. Whether it does, in fact, express itself does not depend solely upon the myth or symbol: other experiences of this reality are needed in order to be certain that we are not dealing merely with a projection. At any rate, the present discussion shows that rationalistic devaluation of myth has run its course. Cf. H. Blumenberg, *Arbeit am Mythos* 2d ed. (Frankfurt: 1981); K. Hübner, *Die Wahrheit des Mythos* (Munich: 1985).

4. The concept is from J. L. Austin and J. R. Searle; it is gradually making itself at home in theology. Cf. D. Zadra, "Symbol und Sakrament," 101ff.; J.-M. R. Tillard, "Les sacrements de l'Eglise," *Initiation* II (see Bibliography 1), 392ff.

5. H. G. Hubbeling, "Der Symbolbegriff bei Gerardus van der Leeuw," *Neue Zeitschrift für Systematische Theologie* (see n. 1 above) 100–110, at 106 and 104.

6. Cf. the detailed studies on the function of myth: H.-P. Müller, "Mythos— Anpassung—Wahrheit. Vom Recht mythischer Rede und deren Aufhebung," *Zeitschrift für Theologie und Kirche* 80 (1983) 1–25; idem, "Das Motiv für die Sintflut. Die hermeneutische Funktion des Mythos und seiner Analyse," *Zeitschrift für die alttestamentliche Wissenschaft* 97 (1985) 295–316 (with important remarks on the "image" of God in mythical structures of seeing); idem, "Mythos und Kerygma. Anthropologische und theologische Aspekte," *Zeitschrift für Theologie und Kirche* 83 (1986) 405–435 (including the recognition of God in myth). H.-P. Müller correctly points out that, for an adequate analysis and interpretation of myth, a recovery of metaphysics is necessary.

From the point of view of the philosophy of religion, the presence of the holy occurs when it is symbolically "presented" or narrated. What, then, distinguishes a sacrament in Christian faith from this point of view?

The sacrament is a symbolic action in which human beings are engaged as believers, as those who celebrate liturgy, as narrators, as persons who act symbolically; but the divine Spirit uses this human action as a means and a way by which to make Jesus Christ, with his historically unique saving activity, memorially, really, and actually present.

This making-present thus does not happen without human beings, but neither does it happen simply *through* them (as happens from the point of view of religious studies or history of religions). Instead, it is the Spirit of God who takes the initiative and supports the whole event, causing the effects in the human persons; but instead of depriving those human persons of their own activity, the Spirit actually strengthens them for what they do.

The manner in which the sacraments as symbolic actions mediate the presence of God can be still more precisely described. Theoretical objections to Christian sacramental practice repeatedly reveal the same doubts: how can human symbols or gestures "compel" God to be present here? How can human beings who perform such symbolic actions claim to have divine grace at their disposal? These questions reveal mistaken ways of thinking. Sacramental theology does not claim that the sacraments cause a nearness to God, who would "otherwise" be absent. The error here is in attributing to God a spatial distance from the world and human beings that is overcome by the sacraments. Sometimes God is also thought of as standing intentionally at a distance, as if God were at the same time neutral to and waiting for human beings, until the sacrament causes him to be gracious to them. In reference to the saving event in Jesus Christ, this mistaken line of thought often supposes an additional distance of time, as though the sacrament could uproot from the past an event that has faded into the misty distance. We sometimes hear utterances even in the churches that give encouragement to such ideas, as when there is talk of the privation or distance of God that is said to exist in places where the sacraments cannot be administered. Here some basic theological preconditions are being forgotten: That God, in the Holy Spirit, is really present to God's creation, to God's humanity, and not in the shape of a static Other, but in the dynamism of God's loving desire, in constant self-communication. For God, who transcends time, God's unsurpassable presence in creation and in humanity in Jesus Christ is not past, but clearly present. In this "attitude," God has no need of a constantly-renewed motivation, an increase of intensity, or any other change. Instead, change is needed on the part of the human beings to whom, because of their own makeup, God's presence, God's desire for self-communication, and the saving event in Jesus Christ are never equally vivid nor equally intensive. In the symbolic sacramental actions—but not only in them—God's Spirit effects the "opening" of the bars that human beings set up against God's presence. The Spirit actualizes and intensifies what "always already" is. A part of this process is the ability of symbolic actions, already described several times, to externalize and make visible that which, from their very inner constitution, demands actualization.

Despite the existence of false notions of sacraments as material containers or "channels" for a divine grace that remains indefinite, there is an increasing trend in theology to consider that sacraments are best and most accurately described as symbolic actions that mediate the presence of God.[7] Special mention should be made of two theologians who have played a particular role in this field. Among Lutherans, Paul Tillich (1886–1965) devoted himself in outstanding fashion to religious symbols and the realm of the sacramental.[8] Tillich not only emphasized the effective character of the symbols and their expository function; he also spoke expressly of God's action by means of symbols: "God, in revealing himself, creates symbols and myths through which he can be recognized and through which human beings can approach him,"[9] not through an autonomous human initiative, but because human beings "are taken up into the sacramental unity with the divine Spirit."[10] Symbol and sacrament are synonymous concepts for Tillich. He saw the finite world as full of symbols; he was convinced that human beings can encounter the sacramental everywhere. The Church's sacraments he regarded as places in which the sacramental,

7. See the overviews in A. Schilson, "Sakrament als Symbol"; A. Schmied, "Perspektiven"; U. Kühn, Sakramente.

8. Cf. P. Lengsfeld, "Symbol und Wirklichkeit. Die Macht der Symbole nach Paul Tillich," in W. Heinen, ed., Bild—Wort—Symbol (Würzburg: 1969) 207–224; U. Reetz, Das Sakramentale in der Theologie Paul Tillichs (Stuttgart: 1974).

9. P. Tillich, Gesammelte Werke VIII (Stuttgart: 1970) 79.

10. P. Tillich, Systematische Theologie III (Stuttgart: 1966) 146.

which can be encountered everywhere, is especially concentrated. This is connected with the idea that not all effective religious symbols are recognized and acknowledged in the same way by human persons. The sacrament is also characterized by the fact that it is accepted by a group—namely, believers.

On the Catholic side, Karl Rahner (1904–1984) not only developed the concept of real symbol (see also 1.2 above), which describes the "expression" of a particular, present reality in symbol, as distinct from an arbitrarily chosen sign;[11] Rahner also understood the symbol as an event, and the following examples he gives of symbolic events make this clear: "In the Trinity the Father is himself when he utters himself in the Son who is distinct from him. The soul exists, that is to say, fulfils its own being, when it embodies and expresses itself in the body which it 'informs' and which is different from it. A person succeeds in adopting a certain attitude when [she or] he expresses it a gesture: by 'expresses' itself the attitude comes into being, or acquires existential depth."[12] If the Reformers said that a sacrament is only a sign or a symbol of the promise of faith which *alone* is effective for salvation, this conception of the sacrament as a complex, effective symbolic event would, of course, be contrary to their ideas.

The sacramental theology of real symbols described above is ecumenically open to the extent that the symbolic action must be borne by the faith that is given by God *alone*, and only in God does it find its ultimate guarantee.

5.1.2 *Jesus Christ as Author of the Sacraments*

The modern notion of an "institution" or "inauguration" of the sacraments by God in Jesus Christ is deceptive, because it suggests a juridical action at a particular point in time. Although it is true that Jesus, and the Judaism of his time, had a positive attitude toward symbolic actions, practiced them and thus gave a certain preference to some of them, it is impossible to make a case for his having, at a particular historical time, performed special juridical actions. Scholasticism, from

11. K. Rahner, "Zur Theologie des Symbols," *Schriften* IV, 275–311.
12. K. Rahner and H. Vorgrimler, *Kleines theol. Wörterbuch* (Freiburg, 15th ed., 1985) 398 (art. "Symbol"). English trans.: *Dictionary of Theology* 2d ed. (New York: Crossroad, 1981) 491.

which the Council of Trent took the concept of *institutio* (see above at 4.2.5), was unacquainted with any narrow, punctual idea of institution. Instead, it embedded the sacraments in a context going back far beyond Jesus Christ, to the very beginning of creation. Of course, it tried so far as possible to discover words of institution during the life of Jesus, but where it found none, it pointed instead to apostolic tradition. *Institutio*, for the Scholastic tradition, could also be seen in the fact that God gave the sacraments their effective power, something that is equally impossible to fix at a particular moment in time, and that in some instances this is ascribed to the work of the exalted Christ through the Spirit.[13]

Sacramental theology is spared any legalistic narrowing in terms of a special moment and particular words of institution, if it follows the suggestion of Karl Rahner: this presupposes an internal and external connection between Jesus Christ and the Church. The essence of that connection is that the incarnation of God in Jesus constitutes the primordial symbol or primordial sacrament of divine grace; that Jesus is the effective pledge of the gracious word of God; that God's Spirit wills a continuation and a palpable appearance of God's promise of salvation in Jesus Christ, which is the Church. "Through its belief in God's grace that is eschatologically victorious in Jesus Christ, a belief that it hears and proclaims in faith, the Church is the sacrament of the world's salvation, since it proclaims and makes present, as eschatologically victorious in the world, that grace which will never again disappear from this world and that invincibly is moving this world towards the fulfillment of the kingdom of God."[14] Given this precondition, the individual sacraments can be regarded as further developments and effective fulfillments of this fundamental, sacramental essence of the Church (see 3.4 above). They originate, accordingly, from God in Jesus Christ through the Holy Spirit, insofar as the Church itself originates from God. Thus it is easy to understand why the

---

13. J. Finkenzeller I, 173–184; A. Schmied, "Was ist ein Sakrament?" (see Bibliography 1) 151–152.

14. K. Rahner and H. Vorgrimler, *Wörterbuch*, 366–367 (Sakrament) (pp. 452–453 of the English translation). "Eschatological" here means what even in the future is unsurpassable and finally valid. See also the summary of Rahner's sacramental theology in K. Rahner, "Das Grundwesen der Kirche," *Handbuch der Pastoraltheologie* I (Freiburg: 1964) 118ff.; idem, "Die Sakramente als Grundfunktionen der Kirche," *Handbuch*, 323–332.

Church arrived at its own unique symbolic actions only through a long process, and learned in that process how to distinguish those of central importance from those of less importance. This process has parallels in the discernment of the canon of biblical books: the process of meditation and reflection on which writings, in the sacramental form of human words, contain the Word of God went on, with much wavering back and forth, until the end of the seventh century. In the case of the individual sacraments, the process lasted until the twelfth century. If we consider the ecumenical differences with regard to both these matters (the biblical canon and the number of the sacraments), we can say that this process of clarification has not been completed even now.

In this process of recognition we can discern those structures that we have already noted several times in connection with the sacraments: the symbolic actions are not "invented" or "decreed," but have grown gradually and have been combined with narrative and explanatory words. They therefore possess many traits of what is conditional and accidental, but that which is essential and absolutely important in them is present in precisely *this* shape and form. That raises the question of the Church's authority to interfere by making changes in the form of the sacramental symbolic actions, which has developed over time. The answer is quite different, depending on which of the individual sacraments is in question, and it presupposes historical knowledge and respect for traditions.[15]

5.1.3 *The Number Seven and the Inequality of the Sacraments*

The total of seven sacraments in the Catholic Church, which was definitively maintained by the Council of Trent (see 4.2.5 above), is the product of a long process of reflection. There are no compelling reasons for maintaining that number as absolute: it developed historically, and even its symbolic value (i.e., 3 persons in God + 4 elements of the world = 7 as the fullness of God's salvific activity) is not per-

15. The Church moved with extreme caution in regard to the Eucharist because of the venerable tradition of the Last Supper accounts; on the other hand, it has shown the greatest flexibility in the case of the sacraments of orders. Cf. also the principle of the liturgical reform, that the rites must be expressive and intelligible (SC 21, which also speaks of "unchangeable elements divinely instituted").

suasive.[16] Nor is it so rigid that it could not, in fact, be expanded through a series of "unfoldings" out of one or another of the individual sacraments. The passage into areas in which we no longer have sacraments in the strict, Roman Catholic sense, but where, in fact, sacramental structures are present, is not really material; they are merely fixed because of a traditional insistence on acts of institution (that is, on what was taken to indicate divine origin) as guarantees of unfailing effectiveness. Quite apart from the problematic development of confirmation, Karl Rahner is probably accurate in observing that the individual sacraments have their locus in concrete situations in the history of salvation of individual human persons, who enfold their (new) decisions in the liturgical symbolic actions of the Church and for that very reason are prepared to accept from the Church the assurance of salvation.

The greater number of sacraments in the Catholic Church is accompanied by a differentiation in their rank (see 4.2.5 above). Traditionally, baptism and Eucharist are regarded as the "greater" or "major sacraments."[17] This emphasis, so important in relations with the Churches of the Reformation, also has an objective foundation. In particular, on the basis of the important biblical witnesses to baptism and Eucharist, we can say of both these sacraments that in them as nowhere else, the whole saving action of Jesus Christ and especially the paschal mystery is made present in the manner of real symbols, and that in their liturgy the invitation to participate in the life and fate of Jesus Christ (in the sense of a Jesus mysticism) is particularly intense. Baptism and Eucharist also take precedence in the Church's ranking: baptism as the symbolic action of incorporation into the Church, and the Eucharist as the liturgical actualization of the community of believers.

5.2 Sacrament—Event of the Word of God

The word of God is intensively involved in the sacramental structure: it causes what it perceptibly "signifies," namely the grace of God

16. A new effort in this speculative direction was made by J. Dournes in "Die Siebenzahl der Sakramente—Versuch einer Entschlüsselung," *Concilium* 4 (1968) 32–40.
17. Cf. Y. Congar, "Die Idee der sacramenta maiora," *Concilium* 4 (1968) 9–15, with extensive material cited.

through Jesus Christ in the Holy Spirit. Reflection on the salvific quality of the word of God begins, from the nature of things, with the holy Scriptures. It gives special attention to its Trinitarian origins: before time, the expressibility of God implies the eternal Logos who, as word of the Father, became human, and who is in one person, the promise of God to humanity and the acceptance of that word of promise by humanity. Hence in every saving event, including the sacramental events, word and materiality are enduringly tied to one another. The word of God (always clothed in human words), however it is communicated, is not limited to demonstrative or informative function: it effects what it says; it brings what it announces.[18]

As long as there have been sacraments, the sacramental symbolic action has always been accompanied by words—not merely interpretive words in the liturgical petition and other explanations (for example, in a homily), but also the narrational, reciting, proclaimed word of *God.* From the beginnings of sacramental theology (Augustine) to the present, this has led to reflection on the more precise relationship between this sacramental word and the external sign. Even at a time when the non-verbal part of the external sign was regarded statically, as element or matter, the accompanying sacramental words (the *forma*) were taken to be decisive in the accomplishment of the sacrament. With reflection on the entirety of the sacramental economy of salvation, the primacy of the word of God became even clearer.[19] On the basis of Christology, the proclamation of the word was seen as the Church's essential function, and the sacrament was recognized as the highest and most compressed form of the Church's word of proclamation. Karl Rahner could even say that "the fundamental essence of the sacra-

18. See the overview of recent theology of the word of God: F. Sobotta, *Die Heilswirksamkeit der Predigt in der theologischen Diskussion der Gegenwart* (Trier: 1968), with bibliography; H. Jacob, *Theologie der Predigt. Zur Deutung der Wortverkündigung durch die neuere katholische Theologie* (Essen: 1969); F. Eisenbach, *Systematische Studien* (see Bibliography 1), 502–533, with bibliography; U. Kühn, *Sakramente*, 218, n. 61, with references to works by L. Scheffczyk, O. Semmelroth, and H. J. Weber; J. Thomassen, "Überlegungen zur Heilswirksamkeit der Verkündigung," in L. Lies, ed., *Praesentia Christi* (Düsseldorf: 1984) 311–320, with bibliography; idem, *Heilsworksamkeit der Verkündigung. Kritik und Neubegründung* (Düsseldorf: 1986).

19. R. Schulte, "Die Wort-Sakrament-Problematik in der evangelischen und katholischen Theologie," *Theologische Berichte* 6 (Zürich: 1977) 81–122; F. Eisenbach, *Systematische Studien*, 542–555 (with bibliography, especially works of K. Rahner and O. Semmelroth).

ment is to be found in the words used,"[20] in the absolute promise of salvation. When in these newer reflections the sacramental and extra-sacramental proclamation of the word of God are compared with one another, and when the absolute high point is found in the sacrament, it is important not to overlook the fact that the difference is not in what is effected; it is not in the gift. The effective word of God, as proclaimed and accepted in the Church, is effective *to the extent that* it is the word of God (and not human communication, teaching, etc.), and it is in *every* form and manner of proclamation the true presence of God's grace, of the saving event in Jesus Christ, through the power of the Holy Spirit. What is different, especially with regard to the intensity, the "compression" of the fulfillment, is the manner in which the gift is communicated[21]—different, then, not because of the gift itself, but because of its reception.

For sacramental theology and praxis it is of decisive importance that the word event in the sacrament not be thought of as restricted to the speaking of a brief "formula," something which may be justified, at most, in cases of extreme necessity and under particular conditions. A sacrament is always liturgy, and therefore must always be seen in a verbal context. In addition to the petition for the coming of the divine Spirit, it includes the proclamation of the effective word of God and the human response.[22] The sacraments are also, in their essence, "actions of response arising from faith and effected by the Spirit."[23]

These reflections on the sacrament as word event are valid, of course, in different ways in accord with the differences among the individual sacraments. The word event in a sacrament touches a particular situation in a community and/or in the life of a concrete individual human being; it is a promise of salvation within that situation, and it makes present the corresponding situation in the life of Jesus Christ.

20. K. Rahner and H. Vorgrimler, *Wörterbuch*, 366 (English trans., p. 452). In *Schriften* XVI, 389, Rahner says that the sacrament is "the most intensive case of God's revealing word." There are related reflections from the Lutheran point of view in the works of G. Ebeling: see M. Raske, *Sakrament, Glaube, Liebe. Gerhard Ebelings Sakramentsverständnis—eine Herausforderung an die katholische Theologie* (Essen: 1973); U. Kühn, *Sakramente*, 215–218.

21. Cf. U. Kühn, *Sakramente*, 218–219.

22. Cf. E. Lessing, "Kirchengemeinschaft und Abendmahlsgemeinschaft," *Wissenschaft und Praxis in Kirche und Gesellschaft* 69 (1980) 450–462, at 458–459; A. Schmied, "Perspektiven," 32.

23. U. Kühn, *Sakramente*, 219.

It draws the believers into this Jesus-situation and thereby alters their situation and, through these changed believers, it alters the situation of the world.

5.3 *Sacrament, Prayer, and Discipleship*

In the course of history, the Latin Church created formulae for the administration of the sacraments and (with some exceptions that will be discussed in connection with the individual sacraments) gave them an indicative form.[24] When, subsequently, the question about the exact moment at which the sacrament is accomplished arose, the answer was: when the minister utters this formula in connection with the physical action.[25] This minimalizing was unjust to the total sacramental event. We should again become aware that, apart from cases of pure necessity, the *whole* liturgical symbolic action constitutes the fulfillment of the sacrament, and that individual elements cannot be dispensed with at will. Beyond that, it is also desirable that the "core words" in the "administration of the sacraments" should (re)acquire the optative form of petitionary prayers. That is not some extra, spiritual, but basically superfluous desideratum. We are dealing here with the basic form of the sacraments: they are prayers, and more precisely, they are prayers "in the name of Jesus," spoken by the community of believers, from "minister" and "recipient," with a content that depends on the situation in which each individual sacrament is given. Such a prayer calls on the God who has revealed the one name that brings salvation (Acts 4:12). *This* prayer[26] is assured of a unique effectiveness; it will certainly be heard (John 14:13-14; 16:23-24; cf. Mark 11:24; Matt 7:7-11; 21:22, and others). It is the most ancient form of the liturgy. In recovering the sacraments as prayer, we could learn a great deal, from a religious and theological point of view, from the Eastern Churches' epiclesis, the petition for the coming of the divine spirit to sanctify the earthly matter. We would thus be made aware, once again, of the Spirit

24. The old Roman liturgy hesitated over this for a long time. The first appearance of indicative formulae cannot be demonstrated in the Roman liturgy before the end of the seventh century. See A. Angenendt, "Bonifatius," 135.

25. Cf. the decree for the Armenians: NR 503/DS 1312.

26. R. Schwager, "Wassertaufe, ein Gebet um die Geisttaufe?" *Zeitschrift für katholische Theologie* 100 (1978) 36–61, at 56–59 on the prayer "in the name of Jesus," precisely in the context of the sacraments.

of God as the one who is at work in the sacraments for the salvation of human beings. At the same time, we could avoid the misunderstanding, whereby it appears that the person, whether man or woman, who, according to the prescribed order of divine service, is entitled to speak these "core words," has the sacraments, with all their effects in the realm of grace, at his or her disposal, or possesses a magical power that serves to distinguish him or her from the others who participate in the celebration. The renewal of the sacraments as a liturgy of prayer would be of great ecumenical importance, both as regards the Eastern Churches and the Churches of the Reformation, and even in relation to Judaism, from which the Church received the structure of its highest sacrament, the form of the Eucharistic prayer.[27]

As long as the perduring common practice, which at the very least displays a "magisterial" mentality,[28] remains unchanged, we must give special attention to the prayers that accompany the sacraments. They are not some kind of superfluous ornamentation; rather, they are a special opportunity for those who celebrate the sacraments and hope to receive some benefit from them to be subjects, to be able to speak for themselves in the presence of God. It would be a far too narrow conception of the sacraments to restrict the subjective participation of those who carry out the sacramental actions, and especially the so-called recipients, to nothing but faith. The sacraments are places for encounter with Jesus Christ, as sacramental theology correctly says. But "encounter" here means more than simply a momentary meeting. It has a mystical meaning, i.e., human beings unite themselves as intensively as possible with the person and destiny of Jesus Christ. The older theology was aware of this when it described the sacraments as renewed fulfillment of the events in the life of Jesus, of the mysteries of Jesus' life,[29] a dimension that has been totally forgotten today.

27. K. Rahner's important ideas on the subject of sacraments as prayer *of the church*, using all the sacraments as examples, but with special concentration on the sacrament of anointing the sick, are found in *Kirche und Sakramente* 22–30, 52–62. For an epicletic and pneumatological understanding of the sacraments, from the point of view of the Eastern Churches, cf. R. Hotz, *Sakramente* (see Bibliography 1) 173–300. See further B. McDermott, "Das Sakrament als Gebetsgeschehen," *Concilium* 18 (1982) 626–630.

28. A. Angenendt, "Bonifatius," 161, with reference also to the opinion of J. Ratzinger.

29. On this, see G. Lohaus, *Die Geheimnisse des Lebens Jesu in der Summa theologiae des heiligen Thomas von Aquin* (Freiburg: 1985). There are some more extensive

The sacraments are the places at which the events that make up the living and dying of a human being are inserted and enfolded in the events of the living and dying of Jesus, and human hopes of resurrection become part of his accomplished triumph. At this point we are again taking up a suggestion of Karl Rahner, when he said that grace is only understood in a Christian way if it is seen not as a metaphysical divinization, but as an assimilation to Jesus Christ, which is existentially transformed into discipleship in his followers.[30]

This mysticism begins in the language event of the sacraments. In making present the events of the living and dying of Jesus, it is (also) a spoken adoration of the Father and at the same time (also) a placing oneself at the disposal of the impulses of the divine Spirit. But it is not restricted to the realms of language and of mental reflection. Johann Baptist Metz is right to call the sacraments "tangible praxis of grace, without which there can be no mysticism of grace."[31] In their physically perceptible, comprehensible form, the sacraments assist the mystical making-present of the tender God, of the body-caring praxis of Jesus; they are "the appeal of grace in the senses."[32] Thus it is clear that this view of things does not imply a mere notion of interiority and otherworldliness; instead, as with Jesus, this mystical dimension is united to a concrete, practical, and even political dimension.

The following reflections may also contribute to the support of this idea. Ordinarily, when people are praying they project the divine dimension into a distant "heaven," a heavenly liturgy far removed from the trials of this earth. In this way, the real nearness of God to creation, to humanity in its concrete situation of need, is not taken seriously enough. For Jesus, as Pascal said, this nearness means that his suffering and death endure to the close of history. The one who is present through the Spirit, in the liturgy as well, is not simply the Exalted One in his glory, but the one who suffers and is oppressed in and with all creatures.

suggestions on this topic also in L. Lies, "Trinitätsvergessenheit gegenwärtiger Sakramententheologie?" *Zeitschrift für katholische Theologie* 105 (1983) 290–314.

30. K. Rahner, *Schriften* I, 220–221.

31. J. B. Metz, *Jenseits bürgerlicher Religion* (Munich and Mainz: 1980) 78.

32. Ibid., 73; cf. the whole section from pp. 73–79.

5.4 *Sacraments of Faith*

We have already discussed faith as one of the preconditions for sacramental theology (1.5 above). Now we need to reflect more directly on the connection between faith and sacraments.

In a very general sense, faith means freely accepting what a person says because of one's confidence in that person.[33] It is thus an essential element in the relationship between persons; it has the character of a response and it rests on the trustworthiness of the person speaking. If God is the speaker, the utterance is always mediated (see 1.1 above), so that from the human point of view God's communication is always more opaque than that of a human being. Because of the infinite distance between God and human beings, Jewish and Christian tradition insists that humans are only able to accept this communication of God in freedom, if God himself enables their acceptance. The word most often used in the Old Testament for faith means "to know myself secure." To God's call and to the experience of security correspond, at the same time, God's claim on the human person in all his or her dimensions, a claim that, in the final analysis, demands that humans love God (so that it is not mere acceptance and obedience) and that finds its fulfillment in the union of divine and human love. In the New Testament conception of faith, it is never a question of founding one's faith on the Church in addition to or instead of on God, so that one trusts totally and completely in the Church. Faith rests always and exclusively in God. But, from God's very first revelations until now, faith is always given also to *what* God reveals as God's will; faith is not only an attitude of unshakable trust, for it also has a content. Christians are convinced that the Church is part of that content,[34] but a Church neither as an autonomous entity nor as something for its own sake; rather, as a reality living entirely from its head, Jesus Christ, and in the Holy Spirit. From this point of view there is, even in the New Testament, an attested connection between faith and sacrament, so that the sacrament can be understood as a tangible fulfillment or confession of faith (Rom 6:1-11; Gal 3:26-27; Acts 8:35ff.; Mark 16:16; John 6:47-51).

---

33. K. Rahner and H. Vorgrimler, *Wörterbuch*, 149–155 (Glauben); English: 167 (Faith).

34. H. de Lubac, "Credo Ecclesiam," in J. Daniélou and H. Vorgrimler, eds., *Sentire Ecclesiam* (Freiburg: 1961) 13–16.

Therefore, in accepting and affirming the sacraments, the Church's tradition has seen participation in them as primarily a confession of faith and in this sense speaks of "sacraments of faith."[35] When the tradition up to Vatican Council II (SC 59) also says of the sacraments that they nourish and strengthen faith, that is not an inappropriate expansion: why should the physically tangible, visible witness to faith not strengthen the inner attitude, which is never purely spiritual, especially since the one who acts in both is one and the same, namely the Holy Spirit of God? The original connection between faith and sacrament is so close that the question whether faith is necessary for the carrying out of the sacrament must be utterly bewildering. However, this question lies at the heart of a common teaching in the Catholic Church, even though it can only be understood against the background of its historical development: the teaching about the minimal conditions for administering a sacrament. The teaching contains a number of problematic distinctions or divisions.

The first distinction to be discussed in this connection is that between the "minister" and the "recipient" of the sacrament. The full ugliness of the phrase is apparent only in German, where the two terms are *Spender* and *Empfänger*. The Latin (and English) term "minister" still has some aura of the meaning of one who gives aid or service. But the development of sacramental theology has made it impossible to dispense entirely with this pair of concepts. At the beginning of sacramental praxis, there was a liturgy performed by all, the community celebration of the sacramental symbolic action; but with the development of the episcopal and priestly offices, for the sake of unity and order in the communities, the question of competence in regard to the sacraments quickly arose. It is certainly evident by the time of Hippolytus of Rome (d. ca. 236). In line with Latin legal theory, it appeared that the single condition that must be fulfilled by the minister of the sacrament was the possession of *authority* (*Vollmacht*).[36] In the wake of divisions within the Church, and the appearance of heretical clerics, who had previously been endowed with genuine authority,

---

35. The standard work is L. Villette, *Foi et Sacrement* I [NT to Augustine] (Paris: 1959); II [Thomas Aquinas to K. Barth] (Paris: 1964). Cf. also H. J. Auf der Maur and others, eds., *Fides sacramenti sacramentum fidei. Studies in honour of Pieter Smulders* (Assen: 1981), containing ten articles on the history of dogma and four systematic studies on the connection between faith and sacrament.
36. J. Finkenzeller I, 103ff.

the further question arose whether sacraments administered by a heretic were not invalid. Augustine dealt with this problem, which was an acute one for him because of the Donatists, with the thesis that even such a sacrament was valid so long as it was administered in the form recognized by the Church.

Thus another distinction entered the picture: that between "valid" and "invalid" administration of a sacrament. The Church claimed the ability to be able to decide whether a sacrament occurs or not. On the basis of the Augustinian position concerning the minister of the sacrament there developed, in the thirteenth century, the teaching about the proper *intention* as a second condition to be fulfilled by the minister of the sacrament.[37] At that time, the problems were less pressing than they had been for Augustine. People inquired theoretically what would happen if a mother, while bathing her child, should jokingly baptize it in the name of the Trinitarian God, or if a priest gave absolution in jest. The theological consensus was that, presupposing that the minister of a sacrament *could* administer it (i.e., had the necessary authority), he or she administers it validly if he or she has the intention, i.e., the purpose, "of doing what the Church does." This view was adopted also by the Council of Trent (see 4.2.5 above).

The Catholic Church had thus established a minimum, which did not do justice to the sacramental event as a whole. The Church did not inquire about the beliefs of the minister of the sacrament; thus faith, on the part of one of the principal actors in the sacramental liturgy, was not regarded as necessary. In critical cases the Church is even prepared to accept the absence of authority in the minister of the sacrament, since it recognizes a sacrament received in good faith, though "invalidly" administered, as having the same saving effects as a "validly" administered sacrament. In this case the Church itself intervenes in favor of those in good faith and supplies what is lacking.[38] As strange as this position may seem, it still bears powerful witness to the conviction that the essential actor in the sacrament is not the human being, but Jesus Christ through the divine Spirit, which will not be thwarted in its effects even by the greatest possible unworthiness, or even lack of faith on the part of the official minister. And this

37. Ibid., 108–111, 190–195; J.-M. Tillard, "Zur Intention des Spenders und des Empfängers der Sakramente," *Concilium* 4 (1968) 54–61, with bibliography.
38. H. Herrmann, *Ecclesia supplet* (Amsterdam: 1968).

conviction is, once again, one of faith—the faith of the Church as a whole.

A parallel question related to the "recipient" of the sacrament. Its origins were in the New Testament communities, who in turn could refer directly to Jewish principles: the desire to belong to the community of God included the will to orient one's life on the faith of that community. In turn, the community cannot accept any and all behavior on the part of its members. Paul's remarks (1 Cor 11:27ff.) on the "worthy" reception of the Eucharist should be understood against this background. From frequent meditation on these statements, which were tangibly expressed in the institution of penance and reconciliation in the ancient Church, there arose a distinction between "worthy" and "unworthy" reception of the sacraments, the latter leading to a harmful result. The ancient Church had very concrete ideas about the "worthiness" of the recipients of a sacrament. They must confess their faith publicly and offer tangible evidence of a Christian way of life.

For theology, the initial question was not whether too much importance was thus given to human achievements and claims, since there was an unbroken consensus, based on a clear theology of grace, that no human being could do anything good unless God gave him or her the ability, the will, and the means to accomplish it. Theologians were more inclined to discuss whether people could "worthily" receive sacraments, if they were not in a position to give a clear expression of their purpose (intention) to receive them. The practice of baptizing infants or anointing unconscious persons evoked this question about the minimal *disposition* (appropriate readiness). The Catholic Church adopted a theory that was mainly worked out by Albert the Great and Thomas Aquinas, which said that a negative disposition was sufficient for the valid and worthy reception of a sacrament. More precisely stated, the negative disposition exists so long as a human being places no obstacle (*obex*) to God's saving will. Clear obstacles were an expressed will not to receive the sacrament, or a disposition of serious and unrepented guilt. At the Council of Trent this teaching about the minimal disposition was officially accepted by the Church (see 4.2.5 above).

Once again, this conception, one-sidedly oriented as it is to borderline cases, does not do justice to the whole process of sacramental liturgy. It does express, in its own way, the conviction that the faith of the Church as a whole, the gift of the divine Spirit, accomplishes the sacramental events, and that God's gracious action always anticipates the human part, embracing even those who are unconscious or incapable of independent action. But faith, as it is searchingly portrayed in the revealed word of God, must be accepted by individual, concrete subjects and accomplished in the forms of profession, liturgy and the praxis of life. This insight gave rise to the generally accepted teaching about the "fruitful" reception of a sacrament, which only happens when a human being, led by the grace of God, makes the sacrament a sign of his or her faithful acceptance of God's promise of salvation. This can also occur when the person consciously accepts a sacrament that was previously bestowed on him or her, thus "ratifying" or "renewing" it. This is sensible and even necessary for Christian life, not only in the case of baptism, but also for other sacraments that can only be received once but are to have real effects throughout a person's whole life, such as marriage or orders.[39] The sacraments are delivered from momentary or mechanical conceptions, if we see them as dynamically embedded in the whole dialogical life-story of a human being with God, which never remains at the same level of intensity, but has its heights and depths. In this sense, the Council of Trent said of the sacraments that, through them, "every true justice begins, grows or, having been lost, is restored" (NR 505/DS 1600).

5.5 *Sacrament as Mediation of Divine Grace*

If, according to Catholic belief, the sacraments mediate divine grace, and do so "by the power of the completed ritual" (*ex opere operato*) this conviction needs to be protected against a variety of possible misinterpretations. God's grace exists where God is, and since God is in creation and with God's people, God's grace is "always already" there, is always present to human beings. This is quite clear when grace is understood primarily as that uncreated grace that is Godself, who desires to communicate himself to creation and to human beings, and

39. On the connection between faith and sacrament, see also K. Rahner, "Personale und sakramentale Frömmigkeit," *Schriften* II, 115–141, as well as his "Glaube und Sakrament," *Schriften* XVI, 387–397. Also important is Rahner's *Kirche und Sakrament* 30, regarding a "revival" of the sacraments when the "obstacle" has been removed. This idea of "revival" or "revivification" can be found as early as Augustine with regard to the sacraments that imprint a "character" (see 5.7 below) and cannot be repeated.

who has "always already" made that communication. Sacraments are thus neither means whereby God is moved to change something, nor means for bringing about the presence of God. But God's presence, which is "always already" guaranteed, seeks concrete ways of inserting itself in particular human situations. Concretely that means: ways that are perceptible and evident to human beings in a human way, and ways that people can follow. God desires to be present in particular human situations since God is not merely an incomprehensible, transcendent presence, but has already entered concretely into humanity in God's word made human and in the Holy Spirit, has already given tangible expression, in the community of believers, to that divine "arrival" within humanity. What is still lacking and has to be made clear again and again is that this "arrival" of God happens concretely in particular situations touching the community and individual persons. This concretion occurs in the liturgical symbolic actions of the sacraments: the express promise rests on them, because the effectiveness of prayer and of the community assembly (no matter how small) are secured by divine revelation. The difference in situations means that the presence of God is effective in different ways, which in itself justifies a differentiated view of sacramental grace according to the variety of the sacraments.

"By the power of the completed ritual" (*ex opere operato*) thus means that the sacrament derives its validity and effectiveness from the power of God. Human religious subjectivity, human faith, human readiness to accept pardon and salvation from God are *not* the *cause* of the sacrament's effective power; they are the *condition*, brought about by the Spirit of God, for the effective application of the grace of God that is offered in the sacrament. The sign stands under the promise of God and is at God's disposal: God means it with full sincerity, it will never lead human beings astray, and thus it can never lose its real sign value—its significance as symbol of God's unconditional promise of salvation in Jesus Christ—even through the negligence of the Church's official ministers.

This connection between sacrament and concrete realization of the grace of God, of course, suggests the question whether this means that the sacraments are *necessary* for human salvation. The answer to this question about the necessity of the sacraments for salvation must be subtly differentiated. On the one hand, if God had decreed by some legal action the necessity of one or several sacraments for salvation,

God would at the same time have condemned countless human beings, since it would be clear to God how many obstacles there are to
sacramental life for myriad humans. This kind of negative predestination would contradict the revelation of the divine salvific will, which
is effective for *all* people (Rom 11:32; 1 Tim 2:1-6). On the other hand,
the promptings of the divine Spirit in revelation, in choice, and in call
show that God effects his promise of salvation and saving presence
on a path that leads to a people of God and a Church, a path that individuals undertake "for" the others, and which they, as God's witnesses, must invite others to follow. From that point of view it is
impossible to conceive of many roads to salvation running so independently parallel to one another that they simply have nothing to do with
each other. This leads us in the direction of the Catholic conviction
that the sacraments as a whole may not be regarded as optional and
superfluous (Council of Trent: NR 509/DS 1604).

The high Scholastic theologians of the thirteenth century discussed
the question of the necessity of the sacraments for salvation and arrived at a consensus.[40] They often quoted the statement that God has
not bound divine grace exclusively to the sacraments, and concluded
from this that the sacraments are not absolutely necessary, but only
an appropriate way to salvation. Their suitability is given anthropological foundation: it is fitting for human beings to arrive at spiritual
realities by means of material things. When a person does not recognize the Church's way of salvation as obligatory, there can be no question of the sacraments' being necessary for salvation. But when a
person acknowledges the appropriateness and importance of a sacrament, she or he may not neglect it. A particular sacrament can become
necessary for an individual person (Council of Trent, NR 509/DS 1604).
A study of and reflection on the existence of sacraments can be an occasion for some individuals to acknowledge their humanity with its
sense-oriented nature, their dependence on others, and their need for
God's assistance. The fact that such a reflection is a process that occurs over time and is subject to ups and downs, depending on the particular Church and the stages of a person's life—briefly, that in an
individual's life there may also be periods of distancing from the sacraments, is as obvious as is the appropriateness of the sacraments for

40. J. Finkenzeller I, 144-147.

the Church, which as a community of faith, like every community, has a need for symbolic actions of its own. The connection between the different ways of salvation is expressed in the Church's teaching in terms of a desire (*votum*) for the sacraments. Even without visible connection to the Church, and even without the reception of a sacrament, a human being may receive sacramental grace if she or he—prompted by God—has a serious, positive will directed toward Church and sacraments. In the cases of baptism and reconciliation the Council of Trent expressly declared that these sacraments can be replaced by a desire for them. But this desire may only intend the sacraments and the Church in an inclusive sense, that is, when a person is prepared to follow the dictates of his or her own conscience in fulfilling the will of God. The possibility of living in God's grace, of being justified and attaining eternal life thus does not necessarily presuppose a specific knowledge of Church and sacraments (NR 371/DS 3870ff.). This teaching does not deny a unified concept of divine grace: the grace that effects such a desire is the unique grace of God the Father *in Jesus Christ* through the Holy Spirit, the grace that in the Son and for his sake has come to and been accepted by humanity, that continues to seek its tangible expression, its concrete "bodiliness" in the Church and in the individual sacraments, but that in some people already anticipates this embodiment as an abiding basis for its effectiveness.[41]

5.6 Sacrament and History

In the sacramental symbolic actions, concrete situations in an individual human life or in the life of a community are brought before God, the God who is not distant, but rather is present in a love that anticipates all needs. The presence of God is different from the intermittent presence of human beings: with God, past and future are "present" together. If the sacraments are signs that effect what they signify— that is, if they mediate the saving presence of God through Jesus Christ in the Holy Spirit—then they make "present" the past, present and future; and these are not simply some historical events, but the history that is defined by God.

---

41. K. Rahner and H. Vorgrimler, *Wörterbuch*, 439 (Votum), English: 531 (Votum).

Scholastic theology was aware of this.[42] It spoke about a threefold symbolic function of the sacraments. It is certainly not wrong to expand the medieval vision in a Trinitarian context, so that the structure of faith-love-hope is made clear. A sacrament is, in the first place, always a memorial symbol (Thomas Aquinas: *signum rememorativum*). That is, it is remembering, a narrative recall[43] of a past that, through the effective sign, becomes present. This is the past in which the source and origin of all saving and forgiving grace is to be found. Medieval theology, in its mystical view, took as this source the suffering of Jesus Christ that becomes present reality. Beyond that, the memory of the whole life of Jesus, his adherence to his own people, his origin as Son and Word of God from eternity, in which "always already" the salvation of creation and humanity, was intended. A sacrament is, secondly, a sign of grace at work in the present (*signum demonstrativum*). It points to the divine Spirit who, here and now, is effecting divine love, human love and forgiveness in the human person. A sacrament is, thirdly, an effective anticipation of the future (*signum prognosticum*). It points to the accomplishments of God's purpose, the perfection of creation, the universally-realized reign of God and, included in that, the perfection of the individual life in death and in eternal blessedness. And so this making-present of the future results in the praise and adoration of God the Father.

Sacramental praxis easily overlooks this making-present of all history as salvation history in every individual sacrament. Especially when a sacrament is administered only in an attentuated rite, all attention is drawn to the grace-filled event of the moment. When it is really celebrated, as liturgy, which is normally the case only with the Eucharist, it attains to its fullness as a recovery of the abiding past in the present and a stretching forward into the future already begun.

5.7 *Sacraments of the Church*

From what has been said it is probably clear that the sacraments can be understood as fulfillments of the Church's life or forms of the

42. J. Finkenzeller I, 128–129.

43. J. B. Metz, *Glaube in Geschichte und Gesellschaft* (Mainz: 1977) 185, speaks of the fundamental narrative character of the sacramental event. [English translation: *Faith in History and Society* (New York: Seabury, 1980) 206.]

Church's self-actualization, without detracting in the least from the sovereignty of God in communicating divine grace. Under the always valid precondition tht God alone guarantees that divine grace will be given, by sacramental or nonsacramental means, according to God's will, we can recognize a manifold involvement of the Church in the field of sacraments.

First we ought to mention that, according to Catholic belief, it is the Church's task to recognize the necessary conditions for the validity and liceity of a sacramental action and to establish appropriate norms. Since the sacraments are the Church's liturgy, there is no doubt that the Church has charge over the design, ordering, and reform of sacramental liturgy. That does not exclude the possibility that there could be improvements as regards the concrete application of this principle, for example, regarding the minimalizing and juridical points of view discussed above (4.2.3), or as regards the exclusion of most Christians from the designing of a liturgy that remains largely that of a clerical hierarchy. It must be admitted that the liturgical reforms, begun by Vatican II, have created the preconditions for changing this narrow viewpoint. In the reform of each sacramental rite (as will be indicated below in connection with each individual sacrament), blessings were incorporated in the essential rite which, in their structure, correspond to the Eucharistic prayer as the "quintessence" of all liturgy—i.e., consisting of a memorial of God's saving acts, an *anamnesis*, a praise of thanks, as well as the petition for the coming and action of the divine Spirit (*epiclesis*). When the essential action is the common prayer, the question of the "minister" is relatively unimportant in principle. At least there are signs of a future possibility whereby the blessing-prayer could be seen as that which constitutes the sacrament, with no restriction, without reason, on the number of those who can pray that prayer. However, we cannot overlook the fact that from the Middle Ages to the present the center of the Church's interest has been focused on the possession of authority, the proper intention of the "minister," and the disposition of the "recipient." We have already discussed this above (5.4). This overemphasis on legality is nonetheless an expression of reverence for the sacrament.

Besides this regulatory function of the Church, sacramental theology perceives an internal ecclesial shaping of the sacraments. This means that when a human person enters into the sacramental action (asks to "receive" a sacrament), that person expresses a willingness

to be a living member of the Church; that the one who desires to encounter Jesus Christ in the sacraments also expresses a positive desire
to encounter the Church, and neither can nor wishes to exclude the
Church from this encounter. The theological basis for this connection
between the fully dissimilar realities of Jesus Christ and the Church
is to be found in the New Testament teaching about the Body of Christ
(see 4.2.1 above). Theology has described this connection, in the
sacramental context, with the Scholastic concept *res et sacramentum* (see
4.2.3 above). *Res et sacramentum*, a kind of middle term between the
sacramental sign (*sacramentum tantum*) and the final effect of grace (*res
sacramenti*), must participate both in that final effectiveness and in the
visibility of the sign, but in such a "middle" way that *res et sacramentum* is not identical with either. This "middle" is seen by some
theologians[44] in the special ecclesial relationship in which the first effect also participates, for example, in baptism, the acceptance into the
Church as the Body of Christ and *thereby* the remission of all sins; in
the Eucharist, the communion with the Church as community of love
and *thereby* the communion with Jesus himself; in penance, the reconciliation with the Church injured by sin and *thereby* the eradication of
the sin by God. Accordingly, an individual sacrament always actualizes the fundamental sacrament that is Church and incorporates those
celebrating the sacrament, in a way unique to each sacrament, into that
fundamental sacrament. An acceptance of these ideas, which need not
be couched in Scholastic terminology, could liberate the sacraments
from any ideological form of individualism in their saving application.
In addition, from this point of view it is theologically plausible that
the Church can refuse the sacraments to those who do not have the
desire to participate actively in the Church community. In doing so,
it does not deny these people the grace of God, which is in no way
at the disposal of the Church.

A further implication of this conviction about an internal connection between Church and sacraments is the Catholic teaching that three
sacraments (baptism, confirmation, and orders) bestow a "sacramen-

44. Consistently treated by K. Rahner in *Kirche und Sakramente*; he has a number
of followers. Cf. L. Bertsch and G. Gäde, " 'Res et sacramentum.' Zur Wiederentdeckung der kirchlichen Dimension in der Sakramentenkatechese," in W. Löser
and others, eds., *Dogmengeschichte und katholische Theologie* (Würzburg: 1985)
451–478.

tal character."[45] The Greek word "character" or "sign of recognition" indicates that "spiritual and indelible sign" that, according to the Councils of Florence (NR 504/DS 1313) and Trent (NR 514/DS 1609), is marked on the human soul. This teaching arose from the conviction of the ancient Church in the third and fourth centuries, that baptism and orders, even if conferred by heretical or unworthy officials, could not be repeated. It is, in its own way, a witness to the fact that the initiative of God, which lays hold of human beings, anticipates every human decision. But in particular it tells us that God's promise of salvation in the sacrament also represents a call to individual human persons to accept their "likeness to Christ" (Gal 3:27) beyond the individual level as ecclesial existence, and that they accept the duties that fall to them within the Church. In terms of the three sacraments mentioned, the first duty is to celebrate the liturgy, but that is not the only obligation. (According to Thomas Aquinas, in each of the three sacraments the "character" gives a share in the priesthood of Jesus Christ, but that priesthood includes witnessing both through word and through the work of one's life.)[46] The call remains—that is, it does not need to be repeated in the future, in so far as it cannot be lost, nor can it be surpassed by anything greater or better.

45. E. Ruffini, "Der Charakter als konkrete Sichtbarkeit des Sakraments in Beziehung zur Kirche," *Concilium* 4 (1968) 47–53 (with bibliography).

46. K. Rahner, *Kirche und Sakramente*, and E. Schillebeeckx, *Christus, Sakrament der Gottbegegnung* [*Christ the Sacrament of the Encounter with God*] 160, 170, etc.; Vatican Council II, *LG* 11.

Bibliography 1

Sacraments in General

a) Books

Adam, A. *Grundriß Liturgie.* Freiburg: 1985 (Bibliography).

Ambaum, J. *Glaubenszeichen. Schillebeeckx' Auffassung von der Sakramenten.* Regensburg: 1980.

Auer, J. *Allgemeine Sakramentenlehre und das Mysterium der Eucharistie.* 3d. ed. Regensburg: 1980.

――――――. *Die Sakramente der Kirche.* 2d ed. Regensburg: 1979.

Baudler, G. *Korrelationsdidaktik: Leben durch Glauben erschließen.* Paderborn: 1984 (Also on symbol and sacraments).

Biemer, G. *Katechetik der Sakramente.* Freiburg: 1983.

Boff, L. *Kleine Sakramentenlehre.* 5th ed. Düsseldorf: 1982.

Borobio, D., and others. *La Celebración en la Iglesia* I. Salamanca: 1985 (Liturgical theological foundations; the individual sacraments are to be discussed in volume II).

Browning, R. L., and R. A. Reed. *The Sacraments in Religious Education and Liturgy: An Ecumenical Model.* Birmingham, Ala.: 1985.

Chauvet, L.-M. *Du symbolique au symbole.* Paris: 1979.

Chauvet, L.-M., and others. *Sacrements de Jésus-Christ.* Paris: 1983.

Denis, H. *Sacrements, sources de vie.* Paris: 1982.

Duval, A. *Des sacrements au Concile de Trente.* Paris: 1985 (On all the sacraments except confirmation).

Eisenbach, F. *Die Gegenwart Jesu Christi im Gottesdienst. Systematische Studien zur Liturgiekonstitution des Zweiten Vatikanischen Konzils.* Mainz: 1982.

Finkenzeller, J. *Die Lehre von den Sakramenten im allgemeinen. Von der Schrift bis zur Scholastik* (HDG IV/1a). Freiburg: 1980.

————. *Die Lehre von den Sakramenten im allgemeinen. Von der Reformation bis zur Gegenwart* (HDG IV/1b). Freiburg: 1982.

Francesconi, G. *Storia e simbolo. "Mysterium in figura."* Brescia: 1981 (Ambrose on Sacraments).

Frenkle, N. J., and others. *Zum Thema Kult und Liturgie.* Stuttgart: 1972.

Ganoczy, A. *Einführung in die katholische Sakramentenlehre.* Darmstadt: 1979.

Heumann, J. *Symbol—Sprache der Religion.* Stuttgart: 1983.

Hotz, R. *Sakramente—im Wechselspiel zwischen Ost und West.* Zürich: 1979.

Jetter, W. *Symbol und Ritual. Anthropologische Elemente im Gottesdienst.* Göttingen: 1978.

Jourjon, M. *Les sacrements de la liberté chrétienne selon l'Eglise ancienne.* Paris: 1981.

Jüngel, E., and K. Rahner. *Was ist ein Sakrament?* Freiburg: 1971.

Kirchhoff, H., ed. *Ursymbole und ihre Bedeutung für die religiöse Erziehung.* 2d ed. Munich: 1985.

Klöckener, M., and W. Glade, eds. *Die Feier der Sakramente in der Gemeinde* (FS H. Rennings). Kevelaer: 1986.

Knoch, W. *Die Einsetzung der Sakramente durch Christus. Eine Untersuchung zur Sakramententheologie der Frühscholastik von Anselm von Laon vis zu Wilhelm von Auxerre.* Münster: 1983.

Koch, G., and others. *Gegenwärtig in Wort und Sakrament. Eine Hinführung zur Sakramentenlehre.* Würzburg: 1976.

Kress, B. *The Church. Communion, Sacrament, Communication.* New York: 1985.

Kühn, U. *Sakramente.* (Handbuch Systematischer Theologie 11). Gütersloh: 1985.

Lligadas Vendrell, J. *"Ex opere operato." El significado de la doctrina tridentina sobre la eficacia de los sacramentos.* Rome: 1981.

————. *La eficacia de los sacramentos: "Ex opere operato" en la doctrina del concilio de Trento.* Barcelona: 1983.

Lorizio, G., ed. *Ecclesiae sacramentum* (FS A. Marranzini). Naples: 1986.

Luthe, H., ed. *Christusbegegnung in den Sakramenten.* 2d ed. Kevelaer: 1984.

Martimort, A. G., ed. *L'Eglise en prière.* New edition. III: *Les sacrements,* by R. Cabié and others. Paris and Tournai: 1984.

Martos, J. *Doors to the Sacred. A Historical Introduction to Sacraments in the Christian Church.* London: 1981.

Mens concordet voci (FS A. G. Martimort). Paris: 1983 (several articles on sacramental theology).

Müller, A. *Die Sakramente der Kirche.* Fribourg: 1975.

Neue Zeitschrift für systematische Theologie und Religionsphilosophie 27 (1985) no. 2: special issue on modern symbolic theories.

Nocke, F.-J. *Wort und Geste. Zum Verständnis der Sakramente.* Munich: 1985.

O'Neill, C. *Sacramental Realism. A General Theory of the Sacraments.* Wilmington: 1983.

Rahner, K. *Kirche und Sakramente.* Freiburg and Breisgau: 1960.

Reetz, U. *Das Sakramentale in der Theologie Paul Tillichs.* Stuttgart: 1974.

Ries, J., ed. *Le symbolisme dans le culte des grandes religions.* Louvain: 1985.

Rordorf, W. *Liturgie, foi et vie des premiers chrétiens. Etudes patristiques.* Paris: 1986.

Rosenberg, A. *Einführung in das Symbolverständnis.* Freiburg: 1984.

Ruster, T. *Sakramentales Verstehen.* Frankfurt and Bern: 1983 (especially important on the relationship between word and sacrament).

Die Sakramentalität der Kirche in der ökumenischen Diskussion. Ed. Johann-Adam-Möhler Institute. Paderborn: 1983.

Scharfenberg, J., and H. Kämpfer. *Mit Symbolen leben.* Olten: 1980.

Schillebeeckx, E. H. *Christus, Sakrament der Gottbegegnung.* Mainz: 1960.

Schilson, A. *Theologie als Sakramententheologie. Die Mysterientheologie Odo Casels.* Mainz: 1982.

Schmid-Keiser, S. *Aktive Teilnahme: Kriterium gottesdienstlichen Handelns und Feierns.* 2 vols. Bern and Frankfurt: 1985.

Schneider, T. *Zeichen der Nähe Gottes.* 4th ed. Mainz: 1984.

Schönborn, C. von. *L'Icône du Christ.* 2d ed. Fribourg: 1978.

Schupp, F. *Glaube—Kultur—Symbol. Versuch einer kritischen Theorie sakramentaler Praxis.* Düsseldorf: 1974.

Semmelroth, O. *Vom Sinn der Sakramente.* Frankfurt: 1960.

Skowronek, A. *Sakrament in der evangelischen Theologie der Gegenwart.* Paderborn: 1971.

Snela, B. *Das Menschliche im Christlichen. Elementare Strukturen der religiösen Zeichen.* Munich: 1986, especially 42–59 (an effort toward a structuralist approach to the elementary structures and semantic units of the Church's sacramental system).

Spiegel, Y. *Glaube wie er leibt und lebt.* Vol. 3. Munich: 1984, 8–38 (on symbols).

Stöhr, J. *Wann werden Sakramente gültig gespendet?* Aschaffenburg: 1980.

Stock, U. *Die Bedeutung der Sakramente in Luthers Sermonen von 1519.* Leiden: 1982.

Symbolische und künsterliche Ausdrucksformen im Gottesdienst: Concilium 16 (1980) no. 2.

Symbol und Kommunikation: Liturgisches Jahrbuch 35 (1985) no. 4.

Zur Theologie der Sakramente: Concilium 4 (1968) no. 1.

Theologische Berichte 9: Kirche und Sakrament. Zürich: 1980.

Tragan, R., ed. *Fede e sacramenti negli scritti giovannei.* Rome: 1985.

Triacca, A. M., ed. *Trinité et liturgie.* Louvain: 1984.

Van Beeck, F. J. *Grounded in Love: Sacramental Theology in an Ecumenical Perspective.* London: 1982.

Villalón, J. *Sacrements dans l'Esprit. Existence humaine et théologie sacramentelle.* Paris: 1977.

Wehrle, P. *Die Bedeutung des Symbols für die religiöse Erziehung.* Munich: 1980.

Worgul, G. S. *From Magic to Metaphor: A Validation of Christian Sacraments.* 2d ed. London: 1986.

b) Articles and Essays

Baumer, I. "Interaktion, Zeichen, Symbol. Ansätze zu einer Deutung liturgischen und volksfrommen Tuns." *Liturgisches Jahrbuch* 31 (1981) 9–35.

Beinert, W. "Die Sakramentalität der Kirche im theologischen Gespräch." *Theologische Berichte* [Zürich] 9 (1980) 13–66.

Borobio, D. "Cristología y sacramentología." *Salmanticensis* 31 (1984) 5–47.

Brinkman, B. R. "For an aesthetic of sacramentology: a retrospective." *Zeitschrift für katholische Theologie* 107 (1985) 341–364 (extensive bibliography).

Chauvet, L.-M. "Sacrements et institution." In M. Michel, ed., *La théologie à l'épreuve de la vérité* (Paris: 1984) 201–235.

Dalmais, I.-H. "Le 'Mysterion,' contribution à une théologie de la liturgie." *La Maison Dieu* 158 (1984) 14–50.

De Margerie, B. "Vers une relecture du Concile de Florence grâce à la reconsidération de l'Ecriture et des Pères grecs et latins." *Revue Thomiste* 94 (1986) 31–81.

Dulles, A. "The Symbolic Structure of Revelation." *Theological Studies* 41 (1980) 51–73.

Fransen, P. "Modellen in de theologie van de sacramenten" *Collationes* 12 (1982) 131–155.

————. "De sacramenten als gemeenschapsviering van de goddelijke mysteries." *Collationes* 13 (1983) 139–163.

Ganoczy, A. "Sakrament." *Neues Handbuch theologischer Grundbegriffe* IV (1985) 94–104.

Gamber, K. "Die Christus- und Geist-Epiklese in der frühen abendländischen Liturgie." *Praesentia Christi*, FS J Betz (Düsseldorf: 1984) 79–100.

García Prada, J. M. "Hermenéutica de los símbolos y crisis del lenguaje religioso." *Ciencia tomista* 111 (1984) 515–550.

Garijo Guembe, M. M. "Sakrament und Sakramentalität." *Catholica* 40 (1986) 110–124.

"Gottesdienst." *TRE* XIV (1985) 1–97 (bibliography).

Houssiau, A. "La rédecouverte de la liturgie par la théologie sacramentaire (1950–1980)." *La Maison Dieu* 149 (1982) 27–55.

Hotz, R. "Religion, Symbolhandlung, Sakrament." *Liturgisches Jahrbuch* 31 (1981) 36–54.

Hünermann, P. "Reflexionen zum Sakramentenbegriff des II. Vatikanums." Eds. E. Klinger and K. Wittstadt. *Glaube im Prozeß* (Freiburg: 1984) 309–324.

Irwin, K. W. "Recent sacramental theology." *Thomist* 47 (1983) 592–608.

Jüngel, E. "Die Kirche als Sakrament?" *Zeitschrift für Theologie und Kirche* 80 (1983) 432–457.

Lengeling, E. J. "Wort, Bild, Symbol in der Liturgie." *Liturgisches Jahrbuch* 30 (1980) 230–242.

Lies, L. "Kultmysterium heute—Modell sakramentaler Begegnung." *Archiv für Liturgiewissenschaft* 28 (1986) 2–21.

McKenna, J., and others. "The epiclesis." *Ephemerides Liturgicae* 99 (1985) 314–382.

Oñatibia, I. "De la dialéctica al simbolismo." *Estudios eclesiásticos* 56 (1981) 1398–1431.

Paprocki, H. "Le Saint Esprit dans les sacraments de l'Eglise." *Istina* 28 (1983) 267–281.

Pesch, O. H. "Das katholische Sakramentsverständnis im Urteil gegenwärtiger evangelischer Theologen." In *Verifikationen*, FS G. Ebeling (Tübingen: 1982) 317–340.

Rahner, K. "Personale und sakramentale Frömmigkeit." *Schriften* 2 (1955) 115–141.

―――. "Theologie des Symbols." *Schriften* 4 (1960) 275–311.

―――. "Überlegungen zum personalen Vollzug des sakramentalen Geschehens" *Schriften* 10 (1972) 405–429.

Richter, K. "Riten und Symbole in der Industriekultur." *Concilium* 13 (1980) 108–113.

Schillebeeckx, E. "Sakramente als Organe der Gottbegegnung." In J. Feiner, J. Trütsch, and F. Böckle, eds., *Fragen der Theologie heute* (Einsiedeln 1957) 379–401.

Schilson, A., "Sakrament als Symbol." *Christlicher Glaube in moderner Gesellschaft* (Freiburg) 28 (1982) 122–150.

Schmied, A., "Was ist ein Sakrament?" *Theologie der Gegenwart* 20 (1977) 143–152.

―――. "Perspektiven und Akzente heutiger Sakramententheologie." *Wissenschaft und Weisheit* 44 (1981) 17–45 (bibliography).

Schneider, T. "Die dogmatische Begründung der Ekklesiologie nach dem Zweiten Vatikanischen Konzil." *Renovatio et Reformatio*, FS L Hödl (Münster: 1985) 80–116.

Schütz, C. *MySal Ergänzungsband* (1981) 347–355.

Schützeichel, H. "Calvins Stellungnahme zu den Trienter Canones über die Sakramente im allgemeinen." *Catholica* 38 (1984) 317–339.

Schulte, R. *MySal* IV/2 (Einsiedeln 1973) 46–155.

————. "Die Wort-Sakramente-Problematik in der evangelischen und katholischen Theologie." *Theologische Berichte* (Zürich) 6 (1977) 81–122.

Schulz, F. "Die jüdischen Wurzeln des christlichen Gottesdienstes." *Jahrbuch für Liturgik und Hymnologie* 28 (1984) 39–55.

Seybold, M. "Die Siebenzahl der Sakrament." *Münchener Theologische Zeitschrift* 27 (1976) 113–141.

Standart, B., and others. "Le mystère de l'Esprit." *Questions liturgiques* 67 (1986) 87–179.

Strebel, A. "Symboldenken und Symbolverständnis in der neueren evangelischen Theologie." *Symbolon* (Cologne) n. s. 6 (1981) 129–144.

Tillard, J.-M. R. "Les sacrements de l'Eglise." *Initiation à la pratique de la théologie* 2 (Paris: 1983) 385–466.

————. "Eglise et salut. Sur la sacramentalité de l'Eglise." *Nouvelle Revue Théologique* 106 (1984) 658–685.

Van Eijk, A. H. C. "De Kerk als sakrament en het heil van de wereld." *Bijdragen* 45 (1984) 295–330.

Zadra, D. "Sakramente und Zeit." *Probleme und Perspektiven dogmatischer Theologie*, ed. K. H. Neufeld (Düsseldorf: 1986) 250–272 (on the system of symbols).

Bibliography 2

Ecumenical Dialogue on the Sacraments, with Particular Reference to the Lima Documents

Dantine, J. "Zur Konvergenzerklärung." *Ökumenische Rundschau* 32 (1983) 12–17.

De Baciocchi, J. "Les ministères ecclésiaux dans le Texte de Lima." *Mélange de science religieuse* 40 (1983) 73–90.

Eham, M. *Gemeinschaft im Sakrament? Die Frage nach der Möglichkeit sakramentaler Gemeinschaft zwischen katholischen und nichtkatholischen Christen.* Frankfurt and Bern: 1986.

Ephemerides Theologicae Lovanienses 61 (1985) 327–328; 62 (1986) 335–336 (bibliography on the Lima documents).

Fahey, M. A., ed. *Catholic Perspectives on Baptism, Eucharist and Ministry.* London and New York: 1986.

Geldbach, E., and others. *Kommentar zu den Lima-Erklärungen.* Göttingen: 1983.

Gemeinsame röm-kath./ev.-luth. Kommission. *Einheit vor uns. Modelle, Formen und Thesen katholisch/lutherischer Kirchengemeinschaft.* Paderborn and Frankfurt: 1985.

Hinz, C. "Kommentare zu den Lima-Erklärungen." *Theologische Literatur-Zeitung* 109 (1984) 173–180.

Kerygma und Dogma 31 (1985) no. 1 (on the Lima documents).

Kühn, U. "Das reformatorische Proprium und die Ökumene." *Kerygma und Dogma* 32 (1986) 170–186 (on negative reactions to the Lima documents, in particular that of E. Herms).

Lehmann, K., and Pannenberg, W., eds. *Lehrverurteilungen—kirchentrennend?* Part I: *Rechtfertigung, Sakramente und Amt im Zeitalter der Reformation und heute.* Freiburg and Göttingen: 1986.

Mélange de science religieuse 42 (1985) 3-19 (on the Lima documents).

Neuner, P. *Kleines Handbuch der Ökumene.* Düsseldorf: 1984, 141-177.

Pfnür, V. *Die Wirksamkeit der Sakramente sola fide und ex opere operato: Das Herrenmahl.* Paderborn and Frankfurt: 1979, 93-100.

Regli, S. "Ökumenische Konsenserklärungen mit röm.-kath. Beteiligung über Taufe, Eucharistie und Amt: Ergebnisse." *Theologische Berichte* (Zürich) 9 (1980) 129-171.

Seybold, M., and Gläßer, A. *Das "Lima-Papier."* Eichstätt: 1985.

Slenczka, R. "Ökumenische Erklärungen und dogmatische Klärungen." *Kerygma und Dogma* 32 (1986) 207-232.

Studia Liturgica 16 (1986), nos. 1-2, pp. 3-128 (on the Lima documents).

Thurian, M., ed. *Churches respond to "Baptism, Eucharist and Ministry"* I. Geneva: 1986.

Tillard, J.-M. R. "Ecclésiologie de communion et exigence oecuménique." *Irénikon* 59 (1986) 201-230.

Voigt, G., and others. *Lima und das reformatorische Proprium.* Hannover: 1984.

6

Baptism

6.1 *Biblical Foundations*

Baptism is the Christian symbolic action that is most often mentioned in the New Testament. There are two sayings of Jesus referring to baptism; however, both of these are formulations that do not come from Jesus himself, but instead represent a later stage of development: Matthew 28:19 is clearly influenced by the liturgy, and Mark 16:16, from the non-genuine ending of Mark, dates from the second century. Thus we cannot determine any origination or institution of baptism by Jesus. But there can be no doubt that even the earliest Christian communities baptized. The appearance of Christian baptism is, according to the present state of our knowledge,[1] not to be traced either to Hellenistic influences, to purification rituals, or to Jewish proselyte bap-

---

1. G. Lohfink, "Der Ursprung der christlichen Taufe," *Theologische Quartalschrift* 156 (1976) 35–54; R. Schwager, "Wassertaufe, ein Gebet um die Geisttaufe?" *Zeitschrift für katholische Theologie* 100 (1978) 36–61, with bibliography at 36 n. 3; G. Barth, *Die Taufe in frühchristlicher Zeit* (Neukirchen: 1981), is an exegetical treatment.

tism. Instead, Christian baptism is in continuity with the baptism ''of repentance for the forgiveness of sins'' (Mark 1:4) practiced by John the Baptizer.[2] The symbolism—immersion in flowing water with the implication of danger, in this case the destruction of an old, false orientation of one's life—and the inner content, a firm purpose of repentance, a new orientation to the will of God and to the approaching reign of God, are elements of John's baptism that are retained in the Christian rite. In this connection, it was certainly of decisive importance for the earliest Christian community that Jesus himself had been baptized by John and by this gesture of solidarity with ''people from the whole Judean countryside and all the people of Jerusalem'' (Mark 1:5) acknowledged that he regarded the external demonstration of an internal disposition by means of a symbolic action as proper and important. Of course, this is not to say that the Synoptic authors reported the baptism of Jesus in order to give a foundation for the later sacrament of baptism and to depict it in anticipation. Of the highest importance for sacramental theology in general and for baptismal theology in particular is the fact that the Synoptic authors, in composing the baptismal pericope,[3] supplement the scene of baptism with a revelation scene, according to which it is only after baptism that the divine Spirit descended on Jesus and Jesus' mission was made known. It is not only the temporal (real or possible) disjunction of water baptism and Spirit-baptism that is of theological interest, but also the consideration that the Synoptic authors certainly did not intend to deny that Jesus was totally in the power of the divine Spirit even *before* his baptism, and knew of his mission. There are also other places in the New Testament that attest that the communication of the Spirit should not be thought of as limited to an isolated, individual event. In this sense, a distinction is to be made between the communication of the Spirit and the making known of that fact (in one or another manner, which under certain circumstances may be a sacramental one).

If the New Testament nowhere offers us a theology of the early Christian sacrament of baptism, still it contains a great number of state-

---

2. Cf. G. Barth, *Die Taufe in frühchristlicher Zeit*, 22-23, 38ff.

3. The pericope is analyzed with the greatest care and with his accustomed acuity by A. Vögtle, ''Herkunft und ursprünglicher Sinn der Taufperikope Mk 1:9-11,'' in his *Offenbarungsgeschehen und Wirkungsgeschichte* (Freiburg: 1985) 70-108, with a thorough discussion of the literature, especially the recent commentaries on Mark.

ments and hints that were later to contribute to such a theology.[4] These
are the most important:

1. The Acts of the Apostles distinguishes between water baptism
and Spirit-baptism; baptism of the Spirit can even precede water baptism (10:47; 11:16). The time interval between the two in 8:12-17 later
served as a biblical argument for the separation of confirmation from
baptism. Baptism is given "in (into) the name of Jesus" (2:38; 8:16;
10:48; 19:5; cf. 22:16). In line with the theology of names in the New
Testament and especially in Acts, the decisive point about this process is that it is something done in the name of Jesus, for it is in that
name that forgiveness of sins and salvation take place.[5] In the name
of Jesus, the event of salvation in Jesus is summarized in its briefest
and most concentrated form.

2. Romans 6:1-11 is a comprehensive exposition of the reasons for
the new ethical life of Christians; this passage is not a sacramental-
theological explication of baptism.[6] From Pauline theology in general,
not only from this passage, it appears that the saving event in Jesus
Christ immediately touches all human beings, and not first those who
came to believe and were baptized; Paul could say that "we" have
died on the cross with Jesus Christ even *before* baptism (cf. Romans
5:6-10; 7:4; 2 Cor 5:14). Paul is thus aware of a communion of believers
with Jesus Christ, a union with him in his whole destiny—life, death,
and resurrection—a real incorporation into him that surpasses space
and time and is decisive for the Christian life. This meditation, rooted
in a strong personal love of Jesus, used to be called "Christ mysticism,"
a concept that has been unjustly devalued. In Romans 6:4-8, Paul
describes an event in which "we" are quite concretely[7] united with
the crucifixion, burial, and raising up of Jesus. Within this event, baptism represents a certain moment in the death of Jesus, namely a unity
with Jesus' burial, a real being-buried-with Jesus (as reflected also in

4. In what follows, I am indebted to the solid treatment by R. Schwager (see
n. 1 above).
5. Ibid., 39–40.
6. The exegetical literature on this passage is listed in R. Schwager, "Wassertaufe," 41, nn. 14 and 15. On what follows, see the same work, pp. 41-47. On
Rom 6:1-11, cf. also A. Schilson, *Theologie* (Bern and Frankfurt: 1985) 234–245, with
bibliographical notes.
7. Rom 6:5 does not speak of a similarity, imaging or reflection, but a very concrete being-in-unity; R. Schwager, "Wassertaufe," 46.

the baptismal statement of the Pauline school found in Col 2:11-12). The burial, which in itself is not a saving event, points to the reality of having died, so that the content of the symbolic action of baptism is as follows: in it the one being baptized recognizes that she or he has died on the cross with Jesus Christ *long before* this present action. The salvation of humanity consists in this unity with Jesus, here made tangible, so that baptism is really a saving event, and not a mere memorial. Again, however, this should not be understood in terms of a particular point in time, for the recognition that one is united with the death of Jesus on the cross arises out of the faith that already brings salvation. In faith, the one baptized is also united with the resurrection of Jesus: in faith, rising with Jesus and the beginning of new life have also occurred. Paul offers us here an important indication of the way in which, despite all differences, the saving event in Jesus Christ is united and made one with the symbolic action and praxis of Christians who are dead to sin.

Other Pauline texts referring to baptism indicate also that saving faith precedes baptism: if it is true that all of us, in the one Spirit, were baptized into one body (1 Cor 12:13), then it is not baptism that first communicates the divine Spirit.[8] According to Galatians 3:26-27, faith causes human beings to become "children of God"; baptism announces (publicly) the condition of being buried with Jesus and the will to remain united with him in new life.[9] Even this brief survey shows that Paul assigns much greater weight to faith than to baptism.[10] Also important in this connection is the distinction Paul makes between reconciliation and salvation: reconciliation occurred on the cross, but salvation will occur in the future, through faith. Baptism, when distinguished from the confession of faith and regarded in itself as a symbolic action, represents the sense-perceptible expression of the fact that, on the cross, the power of sin was destroyed and the world reconciled with God, *before* individual conversion in faith. It is obvious for Paul that this symbolic action is an action of the Church (see the context of 1 Cor 12).

8. On this, see ibid, 50–51.

9. Ibid., 52–53.

10. One could add to this his statements on the saving character of proclamation and his pneumatology, as well as his remarks on the "power of God" that was proclaimed by the gospel message from the cross, and not by baptism (ibid., 53).

3. In 1 Peter 3:19-21, baptism is designated an image of salvation through water, the counterpart of the ark in the flood, in the days of Noah; the text adds the explanation that it acts "not as a removal of dirt from the body, but as an appeal to God for a good conscience, through the resurrection of Jesus Christ" (v. 21). Here the important idea of calling on God, which was only implied in the formula "in (into) the name of Jesus," is expressly stated. The later expansion, "in the name of the Father, the Son, and the Holy Spirit" (Matt 28:19) is a Trinitarian development of the Christological confession. What happens in baptism into the name of the triune God and in the proclamation of the word, as the context of Matthew 28:18, 20 shows, is the making-present of Jesus, his resurrection and rule over heaven and earth, a making-present that encompasses all space and time and is therefore spiritual (pneumatic).

4. The *whole* event, the symbolic action of water baptism and the Spirit-baptism in faith to a new Christian life, can be summarized as "being reborn" or the "washing of rebirth" (John 3:5; Titus 3:5).

It is clear on the basis of this New Testament evidence[11] that the action of baptism in water may not be regarded *exclusively* as the decisive communication of the grace of God, the Holy Spirit, justification, etc. The symbolic action of water baptism, which refers to the death of Jesus on the cross for us, is dialogically embedded in faith in the act of God that anticipates all conversion and all faith, and in the prayer of petition to the Father through the Son in the Holy Spirit that asks especially for the assistance of the divine Spirit in the new life to be lived, and that may be most briefly described as a prayer "in the name of Jesus."[12] What happens here is a common confession of faith, a common prayer of the community, the Church, but not a common act of baptizing. In this symbol of burial, the one being baptized allows something to happen to himself or herself; the person acts as a *recipient*,

11. Ibid., 58–59.

12. R. Schwager (ibid., 56–59) gives an extensive treatment of the effective prayer "in the name of Jesus" that is certain to be heard (John 14:13-14; 16:23-24; cf. Mark 11:24; Matt 7:7-11; 21:22; James 1:6; 1 John 3:22). See also F. Courth, "Die Taufe 'auf den Namen Jesu Christi' in den Zeugnissen der Dogmengeschichte bis zur Hochscholastik," *Theologie und Glaube* 69 (1979) 121–147. Courth expresses a wish (p. 147), and rightly so, that the baptismal formula be made a summary expression of the priestly prayer of petition (epiclesis) and the Church's acceptance of the faith of the one to be baptized.

as the one who, through this renunciation of the old, accepts the strength for new life (both renunciation and acceptance being effected by the Spirit), and as the one to whom is guaranteed an acceptance into the body of Christ, which is the Church. Raymond Schwager's conclusion is grounded in the New Testament: the symbolic action of water baptism is an ecclesial "primal prayer" for Spirit-baptism that is certain to be heard, but God can also give the baptism in the Spirit to a person even in the absence of such a prayer.[13]

6.2 The Rite of Initiation

The saving event that touches an individual human person and allows that person to begin the practice of Christian life is also designated, in the language of the history of religions, as "initiation" (dedication, induction). Since it is a truly fundamental event, it is not restricted to a momentary action, but lasts throughout a lifetime. From a New Testament point of view, and thus in current theology as well, it can be addressed under various aspects: as a mystical union with Jesus Christ, more than a merely figurative entering into him, remaining in him, having "put him on," but as an entry into sharing his destiny, as a linguistic-dialogical event in which the preached word calls out and faith responds to it, as acceptance into the Church as the body of Christ, as being seized by the Spirit sent by the exalted Jesus Christ.

The concept of "initiation" can be an aid to us in not directing our attention simply to the symbolic action of baptism, but instead to the total, fundamental event. Even in the old rite of initiation, this connection was expressed.

The oldest postbiblical witnesses[14] for the celebration of baptism indicate a connection between the immersion in the water and a threefold (Trinitarian) calling upon God (epiclesis) spoken over the person being baptized. According to the *Apostolic Tradition* of Hippolytus (ca. 215), the solemn initiation followed a three-year catechumenate.[15] It

13. R. Schwager, "Wassertaufe," 60.
14. I refer especially to Justin (d. 165). The *Didache* (ch. 7) should, in my opinion, be assigned a late date. It speaks of a previous fasting and instruction and contains only one reference to Matt 28:19.
15. A. Angenendt, *Kaiserherrschaft und Königstaufe* (Berlin: 1984). Part I: "Das Sakrament der Initiation im frühen Mittelalter," 21–164 (with bibliography).

included baptism with preceding and following rites and a conclud-
ing celebration of the Eucharist. Among the rites of preparation, in
order to make the "change of rulership" externally visible, was an exorcism and renunciation of the devil[16] as well as a "prebaptismal"
anointing. Baptism consisted of a combination of threefold immersion
and confession of faith in three (Trinitarian) steps and in dialogical form
("interrogative conferral of baptism"). From Hippolytus' testimony it
is clear that it was not the one baptizing who was important, whatever that person's intention or moral qualities; the significant person
was the one being baptized, and his or her acceptance in faith.[17] After
baptism, the newly baptized person received a (postbaptismal) anointing by the priest, and then an imposition of hands, signing of the forehead and anointing with chrism by the bishop. The celebration of the
Eucharist, with the community's prayer for the newly baptized, was
an essential part of initiation.

There is no question of a baptismal formula as the central point of
the whole event. The indicative formula, "I baptize you," which is
easily explained on the basis of the baptism of infants, is not found
in the Roman liturgy before the end of the seventh century.[18] The blessing of the baptismal water was developed as early as the third and
fourth centuries. (The important witnesses are Tertullian in the West
and Basil in the East.) This consisted of an exorcism of evil and an
epiclesis as a blessing of the water. At this point, material stipulations
first begin to restrict the dynamic conception of the whole event. Problems arose concerning those who conferred baptism (in the countryside, these could include deacons and lay people) in connection with
the question of baptism by heretics and the Donatist controversy (see
6.3), but the imposition of hands continued to be reserved to the
bishop.[19] In the Roman liturgy the imposition of hands was combined
with a second, postbaptismal anointing, which also became the
prerogative of the bishop. This (postbaptismal) anointing was other-

16. A. Angenendt, "Der Taufexorzismus und seine Kritik in der Theologie des
12. und 13. Jahrhunderts," in A. Zimmermann, ed., *Miscellanea Mediaevalia* 11 (Berlin: 1977) 388–409.

17. Angenendt, *Kaiserherrschaft*, 27.

18. A. Angenendt, "Bonifatius und das Sacramentum initiationis. Zugleich ein
Beitrag zur Geschichte der Firmung," *Römische Quartalschrift* 72 (1977) 133–183,
at 135.

19. Ibid., 143.

wise unknown in the Western Church, but it was probably customary everywhere to use only oils blessed by the bishop for the purpose of anointing. As with the baptismal water, attention was diverted from the liturgical action as a whole and concentrated on this oil, which was regarded as the real vehicle of grace.[20] Practical problems arose out of the question whether the bishop had to be present at all baptisms in his (often very extensive) diocese, or if not, how he was to be represented. In the Western Church this was complicated by a multiplication of dates for baptism, since the new teaching on original sin created anxiety about salvation, so that it no longer seemed advisable to baptize only in the Easter season. We find the first evidence of a separation of baptism and episcopal imposition of hands with signing of the forehead in Novatian, around the middle of the third century.[21] This separation was obviously promoted by the baptism of infants, which by the third century was already an old custom. A letter of Pope Innocent I to the bishop of Gubbio in the year 416 (only in Latin, DS 215) was of great importance. Here the priests are permitted to anoint, but only with oil consecrated by the bishop; however, they are forbidden to sign the forehead with oil, since this is reserved to the bishops who thus confer the Holy Spirit. At this point, evidently, the unity of the rite of initiation had been destroyed and the sacrament of confirmation was born. When the Roman version of the liturgy was adopted by the Carolingian reformers, the process was complete.[22]

6.3 *Historical Decisions*

The first questions to which the Church gave definitive answers were those regarding the validity of baptisms administered outside the Catholic Church after a schism. Pope Stephen I defended their validity in 256 against Bishop Cyprian of Carthage in the so-called controversy over heretical baptism (only in Latin, DS 110–111); similarly, Silvester I, in 314, forbade the rebaptism of Donatists who returned to the Great Church, unless they had not been baptized in the name of the Trinity (only in Latin, DS 123). This topic was broadened later: now the question was not merely about baptism by unworthy priests, but doubts

20. Ibid., 145–146.
21. Ibid., 157.
22. Ibid., 157–158.

were raised whether baptisms by Jews or pagans were valid. In 866, Nicholas I sent an answer to Bulgaria, where such cases were supposed to have occurred, that whenever someone had been baptized in the name of the holy Trinity or in the name of Christ,[23] the person was not to be rebaptized (only in Latin, DS 644–646). In theology, this teaching accorded very well with the notion of a sacramental "character," as developed by Augustine: a mark imprinted once and for all by baptism (see 5.7 above).

The baptism of small children who were unable to make decisions for themselves had been sharply and repeatedly criticized, beginning with Tertullian in the third century. It was defended by Church authorities, for example Innocent III in 1201 (NR 526/DS 780) and 1208 (NR 527/DS 794), with reference to original sin: as a human person acquired original sin without consenting to it, so without his or her consent it would be forgiven by the power of the sacrament. But it was also taught, in this connection, that it was contrary to the Christian religion to force anyone to accept Christianity;[24] adult people who were baptized against their will and had never given their consent to it received neither the mark of the sacrament nor its effects (Innocent III, 1201: NR 526/DS 781).

The first summary teaching on the sacrament of baptism is contained in the Council of Florence's Decree for the Armenians (NR 528-531/DS 1314–1316). This text, which rests on the work of Thomas Aquinas, reads:

> Among all the sacraments holy baptism holds the first place because it is *the gateway to the spiritual life*; by it we are made members of Christ and belong to His body, the Church. And since through the first man death has entered into all (cf. Rom 5:12), unless we are born again of water and the Spirit, we cannot, as the Truth said, enter into the Kingdom of heaven (cf. Jn 3:5).
>
> The *matter* of this sacrament is true natural water; it does not matter whether it is cold or warm. The *form* is: "I baptize you in the name of the Father and of the Son and of the Holy Spirit." We do not deny, however, that true baptism is also effected by these words: "May the servant of Christ, N., be baptized in the name of the Father and of the Son

---

23. On the hesitancy of high Scholastic theologians regarding baptism in the name of Jesus Christ, cf. F. Courth, "Die Taufe 'auf den Namen Jesu Christi.' "

24. Augustine had misinterpreted Luke 14:23 to say that violence could be used in religious matters. Cf. O. Karrer, "Compelle intrare," *LThK* III, 27–28.

and of the Holy Spirit," or: "By my hands N. is baptized in the name of the Father and of the Son and of the Holy Spirit." For as the principal cause from which baptism derives its virtue is the Holy Trinity, while the instrumental cause is the minister who confers the sacrament externally, the sacrament is performed whenever the act carried out by the minister is expressed along with the invocation of the Holy Trinity.

The *minister* of this sacrament is the priest, to whom by reason of his office it belongs to baptize. But in case of necessity not only a priest or deacon, but also a layman, or a woman, or even a pagan and a heretic may baptize, provided [she or] he observes the Church's form and intends to do what the Church does.

The *effect* of this sacrament is the remission of all guilt, original and actual, and also of all punishment due to the guilt itself. For this reason, no satisfaction is to be enjoined on the baptized for their past sins; and if they die before committing any fault, they immediately gain access to the Kingdom of heaven and the beatific vision.[25]

This text speaks entirely as if adult baptism were still the norm. The relationship between faith and baptism is not discussed. The reference to John 3:5 reveals a total obliviousness to the previously-held conviction that the process of "rebirth" includes both descent of the divine Spirit and coming to belief, and that Spirit-baptism is not simply identical with water baptism.

The Council of Trent, in its seventh session in 1547, accepted fourteen statements (canons) on baptism that do not represent a summary or connected doctrine of baptism. Rather, they take positions on questions which were seen at the time as threatening to Catholic teaching (NR 532–545/DS 1614–1627). Some of them deal with topics that belong more properly to the theology of grace, such as the relationship among faith, law, and loss of grace (canons 6–10). The council reiterated the teaching that even "heretics" can administer true baptism (canon 4), and declared that baptism is necessary for salvation (canon 5) and cannot be repeated (canon 11). The practice of infant baptism is defended—against, among others, the sixteenth-century "Anabaptist movement"—with a statement that little children are baptized in and because of the faith of the Church, without their having made an act of faith of their own (canons 12–14).

---

25. Translation adapted from J. Neuner, S. J. and J. Dupuis, S. J., *The Christian Faith in the Doctrinal Documents of the Catholic Church* (Westminster, Md: Christian Classics, Inc., 1975).

What is said in these statements about faith is inadequate as a response to the Reformers' theology of faith. A proper evaluation of the Council of Trent's efforts would require us to examine its important decree on justification. Even so, it is regrettable that the council's attention is concentrated on questions of the legality and validity of baptism, and of its necessity for salvation, in the absence of any theological basis or context. The introduction of the baptized in the destiny of Jesus Christ and their incorporation in the Church are not mentioned. Part of what is lacking here was supplied by the council in its teaching on original sin in 1546 (NR 356–357/DS 1514–1515). In the first section, which is here cited, it simply took over, word for word, the teaching of a synod in Carthage, in North Africa, held in the year 418:

> 4. If anyone denies that *infants* newly born from their mothers' womb are to be baptized, even when born from baptized parents, or says that, though they are baptized for the remission of sins, yet they do not contract from Adam any original sin which must be expiated by the bath of regeneration that leads to eternal life, so that in their case the formula of baptism "for the forgiveness of sins" would no longer be true but would be false, *anathema sit.* For, what the apostle says: "sin came into the world through one man and death through sin, and so death spread to all because all have sinned" (Rom 5:12), should not be understood in another sense than that in which the Catholic Church spread over the whole world has understood it at all times. For, because of this rule of faith, in accordance with apostolic tradition, even children who of themselves cannot have yet committed any sin are truly baptized for the remission of sins, so that by regeneration they may be cleansed from what they contracted through generation. For "unless one is born of water and the Spirit, he cannot enter the kingdom of God" (John 3:5).
> 5. If anyone denies that *the guilt of original sin* is remitted by the grace of our Lord Jesus Christ given in baptism, or asserts that all that is sin in the true and proper sense is not taken away but only brushed over or not imputed, *anathema sit.* For, in those who are reborn God hates nothing, because there is no condemnation for those who were buried with Christ through baptism into death (cf. Rom 8:1 and 6:4), "who do not walk according to the flesh" (Rom 8:4) but who, putting off the old human and putting on the new human, created after the likeness of God (cf. Eph 4:22-23; Col 3:9-10), innocent, unstained, pure and guiltless, have become the beloved sons of God, "heirs of God and fellow heirs

with Christ" (Rom 8:17), so that nothing henceforth holds them back from entering into heaven.[26]

The essential contribution of Vatican Council II to the theme of baptism is in the ecumenical area (see 6.5). But here we should also mention the reform of the liturgy, which led to a rite for the baptism of children that is not an imitation of adult baptism, and which also developed a special form of initiation for adults.[27]

6.4 *Baptism of Children*

The practice and theology of baptism of children have been of major importance for sacramental theology. Since the baptism of children (and particularly the baptism of infants) disrupts the process by which a person comes to believe and begins the practice of a Christian life, and disregards the order of things posited in the New Testament, in which hearing the word is followed by conversion, coming to faith, and symbolic action, it contributed heavily to a separation between faith and personal action on the one hand, and the sacrament on the other. It strengthened the impression that the "real" event is the ritual. Thus the baptism of infants became the classical model of a sacrament, since it appeared that here the effectiveness of the sacrament was clearly independent of the worthiness of the minister, independent of the consciousness of the recipient, so long as the latter placed no "obstacle" to its reception, and dependent only on the relationship between valid matter and correct form. The deficiency and danger in this development gave rise to repeated discussions on the legitimacy of infant baptism, the circumstances under which baptism might legitimately be delayed, etc.[28]

---

26. Ibid.

27. R. Kaczynski, *Enchiridion Documentorum Instaurationis liturgicae* I (1963-1973) (Turin: 1976), "Kindertaufe" 556-572, "Initiation Erwachsener" 830-859. Cf. also A. E. Hierold, "Taufe und Firmung," *HKR*, 659-675, at 660-661 on the baptism of adults (with catechumenate) since 1972, in the old order of baptism, confirmation, Eucharist; ibid., 665-666 on the preconditions for baptism, especially among adults.

28. From the literature on this subject in Bibliography 4, see especially the works by F. Reckinger, W. Molinski, H. Hubert, and E. Nagel.

In all this, an extended discussion that has taken place since the middle of the twentieth century on the New Testament sources remained inconclusive. There is no certain witness in the New Testament for the probability of a baptism of children; neither the mention of the baptism of a "whole house," nor Jesus' hospitable welcome of children (Mark 10:13-16), nor Paul's statement that the children of believing parents are "holy" (1 Cor 7:14) provides unimpeachable proof.[29] Clear statements about baptism of children around the end of the second and beginning of the third century presume a practice that has already become customary. In the important witnesses from that period onward (Tertullian, Hippolytus, Augustine) we also read of godparents: at first these are the natural parents.[30] It was out of this practice that Augustine, in his controversy with Pelagius and his followers over the theology of grace, developed his teaching about the necessity of baptism for salvation even of the youngest children. Why, he asked, are children baptized if they are not burdened with guilt and in need of pardon for the sake of salvation? The idea that those closest to these children must come to their aid was more important than the question of individual decision. Thus the conviction arose that the faith of the Church can and must substitute for the faith of the children. Scholastic theology introduced here the distinction between faith as a capacity given or "poured into" one by the grace of God (*habitus*) and faith as a responsible realization of this capacity (*actus*): in baptism, children receive faith as *habitus*, but this does not dispense them from the necessity, as adults, of awakening and exercising this *habitus* of faith as *actus*.

The great anxiety that resulted, in theology and in the Church, about the eternal salvation of children who may die without baptism has been relieved, in the present century, by a deeper reflection. It is not that the teaching about original sin and its dangers has been abandoned, but rather that it has been traced back to its true essentials.[31]

29. In A. Angenendt, *Kaiserherrschaft*, 67, we find the note that the Christian family of the early days, unlike the early Middle Ages, was a nuclear family, in which it would be unlikely that the father would make the decision regarding baptism.
30. Ibid., 92.
31. Cf. H. M. Köster, *Urstand, Fall und Erbsünde in der kath. Theologie unseres Jahrhunderts* (Regensburg: 1983), (principal texts, bibliography); idem, "Urstand, Fall und Erbsünde. Von der Reformation bis zur Gegenwart," *Handbuch der Dogmengeschichte* II/3c (Freiburg: 1982); idem, "Paradies, Urund Erbsünde im Denken

The doctrine of original sin on the basis of Pauline theology (especially in Rom 5) and the Council of Trent says that humanity has, from
the beginning, rejected the clearly-acknowledged will of God and so
from the beginning there has existed a context of evil which affects
all human beings. Every human being, without being consulted, is born
into a situation that is marked by a "no" to God, and by a general
lack of peace, by injustice, and by temptation. This situation did not
arise of itself, but was created by conscious, wrong human decisions,
and is constantly being augmented by such decisions. To that extent
it can be called a "sinful" situation, and the word "inherit" [original
sin is referred to in German as *Erbsünde*, i.e., inherited sin] refers to
the entry of newborn human beings into this negatively warped situation. There is no question here of a personal sin for which the newborn is responsible. The situation only becomes one of attributable guilt
when a human being consciously adopts it as his or her own and becomes a wrongdoer in person. However, no human being is born into
a situation that is exclusively and completely evil. Instead, from the
beginning of its life, the child and later adult is called by the grace and
mercy of God, the Father, whose universal salvific will includes all
human beings without exception. The child is born into a humanity
that, as a whole, has been hallowed by the incarnation of the eternal
Son of God, and was so hallowed even in anticipation of that incarnation. It belongs to a humanity in which God's Spirit is continually at
work. We may not think of these two preexisting conditions of the
human situation (what Karl Rahner called "existentials"), one negative and one positive, as equal in status and power. Instead, according to faith, God is much more powerful than evil, and God's grace
is and will remain victorious.

From this point of view baptism is the effective symbolic action by
which the Church makes known that God's grace is victorious even
for newborn human beings, and that this human being is incorporated
in that human community in which God's will is acknowledged, and
which stands in resistance to the powers of evil. Should baptism not

repräsentativer Theologen der Aufklärungszeit," *Trierer Theologische Zeitschrift* 91
(1982) 116–132, 195–205, 281–290; idem, *Urstand, Fall und Erbsünde in der evangelischen
Theologie des 19. Jahrhunderts* (Frankfurt and Bern: 1983); see also A. de Villalmonte,
El pecado original (Salamanca: 1978), with commentary on ca. 800 publications since
1950; N. Lohfink and others, *Zum Problem der Erbsünde* (Essen: 1981); A.-M. Dubarle,
Le péché originel (Paris: 1983).

be given to a newborn child for some reason, this does not mean that this person stands outside God's grace and is rejected by God.

Even though we thus avoid placing undue theological weight on baptism, still there are important reasons in favor of the baptism of infants and children. No newborn human being is born into a neutral family, a neutral social or human situation. No human life begins at an absolute zero. Each of us is subjected to the influence and the decisions of other people. If those who are responsible for the child are convinced of the positive quality of Christian relationships, they will desire to include their child in those relationships; in that case, baptism represents their recognition both of the dangerous context of evil to which they do not wish to deliver up their child, and of the protective community of faith in which they wish to see their child grow up. Since the child must live in some concrete place, no matter what, they decide for the place they find to be good, and they would not regard this as robbing the child of its freedom. So baptism also represents the relatives' acknowledgement of the prevenient grace of God, of God's choice and call. If the sacrament of baptism is understood in line with what was said above (6.1) as a prayer of petition, then when a child is baptized the Church's petition intercedes for the child in order that, when it comes to the age of decision, it may choose the way of Jesus Christ. A positive, faith-filled tutelage of the child by those who are responsible for its upbringing does not exclude an education toward freedom and does not necessarily mean a spiritual rape or a denial of self-determination.

6.5   *Ecumenical Perspectives*

The quarrels of the third and fourth centuries left behind them the impression that baptism is the last remnant that separated Christians have in common. Since the primary actor in baptism is Jesus Christ himself, the validity of a baptism inside or outside the Church must be acknowledged, and baptism may not be repeated. This conviction could not be shaken even by the great Church divisions of the sixteenth century. The ecumenical movement that has emerged more and more strongly since 1910 has made clear that baptism is not so much a meager remnant of unity as it is the expression of an existing community in faith and a promising beginning.[32] That was also Vatican II's view of baptism: "By the sacrament of baptism, whenever it is properly conferred in the way the Lord determined, and received with the appropriate dispositions of soul, a [human being] becomes truly incorporated into the crucified and glorified Christ and is reborn to a sharing of the divine life, as the apostle says: 'For you were buried together with him in Baptism, and in him also rose again through faith in the working of God who raised him from the dead' (Col 2:12; cf. Rom 6:4). Baptism, therefore, constitutes a sacramental bond of unity linking all who have been reborn by means of it. But baptism, of itself, is only a beginning, a point of departure, for it is wholly directed toward the acquiring of fullness of life in Christ. Baptism is thus oriented toward a complete profession of faith, a complete incorporation into the system of salvation such as Christ Himself willed it to be, and finally, toward a complete participation in Eucharistic communion" (Decree on Ecumenism 22; cf. also par. 3).

In the struggle toward an ecumenical common declaration that culminated in the so-called Lima texts of 1982, baptism offered the fewest difficulties.[33]

6.6 *Summary*

Baptism, as the first symbolic action of the Church in the life of a Christian, is part of a comprehensive process that in the narrower sense consists of the beginning of the Christian way of life, but in a broader sense encompasses the whole of that life. Within this process, the symbolic action *means* primarily the rejection of a way of life that is shaped by the evil situation in which humanity exists. But the process as a whole, and thus baptism as well, is first of all an action of God and not a human initiative. This means in detail that: (1) Baptism *indicates*—and brings about by indicating it—the incorporation of a human being

32. Cf. J. Trütsch, "Taufe, Sakrament der Einheit—Eucharistie, Sakrament der Trennung?" *Theologische Berichte* (Zürich) 9 (1980) 67–95.

33. Text edition: *Taufe, Eucharistie und Amt. Konvergenzerklärungen der Kommission für Glauben und Kirchenverfassung des Ökumenischen Rates der Kirchen* (Frankfurt and Paderborn: 1982): on baptism, 9–17; cf. also the commentary on the text: G. Voss, ed., *Wachsende Übereinstimmung in Taufe, Eucharistie und Amt* (Freising and Paderborn: 1984): on baptism, 22–36; see also Bibliography 2.

in the body of Jesus Christ, i.e., in the renewed humanity of those who believe in Jesus Christ. This process takes place, in indissoluble unity, both on the internal-spiritual and the external-social level; it includes belonging to and solidarity with the multitude of unknown believers in past, present, and future, as well as a legal induction into the Church and membership in a particular community. (2) By this very fact, baptism makes visible the fact that God's salvation in Jesus Christ through the divine Spirit has taken hold of this person, so that, by the power of the prevenient grace of God, sins (if this person is a sinner) are forgiven and justification is bestowed on him or her. (3) Baptism places the whole life of this person within the prayer of the Church. It indicates the Church's desire that the one being baptized may assent by a free decision to the faith that God's Spirit has awakened in the Church, and may affirm and deepen this faith in his or her life. Baptism indicates the ongoing call of the one baptized ("sacramental character") to witness this faith not only in word, but also in practice: in the unity of love of God and love of human beings, in following Jesus, and in service of justice.

Where these three effects of baptism are found together, baptism can truly be called the beginning of a new life by the power of the Holy Spirit, and given the biblical designation of "rebirth."

Bibliography 3

Sacraments of Initiation

Angenendt, A., "Bonifatius und das Sacramentum initiationis. Zugleich ein Beitrag zur Geschichte der Firmung," *Römische Quartalschrift* 72 (1977) 133–183.

Baptism, Confirmation, International Bibliography 1975–1984. Strasbourg: 1985.

Bourgeois, H. *L'initiation chrétienne et ses sacrements.* Paris: 1982.

Brosseder, J. "Taufe und Firmung." *NHthG* IV (1985) 167–182.

Farnedi, G., ed. *I simboli dell'iniziazione cristiana.* Rome: 1983.

Schmitz, H. "Taufe, Firmung, Eucharistie. Die Sakramente der Initiation und ihre Rechtsfolgen in der Sicht des CIC von 1983." *Archiv für katholisches Kirchenrecht* 152 (1983) 369–407.

Sprinks, B. D., ed. *The Sacrifice of Praise.* Louvain: 1981. Studies on baptism and Eucharist.

"Strukturen christlicher Initiation," *Concilium* 15 (1979) n. 2.

Thurian, M., and G. Wainwright, eds. *Baptism and Eucharist.* Geneva: 1983. Collection of texts on liturgical traditions.

Bibliography 4

Baptism

Angenendt, A. "Der Taufexorzismus und seine Kritik in der Theologie des 12. und 13. Jahrhunderts." In A. Zimmermann, ed., *Miscellanea Mediaevalia* (Berlin) 11 (1977) 388–409.

_____. *Kaiserherrschaft und Königstaufe.* Berlin: 1984.

Aubin, P. *Le Baptême.* Paris: 1980.

Barth, G. *Die Taufe in frühchristlicher Zeit.* Neukirchen: 1981.

Burnish, R. *The Meaning of Baptism.* London: 1985.

Courth, F. "Die Taufe 'auf den Namen Jesu Christi' in den Zeugnissen der Dogmengeschichte bis zur Hochscholastik." *Theologie und Glaube* 69 (1979) 121–147.

Delling, G. *Die Taufe im Neuen Testament.* Berlin: 1963.

Duggan, R. D. "Conversion in the 'Ordo initiationis christianae adultorum.'" *Ephemerides Liturgicae* 96 (1982) 57–83, 209–252.

Hierold, A. E. "Taufe und Firmung." *HKR* 659–675.

Hossiau, A., and others. *Le baptême, entrée dans l'existence chrétienne.* Brussels: 1983.

Hubert, H. "Kirchenbild, Sakramentsverständnis und Kindertaufe." *Münchener Theologische Zeitschrift* 20 (1969) 315–329.

_____. *Der Streit um die Kindertaufe. Eine Darstellung der von Karl Barth 1943 ausgelösten Diskussion um die Kindertaufe und ihre Bedeutung für die heutige Tauffrage.* Frankfurt: 1972.

Jüngel, E. *Barth-Studien.* Zürich: 1982, 246–314 (on Karl Barth's view of baptism).

Labourdette, M.-M. "Le péché originel dans la tradition vivante de l'Eglise." *Revue Thomiste* 92 (1984) 357–398.

Lienemann-Perrin, C., ed. *Taufe und Kirchenzugehörigkeit.* Munich: 1983 (with historical material as well).

Lohfink, G. "Der Ursprung der christlichen Taufe." *Theologische Quartalschrift* 156 (1976) 35–54.

Mäki, P., ed., *Taufe und Heiliger Geist.* Helsinki: 1979.

Molinski, W., ed. *Diskussion um die Taufe.* Munich: 1971.

Nagel, E. "Die 'Heiligkeit' der Christenkinder nach Tertullian." *Zeitschrift für katholische Theologie* 100 (1978) 62–68 (with bibliography on infant baptism).

_____. *Kindertaufe und Taufaufschub. Die Praxis vom 3.-5. Jahrhundert in Nordafrika und ihre theologische Einordnung bei Tertullian, Cyprian und Augustinus.* Frankfurt: 1980.

Nepper-Christensen, P. "Die Taufe im Matthäusevangelium." *New Testament Studies* 31 (1985) 189–207.

Neunheuser, B. *Taufe und Firmung.* Handbuch der Dogmengeschichte IV/2. 2d ed. Freiburg: 1982.

Orbanic, Z. *L'atteggiamento e la prassi della chiesa sull'età del battesimo.* Rome: 1983.

Quesnel, M. *Baptisés dans l'esprit. Baptême et Esprit Saint dans les Actes des Apôtres.* Paris: 1985.

Reckinger, F. *Kinder taufen—mit Bedacht. Eine Darstellung der Diskussion um die Kindertaufe im katholischen Raum seit 1945 mit kritischen Stellungnahmen und pastoralen Ausblicken.* Steinfeld-Kall: 1982.

Schenke, L. "Zur sog. 'Oikosformel' im NT." *Kairos* 13 (1971) 226–243.

Schillebeeckx, E. "Begierdetaufe." *LThK* 2:112–115.

Schulte, R. "Die Umkehr (metanoia) als Anfang und Form des christlichen Lebens." *MySal* 5 (1976) 117–221.

Schulz, H.-J. " 'Wann immer einer tauft, ist es Christus, der tauft!' " In *Praesentia Christi,* FS J. Betz, Düsseldorf: 1984, 240–260 (on Greek patristics).

Schwager, R. "Wassertaufe, ein Gebet um die Geisttaufe?" *Zeitschrift für katholische Theologie* 100 (1978) 36–61.

Stenzel, A. *Die Taufe. Eine genetische Erklärung der Taufliturgie.* Innsbruck: 1958 (historically important).

Trütsch, J. "Taufe, Sakrament der Einheit—Eucharistie, Sakrament der Trennung?" *Theologische Berichte* (Zürich) 9 (1980) 67–95.

7

Confirmation

7.1 Biblical Foundations

Since the sacrament of confirmation is the liturgical symbolic action that, according to Catholic belief, visibly confers the divine Spirit, an understanding of the sacrament and the problems connected with it presupposes knowledge of the biblical statements about the Holy Spirit. Particularly important for the connection between New Testament pneumatology and confirmation is the two-volume work called Luke-Acts.[1] It was the Spirit of God who produced the man Jesus (Luke 1:35) and visibly descended upon him (Luke 3:22), and who (certainly *before* that "descent") filled him (Luke 4:1). In the power of this Spirit, Jesus undertook his public work (Luke 4:14); to the Spirit he traced his mission, at the same time religious and secular, in the sense of the words of the prophet Isaiah (Luke 4:18-19). Jesus taught, concerning this divine Spirit, that God the Father will give the Spirit to those who

1. See the commentaries on Luke and Acts: M. Rese, "Das Lukas-Evangelium. Ein Forschungsbericht," *Aufstieg und Niedergang der römischen Welt* II/25 (Berlin: 1985) 2258-2328 (bibliography); F. Hahn, "Der gegenwärtige Stand der Erforschung der Apostelgeschichte," *Theologische Revue* 82 (1986) 177-190 (bibliography).

ask (Luke 11:13). Here we can discern a twofold view of the divine Spirit: it comes upon individual human beings, fills them and inspires them to a particular mission, but at the same time it is necessary for all who desire simply to live within the humanity renewed by God, since God's Spirit is *the* prophetically promised messianic gift of salvation.[2] Acts refers explicitly to the promise of the divine Spirit in the prophet Joel (2:28-32) and has Peter explain the experience of the Spirit on the first Pentecost in this way: "This Jesus God raised up, and of that all of us are witnesses. Being therefore exalted at the right hand of God, and having received from the Father the promise of the Holy Spirit, he has poured out this that you both see and hear" (Acts 2:32-33; the entire sermon of Peter is in vv. 17-36). It is necessary to receive the divine Spirit in order to be rescued from the peril of death and brought to God; certainly, no one but God alone decides for how many this promise of salvation will be realized, but Peter gives assurance that those who repent and are baptized "in the name of Jesus Christ so that your sins may be forgiven" will receive the gift of the Holy Spirit (vv. 38-39). Here the twofold manner of the divine Spirit's coming is made clear: the Spirit comes spontaneously, from the limitless sovereignty of the divine Father who gives the Spirit through Jesus, and it is given in connection with the sacrament and the reorientation of one's life. Neither way of receiving the Spirit is understood as exclusive of the other. In both instances it is God who gives; God remains sovereign in the sacramental action as well, since it is God who decides about the Spirit's coming to human beings and its activity within them. Thus these New Testament texts concerning the Spirit offer no basis for the opinion that the Church claims to have the divine Spirit at its disposal and to be able to "channel" it.

We should also take note of these conclusions in connection with the text that in Catholic theology has served as the classic witness for the sacrament of confirmation: Acts 8:14-17. In Samaria[3] there were

2. Documentation can readily be found in works on pneumatology, e.g., those of Y. Congar (*Der Heilige Geist*) and C. Schütz (*Einführung*) (see ch. 1, n. 22 above), or in encyclopedia articles on "Pneuma."

3. Here we cannot go into the question of the purpose of the author of Acts in telling this story. The idea that the Holy Spirit, promised by the prophets at the end-time, had already been poured out on the earliest Christian community, and the assumption of the power to impose hands by agents of that community are certainly to be read in the context of the separation of the Church from Israel.

believers who had accepted the word of God and been baptized, but on whom the Holy Spirit had not "fallen." The Jerusalem apostles sent Peter and John to them; these apostles prayed for the coming of the divine Spirit, laid their hands on the believers, and these Christians also received the Holy Spirit. Afterward it is said that the divine Spirit was given "through the laying on of the apostles' hands" (vv. 18-19). The statement should certainly not be understood in an exclusive sense, so that the rite of imposition of hands is contrasted with the prayer for the coming of the Spirit. The ancient gesture of blessing, the imposition of hands (Gen 48:15) was combined with prayer.[4] This is mentioned in Acts without any theological reflection, as a matter of course (cf. 6:6: imposition of hands following prayer; 9:12-18; 19:6), but nowhere does it suppress the saving and Spirit-communicating quality of faith in the gospel (cf. 15:7-8).

Thus these New Testament witnesses to the Spirit authorize the conclusion that God's Spirit, as the gift of the Father through the Son, is on the one hand promised and really given to human beings who represent God's new humanity and in whom, by the power of the Spirit, eternal life has already begun, but that on the other hand the Church can effectively pray for the coming of the divine Spirit for a particular purpose. Acts speaks unsystematically of special tasks for whose fulfillment the divine Spirit is needed: giving witness to the faith (2:22-36; 4:8-12, etc.), missionary work to win new people to the faith (8:29, 39; 13:2ff., etc.), making important decisions for the life of the Church (10:19; 11:12; 15:28; 20:28).

The other New Testament passages concerning the Spirit (primarily in Paul and John) do not contradict the viewpoint of Luke's volumes. But they concentrate on the creative divine Spirit who gives new life, who changes human beings, leading them to faith and ever deeper insight, who continually seeks to produce practical "fruits of the Spirit" in human attitudes, who strengthens them to use the freedom that has been given them, who bestows different gifts for the upbuilding

4. See the standard work on imposition of hands: K. Groß, *Menschenhand und Gotteshand in Antike und Christentum* (Stuttgart: 1985). In connection with the discussion of the sacrament of orders we should also pose the question, still unanswered at the present, whether the instances of laying on of hands mentioned in the New Testament all, or in most cases, were not gestures of blessing, but signs of election (lifting up of hands). Cf. also A. T. Hanson and others, "Handauflegung," *TRE* XIV (1985) 415-418.

of the Christian community and thus guarantees the unity of believers. In short: they describe the Spirit as the essence of God (John 4:24), as the way in which God, after the exaltation of Jesus Christ, is present in humanity. In this way of coming and remaining, God, the Spirit, is absolutely free, not at anyone's disposal and unpredictable. It would contradict the New Testament to try to make the presence of the divine Spirit in human hearts dependent on the administration of a sacrament. But it would not be contradictory to regard a sacrament as the prayer for the Spirit's coming and acting in a special way.

7.2 *Historical Decisions*

In the Latin Church, the detaching of the postbaptismal anointing—as symbol of the strengthening and claiming of a human being for God (consecration)—and the imposition of hands by the bishop from the act of baptism with water (see 6.2 above) made confirmation a separate sacrament. This division was finalized by the Carolingian reform.[5] The theological reflections that on rare occasions accompanied this process of division concentrated on the actions of anointing (which was also understood pneumatologically) and imposition of hands. The connection with baptism was retained: the detached rite was regarded as the completion of baptism, reserved to the bishop, according to a synod at Elvira (present Granada), around 300 (only in Latin, DS 120-121). The first reasoning for this imposition of hands as the prerogative of the bishop was given by Cyprian of Carthage (d. 258), citing Acts 8:14-17. In addition, the consecration of the chrism (composed of olive oil and balsam) was always reserved to the bishop.

In the patristic period we find witnesses who understand the rite after baptism not merely as an external expansion or completion, but as an intensification of the baptismal action. The theological meditation concentrated on two symbolic concepts, *chrism* and *sphragis*. The anointing was seen as a visible communication of interior power, even the strength that made it possible to undergo martyrdom, a witnessing to faith that endures even to death. Baptism, in its complete form, including episcopal imposition of hands, was understood as the transfer of a human being into the ownership of Jesus Christ and to his service, as the sealing (*sphragis*) of a decision made once and for all. From

5. Cf. A. Angenendt, *Kaiserherrschaft und Königstaufe* (Berlin: 1984) 75-91.

that point of view we can understand how the indelible mark (character) attributed to baptism was also attached to confirmation, after it was detached from baptism. It was this understanding of the sacrament that gave it its name in Latin theology: *confirmatio*.

Scholastic theology was at pains to define the inner content of confirmation: it was said to show that human beings were spiritually and religiously mature, to give them the strength to witness to faith in the broader sense and to bestow on them the irrevocable task of participation in the life and mission of the Church (hence the non-repeatability of confirmation implied by the "character"). The relationship to baptism was always preserved, and it was never said that confirmation was the exclusive or even a preferred way in which the Holy Spirit comes to a human person.

The Church's dogmatic statements on confirmation arose out of the efforts toward unity with the separated Eastern Churches in the fourteenth and fifteenth centuries. In Eastern theology, the "anointing with myron" was strictly distinguished from baptism, but it was connected with it, as it still is in the Eastern Churches, where it was and is bestowed on the infant by a simple priest. In 1351 the Pope expected the Armenians to acknowledge that chrism could only be consecrated by the bishop (NR 548/DS 1068), and that the sacrament of confirmation could "by reason of his office" and "ordinarily" (i.e., according to the normal order of things) be administered only by the bishop (NR 549/DS 1069), but the Pope, and he alone, could also empower simple priests to administer it (NR 550/DS 1070); candidates who had not been confirmed according to these rules must be reconfirmed by a bishop (NR 551/DS 1071). The Council of Florence in 1439 also sought, in its teaching for the Armenians, to compel them to accept the Latin view of confirmation (NR 552-553/DS 1317-1318). In this text, which relies on Thomas Aquinas, we also read of the special effects of confirmation. It states that "through confirmation our grace is increased and our faith strengthened" (NR 502/DS 1311), and further: "The effect of this sacrament is that in it the Holy Spirit is given for strength, as . . . to the apostles on the day of Pentecost, in order that the Christian may courageously confess the name of Christ. And, therefore, the one to be confirmed is anointed on the forehead which is the seat of shame, so that [she or] he may not be ashamed to confess the name of Christ, and chiefly His cross, which according to the apostle, is a stumbling block for the Jews and foolishness for the Gentiles. This is why [she or] he is signed with the sign of the cross'' (NR 554/DS 1319). Along with its teaching about the sacramental character of confirmation, this council emphasized that the sacrament could not be repeated (NR 504/DS 1313).

The next occasion for official Church statements about confirmation was the rejection of this sacrament by the Reformers: the latter saw in confirmation a devaluation of baptism and, in accord with their principle that a sacrament must have been expressly instituted by Jesus Christ and bear a promise of grace, they could not recognize confirmation as a sacrament. The seventh session of the Council of Trent (1547), in its teaching on the sacraments in general, counted confirmation among the seven sacraments instituted by Jesus Christ (NR 506/DS 1601) and repeated the teaching about the sacramental character imprinted by confirmation (NR 514/DS 1609). In the same session it produced three doctrinal statements on confirmation:

> 1. If anyone says that the confirmation of those baptized is a useless ceremony and not a true and proper sacrament; or that of old it was nothing more than a sort of catechesis in which those nearing adolescence gave an account of their faith before the Church, *anathema sit.*
> 2. If anyone says that those who ascribe any power to the sacred chrism of confirmation are offending the Holy Spirit, *anathema sit.*
> 3. If anyone says that the ordinary minister of holy confirmation is not the bishop alone but any simple priest, *anathema sit* (NR 555-557/DS 1628-1630).[6]

The third sentence was not intended to condemn the Eastern Church's usage of confirmation by the priest, but to designate it as an ''extraordinary'' procedure.

In the Protestant Churches, confirmation was known even in the sixteenth century as a non-sacramental service of worship, in which young people (about fourteen years old) were recognized by the community as full members of the Church; it was combined with a commemoration of baptism and an explicit, confessional-type dedication of those being confirmed to the way of Jesus Christ. This custom, which has been in general use since the eighteenth century, reveals a need (found also in the Catholic Church) to ask of those approaching adult-

6. Translation adapted from J. Neuner, S.J. and J. Dupuis, S.J., *The Christian Faith in the Doctrinal Documents of the Catholic Church* (Westminster, Md.: Christian Classics, Inc., 1975).

hood a personal, responsible statement of their attitude toward the baptism conferred on them as infants, and if that response is positive, to obligate these young Christians to a life of conscious witness. The insight that in this sense baptism needs an expansion and completion led, among Catholics, to extended discussions in the field of practical theology about the right age for confirmation. The more confirmation is seen as a public act of conscious, inner affirmation of conversion and faith, a making-present of the baptismal event, and a freely-chosen entry into an ecclesial and missionary existence, the stronger is the inclination to advance the suggested age for confirmation to the threshold of genuine adulthood.

Vatican Council II expressed itself on several individual aspects of confirmation. In the Constitution on the Liturgy we read: "The rite of confirmation is to be revised and the intimate connection which this sacrament has with the whole of Christian initiation is to be more lucidly set forth; for this reason it will be fitting for candidates to renew their baptismal promises just before they are confirmed" (SC 71). In the dogmatic Constitution on the Church, what is said about the effects of confirmation is evidently based on a comparison with baptism. It is said of the faithful that "bound more intimately to the Church by the sacrament of confirmation, they are endowed by the Holy Spirit with special strength" (LG 11); their special ecclesial mission is also expressed when their calling to an apostolate of the laity by baptism and confirmation is traced to the exalted Lord (LG 33). The practical situation in the Catholic Church has become such that not only bishops, but priests authorized by them can confirm (and in case of need, any priest, even without authorization). Vatican Council II clarified the question of the "minister" in part, by saying of the bishops: "they are the original ministers of confirmation" (LG 26), and therefore in no way the exclusive ministers; moreover, the Eastern Church practice of confirmation by priests with chrism blessed by the patriarch or bishop was expressly acknowledged (OE 13–14). In the reformed rite of confirmation,[7] the sacrament is administered, after a prayer for the

7. The new order of confirmation was established by the apostolic constitution *Divinae consortium naturae* (15 August 1971): AAS 63 (1971) 657–664. The corresponding liturgical order is found in R. Kaczynski, *Enchiridion Documentorum Instaurationis liturgicae* I, 1963–1973 (Turin: 1976) 814–820; cf. A. E. Hierold, "Taufe und Firmung," *HKR*, 659–675, at 671–675 on confirmation, especially the new regulation regarding the "minister of confirmation," 672–673.

coming of the divine Spirit, by an anointing on the forehead with chrism, accompanied by an imposition of the hand, as the words are spoken: "Be sealed with the gift of God, the Holy Spirit." When adults are baptized and confirmed, the old order of initiation (baptism, confirmation, Eucharist) is to be observed.

7.3 *Summary*

On the basis of the origins of confirmation, it is possible to regard this sacrament as that symbolic action in which the Church prays for a special effectiveness of the Holy Spirit in and for a baptized person. The Church is, in principle, free to determine the particular aspiration of this prayer more precisely. On the basis of tradition, an interpretation in terms of the completion of baptism suggests itself, in the sense that, in confirmation, the baptized recall their own baptism, become conscious of an intimate union with Jesus Christ, and strengthen both the orientation of their whole lives to Jesus Christ ("conversion") and their acceptance of the faith of the Church. This can be accompanied by a new, personal commitment to live as a witness for that faith in the world, the acceptance of a mission, or "apostolate" from the Church. These ways of filling out the content of the sacrament are not mere human inventions; they are guaranteed by God through the exalted Son, to the extent that the latter desires to see his mission continued by the community of believers, in the power of the Holy Spirit who is present among them. If the Church maintains that Jesus Christ is the one really acting in this sacrament, since he gives the Spirit bestowed on him by the Father to those who ask, for the fulfillment of specific tasks, that does not mean that the Church assumes authority of the divine Spirit or regards the Spirit as being at the Church's disposal.

Two misunderstandings ought to be avoided. (1) Confirmation may not be regarded as the first and fundamental communication of the Holy Spirit to any human being. Since God's grace is, in the first place, nothing different from God's own self, and since God's coming to a human being, God's dwelling in the most intimate center of a human person, depends entirely on God's free initiative, the point at which the divine Spirit is communicated to the human person is identical with this gracious coming of God; however, it can never be discovered and pinpointed by any human person. In the grace-filled event of confirmation, the Spirit of God present in the human being moves the believer in a particular direction to the fulfilling of the will of God. (2) But confirmation must not be understood as the sacrament of the lay apostolate. It indicates the beginning of being a Christian in the ecclesial and secular public realm as gift and task, the strengthening of faith and the empowerment to witness to it; thus, together with baptism, it is fundamental for *all* "states" and ministries in the Church. Confirmation is one of the "lesser" sacraments; it was never regarded as necessary for salvation. Nevertheless, as a visible expression of our dependence on God's Holy Spirit, it is of great importance. As an acknowledgment of the prophetic promise of the Spirit and its fulfillment in accord with the mysterious will of God, as a symbolic action incorporating the venerable gestures of anointing and imposition of hands, it documents the enduring connection of the Christian Church with Israel. The desire for confirmation in the Reformed Churches shows that the existence of this sacrament need not stand in the way of ecumenical endeavors.

Bibliography 5

Confirmation

Amougou-Atangana, J. *Ein Sakrament des Geistempfangs?* Freiburg: 1974.

Barral-Baron, N. *Renouveau de la confirmation.* Paris: 1983.

Biemer, G. *Firmung. Theologie und Praxis.* Würzburg: 1973 (bibliography).

De Halleux, A. "Confirmation et Chrisma." *Irénikon* 57 (1984) 490–515.

Ferrari, G. "Teologia e liturgia della confirmazione in Oriente e Occident" *Nicolaus* 12 (1985) 295–316.

"Firmung." *Internationale kath. Zeitschrift* 11 (1982) 409–456.

Il sacramento della confermazione. Bologna: 1983.

Kretschmar, G. "Firmung." *TRE* XI (1983) 192–204.

Lanne, E. "Les sacrements de l'initiation chrétienne et la confirmation dans l'Eglise d'Occident." *Irénikon* 57 (1984) 196–215, 324–346.

Larrabe, J. L. "La Confirmación, sacramento del Espíritu en la teologia moderna." *Lumen* 32 (1983) 144–175.

Ligier, L. *La Confirmation.* Paris: 1973 (criticizes the decline of imposition of hands in favor of anointing; rich in materials).

Meyer, H. B. *Aus dem Wasser und dem Heiligen Geist.* Aschaffenburg: 1969.

Mühlen, H. "Firmung als sakramentales Zeichen der heilsgeschichtlichen Selbstüberlieferung des Geistes Christi." *Theologie und Glaube* 57 (1967) 263–286.

Nordhues, P., and H. Petri, eds. *Die Gabe Gottes. Beiträge zur Theologie und Pastoral des Firmsakraments.* Paderborn: 1974.

Schützeichel, H. *Katholische Calvin-Studien.* Trier: 1980, 9–27 (Calvin's critique of confirmation).

Zerndl, J. *Die Theologie der Firmung in der Vorbereitung und in den Akten des Zweiten Vatikanischen Konzils.* Paderborn: 1986.

8

Eucharist

8.1 *Introduction*

Among the seven sacraments of the Church, the Eucharist has the highest place. For Roman Catholic and Orthodox Christians it is *the* liturgy pure and simple. Here, as with no other sacrament, the objective rite and the deepest subjective, emotional and mystical piety are united; the most important human capabilities (music, architecture, crafts, painting, poetry) are brought into service; all the theological disciplines have striven and are still striving for knowledge, insight, and a way in which to do it justice; and all the doctrines of faith from the theology of creation to eschatology come together in this one sacrament. This intensive and extensive attention makes it impossible to speak adequately of this sacrament and its history in a brief overview.

Similarly, the various crises endured by the Eucharist can only be mentioned here. When there is discussion of resistance to and lack of interest in liturgy and symbols, the Eucharist is the form of worship most affected. To the same degree, it is the object of a newly awakened interest in ''the Lord's supper as an assurance of belonging, an experience of security; the Lord's supper as a new beginning in the snares of guilt and violence; the Lord's supper as the experience of shared life in the bread broken with one another; the Lord's supper as a meal of hope, a dream."[1] In its new forms, Eucharist is to reveal the Church as always young and dynamic, politically and socially active, inviting and missionary; far beyond the inner circle, it should be "an open, public meal of fellowship for peace and God's justice in the world,"[2] in which even the unbaptized can participate by eating and drinking. In efforts to preserve the Eucharist to the fullest extent possible from having a cultic appearance—though the cultic aspect still shows its vitality in huge celebrations with mass participation—the anthropological and sociological meaning of mutual eating and drinking receives special emphasis.[3]

This kind of open praxis (and the more modest form of "unauthorized" alterations in the liturgy), with the discussions surrounding it, not only lead to admonitions and warnings from Church officials and theologians; they also deepen the existing rifts within a single Church and even lead to a splitting off of sects,[4] so that Jesus' legacy becomes a source of strife and disunion. These and similar observations draw attention to the preconditions that must be fulfilled if we are really to speak of Eucharist. Whatever value the memorial of Jesus in a broader form may have for new approaches to Christian praxis and faith, the Christian celebration can only under particular conditions lay claim to the name that, by preference, is given to this sacrament by Catholic and Protestant Christians: Eucharist or Lord's Supper.

A first condition is the genuine and active desire for Church unity. This is threatened, in the first instance, by a lack of reconciliation, by aggressivity and dogmatism (on all sides!). According to a word of Jesus that has been handed down to us, reconciliation is a precondition for liturgy (Matt 5:23-24). At a time when many eyewitnesses and hearers of Jesus were still living, Paul spoke of the impossibility of celebrating Eucharist in the community, as long as divisions existed (1 Cor 11, es-

---

1. U. Kühn, *Sakramente*, 264.
2. J. Moltmann, *Kirche in der Kraft des Geistes* (Munich: 1975) 270.
3. M. Jossutis and G. M. Martin, eds., *Das heilige Essen. Kulturwissenschaftliche Beiträge zum Verständnis des Abendmahls* (Stuttgart and Berlin: 1980).
4. As one example among many, let me mention the activities of the Lefebvre group and the consequences thereof; cf. A. Schifferle's dissertation, written under my direction and entitled *Marcel Lefebvre—Ärgernis und Besinnung* (Kevelaer: 1983), especially 131-166.

pecially 17-20; cf. also 10:17). In an expression that is still often cited, Augustine called the Eucharist "the sign of unity, the bond of love" (Vatican II, SC 47). Walter Kasper writes correctly that: "It is certainly contrary to the essence of eucharist and to the decisions of the early Church on this subject, to make of the eucharist a celebration of race or class, either by making it an exclusive eucharist of the privileged, or by turning it into a revolutionary celebration of the underprivileged. But it contradicts the essence of the eucharist to the same degree, if one ignores the ethical preconditions and consequences of a common eucharistic celebration: *agape* concretely realized (cf. Mt 5:23-24), the *miniumum* of which is the fulfillment of the demands of social justice."[5]

The Eucharist, as the embodiment of our confession of faith, obviously raises the question of the faith of those celebrating it. In many memorials of Jesus it is evident that there is no awareness at all that Jesus was the very model of a "pious Jew," a person who lived entirely from and toward God, filled with his mission and determined to be faithful to that mission, and to the Father who sent him, even to the end. How could we think of Jesus without being conscious of God? We can only speak of Eucharist in any meaningful sense where there is faith in God and in God's all-penetrating presence. That may sound more obvious than it is for many people. Do not many notions of the Eucharist contain the implicit idea that in this sacrament Jesus (and, with Jesus, God) is present, though he is otherwise distant, taken up into "heaven"? That he is "made" or "caused to be" present by a human agent? It is a precondition for Eucharist, as for every sacrament, that one believe firmly that God is the reality who determines all things and who is present at all times and everywhere.

The presence of the triune God is a *real* presence. The opposite of a real, that is, a fully genuine presence would be a presence only in thought, perhaps illusory, in any case uncertain. But how could God be thought of in terms of spatial distance, beyond some abyss that our thought might be able to bridge? God is really present to everyone and everything, and even if Jesus were nothing more than one human being rescued and taken to God, he would be where the dead who are saved for God are, namely, with God. And so he would in any case be really present for those who believe in God's real presence. But Jesus

5. W. Kasper, "Einheit und Vielfalt der Aspekte der Eucharistie," *Internationale katholische Zeitschrift* 14 (1985) 196–215, at 212–213. Emphasis supplied.

is immeasurably more than merely a human being who has been rescued from death and taken to God, since he is the human being with whom that in God which can be uttered, the eternal "logos" has united itself inseparably and without confusion. Where God truly is present, there is the real presence of Jesus.

This presence of God cannot be comprehended in ideas of space and time. The question: "When does God begin and end?" is as senseless as the question: "Where is God?" On the basis of biblical testimonies about God, Christian faith speaks of God as spirit or *pneuma* (John 4:24); God's presence for us is thus a pneumatic presence (see 2.3 and 5.1.1 above). When we say of a human being that he was awakened by God from death to eternal life, and that he was wholly saved, that is, raised from the dead, we obviously include his body. But the body that has been definitively taken up into God's glory, as so impressively described in 1 Corinthians 15:35-55, is of an entirely different quality from that of our bodies, limited as they are by space and time. The body hidden in God is "the work of the Spirit" (*pneumatikos*: not "spiritual," as so many translations say, but "Spirit-empowered"). Thus the presence of God and the presence of Jesus, as Son of God and as glorified human being, can always and only be a *pneumatic* presence.

It is fundamental to Christian faith, and thus also to the faith-preconditions for the Eucharist, that God's presence is only made evident for us through God's holy *pneuma*, the divine Spirit. This Spirit is not to be sought here or there, but in the innermost depths of ourselves, in our "hearts" (Rom 5:5). There, through the Spirit, and not through our own effort or achievement, occurs that opening, that disclosure that we call "faith," and that indwelling of God in a union or *communio* that cannot be described in words. This is the goal of Christian faith and of its praxis, the goal of all devotion, all liturgy and thus of all the sacraments, but especially of the Eucharist. If a Christian celebration is not oriented toward the real, pneumatic presence of God in Jesus through the Spirit, and if this union with God is not its final and highest end, it should not be called "Eucharist."

We should mention one other pneumatological precondition for Eucharist. It is God's Spirit who awakens faith in the hearts of human persons, who leads them to acknowledge and witness to this faith, and thus forms the Church. The fundamental features of the Church are the work of the Spirit of God. There the Spirit not only brings about the encounter of individuals with God, but is continually at work in them to bring together the Church as community. A certain trust in this work of the Spirit is part of any sacramental celebration: trust that those celebrating are not the victims of error or illusion. One aspect of this trust in the Holy Spirit is the confidence that the Church in its *fundamentals* need not be disturbed by historical research. Historical findings in the context of faith can never be so clear and certain that they compel any person to accept a particular conviction; in that case we could no longer speak of a freedom of belief. In the case of the Eucharist, historical-critical research has produced well-founded doubts as to whether we can speak of a direct, immediate "institution" or "origination" by the historical Jesus, whether he had instructed his friends to celebrate "this" in his memory, whether the words of institution over bread and cup could have been the same ones used by him, and so on. The traditional witnesses for the essential statements on the Eucharist lead us back so close to Jesus, both in time and in content, that faith still has enough historical points of contact to retain its intellectual integrity. Historians cannot explain how the earliest Christian community could simply have invented the heart of the Eucharistic tradition in so short a time after Jesus' departure. But it is not only historians who establish an "institutional connection" between Jesus and the Eucharist; that guarantee is really the work of the Spirit of God.

It follows from what has been said that the Church has the right, in principle, to restrict access to the Eucharist, and that there can be no objective injustice involved when that is done. In forbidding access, the Church does not decide whether God will be intimately present to a human person, in love and favor, and this barring of access need not necessarily mean that Christians within the Church keep their distance even at the level of human contacts and Christian charitable activities from those who think differently. For atheists or adherents of non-Christian religions the Church can be inviting and humanitarian in many ways, but it can and may not alter the function of the Eucharist to make it a supper open to the whole world.

The case of the Eucharistic communities of Christians who still live in separated Churches is different.[6] Must we demand of them a com-

---

6. There are some good overviews of the current situation, e.g., U. Kühn's in *TRE* I (1977) 145–212 or that of G. Wainwright in *EKL* I (1986) 29–32, both with bibliography. Cf. also T. Schneider, *Zeichen* (Mainz: 1984) 173–183.

mon creed? That they also hold a Trinitarian faith and acknowledge the real presence of God through God's Son Jesus in the Holy Spirit is an obvious precondition for celebrating the Eucharist and for Eucharistic communion. Beyond this, some Churches, for example the Orthodox and Roman Catholic, require that full Church unity be accomplished before there can be full Eucharistic community.[7] Although ecumenical dialogue has made astonishing strides in the last twenty-five years, our historical inheritance includes some dogmatic statements that, in the opinion of many Church leadership bodies, cannot be surrendered without loss of Church identity. Thus the Roman Catholic Church demands, for reception of the Eucharist, the acknowledgement that Jesus Christ is present in a special and unique manner (see below, 8.4.2 and 8.4.3), and requires, for a "valid" celebration of the Eucharist, that it be conducted by a "validly" ordained priest,[8] although the lack of this "validity" certainly cannot mean that God's gracious presence would be lacking or that the priestless celebration would be without any value. Small groups or individual theologians are powerless in face of such demands. But in the Christian tradition there are other witnesses that do not make a full unity of Church and creed the precondition for Eucharistic communion, and that see the Eucharist not only as a sign of full unity, but also as a means and a way to continually deepen a fundamental unity that, because of faith and baptism, already exists—so that the Eucharist *reveals* and *causes* the Church's unity (Pope Innocent III, d. 1216; PL 217, 879).

8.2 Biblical Foundations

8.2.1 *The Last Supper Accounts*

The Last Supper accounts found in the New Testament are regarded in all Christian Churches as the historical and theological basis for the

7. The Catholic Church is more prepared than the Orthodox to extend Eucharistic hospitality without mutuality, as the literature reveals. Cf. also A. Mayer, "Die Eucharistie," *HKR* 676–691.

8. U. Kühn, *Sakramente*, 302, is pleased to note that Vatican II did not use the word "validity," but instead spoke of a "deficiency" in the Protestant Eucharist, and not of a total absence or lack. The *Catechism for Catholic Adults* prepared by the German bishops' conference in 1985, however, referring to NR 920 and 713, again speaks of the only "valid" celebration by the "validly" ordained priest (359).

Eucharist or Lord's Supper.[9] However, they are not historical reports
in the sense of the term used by modern historians. They presuppose
the earliest Christian liturgy, the assembly gathered "in the name of
Jesus" and in faith in his real presence, in memory of that which God
accomplished in him, and in the experience of real community with
him, with hope of a continuing communion with him. They are evidently intended to serve the concrete shaping of this liturgy and its
religious-theological understanding.[10] Historically, the Eucharist goes
back to that last meal that Jesus ate with his most intimate circle of
disciples on the evening before his death. We may regard it also as
historically certain that Jesus had at least a strong premonition of his
approaching violent death, now that, in obedience to his mission, he
had offered the most extreme provocation to the Temple hierarchy.
It is scarcely disputed that it was Jesus' expectation and interpretation
of his violent death that distinguished this last meal from other meals.
"It is true that Jesus' last meal was much like the meals he had shared
with his disciples, as well as with toll collectors and sinners (Mk 2:16;
Lk 15:2), and in which, in anticipation of the messianic time of salvation, they all shared in the saving community of God, but this meal
also marked a turning point: while before this occasion the community was made possible by the presence of Jesus, this farewell meal
looks forward to the new situation that will be brought about by his
approaching death."[11] There can be no reasonable doubt that Jesus
also couched this meal within Jewish table liturgy. According to the
reports of the Last Supper, he combined the breaking and giving of
bread and the offering of the blessed cup with interpretive words.
While these words can no longer be reconstructed in their precise form,
there are no good grounds to think that such words were *not* spoken

9. For an introduction to what follows, see: G. Delling, "Abendmahl III," *TRE*
I (1977) 47–58; H. Frankemölle, B. J. Hilberath, and T. Schneider, "Eucharistie,"
NHthG I (1984) 297–317, especially 297–305; J. Roloff, "Abendmahl 2," *EKL* I (1986)
10–13, all with bibliography. For more detail, see T. Schneider, *Zeichen*, 128–173;
X. Léon-Dufour, "Das letzte Mahl Jesu und die testamentarische Tradition nach
Lk 22," *Zeitschrift für katholische Theologie* 103 (1981) 33–55; idem, *Le partage du pain
eucharistique selon le Nouveau Testament* (Paris: 1982); H.-J. Klauck, *Herrenmahl und
hellenistischer Kult. Eine religionsgeschichtliche Untersuchung zum ersten Korintherbrief*
(Münster: 1982); U. Kühn, *Sakramente*, 266–278.
10. Form-critically, they belong to the category of cult etiologies, a not very attrac-
tive title. But see what X. Léon-Dufour has to say about Luke 22.
11. J. Roloff, "Abendmahl" (see n. 9 above), 11.

by Jesus or that he was not referring to himself and his own destiny.[12] Therefore in their essence they may be regarded as historically certain. Jesus could have spoken words of interpretation when giving the bread: "This is my body"; for the cup: "This cup is my blood for many."[13] The saying over the bread, with the Aramaic word *gufa*, would refer to the whole, historically existing person; the word over the cup "extends" the movement of Jesus' life for others, and particularly for those who are far from God, even into death: this death, as well, will be for the benefit of the many, of those who are far from God. The presentation of gifts thus interpreted in the context of the meal promises that, beyond Jesus' death, community will be maintained with him, with his whole person and not only his "cause," and that the community of those who take part in the meal will be possible in view of that for which Jesus lived and died, namely, the reign of God.

"The post-Easter community, led by the exalted Lord present in the Spirit, by continuing in a new form the pre-Easter meals and especially the feast of Jesus' death with his disciples (i.e., in the form of thanksgiving, 'in memory,' calling on the Spirit), rightly laid claim to those pre-Easter celebrations (and especially the last meal) as a gift of the Lord to the Church."[14]

The reports of the Last Supper, as we have them, preserve both the liturgical practice of the early Christian communities and certain religious-theological interpretations drawn from that practice. The report in Mark (Mark 14:22-25) and that in Paul's Letter to the Corinthians (1 Cor 11:23-26) are regarded by scholars today as ancient versions, independent of one another, drawn from an original version that is no longer extant.[15] Whether Jesus' last meal was a Passover supper as the Synoptics say, in disagreement with John (18:28; 19:14), can no longer be determined. There is no tradition of Jesus' giving an interpretation in terms of Passover. Only later did theologians think it

12. For example, see J. Roloff, "Abendmahl," 10–11, against efforts in this direction by H. Lietzmann and W. Marxsen. H.-J. Klauck gives a detailed critique of the thesis of Hellenistic origins. According to his findings, in the actions with bread and cup Jesus conveyed the significance of his surrender to death as a prophetic sign of fulfillment, which they understood only in light of the Easter experience: Klauck, *Herrenmahl*, 365–374.

13. J. Roloff, "Abendmahl," 10, with regard to a possible "original form."

14. U. Kühn, *Sakramente*, 269.

15. Cf. J. Roloff, "Abendmahl," 10.

proper to devalue the Jewish Passover as a mere foreshadowing of the ''Paschal mystery'' of Jesus. The word over the cup in Mark (14:24): ''This is my blood of the covenant, which is poured out for many,'' interprets Jesus' violent death in terms of Exodus 24:5-8 as a new covenant, and understands Jesus as the servant of YHWH depicted by Isaiah, who as mediator of the covenant (cf. Isa 42:6; 49:8) bore the sins of ''the many,'' that is, of all, and who interceded for the guilty before God (Isa 53:12). The eschatological point of view (Mark 14:25; Matt 26:29; Luke 22:18), even if it does not go back to Jesus himself, bears the marks of his spirit: it reflects the certainty of Jesus' conviction about the realization of the reign of God, and it reveals the confidence with which Jesus, as a just Jew, went to his death, in the firm faith that YHWH would not abandon those who are faithful.[16]

Matthew's report (Matt 26:26-29) is completely dependent on Mark, but reveals still stronger marks of liturgical stylization.[17] It expands the shedding of the blood of the covenant for the many with the explanation, ''for the forgiveness of sins.''

In the ancient account of the Last Supper in Paul's writing (1 Cor 11:23-26), we probably find the earliest tradition that the interpretive words were directly connected with the cup, not with the blood.[18] Otherwise this is a stylized, theologically weighted text that serves Paul's purpose of opposing abuses in the Eucharistic celebration at Corinth. But for that very reason it is of great value in revealing the early development of an interpretation of the Eucharist. The ''supper of the Lord'' is already clearly distinguished from ordinary meals. Undoubtedly, Paul and the addressees of the letter share a belief in a real, ''sacramental'' presence of Jesus (cf. 11:27). The recipients of the letter evidently had a well-developed understanding of sacrament, but had forgotten that the Eucharistic meal involved a personal encounter with the Crucified, which presupposed and resulted in a companionable attitude in solidarity with others. In his urgent warning, Paul uses the word ''memorial'' (*anamnesis*) in order to point out that in this meal the event of the cross is made present, so that those who eat and drink may participate in it. The immediate effect of the event of the cross is, according to the word over the cup, the ''new covenant,'' in fulfill-

16. Cf. H. Vorgrimler, *Hoffnung auf Vollendung*, 2d ed. (Freiburg: 1984) 41–42 (with literature on Jesus' eschatology).
17. J. Roloff, ''Abendmahl.''
18. Ibid.

ment of the prophecy of Jeremiah 31:31-34. The liturgy makes this covenant present, whenever it is celebrated, and thus keeps before our eyes the fact that God expects of the partners in the covenant a particular ethical standard of behavior. In this memorial-that-makes-present, the participants (if they celebrate the Eucharist "worthily") proclaim "the death of the Lord, until he comes" (11:26). It is in this form that Jesus' eschatological point of view is retained.

In recent research[19] it has been pointed out that this report reveals an accommodation of the Eucharist to Hellenistic memorial meals for the dead. It is true that the reference to a historical institution by Jesus and the influence of Jewish historical thinking are of primary importance, but a process of Hellenizing can be demonstrated at many levels. This Hellenizing is represented especially by the development of the Eucharist into a stylized cultic action and, with regard to the "anamnesis," the increasing similarity to a Hellenistic memorial meal. These findings, however, should at least be supplemented by the observation that even Jewish festival meals were liturgically stylized (and that the concepts of "cult" and "cultic" should be reserved for pagan rituals), as well as the fact that memorials that made present the mighty works of God were and are an essential component of Jewish liturgy. The memorial celebration of Eucharist does not depend on the concept of "anamnesis." Even if Jesus did not say, in good Hellenistic style, "do this in memory of me," his symbolic action within the format of a Jewish festival meal could have served as a basis for the memorial structure of the Eucharist. In any case, it seems a false direction for research to attempt to make the "institution" of the Eucharist by Jesus, the Jew, more historically credible by seeking to find formal rituals in the Judaism of Jesus' time, involving bread and wine if possible, to which Jesus only had to give a new meaning—whether that ritual be the table blessing (*bere akha*),[20] or the historically dubious sacrifice of praise (*todâ*).[21]

19. Cf. H.-J. Klauck, *Herrenmahl*, 285-364.
20. A derivation of the Eucharist from the *berakah*, influential among Catholics, was attempted by L. Bouyer, *Théologie et spiritualité de la prière eucharistique* (Paris: 1966).
21. H. Gese, "Die Herkunft des Herrenmahls,"in his *Zur biblischen Theologie* (Munich: 1977) 107-127 posits an origin in the *todah*; in agreement with him is J. Ratzinger, *Das Fest des Glaubens* (Einsiedeln: 1981) 47-54; against this interpretation is H.-J. Klauck, *Herrenmahl*.

Luke's account (Luke 22:15-20) incorporates concepts from sacrificial theology in the interpretive words ("given," v. 19, "poured out," v. 20) and, like Paul, the statement that the "new covenant" is completed in the blood of Jesus (v. 20). The command to "do this in memory of me," repeated twice by Paul, is found once here. Xavier Léon-Dufour has made an important contribution with his study of the Lukan account.[22] According to him, in the earliest Christian communities there was a twofold response to the question: How could a genuine and effective memorial of Jesus, who had entered into death, be maintained? how could a personal union with the living but absent Jesus be possible? One answer is reflected in cultic tradition, the other is echoed in testamentary tradition. The two are not mutually exclusive. The cultic tradition, which might better be called a "liturgical tradition," concentrated on the new manner of Jesus' presence and the event of the cross; the group of disciples became the community assembled around Jesus at a liturgical meal. This liturgical concentration is found in the Last Supper accounts of Mark and Matthew. The testamentary tradition, in contrast, places the emphasis on the "testament" that the departed had left behind. Léon-Dufour is able to point to a number of examples of testamentary tradition in Jewish writings. In the New Testament, he finds, it exists in the literary genre of Jesus' farewell speeches. John's Gospel has deliberately and completely replaced the liturgical tradition with the testamentary tradition. Luke, on the other hand, has incorporated the liturgical tradition (presence of Jesus in 22:19 and, in a present, symbolic action, his death in 22:20) within a farewell speech and thus given the whole a testamentary form (extending from 22:15 to 22:38). The evangelist is concerned to emphasize that the institution of the sacramental action is not the whole of Jesus' testament, which also includes the urgent admonition to service in thought and deed (22:24-30), to watchfulness in times of peril (22:31-38), and to expectation of the completion of the meal in the reign of God (22:15-16). Thus the evangelist reminded the Christians of his time of that which was essential for Jesus, namely that their relationship with God was not to consist wholly in liturgical devotion.

22. X. Léon-Dufour, "Das letzte Mahl Jesu," on Luke 22; also his *Le partage*, 211-317 (see n. 9 above).

8.2.2 *Other New Testament Texts*

The experience of knowing that Jesus, although he had been killed by human beings, lives and can be present in another manner, which is also perceptible to the senses, is reflected in the stories about table fellowship with the One whom God had raised up (Luke 24:13-35; John 21:1-14). These encounters at table have the function of "opening up" the Easter experience: just as Jesus' meals with outcasts and public sinners had been evidence of God's will to forgive and bestow mercy, so the post-Easter experiences made it possible to understand God's mighty deeds in and for Jesus more and more profoundly; as the Emmaus story says, they gave people the courage to be witnesses (cf. also Acts 10:41).

The New Testament texts that already contain theological reflection on the Eucharist quite clearly presume a transformation of the gifts, but they do not say *what* it is that happens to them. They are more interested in the communion with Jesus Christ that is made possible precisely through sharing in these gifts. For Paul, that communion is soteriological and Christological in character: it is a saving communion in the blood of Christ (1 Cor 10:16) and membership in the glorious realm of the divine Lord (1 Cor 10:21); but it is also ecclesiological in character: communion in the one bread brings about (not "crowns") the unity of that body of Christ that is the Church (1 Cor 10:17). The Johannine Gospel portrays a theological origin of the two major sacraments, and thus of the Church, in the Crucified (John 19:33-37). This Gospel speaks of the Eucharist in the great bread discourse (John 6:22-65), which is placed in the context of Passover (6:4) and the feeding of five thousand (6:5-15). The "true bread from God" is compared to the manna in the desert, which nourished but could not prevent death and thus was at best a prefiguring (*typos*) of the true bread. A Christological and a sacramental aspect are to be distinguished in the discourse. What they have in common is the statement that whoever has a living ("personal") relationship to Jesus already has eternal life and will be raised up from physical death. In the Christological section (vv. 32-51b), the true bread of life is described as a gift of the divine Father; the meal, which gives eternal life, is faith in the Son (a faith that is also given by the Father; 6:44). In the sacramental section it is Jesus who gives himself in the two Eucharistic gifts, which are his flesh and blood (51c-59). Eating and drinking these gifts causes a mutual and continuing indwelling in one another (v. 56). From the beginning, a soteriological expansion is evident: "and the bread that I will give for the life of the world is my flesh" (v. 51c). The realism of incarnational thought in this Gospel corresponds to the realism of its sacramental thought, and the sharp accentuation in both may be traced to the final, anti-Docetic redaction of the Gospel. But the discourse is not content to speak of the salvific content of the sacramental gifts, for it has a strongly dynamic character: it describes Jesus' mission, his coming from and going to the Father, and it assures those who believe and share in the sacrament that they are included in that process. This process that leads to life is the work of the divine Spirit, for "it is the spirit that gives life; the flesh is useless" (v. 63).

8.2.3 *Summary and Problems*

The Eucharist appears in the New Testament as a formal liturgy distinguished from ordinary common meals,[23] even though both may include rituals of blessing and praise. What sets the Eucharist apart from all other liturgies is the gift that goes back to Jesus' actions during his last meal.[24] In the time between Jesus' death and the final, perfect union with him, the Eucharist guarantees (sacramental) communion with Jesus, clarifies the meaning of Jesus Christ's death and resurrection, and creates the community of the faithful.

In relation to the action involving the gifts, three groups of words are of particular importance: the word about repetition, the words about memorial, and the words over the bread and cup respectively. The first two state that God in Jesus is the one who really accomplishes this event; it is God's power alone that can make present what is past, so that this saying always refers the Church back to Jesus. The words over the bread tell us that Jesus gives himself, in his whole historical and personal reality, in the distribution of this bread; they invite us, in taking and eating this bread, to enter into the deepest possible union with Jesus; they are addressed to a group of people and thereby express the fact that real community occurs among those who deliberately eat

23. Cf. W.-D. Hauschild, "Agapen. I. In der Alten Kirche," *TRE* I (1977) 748–753.
24. For what follows I am particularly indebted to X. Léon-Dufour, *Le partage*, and the affirmative review of that book by M. Rese in *Theologische Zeitschrift* (Basel) 40 (1984) 423–425.

of this bread. The words over the cup are intended to express the deeper meaning of Jesus' act: through his blood he has inaugurated a new and definitive relationship between the human community and God, into which those who drink from this cup are incorporated.

Of course, these statements have an internal continuity with other central biblical themes: those that speak of God's benevolent attitude toward human beings, of the presence of God, of God's common history with humanity. The Eucharist is in immediate contact with what has been revealed about the life-giving activity of the divine Spirit, the creative power of the divine Word. Thus proclamation of the Word and a prayer for the action of the Spirit have been part of the Church's Eucharistic celebration from the very beginning, for sound biblical reasons. But in particular the testamentary tradition, recently expounded by Xavier Léon-Dufour, shows that the Eucharist may not be celebrated in isolation from people's concrete lives. The Eucharist not only presupposes an ethical and solidary mind-set and praxis, but also demands certain practical consequences: "Effective love of neighbor is the only 'reality' that is an authentic and living heritage from Christ in the Church."[25] For the New Testament, the points at which the Eucharist is open to people's lives are more important than theological explanations. Léon-Dufour lists some conditions and some ways leading to a better and deeper understanding of the Eucharist from a biblical basis.

The conditions: the eucharist essentially means community and not the relationship of individuals to the "holy sacrament," and the words of institution do not apply to a thing in isolation, but are part of a narrative which aims at a relationship among all participants. Concerning the means of access to this reality, Léon-Dufour points first of all to the rhythm of cult and daily life among Christians, which can be linked up with the cultic and testamentary tradition in the accounts of Jesus' final meal, since in those accounts the gift that is Jesus himself, through his personal sacrifice in cross and resurrection, are joined with the duty of Christians, in effect from then on to love one another. Secondly, Léon-Dufour speaks of a symbolic interpretation of eucharist: bread and wine indicate the two dimensions of daily life and festival in human existence, and food itself represents the new life that is bestowed on the community. Third, for Léon-Dufour the realities of covenant, the blood that has been shed and the sharing in the mystery are appropriate pointers to

25. X. Léon-Dufour, *Le partage*, 114.

the relationship between God and humanity, since all three are first of all and primarily gift.[26]

If we now attempt to clarify these New Testament fundamentals further, using categories drawn from the theological tradition, we may say that a certain variety in the theological interpretations of the Eucharist found in the New Testament, and especially the twofold form of the interpretative words over bread and cup have made it "easier," for a long time, to let theological descriptions of the Eucharist separate into bits and pieces. In official teaching of the Catholic Church, as we will see, there are three pieces: real presence, the sacrifice of the Mass, and sacramental communion. From what has already been said it is clear that, from a New Testament point of view, communion offers the least difficulties. If the New Testament texts are not interested in giving a more precise explanation of the "how" of Jesus' presence in the gifts, they still testify to a sacramental realism, i.e., they hold irrevocably to Jesus' genuine presence as a fully living person. They also presuppose that the purpose of partaking of these gifts is entry into intimate communion with him, and not eating one's fill: that means that in this celebration the gifts are changed into something different from what they were before. It is obvious to those Christians celebrating the Eucharist who formerly had been Jews that it is not the human participants who bring about this change. The one who creates all good things is God, the omnipresent, to whom all things belong. Bread and wine are also God's possession; they are at God's disposal; they are God's gifts. The blessing over the gifts calls on God, and faith trusts that God will act upon them.

The greatest problems are involved with the thematic area that may be briefly designated "the theme of sacrifice" (with the caution that here, in relation to the Bible, we are only talking about Jesus' sacrifice). The difficulties derive from the New Testament texts and the disparate interpretations we find there. It is certain that the Eucharist makes present the resurrection of Jesus, since it celebrates in faith the presence of Jesus as the Risen and Living One and gives thanks to the Father for raising him up. But as the word over the cup indicates, the Eucharist primarily makes present the death of Jesus and its salvific

26. M. Rese, review of Dufour (see n. 24 above) 425, referring to Dufour, *Le partage*, 321–340.

significance for us and for all. This raises the unavoidable question of Jesus' understanding of his own death. The easiest answer, if it were adequate, would be to see Jesus' acceptance of death simply as the consequence of his obedience to his mission from the Father and his love of humanity, and his death as the high point of his "pro-existence."[27] That would avoid the many objections that Anton Vögtle and others raise against the idea that Jesus understood his death as that of a representative atoning sacrifice, which would be another condition of salvation in addition to Jesus' previous preaching about God.[28] The designations of "sacrifice" and "self-surrender" for Jesus' consistent acceptance of his death are within the framework of what we know of the historical Jesus: they comprehend (even if they do so in a way that is subject to misunderstanding because of their passive sound) Jesus' radical obedience to his mission, his identification with all human beings who are victims of evil, and his intercession for all.[29] But did God demand of Jesus, at the end of his life, that he die as a representative atonement, making this a precondition for reconciliation? The objection to this is that the sacrifice of human life in a death of atonement is absolutely alien to the God of biblical revelation.[30] On the other hand, many witnesses in the New Testament make a close connection between the death of Jesus and the idea of representation and atonement.[31] Helmut Merklein takes up an idea expressed earlier by Rudolf Pesch, that in the death of Jesus God personally atoned for recalcitrant Israel.[32] In this case Jesus' preaching about God would not need correction: God is the one who is already always reconciled, and

27. Cf. the summary of his own previous work by H. Schürmann, "Pro-Existenz als christologischer Grundbegriff," *Analecta Cracoviensia* 17 (1985) 345–371. Cf. also H. Merklein, "Der Tod Jesu als stellvertretender Sühnetod," *Bibel und Kirche* 41 (1986) 68–75, at 68.
28. A. Vögtle, *Offenbarungsgeschehen und Wirkungsgeschichte* (Freiburg: 1985) 141–168. (Basic questions in the discussion about Jesus' understanding of his death as mediating salvation, with arguments by the various authors involved.)
29. R. Schwager, "Der Tod Christi und die Opferkritik," *Theologie der Gegenwart* 29 (1986) 11–20, with bibliography.
30. H. Frankemölle, in *NHthG* I (1984) 303. On this whole problem, see F.-L. Hossfeld, "Versöhnung und Sühne," *Bibel und Kirche* 41 (1986) 54–60, with bibliography.
31. A. Weiser, "Der Tod Jesu und das Heil der Menschen," *Bibel und Kirche* 41 (1986) 60–67, with bibliography.
32 H. Merklein, "Der Tod Jesu," especially 69–70, with bibliography.

from whom all reconciliation comes. God's forgiveness, both logically and temporally, precedes all human conversion.[33] It is God who annuls the law that sin will be visited on the sinners. "Atonement" is thus not a satisfaction demanded for an insult given to God, but is the possibility opened by God for those who, in Israel, rejected Jesus to escape the promised judgment. The elements introduced into the tradition of the supper, including the reference to the servant of God from Isaiah 53, the eschatological covenant sacrifice related to Exodus 24:8, or the fulfillment of Jeremiah 31:31-34, would thus witness to God's steadfast fidelity to Israel. But this would not express the idea of Jesus' death as an additional condition of salvation for all.[34]

8.3 Concept and Basic Form of the Eucharist

8.3.1 *The Fundamental Liturgical Form*

The Church testifies most deeply and comprehensively to its understanding of the Eucharist in the liturgy itself.[35] Therefore it is extremely important that the newest research gives special attention to the theological structure of the Eucharistic liturgy.[36]

A reconstruction of Jesus' last supper is, as we said, impossible. Neither is it possible to reconstruct the form of the Christian Eucharis-

33. H. Merklein, *Die Gottesherrschaft als Handlungsprinzip* (Würzburg: 1978) 204. Cf. 2 Corinthians 5:19.

34. The question whether, as in the German and English translations of the Eucharistic texts, it should be said that Jesus' death was "for all," or whether we should hold to the literal translation "for many," would not thereby be less urgent. No one is or ever has been excluded from the effective, loving will of God, and the Noachic covenant between God and *all* humanity was never cancelled.

35. J. Betz, *Sacramentum Mundi I* (Freiburg: 1967) 1224. Cf. H.-J. Schulz, *Ökumenische Glaubenseinheit aus eucharistischer Überlieferung* (Paderborn: 1976) 24-32 (the Eucharistic Prayer as normative witness of faith); K. Richter, ed., *Liturgie—ein vergessenes Thema der Theologie?* (Freiburg: 1986), especially the dogmatic essays by M. M. Garijo Guembe and H. Vorgrimler.

36. C. Giraudo, *La struttura letteraria della preghiera eucaristica* (Rome: 1981); H. B. Meyer, "Das Werden der literarischen Struktur des Hochgebets," *Zeitschrift für katholische Theologie* 105 (1983) 184-202 (with bibliography); E. Mazza, *Le odierne preghiere eucaristiche*, 2 vols. (Bologna: 1984), and the review by H. B. Meyer in *Zeitschrift für katholische Theologie* 108 (1986) 170-174; J.-M. R. Tillard, "Segen, Sakramentalität und Epiklese," *Concilium* 21 (1985) 140-149.

tic celebration in the first centuries in all its details; too much was left to oral tradition and, even beyond the fourth century, to free formulation. But from the witnesses surviving in the New Testament and thereafter we can be certain that the form of the liturgy was always based on a structural plan. In both theological and liturgical scholarship, there has long been a consensus that this schematic structure is of Old Testament and Jewish origin. Cesare Giraudo succeeded in establishing the details of this underlying theological and theoretical structure and its adoption in Christianity.[37] We find here a prayer addressed to God (in the Christian tradition this is in principle always addressed to the Father), and consisting of two principal parts: a historical commemorative prayer in which both praise and a reminder of God's saving deeds are expressed—and, in accordance with Hebrew ideas, this recollection already includes God's making present of those deeds—(anamnetic part); and a petitionary prayer that calls on God to continue to remember God's people, or the individual offering the prayer (epicletic part).[38]

Sometimes one or the other part is expanded by the introduction of a scriptural citation relating to a particular saving action (called an embolism or insertion). Giraudo was able to show that the Church's Eucharistic prayer reveals precisely this twofold structure and that in the anamnetic part the account of institution is interpolated as a scriptural citation directly addressed to the hearers. This quotation of the account of institution is the "central high point of the dynamic of the prayer," which supports and gives the reason for the whole celebration (though this internal reason for the celebration should be distinguished from its external occasion).[39] The special event that is memorialized and made present by the quotation is God's saving work in Jesus Christ, the paschal mystery of Jesus, that which God accomplished in the death and resurrection of Jesus. The common and primary point

---

37. C. Giraudo, *La struttura*, 11–177, 179–269: structures of prayer in the Old Testament and Judaism; 271–355: the same structures in the Eucharistic Prayers of the East and West. Giraudo's findings are still valid, even if on the basis of Nehemiah 9:6-37 he is too optimistic about the existence of a *todâ*.

38. The memorial is often joined to the petition with the phrase, "and now"; it gives the reason for the petition. The structure is occasionally expanded in the Old Testament by an "opening eulogy" and a "closing doxology." Cf. the forty-five texts presented by C. Giraudo, *La struttura*, 155–159.

39. H. B. Meyer, "Das Werden," 198.

of contact between Jesus' last supper and the Church's Eucharistic celebration is *this* action of God in and for Jesus; the Eucharistic celebration is therefore not *primarily* the memorial of Jesus' last supper.[40] The meaning of the making-present, in praise and anamnesis, of God's saving action in Jesus Christ is not *primarily* to be found in the change wrought in the gifts; rather, its meaning, in the first instance, is that it brings the participants (here we mean the full participants: those who communicate) into a unique communion with Jesus, a community that is, for human persons, a participation, mediated by the Eucharistic gifts, in Jesus' paschal mystery *and* in his present glory.

Thus the Church's liturgy in itself makes clear that the question about the "point in time" at which the change (or consecration) takes place, and what are the precise words that bring it about (i.e., what is the "form" of the sacrament) represent a falsely stated problem for liturgical history and theology. The Eucharistic prayer as a whole, with its three essential parts (anamnesis with thanksgiving, from *"gratias agamus"* on; story of institution; epiclesis) is not directed toward the gifts. It is a prayer directed to God the Father.[41] "In this the eucharistic celebration corresponds to what Jesus did at the Last Supper, when he prayed to the Father over the gifts at table. Because, and to the extent that the Church does the same thing, following Jesus' instructions, the Church's eucharistic celebration participates in the 'sacramental' effects of Jesus' action, when he, through his eternally valid and effective word, accomplished his Passover in anticipation at the Last Supper. That means that the eucharistic prayer as such and as a whole 'eucharistizes' the bread and wine."[42] New light also falls on the priest, who is necessary for the "validity" of the sacramental action: he acts *in persona ecclesiae*, that is, as one authorized to speak for the commu-

---

40. Cf. E. Dekkers, "L'Eucharistie, imitation ou anamnèse de la Dernière Cène?" *Recherches de science religieuse* 58 (1984) 15–23. H. B. Meyer, 1986 (see n. 36 above) calls the Last Supper a (proleptic sacramental) fulfillment in advance, while the Eucharist is an (anamnetic sacramental) subsequent fulfillment (*Nachvollzug*) or reaccomplishment of the Paschal mystery of Jesus.

41. E. Mazza, *Le odierne preghiere* I, 283–317; C. Giraudo, *La struttura*, 361–365. H.-J. Schulz, *"Ökumenische Glaubenseinheit* explains the relationship between this point of view and the declarations of the Councils of Florence and Trent. Cf. also A. Angenendt, "Bonifatius" (Bibliography 3), 163–164: originally the whole canon, including the preface, was consecratory; the narrower concept began with Ambrose.

42. H. B. Meyer, 1986 (see n. 36 above), 173.

nity, when, in the name of the community and supported by its "amen," he proclaims the mighty deeds of God (anamnetic part) and prays that they may become effective in the present celebration (epicletic part).[43]

The Eucharistic liturgy contains still other theologically significant elements. For the anamnetic part recalls not only and not immediately God's saving action in Jesus Christ. It is a memorial of God's name, of creation, of all God's earlier deeds of power, and embedded among these is God's action in and for Jesus that is accomplished in the glorification of Jesus Christ. And that in turn is a prophetic signal of the coming, definitive fulfillment of all creation. In the story of institution and the anamnesis that follows it (which is an "insertion" in the anamnesis) this prophetic sign is "liturgically actualized," and carried forward in the prayer for the dead,[44] in the expectation that God will also fulfill God's creation in them.

Apart from the service of the word that precedes it, the Church's Eucharistic celebration has two centers or crystallization points. Each culminates in an epiclesis, a prayer to God the Father for the action of the Holy Spirit.[45] The account of institution is the center of the anamnesis within which that event is made present. The first epiclesis, the prayer that the gifts be received and that the Spirit will act to change them, is oriented to that account, as is the "extension" of that epiclesis, the petitions in the canon, which ask that the divine Spirit will be active in all who are remembered in view of their ultimate end.[46] The communion epiclesis is oriented to the second center, praying that the Eucharist—this prayer—may reach its goal, which is communion with Jesus Christ in the form of mutual indwelling (not merely his presence), and thus the unity of the Church and "an anticipatory taste of the food of immortality."[47] Both prayers for the Spirit, in turn, show

43. C. Giraudo, *La struttura*; H. B. Meyer, "Das Werden," 200, n. 58.

44. H. B. Meyer, "Das Werden," 199, n. 53. On the Eucharist as eschatological sign, see G. Wainwright, *Eucharist and Eschatology* (New York: 1981).

45. It is theologically incorrect to call the division of the epiclesis into two parts "unfortunate," as does K.-H. Bieritz, *EKL* I (1986), 9 tut.

46. H. B. Meyer, "Das Werden," 200.

47. Idem; see also Meyer, 1986 (see n. 36 above), 174. Cf. also C. Giraudo, *La struttura*, 366–370, where there are some noteworthy remarks on the Eucharist as sacrament for the forgiveness of sins.

that the body of Jesus Christ and his presence in the Eucharist, as well as communion with him, are pneumatic, i.e., the work of the Spirit.[48]

8.3.2   *The Concept of Eucharist*

There is no single word that, of itself, expresses the entire content and meaning of the Eucharist.[49] They all refer to some partial aspect that represents the whole (*pars pro toto*). The term most frequently used in recent Catholic parlance, "Eucharist," is derived from *eucharistein*, meaning to have a grateful demeanor, to be thankful. It is a translation of the Jewish *bere akha*, which refers to the thanksgiving in table prayer (Luke 22:19, par.). By the end of the first and beginning of the second century, "Eucharist" had become established as referring to the whole Eucharistic service of worship, and particularly for the principal prayer (see the important evidence in Ignatius of Antioch and, in the second century, Justin). Paul speaks of the "Lord's supper" (1 Cor 11:20), a title that recent ecumenical discussions have approved as being without confessional overtones. The word "supper," however, describes only one aspect of the event, and the expression incorporates the title "Lord," (German *Herr*), which presents certain problems. Since Luther (1522), the most popular word among German Lutherans has been *Abendmahl* (literally: "evening meal"), which recalls its origins in Jesus' Last Supper: the effect is that the present event is not so readily included. Besides the one-sidedness of the "meal" designation, this expression has the further problem that, as has now been established, the ancient Church even in the first century preferred to hold its Eucharistic celebration early in the morning (on Sunday). The early Christian designations, "breaking bread" (which could also refer to an ordinary meal) and "coming together," have not survived in current usage. Important Greek theologians of the third and fourth

48. Cf. J.-H. Nicolas' contribution in H. Luthe, ed., *Christusbegegnung in den Sakramenten* (see Bibliography 1) 316–317; F. X. Durrwell, *Der Geist des Herrn* (Salzburg: 1986) 140–145 (the Eucharist as, in an eminent way, the sacrament of the Holy Spirit).

49. Cf. J. A. Jungmann, " 'Abendmahl' als Name der Eucharistie," *Zeitschrift für katholische Theologie* 93 (1971) 91–94; J. Talley, "Vor der Berakha zur Eucharistie," *Liturgisches Jahrbuch* 26 (1976) 93–115; L. Lies, "Eulogia—Überlegungen zur formalen Sinngestalt der Eucharistie," *Zeitschrift für katholische Theologie* 100 (1978) 69–97; C. Giraudo, *La struttura*, 260–269; J. Roloff, *EKL* I (1986) 11–12.

centuries called the Eucharist *eulogia*. The word means a gift of bless-ing, the glorification and self-glorification of God, a grateful remem-bering of God's gifts. Expressions that used to be very popular among Catholics, such as "most holy sacrament of the altar," and "sacrifice of the Mass," though earlier in their origins, were unmistakably used to oppose Reformation ideas and expressed only partial aspects of the whole. Equally common in the past was simply "the Mass," a short form of "sacrifice of the Mass," which originated in the sixth century as *missa*, and in emphatic form as *missa solemnia*; at first it referred to the closing act of a worship service with a blessing. In vulgar Latin it could also mean "renunciation," which made it reminiscent of the sacrifice and led to its being applied to the whole Eucharistic cele-bration.

8.4 Historical Stages and Decisions

8.4.1 The Development of a Eucharistic Theology

The history of theological reflection and preaching on the Eucharist has been studied in such an extensive literary corpus and described in so much detail that any brief summary must appear very superfi-cial.[50] The theologians of the ancient Church, who in many cases were themselves liturgists, spoke about the Eucharist primarily in sermons and catecheses. The fundamental contribution to Eucharistic theology in the first centuries resulted from the comparison of the biblical state-ments about the Eucharist with Platonic thought. This did not involve simply "incorporating" a whole philosophical system into Christianity; rather, forms of thought and methods of expression that we tend to think of as "popular philosophy" were used to clarify what was al-ready believed. This popular philosophical view of things included a conviction of the existence of a transcendent, spiritual world, the home of the Divine and the One, the True, the Good, and the Beautiful; a

50. The best easily available description in German is by A. Gerken, *Theologie der Eucharistie* (Munich: 1973) 61–156. For more detail, see the articles by J. Betz in *LThK* III, 1142–1157; "Eucharistie als zentrales Mysterium," *MySal* IV/2 (1973) 185–319 (including the whole history of dogma); *Eucharistie. In der Schrift und Patristik*, Handbuch der Dogmengeschichte IV/4a (Freiburg: 1979).

sober view of our world of experience, with its mutability and its often deceptive appearances; and the presumption that there is communication between the two worlds. While it was possible for human beings to ascend to the higher world by means of severe renunciation and undergoing tests of endurance, following a path that essentially consisted in liberating oneself from the bonds of our world, the coming of the Divine into our world was thought to take place when it transformed earthly realities into its own image and made of them its dwelling place. This image, which one could grasp with the senses, made the divine Original present in its fullness, enabled communication with it, and even participation in it, even though this presence of the Divine might be only temporary and veiled. It is obvious how Christian thought could recognize itself in this (Platonic) world of ideas and how many features of that system are regarded even today as indispensable for Christianity. It was out of this idea of original-and-image that the theory of real symbols, so important for sacramental theology, was developed. In Christian faith, the possibility of making present God and God's world, hidden and yet completely real, is attributed to the activity of the divine Spirit.

The Jewish understanding of the real recalling to present life of past events, in remembering them before God, combined very smoothly with this conception of things. The Jewish way of thinking corresponded to the Greek concept of anamnesis and expanded it with the aid of the historical viewpoint familiar to Jews: now not only could God be believed to be really present, through the Holy Spirit and through persons who had been elevated to divine status, but whole events, the historical deeds of God in power, could be present in images. This presence in image or symbol was, as we have said, temporary and veiled, but it would be wrong to call it "*only* in image, *only* symbolic,*"* for in this view of things it was true to say: the more spiritual it is, the more real it is. To speak of the presence of Jesus Christ in image, parable, symbol, etc., did not imply any weakening of the reality in the eyes of ancient theologians; rather, it was an expression of the hope that in eternity it would finally be possible to encounter God unveiled.

When Greek theologians from Justin to John Chrysostom, the Alexandrians and the Antiochenes, all spoke of the true presence of Jesus Christ and his saving deed, they each emphasized, according to their particular interest of the moment, either the person of Jesus or his work of redemption. Expressions about the real presence of Jesus in the Eucharist show that, from an early period (Justin, Irenaeus, Tertullian, Ambrose), there was belief in a change taking place in the gifts. The fundamental biblical text was John 6. Theological reflection on this aspect of the Eucharist, of course, went hand in hand with the development of Christology. When the Alexandrian theologians (Clement, Origen, Cyril of Alexandria) interpret the Eucharist as the coming of the divine Logos into the bread, and regard communion with the Logos as the essential thing, they allow the memorial of Jesus' death to retreat into the background and be eclipsed by the idea of incarnation. The Antiochene theologians, on the other hand, concentrate on the identity of the Eucharistic body of Jesus with his historical body, and see in the anamnesis (John Chrysostom in particular) the making-present of the deed of redemption on the cross. In it, they see the promise of Malachi 1:11 (an important verse for the Fathers of the Church!) fulfilled; they designate the Eucharist, from the time of *Didache* 14,1, as a sacrifice (*prosphora, sacrificium, oblatio*), referring to the preparation of the gifts as *offere*, although this is not meant to refer to any new and unique sacrifice in addition to the cross of Jesus. It is deliberately stated that the gifts are taken from that which in any case belongs to God; they are, in the memorial, placed before the eyes of God: *memores offerimus*. There was undoubtedly an anti-Gnostic tendency in this attention to the material gifts. But what the Eucharist makes real is primarily the spiritual sacrifice, in the sense of 1 Peter 2:5 or Hebrews 13:15, as the sacrifice of praise of *all* the participants for God's mighty deeds, beginning with creation, and culminating in the Christ event. For Latin theologians like Tertullian and Cyprian, the two separated gifts are already a sign of the passion of Jesus Christ; their interest in the "elements" is much more drastic than that of the Greeks. We find the first explicit theory of transformation (metabolism) in the work of Ambrose (d. 397). Also among the Latins, around 400, we find a neglect of the epiclesis, in connection with the view that the account of institution has a consecratory effect. It is everywhere stated that the action of making present is to be traced to the work of the Holy Spirit, and that Jesus Christ, in the Spirit (according to the Letter to the Hebrews) is the real liturgist who associates human beings with himself in glorifying the Father.

Augustine deserves special mention in two connections. First of all, he studied in the greatest detail the question of the presence of the archetypal divine reality in its sacramental image (see above, 4.1 and 4.2.2), with special reference to the Eucharist. In addition, he presented a combined version of sacramental and ecclesial theology of the body of Christ. In the Eucharist it is always the whole Christ who is present and contained, both the individual body of Jesus and the mystical-universal body that is the Church; it is the sacrament of the *totus Christus caput et corpus*; the Eucharist exists precisely in order that one, holy Church may be created; this Church is therefore the inner reality of grace intended by God in the Eucharist, it is the *res* of this sacrament. This does not mean that the Church is elevated in autonomous self-glorification, since it is her head who is and remains the primary agent, and the Church can do nothing without Jesus Christ. Both concepts, however, took a negative turn as soon as Augustine's original meaning was no longer understood. His theology of symbol and image was simply more influential than that of other theologians because, in the late Middle Ages, he was the greatest theological authority after the Bible. His ecclesial understanding of the Eucharist promoted the idea that, in addition to the making-present of the sacrifice of the cross, the Church was offering itself and acting with Jesus Christ in offering his sacrifice.

8.4.2   *Concentration on the Real Presence*

Eucharistic theology could not always and forever retain the high spiritual level and relatively complete character it had in the Greek theologians we have mentioned and in Augustine. The stronger the development of sacramental realism on the basis of the Christological dogmas, interested primarily in the true presence and palpability of God in the sacrament, the greater was the threat to the concept of images. We find beginnings of this as early as the fifth century. The more Christian people withdrew from frequent communion because of a radical sense of reverence, the more elevated was the position of the celebrant. When the language of worship was no longer understood, as among the peoples designated by the collective name "Germans," there arose a desire for something visible, for a dramatic staging of the worship service. A process began in which the Eucharist was no longer seen within the Trinitarian dynamic of praise, memorial, and petition, but instead was regarded as the principal means of grace, given "from above" (beginning with Isidore of Seville, d. 636). The adoption of the Roman liturgy in France, where its theological content could only be grasped in the grossest form, had serious consequences.[51] "As the idea of the Mass as a new, even independent sacrifice in addition to the one, definitive sacrifice of Jesus Christ developed, something similar happened with regard to the priesthood: in addition to the one priest and mediator, Jesus Christ, we soon find other priests who also refer to themselves as mediators."[52] In the eighth to ninth centuries the Eucharistic celebration was introduced into the system of tariff penance (see 9.4 below) as a means of expiation.[53] Instead of the ancient Christian sacrifice, understood in a spiritual sense as the expression of an attitude of total surrender to God, and therefore celebrated primarily as a sacrifice of praise through the power of the common priesthood,[54] what emerged in the Carolingian period was a sacrifice of atonement offered only by the priest. This shift in theological understanding was one of the primary reasons for the rise of clerics' daily private Masses.[55]

In connection with this critical development, and the inability to understand the liturgical symbolic actions and the symbolic gifts as real symbols, the question of a more precise explanation of the true presence of Jesus Christ in the sacrament, the theme of the "real presence," became the principal issue in medieval Eucharistic theology. It led to two Eucharistic controversies and thus to Church statements to which later official declarations could refer. The first controversy emerged from the Abbey at Corbie, headed by the Benedictine abbot Paschasius Radbertus (d. ca. 859), who is honored by the Church as a saint. In

51. J. A. Jungmann, "Von der 'Eucharistie' zur 'Messe,' " *Zeitschrift für katholische Theologie* 89 (1967) 29–40; H. B. Meyer, *TRE* I (1977) 278–282; A. Angenendt, "Theologie und Liturgie der mittelalterlichen Toten-Memoria," in K. Schmid and J. Wollasch, eds., *Memoria* (Munich: 1984), 79-199, on the Eucharist, 143-148.

52. A. Angenendt, "Missa specialis. Zugleich ein Beitrag zur Entstehung der Privatmessen," in K. Hauck, ed., *Frühmittelalterliche Studien* 17 (Berlin: 1983) 153-221, at 217, with references.

53. Ibid., 213.

54. This is still the sense in Bede (d. 735); cf. A. Angenendt, "Missa specialis," 176, 219.

55. A. Angenendt, "Missa specialis," also discusses the historical background of the problem of Mass stipends in this connection.

the first surviving monograph on the Eucharist, *De corpore et sanguine Domini*, he taught a complete identity between the historical body of Jesus Christ born of Mary, and the Eucharistic Body, and that the suffering of Jesus Christ was repeated every day in a true "slaughter" (*mactatio*). In the same abbey, the monk Ratramnus (d. after 868), at the request of the king, countered with his own writing, *De corpore et sanguine Domini*, saying that bread and wine are not changed by the consecration and thus are only images (*figurae*) of the flesh and blood of Jesus Christ; his Body and Blood are thus, together with their divine power, hidden beneath the veil of these images. Therefore one could not say that the Body of Jesus Christ is really (*in veritate*) received; instead, it is received in image, in mystery, and in power. Ratramnus did not intend to deny a true presence of the Body of Jesus Christ, but only to oppose a complete identification of the historical body with the Eucharistic Body; from this point of view, he also denied the notion of a new passion every day: he spoke instead of a *repraesentatio*, in mystery, of the unique suffering and death. Thus it is wrong to call Ratramnus' position "symbolism."[56]

The second Eucharistic controversy began when the canon Berengar of Tours (d. 1088), citing Augustine and Ratramnus, denied any real presence of the Body of Jesus Christ in the Eucharist, because that glorified Body cannot be "called down" from heaven until the end of the world. On the basis of the appearances of bread and wine he attempted to construct a philosophical proof that nothing changes in the Eucharist, and in doing so he used the concepts of "substance," the spiritual essence or spiritual reality of a thing, and "accidents," the external appearance that, in its assorted components (size, weight, color, taste, etc.) is both "sustained" and held together by the spiritual essence. He referred to the bread and wine of the Eucharist as images of the Body of Jesus Christ, and their reception as a means of spiritual union with the exalted Lord in heaven. These views were condemned by four synods between the years 1047 and 1054. In 1059, at a synod in the Lateran in Rome, Berengar had to sign a confessional statement saying that, after the consecration, bread and wine are not a mere sacrament, but truly the Body and Blood of Jesus Christ, and that these are sensibly, not only in sacrament but in truth (*"non solum*

---

56. K. Vielhaber, "Rathramnus," *LThK* VIII, 1001–1002, including remarks on unjust assessments of his position.

sacramento, sed in veritate!"), "touched and broken by the hands of the priest and crushed by the teeth of the faithful" (only in Latin, DS 690). After returning home, Berengar revoked this confession, with the result that he had to sign a new confessional formula before another Roman synod in 1079: "I, Berengar, believe in my heart and confess with my lips that the bread and wine which are placed on the altar are, by the mystery of the sacred prayer and the words of the Redeemer substantially changed into the true and proper and life-giving body and blood of Jesus Christ our Lord; and that, after consecration, they are Christ's true body, which was born of the Virgin and hung on the cross, being offered for the salvation of the world, and which sits at the right hand of the Father; and Christ's true blood, which was poured forth from his side; not only by way of sign and by the power of the sacrament, but in their true nature and in the reality of their substance" (NR 559/DS 700). This text employs the concepts adopted by Berengar's opponents, Lanfranc of Bec (d. 1089) and Witmund of Aversa (d. 1085): the earthly substances are transformed (while the external appearances [*species*] remain); here we have, in essence, the doctrine of transubstantiation (the substantive *transubstantiatio* was first used around 1140–1142 by Orlando Bandinelli, the later Pope Alexander III). The contrast between *signum* and *virtus sacramenti*, on the one hand, and *proprietas naturae* and *veritas substantiae*, on the other hand, shows the extent to which the theology of real symbols had been lost. However, we cannot overlook the fact that, with the reference to the popular philosophical notion of a final, spiritual reality as the basis for all things, the crass realism of 1059, which was open to the worst kind of misunderstandings, had been overcome. If the presence of Jesus Christ, including his body, was seen in the spiritual dimension—and the concept of "substance" refers only to the spiritual dimension—spatial-material conceptions, including that of a "descent" of the glorified Body from an otherworldly heaven, were excluded. The possibility of getting away from the notion of a means of grace and of recovering the interiority and activity of the divine Spirit in the real symbol was at least not blocked. The timeless, static concept of substance was not and is not suitable for expressing the presence of historical events and of a human person with his relationships, his history, and all that belongs to them.

8.4.3 *Scholastic Theology of the Eucharist*

The "objectivizing"[57] of Eucharistic teaching advanced still further when, in the twelfth century, Scholastic thinkers introduced the concepts of "matter" and "form" in sacramental theology (see 4.2.3 above). Bread and wine were regarded as the matter of the sacrament of the Eucharist; the words of institution were seen as the formal principle that gave the sacrament its essential nature: these were taken to be the words of Jesus in the first person: "This is . . ." These words alone, it was thought, effected the change of substance and thus the presence of the Body and Blood of Jesus Christ. Understandably enough, attention was now concentrated still further on the presiding priest, his power, and his proper intention. The question of faith in the Eucharist was discussed in connection with the reception of communion. In Scholasticism, which was a theology of monks and priests, the community celebration of the Eucharist dissolved into "the sacramental action of the clerics and the 'Mass devotion' of the laity."[58] Two phenomena in this connection led to the development of the "dogma of concomitance," namely the reservation of communion in the cup to the priestly celebrant alone, something which became more and more the rule in the course of the Middle Ages, and the desire to be able to see and receive the *whole* Christ, in his divinity and his humanity. In the twelfth century the "parts" were listed that, together, make up the *totus Christus*: body, blood, soul, divinity. Now the teaching on concomitance or co-presence stated that, by the power of the words of consecration, at the level of spiritual being or substance, the bread is changed only into the Body, the wine only into the Blood of Jesus Christ. But since the other realities are inextricably bound up with the Body and Blood (the Body belongs with the Blood, the divinity with the humanity, unmixed but indivisible, as Christological dogma stated), they are also made present when the words of consecration are spoken, so that in each "part" the whole Christ is present, and, it was thought, nothing was being denied to the laity when the cup was withheld from them.

Official teaching echoed Scholastic opinion. In 1208, in a creed written against the Waldensians, Pope Innocent III emphasized the con-

57. Translator's note: the German is *Versachlichung*, implying the conversion of something into a "thing" or "object."
58. H. B. Meyer, *TRE* I (1977) 281.

ditions for a valid celebration of the Eucharist: the ordained priest
(independently of his moral qualities), the words of consecration, and
the proper intention of the priest (NR 560/DS 794). The Fourth Lateran Council, in 1215, with an eye to the confusions of the time, put
together a confession of faith which also included some statements on
the Eucharist:

> There is indeed one universal Church of the faithful, outside which no
> one at all is saved, and in which the priest himself, Jesus Christ, is also
> the sacrifice. His body and blood are truly contained in the sacrament
> of the altar under the appearances of bread and wine, the bread being
> transubstantiated into the body by the divine power and the wine into
> the blood, to the effect that we receive from what is His in what He has
> received from what is ours in order that the mystery of unity may be
> accomplished. Indeed, no one can perform (*conficere*) this sacrament,
> except the priest duly ordained according to [the power of] the keys of
> the Church, which Jesus Christ himself conceded to the apostles and
> their successors. . . . (NR 920/DS 802).[59]

Against John Wycliffe and Jan Hus, the Council of Constance, in 1415
(NR 561/DS 1198) and in 1418 (NR 563/DS 1257) defended the doctrine
of concomitance, and in 1418 specifically against Wycliffe also defended
the real presence (NR 562/DS 1256).

The Council of Florence, in its Decree for the Armenians of 1439,
intended to serve as the basis for union with that Church, referred to
the Eucharistic teaching of Thomas Aquinas (d. 1274). The Scholastic
elements are obvious: matter and form, change of substance, concomitance. This is the first magisterial text to adopt the formula that
says that at the consecration, the priest acts *in persona Christi*. This rests
on the false Latin translation of 2 Corinthians 2:10, where Paul says
that he has forgiven "in the presence of Christ." This council also
speaks for the first time of the grace effected by the Eucharist. The text
(slightly abridged) reads:

> The third sacrament is the Eucharist. The matter of this sacrament is
> wheat-bread and grape-wine with a small amount of water to be mixed
> in before the consecration. Water is mixed in because . . . it is believed
> that our Lord Himself instituted this sacrament with wine mixed with

59. This and subsequent translations of the Church's official texts adapted from
J. Neuner, S.J., and J. Dupuis, S.J., *The Christian Faith in the Doctrinal Documents
of the Catholic Church* (Westminster, Md.: Christian Classics, Inc., 1975).

water. Furthermore, this is a fitting representation of our Lord's passion. . . . Finally, this is a fitting way to signify the effect of this sacrament, that is, the union of the Christian people with Christ. . . .

The *form* of this sacrament is the words of the Savior with which He effected this sacrament; for the priest effects this sacrament by speaking in the person of Christ. It is by the power of these words that the substance of bread is changed into the body of Christ, and the substance of wine into His blood; in such a way, however, that the whole Christ is contained under the species of bread and the whole Christ under the species of wine. Further, the whole Christ is present under any part of the consecrated host or the consecrated wine when separated from the rest.

The *effect* which this sacrament produces in the soul of a person who receives it worthily, is to unite [that person] with Christ. For, since it is by grace that a person is incorporated into Christ and united to His members, it follows that those who receive this sacrament worthily receive an increase of grace. And all the effects which material food and drink have on the life of the body—maintaining and increasing life, restoring health and giving joy—all these effects this sacrament produces for the spiritual life. As Pope Urban says, in this sacrament we celebrate in thanksgiving the memory of our Savior, we are drawn away from evil, we are strengthened in what is good, and we advance and increase in virtue and in grace (NR 564-566/DS 1320-1322).[60]

It is clear from this text how far sacramental teaching had already been separated from the teaching on the sacrifice of the Mass. The latter is not lacking in Scholastic theology, but in this decree it appears only in connection with the mixture of water and wine (cf. the Latin text in DS 1320).

In its teaching about the sacrifice of the Mass, Scholasticism introduced concepts that would prove fruitful in time to come. It retained the idea of *memoria*, or memorial, and also spoke *repraesentatio*, the making present of the sacrifice of the cross—see the work of the bishop of Paris, Peter Lombard (d. 1160)[61]—and of the *applicatio passionis Christi*

60. Ibid., emphasis supplied. The effects of grace in the Eucharist are even more radically expressed by Thomas Aquinas than in the text cited by the Council of Florence: "Effectus proprius eucharistiae est transformatio hominis in Deum" (*In VI Sent.* d 12 q. 2 a. 1). The council also omits the forgiveness of sins, which Thomas lists in a very prominent place among the effects of this sacrament (*Exp. super Is.* 4 in fine; *Opusc.* 57 c. 24).

61. *IV Sent.* d. 12 c. 5.

ad nos, the application of the passion of Christ to us, in the words of
Thomas Aquinas.[62] Since no one any longer knew what the ideas of
"body" and "blood" had meant in the Hebrew and Aramaic context
in which Jesus lived, they saw the *separate* making of the Body and
Blood of Jesus Christ as a representation of his violent death on the
cross and singled out this feature as constituting the sacrificial character of the Eucharist.[63] This laid the groundwork for the later theories
of the Mass as sacrifice.

In their schematic and often artificial-looking (general) sacramental theology, the Scholastics had retained perspectives from the tradition that could play their part in a later renewal, and this was true also
in the case of their teaching on the Eucharist. Among these perspectives is the language of *sacramentum* and *res* (see 4.2.3 above). The
sacramental sign alone, the *sacrmentum tantum*, is the bread and wine.
The *res et sacramentum*, the second and middle effect of the sacrament,
is *corpus Christi verum*, the true presence of the body of Jesus Christ.
The unique and final reality, the *res*, is twofold: one aspect is indicated
by the sacrament and contained within it, namely Jesus Christ himself, and one is indicated by the sacrament but not contained in it,
namely, the *corpus Christi mysticum* or community of saints.[64] Thus the
connection between Eucharist and Church, so important in antiquity,
was still addressed.[65] The *signum*-teaching retains a condensed version
of the historical dimension when the Eucharist, as *signum rememorativum*, is seen as the sign of God's saving deed in Jesus Christ that
has happened once for all, and when, as *signum prognosticum*, it anticipates in sign-fashion the fulfillment of salvation in the feast in the reign
of God.[66] There is a consensus in historical theology regarding the decline of later Scholastic Eucharistic teaching, the "rack and ruin of practice regarding the Mass" and the necessity of reform. But these negative
developments should not be viewed one-sidedly or blamed on Scholastic theology, which as a whole was more "open" than late- and
neo-Scholasticism reveal.

62. *Post. super Jo.* 61. 6.
63. Thomas Aquinas, *S. th.* III q. 79 a. 7; q. 83 a. 1.
64. Ibid., q. 73 a. 6; q. 80 a. 4.
65. Cf. H. de Lubac, *Corpus Mysticum. Kirche und Eucharistie im Mittelalter* (Einsiedeln: 1969).
66. Thomas Aquinas, *S. th.* III q. 60 a. 3.

8.4.4 *Reformation Teaching on the Lord's Supper*

Theologians of the Lord's Supper among the Reformers were directed by a fundamental consciousness of the word of God, faith, and the forgiveness of sins, which take priority over the sacraments as assurances of the divine promises (see 4.2.4 above).[67] But the attack on Roman Catholic Eucharistic theology was provoked by individual, partial teachings closely related to practice that, in the view of the Reformers, had led to dangerous deviations from true Christian faith. Among these were the doctrine of transubstantiation, the teaching on concomitance, and the theology of the sacrifice of the Mass. The last was the greatest irritant, since it devalued the unique event of the cross and supported the grossest ideas of personal religious achievement. The great Reformers were not united in their ideas about the Lord's Supper, with the result that new oppositions arose; this had the further consequence that even to the present time the Protestant [*evangelische*] Churches are still struggling to achieve a common Eucharist.[68]

For Martin Luther, the New Testament accounts of the Last Supper and the bread discourse in John 6 gave secure reasons to place the real presence of the Body and Blood of Jesus Christ at the center of his statements on this sacrament. He had always understood the words "This is . . ." in the institution accounts as a real identification. He saw the doctrine of transubstantiation as purely private opinion, which he personally denied. His own tentative position assumed a continuation of the substances of bread and wine together with the Body and Blood of Jesus Christ (consubstantiation). The presence of the glorified Body and Blood of Christ meant, for him, the presence of the divinity as well, in whose omnipresence the glorified Body of Christ participates (doctrine of ubiquity). In the sacrament of the altar, Christ unites his glorified Body with the bread and wine. From the words, "take and eat," Luther concluded that the sacrament is a limited event:

67. See the summary treatment by J. Betz in *MySal* IV/2, 243–247.

68. On the current state of the problem, see Bibliography 2; for initial information, see, for example, G. Wainwright, *EKL* I (1986) 29–82, for events up to the Lima documents. For the necessarily brief description of the Reformers' ideas about the Lord's Supper, I am dependent on the precise summary of J. Betz in *MySal* IV/2, 247–251 (with sources). U. Kühn, *Sakramente*, gives more detail. [Translator's note: In saying that "the Protestant (i.e., 'evangelische') Churches are still struggling to achieve a common Eucharist," the author is thinking primarily of the current situation in Germany.]

the promise of Jesus' presence is valid only for the *usus*, i.e., for the time from the words of interpretation until the consumption of the elements. He rejected the Eucharistic devotion that arose from the reservation of consecrated hosts for the sick and had led to such usages as sacramental vigils and Eucharistic processions, because the institutional account says nothing about them. Regarding the sacrificial character of the Mass, he conceded only that it is a sacrifice of thanksgiving for that which is memorialized.

Ulrich Zwingli maintained belief in a presence of the triune God among human beings, but localized the glorified Body of Christ in heaven, whence he cannot really and essentially enter into the bread. Nor, according to John 6:63, could the human soul really be nourished by the flesh of Christ. Thus the bread in the "night meal" is not the Body of Christ, but, like the wine, is a memorial sign that nourishes faith. ("This is . . ." is the same as "this means . . .") Faith alone causes an immediate presence of the whole Christ in the human soul. The sacrificial character of the Mass is to be rejected, according to Zwingli, because of the unique sacrificial deed of Jesus, to which human beings can respond only in memory and thanksgiving.

John Calvin deliberately sought a middle way between Luther and Zwingli. The sacrament is connected with an action of God through the Holy Spirit, and it reveals that action with surety, so that it is neither a mere sign that designates something, nor is it a "means of grace." It is true that, by means of this sacrament, the Body and Blood of Jesus are truly received, but not in the form of something taken with the mouth. Such a view of the substantial real presence, in which Jesus Christ would be imprisoned in mutable elements, Calvin called perverse and a degradation of Christ. For him, the glorified Body of Christ is also located in heaven; participation in him, in communion, is brought about by the Holy Spirit, who lifts those receiving in faith to Christ, with the result that they do not receive the flesh of Christ, but life from the substance of his flesh.

The Council of Trent (1545–1563) attempted to answer the attacks and challenges of the Reformers. From the beginning, they regarded the Eucharist as one of the most important topics. But on the basis of medieval and late medieval theology it was not possible for the council to speak of the Eucharist in a unified way; instead, they treated different parts of it. The only thing that remains uniform is the literary style of the council's utterances. The teaching, obligatory for Catholic Christians, was formulated in brief statements (canons). But in every canon it is necessary for scholars to determine whether an unretractable dogma is being stated, or whether a revered tradition, though reformable in itself, is being protected against novelties. The dogmatic chapters (*Doctrina*) attempt to give more extensive foundation for the canons.

8.4.5 *The Real Presence*

The Council of Trent, in its thirteenth session (1551) adopted a *Decree on the Most Holy Eucharist*.[69] Most of the effort was invested in the formulation of eleven dogmatic statements (canons). These were preceded by eight dogmatic chapters, which were composed in a hurry and do not have the same authority as the canons, but are important in interpreting them. The texts that are still relevant for Eucharistic theology today are cited verbatim:

> 1: The Real Presence of Our Lord Jesus Christ in the Most Holy Sacrament of the Eucharist. To begin with, the holy Council teaches and openly and straightforwardly professes that in the blessed sacrament of the holy Eucharist, after the consecration of the bread and wine, our Lord Jesus Christ, true God and man, is truly, really and substantially contained under the appearances of those perceptible realities. For, there is no contradiction in the fact that our Savior always sits at the right hand of the Father in heaven according to His natural way of existing and that, nevertheless, in His substance He is sacramentally present to us in many other places. We can hardly find words to express this way of existing; but our reason, enlightened through faith, can nevertheless recognize it as possible for God, and we must always believe it unhesitatingly (NR 568/DS 1636).

This is a rejection of Zwingli's and Calvin's views of the presence of Jesus Christ.

After a second chapter on the institution of the Eucharist, there follows:

69. On its history, H. Jedin, *Geschichte des Konzils von Trient*, 3 vols. (Freiburg: 1951-1970); A. Duval, *Des sacrements au Concile de Trente*; on the interpretation of the Eucharistic teaching: K. Rahner, "Die Gegenwart Christi im Sakrament des Herrenmahles," *Schriften* IV, 357–385; J. Wohlmuth, *Realpräsenz und Transubstantiation im Konzil von Trient*, 2 vols. (Bern and Frankfurt: 1975).

3: The Pre-Eminence of the Most Holy Eucharist over the Other Sacraments. In common with the other sacraments, the most holy Eucharist is "a symbol of a sacred thing and a visible form of invisible grace." But the Eucharist also has this unique mark of distinction that, whereas the other sacraments have the power of sanctifying only when someone makes use of them, in the Eucharist the Author of sanctity Himself is present before the sacrament is used. For the apostles had not yet received the Eucharist from the hands of the Lord when He Himself told them that it was truly His body that He was giving them. This has always been the belief of the Church of God that immediately after the consecration the true body and blood of our Lord, together with His soul and divinity, exist under the species of bread and wine. The body exists under the species of bread and the blood under the species of wine by virtue of the words. But the body too exists under the species of wine, the blood under the species of bread, and the soul under both species in virtue of the natural connection and concomitance by which the parts of Christ the Lord, who has already risen from the dead to die no more, are united together. Moreover, the divinity is present because of its admirable hypostatic union with the body and the soul. It is, therefore, perfectly true that just as much is present under either of the two species as is present under both. For Christ, whole and entire, exists under the species of bread and under any part of that species, and similarly the whole Christ exists under the species of wine and under its parts (NR 571/DS 1639–1641).

This chapter is an exposition of the doctrine of concomitance. The next chapter concerns transubstantiation:

4: Transubstantiation. Because Christ our Redeemer said that it was truly His body that He was offering under the species of bread, it has always been the conviction of the Church of God, and this holy Council now again declares that, by the consecration of the bread and wine there takes place a change of the whole substance of bread into the substance of the body of Christ our Lord and of the the whole substance of wine into the substance of His blood. This change the holy Catholic Church has fittingly and properly named transubstantiation [transubstantiation]" (NR 572/DS 1642).

In the fifth chapter, devoted to the veneration of the sacrament, we find the remarkable statement: "*A Christo Domino, ut sumatur, institutum*": "it was instituted, by Christ the Lord, to be eaten" (NR 573/DS 1643). Chapter 6 speaks of the reservation of the sacrament, chapter 7 of preparation for worthy reception, chapter 8 of the "use" of the sacrament, where there is mention of the important connection between "spiritual communion" alone and "spiritual and sacramental communion" (only Latin, DS 1648; see 8.4.9 below).

The canons that are of greatest theological relevance state:

1. If anyone denies that in the sacrament of the most holy Eucharist the body and blood, together with the soul and divinity, of our Lord Jesus Christ and, therefore, the whole Christ, is truly, really and substantially contained, but says that He is in it only as in a sign or figure by His power, *anathema sit* (NR 577/DS 1651).

2. If anyone says that in the holy sacrament of the Eucharist the substance of bread and wine remains together with the body and blood of our Lord Jesus Christ, and denies that wonderful and unique change of the whole substance of the bread into His body and of the whole substance of the wine into His blood while only the species of bread and wine remain, a change which the Catholic Church very fittingly calls transubstantiation [transubstantiatio], *anathema sit* (NR 578/DS 1652).

3. If anyone denies that in the venerable sacrament of the Eucharist the whole Christ is contained under each species and under each part of either species when separated, *anathema sit* (NR 579/DS 1653).

Other statements on the theme of concomitance are found in the teaching on communion under both forms, adopted by the council at its twenty-first session in 1562 (NR 592-595/DS 1731-1734 contain the canons).

4. If anyone says that after the consecration the body and blood of our Lord Jesus Christ are not in the marvellous sacrament of the Eucharist but that they are there only in the use of the sacrament [*in usu*], while it is being received, and not before or after, and that in the consecrated hosts or particles which are preserved or are left over after communion the true body of the Lord does not remain, *anathema sit* (NR 580/DS 1654).

This canon was intended to reject Luther's opinion that the real presence ends with the reception of communion during the worship service.

Canon 5 says that the Eucharist has many effects, and denies that its principal fruit is forgiveness of sins. Canons 6 and 7 deal with the forms of Eucharistic devotion.

8. If anyone says that Christ presented in the Eucharist is only spiritually eaten and not sacramentally and really as well, *anathema sit* (NR 584/DS 1658).

Canon 9 requires an annual communion during the Easter season as a minimum, and canon 10 concerns the communion of the priest.

> 11. If anyone says that faith alone is a sufficient preparation for receiving the sacrament of the most holy Eucharist, *anathema sit*. And, lest so great a sacrament be received unworthily and hence unto death and condemnation, this holy Council determines and decrees that those whose conscience is burdened with mortal sin, no matter how contrite they may think they are, must necessarily make first a sacramental confession if a confessor is available. If anyone presumes to teach, or preach, or obstinately maintain, or defend in public disputation the opposite of this, he shall by the very fact be excommunicated (NR 587/DS 1661).

This canon is to be understood in connection with the teaching about the sacrament of reconciliation (see 9.2 below).

The positive and beautiful things the sixteenth-century bishops and theologians said here are evident from an attentive reading of the texts themselves. But these conciliar statements also have their theological and linguistic limits, which have been pointed out in light of a new consciousness in the twentieth century.[70] These limitations are evident, for one thing, in this council's treatment of biblical and ancient Church tradition, certainly with the best will and according to their best knowledge, but revealing a considerable one-sidedness and narrowness in contrast to earlier perspectives (though the same may be said of the Reformers' opinions as well!). In addition, the council uses categories of interpretation and verbal expressions that, four hundred years later, are scarcely, if at all, appropriate either for advancing an understanding of the truths of faith within the Church, or for promoting communication with others. Thus, as in the case of many other statements of faith, we are faced with the task of seeking what was "really" intended at the time and of reformulating it (incorporating the still older traditions as well) in such a way that the Church does not lose its identity in the process.

70. See the condensed overview of J. Betz in *MySal* IV/2, 256–262, with bibliography; A. Gerken, *Theologie der Eucharistie*, 173–199; J. A. Sayes, *Presencia real de Cristo y Transubstanciación* (Burgos: 1974); B. J. Hilberath and T. Schneider, *NHthG* I (1984) 313–314. Also very good for information on newer models of thought since the 1930s are J. Wohlmuth, "Nochmals: Transsubstantiation oder Transsignifikation?" *Zeitschrift für katholische Theologie* 97 (1975) 430–440; G. Hintzen, *Die neuere Diskussion über die eucharistische Wandlung* (Bern and Frankfurt: 1976); H.-J. Schulz, "Wandlung" (see Bibliography 6).

The core of the statement on the real presence acknowledges the true and genuine presence of Jesus Christ in the celebration and in the sacrament of the Eucharist. It contains as well the Christological confession that the Crucified lives and remains forever the human being who is united in a unique way with God. This statement rejects any "merely" symbolic interpretation, but that in turn points to a historical process of impoverishment: a symbolic interpretation can also be couched in terms of "real symbols," and thereby it can express real presence in symbol.

The conciliar statements on the real presence are not embedded in fundamental considerations about the presence of the triune God among human beings, or about the way in which people can be brought into the presence of the triune God. This would have to include reflection on the way in which Jesus Christ, human being and Son of God, is made present through the Holy Spirit. The presence of his humanity, too, can be "only" pneumatic, when "pneumatic" refers to the highest form of perfection of human bodiliness. The absence of these fundamental considerations on the part of the Council left room for the idea that the triune God "in Godself" is somewhere distant, in an otherworldly heaven, so that inevitably the humanity of Jesus is located outside the world, and the sacrament of the Eucharist is the opportunity to turn spatial distance into spatial nearness. But even when spatial ideas are avoided, theologians are always tempted to play off a presence of God in Jesus against other manners of presence, for example when, using comparative language, someone says that the Eucharistic presence means an increase in the intensity and scope of other ways of being present.[71] Even newer attempts at interpretation reach their verbal limits here: when Jesus' presence in the Eucharist is called "somatic," that is, bodily real presence, we have not yet said what has to be said, namely, that the *soma* of Jesus exists, now and forever, pneumatically. The doctrine of change of substances, with its limited means of expression, pointed to this when it said that a spiritual reality is changed into another spiritual reality. Thus all conceptions of a bodily or somatic real presence have to be thought of within the framework of a pneumatic and spiritual-substantial real presence.

The Council of Trent, together with the Scholastic tradition, no longer understood the fullness of the Jewish concepts of "body" and

71. Thus, in summary form, F. Eisenbach, *Systematische Studien*, 446.

"blood." It took these concepts simply by representing the "parts" of a human being. Only chapter 1 (NR 568/DS 1636) speaks of a presence of the humanness of Jesus Christ, rather than the presence of parts of him. Beyond that, the separation of the teaching about the sacrifice of the Mass from this teaching on the real presence shows that they thought only of the presence of particular persons in their enduring state of completeness, and not of the presence of their whole lives and histories. That had unfortunate consequences for the concept of the Eucharist as a liturgical celebration. The concentration on the making present of the person of Jesus, with divinity and humanity, promoted the notion that the purpose of the Eucharistic celebration was to make the divinity and humanity of Jesus present so that they could be adored and received in communion. This narrows the full content of the "memorial." Veneration of the Eucharist, in the sense in which it has been used, therefore lacked an essential element of any liturgy, namely glorifying God for God's mighty works.

It is part of the core of the faith statement of Trent that what happens in the Eucharist is effected by God, and not by the liturgist or anyone else. Only God can fulfill the promise of this sacrament contained in the "This is . . . ." Human beings can only produce pointers, indications that would be mere signals without the reality present within them. The ancient Church shaped its firm faith in the action of the Spirit in the form of the epiclesis, the prayer for the transforming act of the divine Spirit. The Council of Trent tried to preserve this idea by speaking of an event on the ontological level: only God can change a reality at the level of being; human beings can change the meaning of things at will, but they cannot touch the underlying reality.

The truth contained in this statement is, however, difficult to convey at a time when it is commonly believed that a philosophy of being or essence is no longer possible. Above all, the expressions drawn from natural philosophy about "substance" and "accidents" have become unintelligible. Of course, neither that type of natural philosophy nor the concept of transubstantiation is dogmatically prescribed for Catholic Christians. The Council of Trent only says that this concept is well suited to express the inner, spiritual change in the gifts. That does not forbid us to look for a better concept.

The search for a new formulation of the dogma of the real presence has brought the categories of personal encounter and a relational ontology into the discussion.[72] In this context, it has been observed that the "essence" of a cultural product—and bread and wine are cultural products—can really change with the meaning assigned to it, or, as Bernhard Welte says, the relational context of things and people essentially co-determines the being of what is.[73] A change in purpose or meaning[74] would therefore be the change in being or essence to which the Council of Trent referred. Pope Paul VI felt it necessary to emphasize, in his encyclical *Mysterium Fidei* of 1965, that "as a result of transubstantiation, the species of bread and wine undoubtedly take on a new meaning and a new finality, for they no longer remain ordinary bread and ordinary wine, but become the sign of something sacred, the sign of a spiritual food. However, the reason why they take on this new significance and this new finality is because they contain a new 'reality' which we may justly term ontological" (DS 1580). The context shows that Paul VI wanted to warn against contenting oneself with a subjective change of meaning or function. This warning will be taken to heart, if the new meaning that is bestowed is traced not to human subjectivity, but to the action of God: "The gifts of bread and wine are placed in a completely new relationship to us by Jesus Christ himself, the crucified and risen one, in the power of his Holy Spirit; they receive thereby a new meaning, and acquire a new symbolic function that is given and effected (!) [not by us, but] by him, and is recognized and accepted in faith by us. By being thus taken into the service of the divine, the gifts lose their superficial reference to themselves and experience a definitive change of meaning, bringing with it a change in the 'thing' itself."[75]

8.4.6   *The Sacrifice of the Mass*

At its twenty-second session, in 1562, the Council of Trent adopted a *Doctrine on the Most Holy Sacrifice of the Mass*, consisting of eight chapters and nine doctrinal statements (canons). Those with the greatest theological relevance read as follows:

72. For the former, see J. Betz's note, *MySal* IV/2, 260, on Piet Schoonenberg; for the latter, see A. Gerken, *Theologie der Eucharistie*, 199–210.

73. Cf. J. Betz, *MySal* IV/2, 259.

74. In the newer formulations: transfinalization or transignification.

75. B. J. Hilberath and T. Schneider, *NHthG* I (1984) 314. For a formulation of the real presence in recent Protestant thought, see U. Kühn, *Sakramente*, 278–286.

Chapter 1: The Institution of the Most Holy Sacrifice of the Mass. As the apostle testifies, there was no perfection under the former Covenant because of the insufficiency of the levitical priesthood. It was, therefore, necessary (according to the merciful ordination of God the Father) that another priest arise after the order of Melchizedek, our Lord Jesus Christ who could make perfect all who were to be sanctified and bring them to fulfilment.

He, then, our Lord and God, was once and for all to offer Himself to God the Father by His death on the altar of the cross, to accomplish for them an everlasting redemption. But, because His priesthood was not to end with His death (cf. Heb 7:24, 27), at the Last Supper, "on the night when He was betrayed," in order to leave to His beloved Spouse the Church a visible sacrifice (as the nature of humanity demands) —by which the bloody sacrifice which He was once for all to accomplish on the cross would be represented, its memory perpetuated until the end of the world and its salutary power applied for the forgiveness of the sins which we daily commit—; declaring Himself constituted "a priest for ever after the order of Melchizedek" (Ps 109 [110], 4), He offered His body and blood under the species of bread and wine to God the Father, and, under the same signs [*sub earundem rerum symbolis*] gave them to partake of to the disciples (whom He then established as priests of the New Covenant), and ordered them and their successors in the priesthood to offer, saying: "Do this as a memorial of Me," etc. (Lk 22:19; 1 Cor 11:24), as the Catholic Church has always understood and taught.

For, after He celebrated the old Pasch, which the multitude of the children of Israel offered [*immolabat*] to celebrate the memory of the departure from Egypt, Christ instituted a new Pasch, namely, Himself to be offered by the Church through her priests under visible signs in order to celebrate the memory of His passage from this world to the Father when by the shedding of His blood He redeemed us, "delivered us from the dominion of darkness and transferred us to His Kingdom" (cf. Col 1:13).

This is the clean oblation which cannot be defiled by any unworthiness or malice on the part of those who offer it, and which the Lord foretold through Malachi would be offered in all places as a clean oblation to His name (cf. Mal 1:11). The apostle Paul also refers clearly to it when, writing to the Corinthians, he says that those who have been defiled by partaking of the table of devils cannot be partakers of the table of the Lord. By "table" he understands "altar" in both cases (cf. 1 Cor 10:21). Finally, this is the oblation which was prefigured by various types of sacrifices under the regime of nature and of the Law. For it includes

all the good that was signified by those former sacrifices; it is their fulfilment and perfection (NR 597-598/DS 1739-1742).

Chapter 2: The Visible Sacrifice is Propitiatory for the Living and the
Dead. In this divine sacrifice which is celebrated in the Mass, the same
Christ who offered Himself once in a bloody manner on the altar of the
cross is contained and is offered in an unbloody manner. Therefore, the
holy Council teaches that this sacrifice is truly propitiatory so that, if we
draw near to God with an upright heart and true faith, with fear and
reverence, with sorrow and repentance, through it "we may receive
mercy and find grace to help in time of need" (cf. Heb 4:16). For the
Lord, appeased by this oblation, grants grace and the gift of repentance,
and He pardons wrongdoings and sins, even grave ones. For, the victim is one and the same: the same now offers through the ministry of
priests, who then offered Himself on the cross; only the manner of offering is different. The fruits of this oblation (the bloody one, that is) are
received in abundance through this unbloody oblation. By no means,
then, does the latter detract from the former. Therefore, it is rightly
offered according to apostolic tradition, not only for the sins, punishments, satisfaction and other necessities of the faithful who are alive,
but also for those who have died in Christ but are not yet wholly purified (NR 599/DS 1743).

The succeeding chapters treat liturgical and practical questions: Masses
in honor of the saints (ch. 3), the canon of the Mass (ch. 4), solemn
ceremonies for the celebration of Mass (ch. 5), Masses in which the
priest alone communicates (ch. 6), the mixing of water and wine (ch.
7), celebration of Mass in the vernacular and explanation of the Mass
for the people (ch. 8).

The first four canons are aimed at the teachings of some of the
Reformers:

1. If anyone says that in the Mass a true and proper sacrifice is not offered
to God or that the offering consists merely in the fact that Christ is given
to us to eat, *anathema sit* (NR 606/DS 1751).

2. If anyone says that by the words "Do this as a memorial of Me"
Christ did not establish the apostles as priests or that He did not order
that they and other priests should offer His body and blood, *anathema
sit* (NR 607/DS 1752).

3. If anyone says that the sacrifice of the Mass is merely an offering
of praise and thanksgiving, or that it is a simple commemoration of the
sacrifice accomplished on the cross, but not a propitiatory sacrifice, or
that it benefits only those who communicate; and that it should not be

offered for the living and the dead, for sins, punishments, satisfaction and other necessities, *anathema sit* (NR 608/DS 1753).

4. If anyone says that the sacrifice of the Mass constitutes a blasphemy against the most holy sacrifice which Christ accomplished on the cross, or that it detracts from that sacrifice, *anathema sit* (NR 609/DS 1754).

The remaining five canons are for the protection of the liturgical and practical customs previously mentioned.

With this teaching on the sacrifice of the Mass, the council made some very desirable clarifications and rejected a number of late medieval opinions that had been the source of scandal. It emphasized the unity of the sacrifice of the cross and that of the Mass, secured by the identity of the sacrificing priest and the sacrificial gift, and it made clear that the sacrifice of the Mass is a representation or making present, a memorial and an application of the sacrifice of the cross, and thus is neither a repetition of the unique deed of Jesus Christ nor a new sacrificial action of Jesus taking place at each Mass, an opinion that had been repeatedly asserted in the course of history. The statement that the Mass itself is a true sacrifice in its own right, of course, necessarily sounded objectionable to adherents of the Reformation, especially in the expanded formulation that calls it a propitiatory sacrifice for living and dead. The matter-of-fact use of the concept of "sacrifice" for the event of the cross and the comparison drawn with the sacrificial cult in Judaism, a usage that gives the impression of having disposed all too swiftly of the Old Testament, appeared less offensive in the eyes of the Reformers than it really is. On the other hand, it was not acceptable, within the Reformers' historicizing view of the Bible, to consider Jesus' command at the supper, to remember him in repeating these actions, as proof of the ordained priesthood of the apostles and "their successors in the priesthood" of the Church. Although we have to skip over the developments between Trent and our own century, in order to keep this discussion within limits,[76] and turn to the present state of theological discussion, we begin to see in those developments some important steps toward new formulations, decisive ecumenical approaches of the Churches to one another, but also some difficult problems that still remain.

76. On this process of development, and especially on so-called theories of the Mass as sacrifice, cf. J. Betz, *MySal* IV/2, 254–256 (with bibliography); on new ideas in the twentieth century, idem pp. 256–262 (with bibliography). A clear example of the difficulties involved in this concept, including questions like the distribu-

Expressions like "sacrifice of the cross," or "sacrificial act" of Jesus on Golgotha, and similar phrases, have often been regarded as too technical, too narrow a reference to the Passion alone, and too inappropriate to Jesus' own way of speaking. Many theologians, for example Theodor Schneider, prefer more dynamic expressions that describe Jesus' whole life-process, such as Jesus' "surrender of his life" or "self-surrender" or "self-abandonment."[77] At any rate, there is a growing awareness that the way we talk about this topic decisively affects our image of God, or rather, this or any other way of speaking arises out of a particular image of God. Where there is a strongly Christological consciousness that refuses to see a dramatic division between God the Father and Jesus,[78] his life and destiny to suffer may be seen first of all as an expression of God's love, and the death of Jesus as God's own self-abandonment.[79] The interpretation of Jesus' willingness to bear the consequences of his mission that were imposed by human wickedness, and even to consent to his approaching violent death, in terms of sacrifice and expiation, an interpretation found even in the New Testament, may in this perspective be regarded as secondary. But the discussion of concepts of expiation and representation is still in progress and far from being resolved.[80]

Jesus' whole destiny, in life and death, can be viewed as a twofold movement and thus—though not in ritual terms—as liturgy: from God to human beings and from the human being Jesus to his Father. When

tion of the "fruits of the sacrifice of the Mass," Mass stipends, concelebration, etc., and the limits placed on it, may be found in K. Rahner and A. Häußling, *Die vielen Messen und das eine Opfer* (Freiburg: 1966).

77. Cf. B. J. Hilberath and T. Schneider, *NHthG* III (1985) 288–289, resting on T. Schneider's sacramental theology. In German, the expressions are tainted with an overly pathetic and masochistic flavor.

78. As in the theo-drama of J. Moltmann and H. U. von Balthasar; cf. the overview and bibliography in H. Vorgrimler, *Theologische Gotteslehre* (Düsseldorf: 1985) 160–170.

79. B. J. Hilberath and T. Schneider, *NHthG* III, 290–291. Cf. also 2 Corinthians 5:19; here *God* is the one who reconciles!

80. See the remarks above in 8.2.1 on the New Testament accounts of the Last Supper. On a theology of expiation in the work of H. U. von Balthasar and his circle, see N. Hoffmann, *Sühne. Zur Theologie der Stellvertretung* (Einsiedeln: 1981); idem, *Kreuz und Trinität. Zur Theologie der Sühne* (Einsiedeln: 1982), where a frightful construction of God is evident. Cf. R. Schwager's review in *Zeitschrift für katholische Theologie* 105 (1983) 341–342.

this second movement is expressed in terms of sacrifice, as it is in the Letter to the Hebrews, at least the technical cultic notions of sacrifice that were common in the universal history of religions are abandoned; the sacrificial gift that is identical with the sacrificing priest, Jesus, has a personal character.

The Church's Eucharistic celebration is also called a "sacrifice" by the Council of Trent, under a twofold aspect: first with regard to its intimate connection with Jesus Christ's "sacrifice of the cross," and second with regard to the action of the Church itself.

1. The clarification supplied by Trent, in which concepts like "renewal" or "repetition" of the sacrifice of the cross are deliberately avoided and the Eucharist is understood as a making present (representation), a memorial and an application (or allocation) of the sacrifice of the cross, does not detract from the uniqueness of the event of the cross (Heb 9–10). The new theological movements of the twentieth century have promoted a better understanding of the way in which a unique, past event can be really present without being repeated. Representation (making present)[81] and memorial (*memoria, anamnesis*)[82] here overlap in their essential content, so that either one of these two concepts can stand for the whole. Thus the sacrificial character of the Eucharist can also be re-described, from this initial point of view, as "an anamnesis (memorial) of Jesus Christ's surrrender of his life that causes reality."[83] The statement that the unique event of the cross can be applied to human beings or is allocated to them, and that this happens in the Eucharist—a statement that obviously does not mean "in the Eucharist exclusively"—is accepted by all those who agree that the sacraments bring human beings into the presence of God and open them up to divine grace. The subject of this representation or making present, and of this application, is, of course, Jesus Christ himself, through the Holy Spirit.

2. But to what extent is the Eucharistic celebration also a real and separate sacrifice of the Church? This question leads us to the center of the theology of grace and of ecumenical discussions on that sub-

81. Cf. H. Hofmann, *Repräsentation. Studien zur Wort- und Begriffsgeschichte von der Antike bis ins 19. Jahrhundert* (Berlin: 1974).
82. Cf. 4.2.6 above: the results of the fruitful discussion of Odo Casel's theology of mystery as well as the coincidence of Hebrew memorial and real symbols.
83. B. J. Hilberath and T. Schneider, *NHthG* III (1985) 288.

ject. It was the great concern of the Reformers that the idea of a sacrifice of the Church, especially of an expiatory sacrifice offered by the priest for the sake of the living and dead, detracted from the unique importance of the sacrifice of Jesus on the cross for the justification of sinners, the one expiatory sacrifice whose "fruit" is extended to us in the sacrament.[84] Thus they wished to see the Mass celebration as, at most, a sacrifice of praise and thanksgiving, not endowed with the power to sanctify. On the Catholic side, no one would disagree today with the statement that sanctification comes from God alone and that no ecclesial action can claim to justify sinners. Nor would any Catholic claim that human beings, before receiving justification, were capable of offering their own achievements or gifts of their own to God in the hope of thereby attaining sanctification and divine favor. The fundamental question,[85] which is open for discussion among Catholics, is rather: does God's justifying grace in a human being effect only an attitude of passive, grateful receptiveness, or does it empower that person to an activity that is made possible and supported by God alone? The Catholic response affirms *this kind of* ability to act. Thus, as every prayer is made possible and supported only by God's Spirit, the Church's petition for living and dead is made possible and supported in the same way by Godself, and *in that very way* it is the Church's own prayer brought before God. If we speak of "co-action," we refer to a cooperation that is *posterior* and not simultaneous. With regard to the subject of sacrifice, this ability to act is described as an admission to participation in the existential act of Jesus Christ (in his "loving self-surrender").[86] Enabled and supported by God, this "gift" of the Church's sacrifice would not consist in an additional service "besides" that of Jesus, and certainly not in a material gift. Nor would

84. U. Kühn, *Sakramente*, 286–289.

85. Cf. K. Lehmann and E. Schlink, eds., *Das Opfer Jesu Christi und seine Gegenwart in der Kirche* (Freiburg and Göttingen: 1983); M. Thurian, ed., *Ökumenische Perspektiven von Taufe, Eucharistie und Amt* (Paderborn and Frankfurt: 1983); on the Eucharist, see especially the essays by M. Thurian (pp. 110–123) and J.-M. R. Tillard (pp. 124–137); H. Meyer, H. J. Urban, and L. Vischer, eds., *Dokumente wachsender Übereinstimmung. Sämtliche Berichte und Konsenstexte interkonfessioneller Gespräche auf Weltebene 1931–1982* (Paderborn and Frankfurt: 1983); S. N. Bosshard, "Zur Bedeutung der Anamneselehre für ein ökumenisches Eucharistieverständnis," *Zeitschrift für katholische Theologie* 108 (1986) 155–163 (with bibliography).

86. B. J. Hilberath and T. Schneider, *NHthG* III, 297.

it be only the giving of thanks, but "the state of acceptance, requested of and made possible by God, of the individual person and the whole celebrating community into Jesus' surrender to the Father, which glorifies God and saves the world, participation in his Pasch on which the new covenant is founded."[87] Among Protestants, Ulrich Kühn thinks he can agree with this kind of theology of sacrifice: "The replacement of the 'technical cultic' concept of sacrifice by that of personal surrender to God and human beings, as Catholic theology now uses it, therefore appears appropriate. But this surrender (in a twofold sense) that comprehends not only death but the whole of life is the substance of the reign of God that appears in Jesus. In the supper, Jesus gives us a share in this surrender as well as in his whole life process. Thus those who celebrate the supper are taken up into this total surrender to God (cultic moment) and into his surrender to human beings (explosion of the cult). Here we can see the legitimate meaning of the Catholic teaching about "the Church sacrificing with Christ."[88]

This entry of human persons—made possible by the Spirit of God—with Jesus into his way of life and death is, of course, not accomplished only in the liturgy. But neither does the liturgy itself "revolve" primarily around the Church. Hans Urs von Balthasar, in a pointed expression, directed attention to the real heart of the matter: Jesus did not die for the Church, but for the world, and therefore the Church does not pray primarily for itself when it celebrates the Eucharist, but for those who are far away and for the dead.[89] If this solidarity can be la-

---

87. H. B. Meyer in *Zeitschrift für katholische Theologie* 108 (1986) 172. In a series of publications on the sacrifice of the Church, H. U. von Balthasar opposed this idea about the entry of the Church into Jesus Christ's self-surrender as characterizing the Church's sacrifice. He sees this, instead, in Christ's acceptance of his dismissal on the cross. In this, Mary's "yes" has an important representative role: this "yes" does not seek to accomplish her own justification and thus an independent, redemptive sacrifice. Instead, it is a "yes" to the fact that the most "beloved," Jesus, takes upon himself this sacrifice in place of humanity, a sacrifice that is at the same time the expression of divine love and divine wrath. The essential element in the Church's sacrifice consists in imitating this Marian attitude of total resignation. Cf. the description of this theory, which is not covered by biblical revelation, in G. Bätzing, *Die Eucharistie als Opfer der Kirche nach Hans Urs von Balthasar* (Einsiedeln: 1986).
88. U. Kühn, *TRE* I (1977) 201.
89. H. U. von Balthasar, "Das eucharistische Opfer," *Internationale katholische Zeitschrift* 14 (1985) 193–195, at 195.

beled "expiation," since its intention lies in reconciliation and forgiveness, then the "expiatory sacrifice" would consist in the (subsequent) accompaniment of Jesus in his intercession for those who are far from God, and for the world.

8.4.7   *The Eucharist and the Office of Priesthood*

It follows from what has been said in the general theology of the sacraments and, thus far, about the Eucharist, that the primary agent of any sacrament is Jesus Christ, through the Holy Spirit of God. This was especially emphasized by the Council of Trent, with respect to the sacrificial character of the Eucharist, when it said that he is and remains *the* sacrificing priest in every Eucharistic celebration. In the derivative and subject form just described, the Church can then be described as the wholly secondary subject of the Eucharistic celebration. The Council of Trent expresses this in sacrificial language when it says that Jesus Christ is "offered by the Church through her priests under visible signs" (NR 597). But such a description of human participation remains very abstract: where and how does "the Church" exist? If we start with the two basic components of the Eucharistic prayer, the memorial giving praise and glory to God and the petition for the action of the Spirit, this means that concrete human subjects perform these actions of remembering and petitioning. Thus the concrete community assembled for Eucharist would be the secondary subject of that celebration. That is also the view of the Catholic Church, but we must add that there must be a guarantee that the concrete community acknowledges (1) that it is part of the tradition of faith coming from the apostles as the eyewitnesses and hearers of Jesus, and (2) that it is in communion with all the other communities that live within that tradition. This duty of maintaining a twofold membership in the community of faith is only fulfilled, according to the Catholic point of view, if it is not limited to good will in the hearts of individual community members, but, in addition to that, is also institutionally secured. The institution that, for Catholic believers, maintains this solidarity and thus preserves the identity of the Church throughout history is the college of bishops as successors to the "college" of apostles.

In connection with the Eucharist, this understanding of faith is apparent, at the latest, from the end of the first and beginning of the second century, though at first without the concepts of "sacrifice" or "priesthood." The first witness is Ignatius of Antioch (d. 117 at the latest): "All of you, follow the bishop as Jesus Christ followed the Father, and the presbyters as the apostles; and respect the deacons as you would God's commandment! No one should do anything pertaining to the Church apart from the bishop. Let that be held a valid eucharist which is under the bishop or one to whom he shall have entrusted it. Wherever the bishop appears, there let the people be; just as where Jesus is, there is the universal Church. It is not lawful apart from the bishop either to baptize or to hold a love-feast; but whatever he shall approve is well-pleasing also to God; that everything you do may be sure and valid."[90] Ignatius' ideas about the bishop do not represent any devaluation of "ordinary" Christians or their dignity in offering worship. Ignatius calls them "companions on the way, carrying your God and your shrine, your Christ and your holy things."[91] His statements about the bishop are intended entirely to serve the unity of the Church.[92] It is true that this pointed the way for a certain kind of development, but in the case of the bishop as understood here, too much still depended on subjective qualities; the office of bishop was not yet "objectively" established. Developments in the second and third centuries moved toward that establishment, on the one hand through the demand that bishops be within the apostolic succession— that is, that they stand within a line of tradition that was thought to go back to the apostles—and on the other hand through reliance on the grace of office acquired through consecration (ordination). Both these ideas were first expressly formulated by Irenaeus of Lyons (d. ca. 202).[93]

According to Hippolytus of Rome's Church order, reflecting the Roman situation at the beginning of the third century, the bishop's ordination conveyed both the "spirit of leadership" (*pneuma hegemonikon*) and high-priestly powers; here there is an explicit reference to the Old Testament.[94] In the process of very clear and thorough division

90. *Ign. Smyrn.* 8. See further documentation along these lines in J. Martin, *Der priesterliche Dienst III. Die Genese des Amtspriestertums* (Freiburg: 1972) 89.

91. *Ign. Eph.* 9, 2. Cf. J. Martin, *Der priesterliche Dienst,* 93.

92. J. Martin, *Der priesterliche Dienst,* 94.

93. Ibid., 95–98, with sources. We are leaving the Pastoral Letters out of consideration because of the difficulty of locating them historically. Cf. 11.2.1.

94. Ibid., 98–103; for Hippolytus leadership and priesthood, belonging to the tribes of Juda and Levi, converged in Jesus Christ and descended from him to the apostles and bishops.

of believers into clerics and laity the idea emerged that those who are ordained are able to do things that the non-ordained cannot do. Among the ordained or consecrated it is the bishop who always comes first to mind, since the bishop is regarded as the "high priest" also in the North African theology of Tertullian and Cyprian of Carthage in the third century. As appears even in the writings of Ignatius, the bishop had a subordinate college of lesser officials, to whose members certain duties and powers could be delegated as practical necessity dictated. In earlier days—at the time of Ignatius, for example—they were called "presbyters," but in Hippolytus' Church order they are ordained, like the bishop, for the *sacerdotium* (priesthood), and "rule" the people of God; by the middle of the third century they are clearly designated *sacerdotes* (priests). It is also clear by this point that the offering of the *sacrificium* (sacrifice) is reserved to the *sacerdotes*, the bishops and priests.[95] Their action was in no way understood as in competition with or instead of the sacrifice of the cross; instead, it referred to Jesus' Last Supper and consciously intended to "imitate" Jesus Christ.[96] But this imitation depended on the power bestowed in ordination. In this sense, the first ecumenical council at Nicaea (ca. 325), in its eighteenth canon, speaks of the power to offer the sacrifice (Greek *exousia* and *prospherein*; Latin *potestas offerendi*). The conflicts with heretics and the question of Donatist baptism, and the confrontation with ideas of autonomous power, recalled once more the sense of secondary authority accepted in service, because it is really Jesus Christ who is and remains the true agent in the sacraments.

Scholastic theology introduced a remarkable shift: all the discussions on the "powers" required for the Eucharist centered on the priest, not the bishop. By that time, and for many centuries before, it had been priests and not bishops who were experienced as the normal liturgists at the Eucharist. The concrete reason for theology, and then Church councils, to put so much emphasis on the priest's power was the attack of Cathari, and also of the Waldensians, against the clerics of their time. Criticism of the miserable state of the clergy led to a re-

95. This is absolutely clear in Cyprian. The "offering of the gifts" by presbyter-episcopoi in the 90s of the first century, as found in 1 *Clement* (44,4) is not so definite. Cf. also A. Cunningham's collection of texts, *The Bishop in the Church* (Wilmington: 1985).

96. J. D. Laurance, "The Eucharist as the Imitation of Christ," *Theological Studies* 47 (1986) 286–296 (with patristic texts on the theme of priests/bishops and sacrifice).

vival of the question whether an unworthy minister could perform a valid sacrament, and the denial of that possibility in turn resulted in a rejection of the ordained priesthood, and even, among the Cathari in the twelfth century, in a denial of any change through the consecration of the Eucharist.[97] But theological reaction was not restricted to insistence on a power that guaranteed the completion of the sacrament independently of the worthiness or unworthiness of the minister, or to the establishment of conditions, such as the speaking of the words of consecration, for the reliability of the sacrament's being effected. Even in this narrow view, it was still said that Jesus Christ accomplishes the change that takes place in the Eucharist. A saying attributed to Augustine was frequently cited, whereby the change takes place not through the service of the one consecrating, but through the word of the Creator and the power of the Holy Spirit.[98]

When, in this context, Scholastic theology (on the basis of the false Latin translation of 2 Cor 2:10) said that the priest's liturgical action was done *in persona Christi*, and when it combined this with the teaching about the indelible mark (*character indelibilis*) imprinted by priestly ordination as an "assimilation" to Jesus Christ and empowerment to cultic action, it was pursuing the same object: it wished to indicate that the qualification of the priest conveyed by ordination unites him so closely with Jesus Christ that it is the latter, and not the priest, who is the primary subject of the Eucharistic liturgy.[99] Thus the priest does not have the capacity to cause Jesus Christ, the Exalted One, to continually perform new actions: he himself repeatedly accomplishes "in the person of Christ" the actualization of that which the theology of sacrifice calls the *one* "sacrificial action" of Jesus Christ.

From the perspective of Scholastic theology the priest, through this "quasi-identity"[100] with Jesus Christ, has a place in the Eucharistic celebration that fundamentally differentiates him from all other participants. Beyond that, because of his ordination and his being entrusted with care of a community, he is that community's representative. Thomas Aquinas was the first to say that, to the extent that the

97. K. J. Becker, *Der priesterliche Dienst II. Wesen und Vollmachten des Priestertums nach dem Lehramt* (Freiburg: 1970) 18–43.

98. Ibid., 23 (with sources).

99. On this, see P. J. Cordes, *Sendung zum Dienst* (Frankfurt: 1972); F. Eisenbach, *Systematische Studien*, 405–441.

100. P. J. Cordes, *Sendung zum Dienst*, 185.

cult is a human accomplishment, a confession of faith, and a prayer, the priest acts *in persona ecclesiae*.[101] This Catholic conception of the priest does not really put him in a middle position between God and humanity, which on the basis of the New Testament is not possible, but it does see him as the representative of the one mediator and priest, Jesus Christ, *and* of his community, that is, of the *totus Christus*. But in the concrete celebration of the Eucharist this demands a shift in roles that is difficult to accomplish and is not entirely free of an unanticipated comedy: "Here priest represents the body, to the extent that he represents the head, and his liturgical action depicts the complex relationship between Jesus Christ and his Church, since at one point, in the name of the Lord, he stands over against the congregation, and then, in the name of the congregation, he turns to the Lord, and then again, in the role of the Lord who unites his body with himself, he offers the prayer and sacrifice of the whole mystical body to the Father."[102]

A theological extension of the state of knowledge achieved thus far, to cover the relationship between Eucharist and ordained priesthood, will maintain the historical conclusion: that Jesus Christ, in the Holy Spirit, is the primary subject of the Eucharistic celebration; that there is a legitimate place for an office of service "representing" (but not replacing) him; that this service is part of that office in the Church that, as a whole, stands in service of unity in the faith; that this service is not dependent on the subjective and moral qualities of the ones who serve. This view of things will be careful, not least in ecumenical dialogue, to see that the place of Jesus Christ as the unique head of the Church and thus also of the Eucharistic celebration is not reduced, so that the one who "represents" Jesus Christ in the liturgy (but does not take his place as if he were absent) is theologically located *in*, not *over* the community, as is proper for one whose duty is to hear, to believe, to give thanks in praise and memorial, and to receive.

8.4.8　*Vatican Council II*

The Second Vatican Council dealt with the Eucharist in different contexts and spoke of it in a variety of ways, in an effort to do full

101. F. Eisenbach, *Systematische Studien*, 421, n. 286, with references. "In the name of the Church" is the identical expression.
102. Ibid., 440.

justice to what had been said about the Eucharist in the past. However, in doing so it gave a number of impulses to further theological investigation.[103]

The statements on the subject of sacrifice followed tradition and cited the Council of Trent: "He [Jesus Christ] is present in the sacrifice of the Mass, not only in the person of His minister, 'the same one now offering, through the ministry of priests, who formerly offered himself on the cross,' but especially under the Eucharistic species" (SC 7). In the discussion of the "continuation" of the sacrifice of the cross, the concept of memorial is emphasized: "At the Last Supper, on the night when He was betrayed, our Savior instituted the Eucharistic Sacrifice of His Body and Blood. He did this in order to perpetuate the sacrifice of the Cross throughout the centuries until He should come again, and so to entrust to His beloved spouse, the Church, a memorial of His death and resurrection: a sacrament of love, a sign of unity, a bond of charity, a paschal banquet in which Christ is consumed, the mind is filled with grace, and a pledge of future glory is given to us" (SC 47). The theology of the sacrifice of the Mass is clarified by the inclusion of the Christian people: ". . . they should give thanks to God; by offering the Immaculate Victim, not only through the hands of the priest, but also with him, they should learn to offer themselves too" (SC 48; cf. PO 2; a summary is also found in LG 28).

In one text containing a very impressive Jesus-mysticism, the Eucharist is presented within the context of the theology of the body of Christ (LG 7). The essential difference that, according to this council, exists between the common priesthood of all believers and the hierarchical priesthood, means that at the Eucharist they act together, but also in different ways: "The ministerial priest, by the sacred power he enjoys, molds and rules the priestly people. Acting in the person of Christ, he brings about the Eucharistic Sacrifice, and offers it to God in the name of all the people. For their part, the faithful join in the offering of the Eucharist by virtue of their royal priesthood. They like-

103. We can only mention the most important statements here. Others can easily be located by using a conciliar index (e.g., *Kleines Konzilskompendium* 696-697). The Roman Congregation for Rites attempted, in an instruction on the celebration and veneration of the mystery of the Eucharist (1967), to draw together the essential magisterial teachings: NR 621-625 (German). Let me emphasize the importance of the commentaries on the council, supplementary to *LThK*, which make clear the context and range of the statements.

wise exercise that priesthood by receiving the sacraments, by prayer and thanksgiving, by the witness of a holy life, and by self-denial and active charity'' (LG 10; cf. also 11).

In its theology of the bishop's office, the council attempted a new beginning, with an effort to overcome Scholastic concentration on the priest and to recover the patristic point of view. Representation and conferral of the sacraments are now predicated primarily of the bishop: ''In the bishops, therefore, for whom priests are assistants, our Lord Jesus Christ, the supreme High Priest, is present in the midst of those who believe. For sitting at the right hand of God the Father, He is not absent from the gathering of His high priests, but above all through their excellent service He is preaching the Word of God to all nations, and constantly administering the sacraments of faith to those who believe'' (LG 21, first paragraph). The statements on the subject of bishop, Eucharist, and sacrificial community achieve the level of a Eucharistic ecclesiology:[104]

> A bishop, marked with the fullness of the sacrament of orders, is ''the steward of the grace of the supreme priesthood,'' especially in the Eucharist, which he offers or causes to be offered, and by which the Church constantly lives and grows. This Church of Christ is truly present in all legitimate local congregations of the faithful which, united with their pastors, are themselves called churches in the New Testament. For in their own locality these are the new people called by God, in the Holy

---

104. Ecumenical efforts, especially the dialogue with the Orthodox Churches, made essential contributions to this text (cf. also UR 15). In its thinking on *communio* and collegiality, the council attempted to avoid the disadvantages of the ecclesiology of the Eastern Churches, especially the endangering of the unity of the whole Church by emphasis on autocephaly. A union of all the autocephalic Churches would not be identical with the universal Church as *communio* of local Churches in the Roman Catholic sense. On the consequences of Eastern ecclesiology, see (in addition to R. Hotz, *Sakramente*), P. Plank, *Die Eucharistieversammlung als Kirche* (Würzburg: 1980), especially 145. On this conciliar teaching: K. Rahner, ''Über die Gegenwart Christi in der Diasporagemeinde nach der Lehre des Zweiten Vatikanischen Konzils,'' *Schriften* VIII, 409–425; O. Saier, *Communio in der Lehre des Zweiten Vatikanischen Konzils* (Munich: 1973). We cannot deal here with the practical reforms that also have theological relevance, e.g., the concession of the ''chalice for the laity'' or the use of concelebration to clarify the collegiality of the presbytery. On concelebration, in addition to the trailblazing work of K. Rahner and A. Häußling, *Die vielen Messen*, compare the new work of E. Mazza, *Le odierne preghiere eucharistiche* I, 46–54.

Spirit and in much fullness (cf. 1 Thess 1:5). In them the faithful are gathered together by the preaching of the gospel of Christ, and the mystery of the Lord's Supper is celebrated, "that by the flesh and blood of the Lord's body the whole brotherhood may be joined together."

In any community existing around an altar, under the sacred ministry of the bishop, there is manifested a symbol of that charity and "unity of the Mystical Body, without which there can be no salvation." In these communities, though frequently small and poor, or living far from any other, Christ is present. By virtue of Him the one, holy, catholic and apostolic Church gathers together. For "the partaking of the Body and Blood of Christ does nothing other than transform us into that which we consume."

Every legitimate celebration of the Eucharist is regulated by the bishop, to whom is committed the office of offering the worship of Christian religion to the divine Majesty and of administering it in accordance with the Lord's commandments and with the Church's laws, as further defined by his particular judgment for his diocese (LG 26).

8.4.9 *Communion*

Communio (*koinonia*) with Jesus is, according to current understanding, the second high point, the goal and consummation of the Eucharistic celebration. The external form of this *communio* is eating and drinking the sacramental gifts, but it is not to be understood simply as a meal, since even in the New Testament it was already liturgically stylized and clearly demarcated from ordinary festival meals. Since Jesus is the real and primary agent in *communio* also, the event can be so described in the first instance: Jesus here gives us a share in himself as a concrete, living person with his whole life's destiny, and in the power of the Holy Spirit he accomplishes that being-in-one-another (he in us and we in him) that is the most intimate imaginable form of being together, the greatest possible closeness. This personal sharing occurs, according to the New Testament, primarily through eating his body. We must give careful attention to the manner of his presence and that of the glorified body that exists now in the divine dimension (see 8.4.5 above). It is a real, pneumatic presence, in which Jesus is "otherwise" also present to his own, but that is sacramentally mediated in the *communio*. Christian faith excludes any kind of corporal-material understanding from the start, but it has clung unshakeably to the fact of a sacramental mediation that is perceptible to human senses, in opposition to all interpretations that are inimical to the body or the senses.

The *communio* as *internal process* of union occurs in that part of the relationship between God and the human person in which human beings have no further mediating function and are not "in charge." It is obvious that it can only happen where people are prepared for it, in faith, hope, and love, but this disposition is, in the last analysis, only made possible and supported by God's grace. Thus also the decision whether the faith that, from the human side, must be present to support the union of human persons with Jesus in *communio* is not the province of human agents. Theologically, we can only say that *where*, through the grace of God, the preconditions for this *communio* exist, *where* the Spirit of God brings them to fulfillment, there the gracious *effects* of this *communio*, as given in revelation and the tradition of faith, are perceived to be present. The effect of this sacramental communion that is already mentioned in 1 Corinthians 10:17 and from that point on was always most strongly emphasized in our tradition consists in a union with Jesus Christ that creates community with those who are communicating in faith and love, and thus constantly nourishes the body of Christ which is the Church. The next effect of this sacrament of the Eucharist in those who receive it, according to the Church's traditional teaching, is the increase of grace. This can easily be misunderstood in a quantitative sense. A theology of grace purified of such notions, one that understands "grace" to be God's own self, self-communicated in Jesus Christ through the Holy Spirit, will perceive this "increase" as the opportunity given by God to achieve an ever more intensive *experience* of God's real presence within the human person. There are emotional dimensions to this intensification—the Council of Florence spoke of "rejoicing"—as well as ethical results—the Council of Trent spoke of a "return gift" in exchange for sin—but without doubt it includes also the dissolution of any purely individualistic point of view. "Increase" of grace always means an ever more intensive union with Jesus: in seeking to do the will of God in this world, in the practical unity of love of God and humanity, in following Jesus by beginning to bring about the reign of God, in the service of peace and reconciliation, in standing up against injustice, in attention to the weak, the ostracized, and the strangers. Finally, in connection with the promise of life in John 6 it is said to be an effect of this communion that it is a pledge of our future glory and eternal happiness. Those who receive Jesus are taken into that dimension of God in which the works of God and those who are perfected in God exist in a pure, enduring presence, and into which believers hope someday to be accepted and to abide. Since people often find themselves oppressed and threatened, in a life filled with flaws and contradictions, these mystical and grace-filled effects of the Eucharist cannot endure. That is why the sacrament of the Eucharist, as a memorial celebration that represents and makes present, and as *communio*, must be frequently and continually repeated.

If we now consider this Church teaching about the grace-giving effects of Eucharistic *communio* in terms of the theology of grace and pneumatology, we find that these effects can also be given by God apart from the sacrament (something that, among human beings, can never mean in a purely spiritual manner)—with the exception of the "ecclesial" effect, the visible building up and holding together of the body of Christ that is the Church by the common eating of the one bread. We thus return to a basic insight of general sacramental theology, that is, that the sacraments may not be understood as exclusive (or "monopolistic") means to the grace of God. Here we are also in accord with Augustine's concept of the Eucharist, according to which this sacrament exists precisely because of the ecclesial body of Christ, and not because otherwise it would not be possible for Jesus Christ to be present in his glorified body.

The conception of Eucharist presented here is confirmed by the Church's teaching about "spiritual communion." This could be taken to refer to a form of Eucharistic piety that has existed since the fourteenth century and was popularized especially by French and Spanish mysticism.[105] That is not what I am referring to here. What I mean, instead, is the Church teaching that was developed especially by Thomas Aquinas and adopted by the Council of Trent (Latin only: DS 1648).[106] According to this teaching it is possible to acquire the "fruits" or *res* of the sacrament of Eucharist even without receiving it. This communion is called "spiritual" only in distinction to the communion that is both "spiritual" and "sacramental."[107] It is that union with Jesus

---

105. Cf. H. R. Schlette, *Kommunikation und Sakrament. Theologische Deutung der geistlichen Kommunion* (Freiburg: 1959)—an unsurpassed treatment.

106. Cf. Thomas Aquinas, *S. th.* III q. 73 a. 3; q. 80 a. 1 ad 3.

107. This "spiritual" is completely real, and therefore different from the "only spiritual" mentioned by the Council of Trent in contrast to "real" (NR 584/DS 1658).

in faith and love that "normally" (as a disposition created by grace) precedes sacramental communion for those who live in the Church, and at the same time is the sacrament's supreme fruit. This union is "spiritual" in the same sense as the divine Pneuma, who effects it, is "spirit": something absolutely real that may not be confused with pure human intention or communion in thought. According to the Church's teaching, it cannot exist without a sincere longing for sacramental communion, if such is possible. In Catholic circles this is the only official teaching that can be offered in response to situations in which the sacrament cannot exist:

— in priestless parishes (in which, according to Catholic teaching, the community cannot empower the "non-ordained" to preside);
— for those who are prevented from attending Eucharistic celebrations;
— for those married in the Church who have been civilly divorced and remarried (who are not excommunicated, but are excluded from receiving the sacraments);
— the Protestant Lord's Supper (which, according to Catholic teaching, lacks the original and complete reality of the Eucharistic sacrament, primarily because of the absence of the sacrament of orders, though it is certainly not an ineffective sign).

For people in such situations, the Catholic Church teaches that "when, deeply moved by desire for the sacrament, and united in prayer with the whole Church, they call on the Lord and lift their hearts to him, they commune, through the power of the Holy Spirit, with the Church which is the living body of Christ, and with the Lord himself. United with the Church by their desire for the sacrament, they are, even though externally separated from it, internally and really united with the Church, and thus receive the fruits of the sacrament."[108] Thus, according to this teaching, it is possible to receive all the effects of the sacrament, even the specifically ecclesial effect, "extra-sacramentally."

108. Document of the Congregation for the Doctrine of the Faith, "On some Questions regarding the Service of the Eucharist," 6 August 1983, AAS 49 (Bonn: 1983) III 4, p. 10.

8.5 *The Renewal of Eucharistic Theology*

The most urgent efforts in Eucharistic theology are directed toward achieving a unified view by which the divisions in this teaching can be reversed. This is connected with the hope that the separated Churches might be able to agree on some such fundamental conception. Two theologians will be highlighted in our overview of these efforts.

Among Protestants, Max Thurian has emphasized the central category of memorial (*memoria*) and attempted to interpret the ideas of sacrifice and of presence within that category. He pointed to the connection with Jewish liturgy, which Jesus incorporated in the Eucharist without destroying its ritual. Thus the Eucharist should be understood as a sacrifice of praise and thanksgiving in memory of all God's mighty deeds; in the course of this event there occurs, through the action of the Holy Spirit, the sacramental presence of the unique and single sacrifice of Jesus Christ and thus the person of Jesus Christ himself. The Church's task is, in this view, to place this sacrifice of the Son liturgically before the Father, in order that he may remember his people and give the blessing won by the Son through this sacrifice. Thus the Church unites itself, as a participant, with the Son's prayer for all humanity, praying that the Father grant them salvation so that his kingdom may come. The three elements belonging to the ancient fundamental form of the Eucharist are to be found here: anamnesis and epiclesis, with the "somatic" real presence embedded in them; the "katabatic" or "descending" movement of the blessing implored of God; and the "anabatic" or "ascending" movement of the sacrifice of praise. Max Thurian's ideas were very influential in recent ecumenical discussions of the Eucharist, and in the preparation of the "Lima document." From a Catholic perspective, there remain some questions about the expiatory character of the sacrifice. (Could it not be understood as God's deed of reconciliation?) Catholics are also concerned about the sacramentality of the ordination of priests in Thurian's system.[109]

109. On M. Thurian see, for example, L. Lies' article in *Zeitschrift für katholische Theologie* 100 (1978) 79–82; S. N. Bosshard in *Zeitschrift für katholische Theologie* 108 (1986) 159–161; M. Thurian, "Das Eucharistische Gedächtnis: Lob- und Bittopfer," in M. Thurian, ed., *Ökumenische Perspektiven von Taufe, Eucharistie und Amt* (Paderborn and Frankfurt: 1983) 110–123. Cf. the Lima documents, especially the one

Among Catholics, Johannes Betz has made an effort to bring the manifold results of biblical research, liturgical theology, patristics, and the ecumenical discussions of the present century within a unified, current system. The most important impulses came from the renewal of the theology of the word of God, whose proclamation brings about the presence of what is proclaimed, and from the intuitions of Odo Casel. In spite of the weaknesses revealed in the discussion of historical conclusions and theological arguments,[110] it seemed to many, including Betz, that it is correct to understand the Eucharist as a real-symbolic representation (making present) of the saving act of God that happened once for all in Jesus Christ. Betz attempted to formulate this basic insight of Casel with theological precision, in order to show how both the sacrifice and the real, personal presence of Jesus are "contained" in the whole event. To achieve this, he distinguished three manners of presence, all contained within one another, each of them constituting a real and pneumatic presence: (1) The personal, pneumatic presence in effect of the exalted Christ Jesus, who acts in the Eucharistic sacrament as the principal agent (*principalis agens*) through his Spirit, and making use of the priest as his (secondary) agent. This presence of the Risen One, with its immediate effects without which neither prayer, nor memorial, nor liturgy of any kind would be possible, Betz calls "principal actual presence." (2) The celebrating community, thanks to the One who acts among them, enters into the memorial of the work of redemption, which becomes really present through Jesus Christ, not through subjective memory; the community ratifies the completed sacrifice of Jesus, which was accomplished without its contribution, acknowledges it as a sacrifice done for the benefit of the community and in its place, and in the symbol of the meal makes it its own and renders it fruitful. This Betz calls the "anamnetic memo-

on Eucharist, 3–4 (sacrifice of praise), 5–7 (memorial, anamnesis), 8 (thanksgiving and petition), 13 (real presence), 14 (epiclesis of the Holy Spirit), and on office, 14 (the ordained ministry and the Eucharist). On Catholic critiques of Lima, see M. Seybold and A. Gläßer, *Das "Lima-Papier"* ; L. Lies, "Ökumenische Erwägungen zu Abendmahl, Priesterweihe und Meßopfer," *Zeitschrift für katholische Theologie* 104 (1982) 385–410. For Protestant critiques of newer concepts of the Lord's supper, see E. Volk, "Mahl des Herrn oder Mahl der Kirche?" *Kerygma und Dogma* 31 (1985) 33–64 (Lutheran reservations about Calvinist and Orthodox influences). On ecumenical discussion, see further G. Hintzen, "Das reformatorische Abendmahl aus katholischer Sicht," *Catholica* 40 (1986) 203–288 (with bibliography).

110. See the standard work of A. Schilson, *Theologie als Sakramententheologie.*

rial actual presence.'' (3) In this actual presence of the sacrificial act of Jesus, God, in making present the *whole* act of sacrifice, makes Jesus present as a corporeal person; in the change wrought by the consecration he becomes present in such a way that the deepest personal encounter with him is made possible. This Betz calls the ''somatic, personal real presence.''[111]

Thus in the celebration of the Eucharist the presence of the Risen One in his Holy Spirit causes the presence of his saving act, and with it the corporeal presence of his person, surrendered to death and glorified, for the purpose of achieving the greatest possible community: the person is made present *in* the making present of the events. In more recent developments in Eucharistic theology since Betz, pneumatology is even more strongly emphasized. This brings unmistakably to expression something that Betz always tried to stress: that the Eucharistic celebration does not arise out of human initiative, is not a human achievement or autonomous action, and adds nothing of value to Jesus' saving action. A grounding of Eucharist in pneumatology can also remove the misunderstanding that in this sacrament human beings have God at their disposal and can move Jesus to come to them. It also gives assurance for faith in the real presence of Jesus in the Holy Spirit. That presence is not brought about by subjective consciousness and memory, nor by the prayer for the Spirit's coming, since wherever there is prayer, and wherever God's mighty deeds are praised, God is already present.

In the sacrament of the Eucharist, everything that Christian faith means by ''salvation'' is sacramentally present and united.[112] In this sacrament, the assembled community brings its praise and thanksgiving before God the Father for everything that comes from him: creation and salvation history. In this sacrament, the community is changed into the body of Jesus Christ, the Crucified and Risen One, and thus becomes a place of reconciliation, confession of faith, and festal joy, as well as a place of lament over unfinished salvation, of suffering with those who suffer. In this sacrament individual believers are given the

111. See the summary in *Sacramentum Mundi* I, 1226–1232. Betz met with widespread acceptance, from A. Gerken, *Theologie der Eucharistie* (1973) to W. Kasper, ''Einheit und Vielfalt der Aspekte der Eucharistie,'' 202–203 (1985).

112. ''In hoc sacramento comprehenditur totum mysterium nostrae salutis,'' Thomas Aquinas, *S. th.* III q. 83 a. 4c. On what follows, cf. U. Kühn, *Sakramente*, 293–297: The meaning of the Lord's Supper.

most intimate closeness with Jesus, so that human persons are assured in ever new ways of God's self-communication. In the assembled people and the gifts that are prepared, the hopes, joys, and problems of creation, of all the world, are present, imploring God's blessing, looking forward to the perfection of redemption, and thus occur thanksgiving, memorial, and petition: made possible, supported, and made fruitful by the presence of the Holy Spirit of God.

Bibliography 6

Eucharist

a) Books

Averbeck, W. *Der Opfercharakter des Abendmahls in der neueren evangelischen Theologie.* Paderborn: 1966.

Bätzing, G. *Die Eucharistie als Opfer der Kirche nach Hans Urs von Balthasar.* Einsiedeln: 1986.

Betz, J. *Eucharistie. In der Schrift und Patristik. (Handbuch der Dogmengeschichte* IV/4A.) Freiburg: 1979.

Bistumskommission für ökumenische Fragen Münster, ed. *Die Eucharistie im Gespräch der Konfessionen.* Kevelaer: 1986.

Bode, F.-J. *Gemeinschaft mit dem lebendigen Gott. Die Lehre von der Eucharistie bei Matthias Joseph Scheeben.* Paderborn: 1986.

Bosshard, S. N. *Zwingli—Erasmus—Cajetan. Die Eucharistie als Zeichen der Einheit.* Wiesbaden: 1978.

Bürki, B. *Cène du Seigneur—Eucharistie de l'Eglise.* 2 vols. Fribourg: 1985 (reformed texts).

De Lubac, H. *Corpus Mysticum. Eucharistie und Kirche im Mittelalter.* Einsiedeln: 1969.

Die Eucharistie als Feier der Gegenwart des Herrn: Concilium 4/12 (1968).

Eucharist. International Bibliography 1975-1984. Strasbourg: 1985.

Feld, H. *Das Verständnis des Abendmahls.* Darmstadt: 1976.

195

Felmy, K. C. *Die Deutung der göttlichen in der russischen Theologie.* Berlin: 1984.

Feneberg, R. *Christliche Paschafeier und Abendmahl.* Munich: 1971.

Gamber, K. *Sacrificium Missae. Zum Opferverständnis und zur Liturgie der Frühkirche.* Regensburg: 1980.

_____. *Beracha: Eucharistiegebet und Eucharistiefeier in der Urkirche.* Regensburg: 1986.

Gemeinsame röm-kath./ev.-luth. Kommission. *Das Herrenmahl.* Paderborn and Frankfurt: 1978.

Gerken, A. *Theologie der Eucharistie.* Munich: 1973.

Gesteira García, M. *La Eucharistía, misterio de comunión.* Madrid: 1983.

Gesù e la sua morte (Atti della XXVII Settimana Biblica). Brescia: 1984, esp. G. Ghiberti, "Gesù e la sua morte secondo i raconti della cena. Alcune interpretazioni del XX secolo," 129–153.

Giraudo, C. *La struttura letteraria della preghiera eucaristica.* Rome: 1981.

Grötzinger, E. *Luther und Zwingli. Die Kritik an der mittelalterlichen Lehre von der Messe als Wurzel des Abendmahlsstreites.* Cologne and Gütersloh: 1980.

Heron, A. I. C. *Table and tradition. Toward an ecumenical understanding of the Eucharist.* Philadelphia: 1983.

Hintzen, G. *Die neuere Diskussion über die eucharistische Wandlung.* Frankfurt and Berne: 1976.

Holeton, D. R. *Les Hussites et la communion des petits enfants. Ressourcement patristique et mouvement de piété populaire (1380–1421).* Paris: 1983.

Interkommunion. Hoffnungen—zu bedenken. Fribourg: 1971 (bibliography).

Kann man in jedem Fall die Eucharistie feiern?: Concilium 18/2 (1983).

Klauck, H.-J. *Herrenmahl und hellenistischer Kult.* Münster: 1982.

Léon-Dufour, X. *Le partage du pain eucharistique solon le Nouveau Testament.* Paris: 1982.

_____. *Abendmahl und Abschiedsrede im Neuen Testament.* Stuttgart: 1983.

Lies, L. *Wort und Eucharistie bei Origenes.* Innsbruck: 1978.

Maas-Ewerd, T., and K. Richter, eds. *Gemeinde im Herrenmahl.* Freiburg: 1976.

Macy, G. *The Theologies of the Eucharist in the early scholastic Period (ca. 1080–ca. 1220).* Oxford: 1984.

Martimort, A. G., ed. *L'Eglise en prière.* Ed. nouvelle II: R. Cabié. *L'Eucharistie,* Tournai-Paris: 1983. English: *The Church at Prayer.* New ed. II: Robert Cabié. *The Eucharist.* Collegeville: 1986.

Mazza, E. *Le odierne preghiere eucaristiche.* 2 vols. Bologna: 1984.

Meyer, H. B. *Luther und die Messe.* Paderborn: 1965.

Moll, H. *Die Lehre von der Eucharistie als Opfer. Eine dogmengeschichtliche Untersuchung vom Neuen Testament bis Irenäus von Lyon.* Cologne: 1975.

Nélis, J. *Histoire de la pratique et de la doctrine eucharistiques de l'Eglise Occidentale.* Paris and Brussels: 1984.

Pesch, R. *Das Abendmahl und Jesu Todesverständnis.* Freiburg: 1978.

Piolanti, A. *Il eucaristico*. 3d ed. Rome: 1983.

Plank, P. *Die Eucharistieversammlung als Kirche. Zur Entstehung und Entfaltung der eucharistischen Ekklesiologie Nikolaj Afanas'evs (1893–1966)*. Würzburg: 1980.

Pratzner, F. *Messe und Kreuzesopfer. Die Krise der sakramentalen Idee bei Luther und in der mittelalterlichen Scholastik*. Vienna: 1970.

Pruisken, J. *Interkommunion im Prozeß*. Essen: 1974.

Rahner, K., and A. Häußling. *Die vielen Messen und das eine Opfer*. Freiburg: 1966.

Reumann, J. *The Supper of the Lord*. Philadelphia: 1984 (New Testament, ecumenical dialogue).

Sánchez Caro, J. M. *Eucaristía y historia de la Salvación*. Madrid: 1983 (theology of the Eastern Churches).

Sayes, J. A. *Presencia real de Cristo y Transubstanciación*. Burgos: 1974.

Schäfer, P. *Lebensquelle Eucharistie*. Regensburg: 1985.

Schillebeeckx, E. *Die eucharistische Gegenwart*. Düsseldorf: 1967.

Schneider, T. *Deinen Tod verkünden wir. Gesammelte Studien zum erneuerten Eucharistieverständnis*. Düsseldorf: 1980.

Schulte, R. *Die Messe als Opfer der Kirche. Die Lehre frühmittelalterlicher Autoren über das Opfer*. Münster: 1959.

Verheul, A. *La prière eucharistique dans la primitive église*. Louvain: 1983.

Walter, E. *Eucharistie. Bleibende Wahrheit und heutige Fragen*. Freiburg: 1974.

Wiederkehr, D. *Das Sakrament der Eucharistie*. Fribourg: 1976.

Wohlmuth, J. *Realpräsenz und Transsubstantiation im Konzil von Trient*. 2 vols. Berne and Frankfurt: 1975.

Zizioulas, J. D. *Being in Communion*. Crestwood, N.Y.: 1985 (Eucharistic ecclesiology).

b) Articles and Essays

Angenendt, A. "Missa specialis. Zugleich ein Beitrag Entstehung der Privatmessen." *Frühmittelalterliche Studien* 17 (1983) 153–221.

Beinert, W. "Eucharistie als Sakrament der Einheit." *Catholica* 36 (1982) 234–256.

Betz, J. "Die Eucharistie als Gottes Milch in frühchristlicher Sicht." *Zeitschrift für katholische Theologie* 106 (1984) 1–26, 167–185.

Callam, D. "The frequency of mass in the Latin Church ca 400." *Theological Studies* 45 (1984) 613–650.

Congar, Y. "Lutherana. Théologie de l'Eucharistie et christologie chez Luther." *Revue des sciences philosophiques et théologiques* 66 (1982) 169–197.

————. "Doctrine christologique et théologie de l'Eucharistie." *Revue des sciences philosophiques et théologiques* 66 (1982) 233–244.

Dekkers, E. "L'Eucharistie, imitation ou anamnèse de la Dernière Cène." *Recherches de science religieuse* 68 (1984) 15–23.

Delling, G., and others. "Abendmahl." *TRE* I (1977) 47–229.

Feuillet, A. "L'Eucharistie, le Sacrifice du Calvaire et le Sacerdoce du Christ." *Divinitas* 29 (1985) 103–149 (Synoptics and Hebrews).

Fiedler, P. "Probleme der Abendmahlsforschung." *Archiv für Liturgiewissenschaft* 24 (1982) 190–223.

Frankenmölle, H., B. J. Hilberath, and T. Schneider. "Eucharistie." *NHthG* I (1984) 297–317.

Giraudo, C. "Le récit de l'institution dans la prière eucharistique a-t-il des précédents?" *Nouvelle Revue Théologique* 106 (1984) 513–526.

Greshake, G. "Konzelebration der Priester." In E. Klinger and K. Wittstadt, eds. *Glaube im Prozeß*. Freiburg: 1984, 258–288 (bibliography).

Hauschild, W.-D. "Agapen. I: In der alten Kirche." *TRE* I (1977) 748–753.

Hilberath, B. J., and T. Schneider. "Opfer." *NHthG* III (1985) 287–298.

Kandler, K.-H. "Abendmahl und Heiliger Geist." *Kerygma und Dogma* 28 (1982) 215–227.

Kilmartin, E. J. "The active role of Christ and the Holy Spirit in the sanctification of the eucharistic elements." *Theological Studies* 45 (1984) 225–253.

Klauck, H.-J. "Eucharistie und Kirchengemeinschaft bei Paulus." *Wissenschaft und Weisheit* 49 (1986) 1–14.

Kühn, U. "Abendmahl." In *Sakramente* (see Bibliography 1) 259–304.

Kunz, E. "Eucharistie. Ursprung von Kommunikation und Gemeinschaft." *Theologie und Philosophie* 58 (1983) 321–345.

Legrand, H.-M. "La présidence de l'Eucharistie selon la tradition ancienne." *Spiritus* 18 (1977) 409–431 (evidence before Nicea).

Lessing, E. "Kirchengemeinschaft und Abendmahlsgemeinschaft." *Wissenschaft und Praxis in Kirche und Gesellschaft* 69 (1980) 450–462.

Lies, L. "Ökumenische Erwägungen zu Abendmahl, Priesterweihe und Meßopfer." *Zeitschrift für katholische Theologie* 104 (1982) 385–410.

————. "Verbalpräsenz—Aktualpräsenz." In *Praesentia Christi*, FS J. Betz. Düsseldorf: 1984, 790–100.

Madeja, S. "Analisi del concetto di concelebrazione eucaristica nel Concilio Vaticano II e nella riforma liturgica postconciliare." *Ephemerides Liturgicae* 96 (1982) 3–56.

Mayer, A. "Die Eucharistie." *HKR* 676–691.

Medisch, R. "Kirchliches Amt und Eucharistie." *Theologie der Gegenwart* 28 (1985) 182–188 (bibliography).

Nocke, F.-J. "Wort und Geste" (see Bibliography 1) 59–83.

Rahner, K. "Wort und Eucharistie." In *Schriften* IV (1960) 313–356.

Ramis, G. "El memorial eucarístico (anaphora)." *Ephemerides Liturgicae* 96 (1982) 189–208.

Roux, J.-M. "Corporéité et symbole eucharistique." *Bulletin de littérature ecclésiastique* 86 (1985) 101–126; 87 (1986) 29–56.

Salado, Martínez, D. "La interrelación simbólica Eucaristía-Penitencia en el Organismo Sacramental." *Escritos del Vedat* 16 (1986) 179-215.

Sánchez Caro, J. M. " 'Probet autem seipsum homo' (1 Cor XI, 28). Influjo de la praxis penitencial eclesiástica en la interpretación de un texto bíblico." *Salmanticensis* 32 (1985) 293-334.

Schulz, H.-J. " 'Wandlung' im ostkirchlich-liturgischen Verständnis. Eine Orientierung im Disput um Transsubstantiation und Transsignifikation." *Catholica* 49 (1986) 270-286 (bibliography, esp. B. J. Hilberath and G. Hintzen).

Schwager, R. "Der Tod Christi und die Opferkritik." *Theologie der Gegenwart* 29 (1986) 11-20 (bibliography).

Thunberg, L. "Symbol and Mystery in St. Maximus the Confessor." In F. Heinzer and C. Schönborn, eds. *Maximus Confessor.* Fribourg: 1981, 285-308.

Tilliette, X. "Problèmes de philosophie eucharistique." *Gregorianum* 64 (1983) 273-305.

Trütsch, J. "Taufe, Sakrament der Einheit—Eucharistie, Sakrament der Trennung?" *Theologische Berichte* (Zürich) 9 (1980) 67-95.

Volk., E. "Evangelische Akzente im Verständnis der Eucharistie." *Kerygma und Dogma* 32 (1986) 188-206.

Wenz, G. "Die Lehre vom Opfer Christi im Herrenmahl als Problem ökumenischer Theologie." *Kerygma und Dogma* 28 (1982) 7-41.

9

The Sacrament of Reconciliation

9.1 Preliminary Theological Questions

Certain basics of divine revelation in the Bible and of the Church's faith tradition are in the present context taken for granted: that God has revealed God's concrete will regarding a divine standard for human behavior; that people in general—with numerous exceptions—are able to recognize God's will (Rom 1:18-3:20); that God has not predestined any human being to evil, that is, God offers everyone the opportunity to carry out the divine will; that people in general nonetheless —again with numerous exceptions—have enough freedom to be able to refuse to do God's will. In biblical-ecclesial language, this refusal is called "sin." When the refusal to do God's will is a free, conscious, and radical decision, it is called "serious" or "grave sin" and, if it remains final and unretracted until death, it would lead to eternal separation from God. When God's will is only imperfectly known, or when human freedom is restricted or the thing refused is not an essential value willed by God, Christian tradition speaks of "venial sin." In individual instances, both kinds of sin can take very different forms, ranging from a frontal denial of God, once and for all, to a conglomerate of many small, scarcely noticeable refusals; in both kinds, it is always necessary to decide whether they stem more from the "center" or from the "periphery" of a human person. They need not always be expressly directed against God, since there is a close connection between the relationship of a human person to God and to fellow human beings, so that essential resistance to God is enacted in the realm of human society, the very realm in which, both in the Old and New Testaments, God has made his concrete will known.[1]

The conviction that no one but God can forgive sin is part of the Jewish and Christian faith tradition. It is true that in both testaments we read of God's continually renewed demands for repentance, that is, that people turn away from their false behavior and turn toward God in a new life-orientation. But even this repentance is God's gift to human beings, since it is from God's initiative alone that the will, the ability, and the accomplishment of a new life arises. It is part of the sacramental structure of their relationship to God (see 1.2 above) that human beings, in this instance also, depend on a mediation through the senses, meaning that God must open for them a place or space for forgiveness. For Christian believers this tangible place of divine forgiveness and reconciliation is called Jesus Christ. In his solidarity with sinners, witnessed by his whole life, in his acceptance of John's baptism of repentance, in eating with sinners, in his work of healing and pardoning, in his self-donation to those who are estranged from God, even unto death, the unconditional and anticipatory love of God is made visible in an unsurpassable way. All those who, conscious of their guilt, in full confidence seek refuge in Jesus, are already in the grip of a dynamic initiated and borne by the Holy Spirit of God that assures them of pardon from "the Father of mercies and the God of all consolation" (2 Cor 1:3). This is the common faith of all Christians. But division starts with the question of exactly *what* is forgiven. Is sin a corruption common to all humanity that is not really removed by divine forgiveness, but in view of the cross of Jesus is simply not

1. On theological, psychological, social-psychological, and other insights concerning sin, see the specialized literature. Cf. also H. Vorgrimler, "Der Kampf des Christen mit der Sünde," *MySal* V (1976) 349–448, here especially at 365 n. 34 (bibliography) and 375 n. 60 (bibliography); P. Hoffmann and V. Eid, *Jesus von Nazareth und eine christliche Moral* 3d ed. (Freiburg: 1979); J. Werbick, *Schulderfahrung und Bußsakrament* (Mainz: 1985); J. Blank and J. Werbick, eds., *Sühne und Versöhnung*, Theologie zur Zeit 1 (Düsseldorf: 1986).

attributed to us, so that *after* being pardoned a human being is simultaneously just and sinful?[2] Or is sin a concrete attitude growing out of a false basic decision, both of which are forgiven by God in the sense that afterward both are really removed, so that *after* being pardoned a human being is marked by an evil inclination and certain consequences of sin, but not by the corruption itself?

Christians agree in the belief that when human persons recognize what is false in their way of life and orient themselves anew toward God, this is only possible because of the prior grace of God that takes hold of the human person. This repentance that is granted to a human being expresses itself concretely in that person's spiritual life in the form of contrition, which is at the same time an active will to adopt a new attitude and to turn decisively away from one's former life. This remorse, as reflected in Catholic teaching, is also always a trust in a forgiving God; thus it cannot be interpreted as self-justification. According to the experience reflected in Catholic teaching, a person who conscientiously reflects on his or her conversion may have different motives for contrition, i.e., for condemning his or her sin. In "perfect" contrition this motive is a God-given love of the God who deliberately makes a human person his own possession. In "imperfect" contrition the motive is less than love, but still of ethical value; a crass fear of divine punishment would not be a worthy motive in this sense.

In the Catholic view, repentance is expressed in all the levels or dimensions of the human person, which have been affected by the false orientation, and thus may well have an emotional character ("tears of remorse"). In the same way, and corresponding to the sacramental structure of the relationship between God and humanity, God's forgiveness has a tendency toward a sensibly-evident, perceptible event that takes place in the framework of human community. Here again we must realize that relevant rejection of God's will takes place in the realm of one's environment and social milieu, and therefore it is there that reconciliation with God must find its practical expression. It is also in this dimension of the palpable and the social that prayer for one another finds its place. When forgiveness is seen as happening only in grace-given faith in the gospel, that is, in the internal milieu of an

---

2. For a more nuanced view, see H. Wulf, "Simul iustus et peccator," *LThK* IX 778–780 (bibliography).

encounter between God and an individual human being, the palpable-social dimension of the divine-human relationship slips from view.

9.2 Forms of Forgiveness

God's pardoning of guilt may be considered theologically as a unique gift of God's creative power, mediated through Jesus in the Holy Spirit. This gift can be rejected throughout the course of a long life; it can be made unfruitful; but, within the manifold dimensions of a human life, it can also revive. Correspondingly, the tradition of Christian faith recognizes many forms of forgiveness in which the *one* divine pardon takes concrete shape.[3] As human actions they are supported by the constant petition of the whole Church for the forgiveness of sins. From among these many forms, we may emphasize the following as of primary importance:

1. Reconciliation through hearing the word of God. Because of God's own unique initiative, the divine word encounters us as a word of reconciliation in the form of an offer to everyone who hears, and in the form of real pardon of those who, in a repentance wrought by grace, become aware of their need for forgiveness. The encounter with the forgiving word of God (in preaching, reading, discussion, or the dialogue of prayer) is no less effective or certain than the encounter that takes place, for example, in a sacramental action.

2. Reconciliation through restitution. Reconciliation with the people we have wronged or injured is a precondition for God's effective forgiveness (Matt 5:23-24; 6:12).

3. Reconciliation through productive love. Wherever a person turns away from fixation on himself or herself and the sterility that results from that, wherever such a person undertakes a commitment, individually or socially, on behalf of others, that person's sins are forgiven in this God-given practice of love, even if he or she does not think directly of God and God's forgiving word.

4. Reconciliation through conversational encounter. The New Testament admonitions to speak to one another and to listen to one another

3. Cf. H. Vorgrimler in *MySal* V, 349-448, and the same author's article in *NHthG* I (1984) 154-157.

make it clear that conversation, critique, and self-criticism can be of decisive importance in the reception of the effective word of forgiveness.

5. Reconciliation through dying with Jesus. Concrete practices of penance can often arise out of mistaken or sick ideas. If notions of earning forgiveness and masochistic ideas of reparation are avoided, ascetic forms of life, the acceptance of situations that have no human solution (loneliness, old age) and the endurance of meaningless but unavoidable suffering can be understood as the death of the self and its guilt, a dying with Jesus and an occasion of the forgiveness won for us by Jesus.

6. Reconciliation through the Church. From the beginning, the Church recognized itself as a community of those called by God to be a place of reconciliation and peace in the midst of a godless world. Since there were early signs of a discrepancy between the task of being God's sinless possession, and therefore "holy," and the reality, which was marked by manifold faults and failings, the Church sought for what was "objectively" holy, something that could not be damaged by human sin, and found it primarily in the realm of the sacraments. In more recent times the ideas of Jesus as the primary sacrament and the Church as the fundamental sacrament have been seamlessly integrated into this scheme. The sacraments, as expressions of the Church's life, are symbolic actions perceptible to the senses in which the gift of divine forgiveness is *also* effective. From the early days of the Church, this was predicated in a special way of certain sacraments:

(a) According to common Christian teaching, the primary sacrament for the forgiveness of sins is baptism. Its uniqueness corresponds to the uniqueness of radical conversion effected by the grace of God, which is "embodied" in this sacrament, placed within the context of Church, and thus comes to a socially perceptible and fruitful conclusion. In the Church's tradition, baptism was regarded as the "lighter" penance in comparison with the arduous penances endured after later misdeeds or in the wake of a baptized person's fall from faith and subsequent repentance.

(b) Among the sacraments of reconciliation for those who are baptized, the Eucharist has first place. Its fundamental ideas—the recollection of the life and death of Jesus in union with the forgiveness expressed in his preaching, the joyful anticipation of reconciled life in the reign of God and the realization of the body of Jesus Christ in a human community—include the reconciliation of all participants with one another and with God. Of course, even before Paul's demand (1 Cor 11:28-29) for a "worthy" reception of the Eucharist, the Eucharist was regarded more as a feast of those who were already reconciled and not so much as a way and means to reconciliation. This Pauline idea was adopted in the Church's discipline: there is an obligation to confess serious sins before receiving communion (NR 587/DS 1661). There is a tension between this discipline and the Church's teaching that the Eucharist bestows gifts of repentance and removes even the most serious sins (NR 599/DS 1743).

(c) The sacrament of reconciliation, to which this chapter is devoted, stands in the foreground of the Church's teaching and practice on sacraments that forgive sins.[4] In this sacrament, the repentant sinner returns to "peace with the Church"; the real symbol of the sacrament makes effectively present the truth that God is judge of sins and sinners, that in the death of Jesus sin has been destroyed, and that before the tribunal of grace the sinner is freed from all guilt.

(d) In the sacrament of anointing of the sick the symbolic action unites the petition of the Church community that the sick person be strengthened in face of serious illness with a petition that his or her sins may be forgiven.

9.3 Biblical Foundations

The New Testament, like the Old, witnesses that the community of faith stands under the sign of the forgiving love of God; that this indicative is at the same time an imperative to preserve what has been bestowed; but that the community of believers constantly falls short of this demand and is threatened by failure. This failure takes such a serious form in the case of many members that the Christian identity of the community is concretely endangered. In such cases a process is begun which has as its purpose the preservation of the community from evil by distancing it from the sinner: the means to that end is a declaration to the sinful person that he or she has distanced himself or herself from the community by an attitude that reveals a lack of judg-

---

4. See the brief summary of the reasons for the present critical situation of the sacrament of reconciliation in ibid.

ment. A truly theological understanding of the Church will regard such a procedure as having a deeper effect than some merely legalistic "ecclesiastical punishment." In the Pauline letters we encounter a process carried out in stages: first there are warnings and reprimands; in "ordinary" cases the exclusion is not regarded as final; there is evidence that the separation is removed when the sinners repent. This practice of exclusion was consciously modeled on Jewish practice: 1 Corinthians 5:9ff. bases it on Deuteronomy 19:5. In extraordinary cases the vocabulary (exclusion with a curse) reveals that the community or its leaders had no hope for the repentance of the sinner.[5] This resignation applies only to human judgment; according to the New Testament there are no unforgiveable sins. Even for those guilty of "serious" sin God remains the Father who will deny love to no one and has already extended joyful forgiveness to the one who repents (Luke 15:1-32).

The later sacrament of reconciliation developed against this background. Since the beginning of the third century (penitential conflicts in North Africa) we find, as classical texts for the "institution" of the sacrament of reconciliation by Jesus, the "binding and loosing" in Matthew 16:19 and 18:18, as well as the "forgiving and retaining" of sins in John 20:23. A closer examination of "binding and loosing" in its ancient context indicates the following meanings: rabbinic parallels to "binding and loosing" comprehend the power of the rabbis to declare something forbidden or permissible, and their power to ban sinners or to remove the ban from them. Applied to the Church, that indicates the distancing of the Christian community from sinners and the reincorporation of those who repent. According to Matthew, this process is also effective "in heaven," with God. The expression had a "demonological" background in antiquity: "loosing" indicated the liberation of a human being from the influence of evil; "binding" is the consigning of a person to the evil power, since that person, through obduracy, has already surrendered to evil. Exegetes doubt that the sayings about "binding and loosing" in Matthew 16 and 18 are genuine words of Jesus.[6] What Jesus himself expected of his disciples is clear in Matthew 18: the community rule in 18:15-18, which already reveals

5. This is particularly the case when the person has fallen away from faith or into "sins against the Holy Spirit"; cf. H. Vorgrimler, *Buße und Krankensalbung* (Freiburg: 1978) 21ff.

6. For exegetical literature to 1978, see H. Vorgrimler, ibid., 12–19; also A. Vögtle, *Offenbarungsgeschehen*.

a considerable degree of institutionalization, is placed in a broader context which strongly emphasizes God's forgiveness of sin and at the
same time impresses on the disciples their obligation to forgive without limit (cf. Matt 18:23-34). The "forgiving and retaining" in John 20:23
is regarded by recent New Testament exegesis as a variant tradition
of the "binding and loosing" in Matthew 18. Here again, those addressed are not officials of the Church, but the disciples of the Risen
One. Human "forgiving" of sins is impossible apart from the Holy
Spirit of God who is given by Jesus (John 20:22).

9.4 The History of the Sacrament of Reconciliation

In the complicated history of this sacrament, which we cannot begin
to detail here,[7] we may distinguish two watershed decisions: the introduction of private, repeatable, individual confession, and the teaching on the effects of priestly absolution.

Around the end of the first century, and throughout the second,
we find evidence of the Church's penitential practice (Clement of
Rome, Shepherd of Hermas). There are no theological reflections on this
practice in the early period. In connection with the tendency to reserve
not only the teaching function but also the essential liturgical actions
to the Church's official ministers, we find at the beginning of the third
century (according to the evidence of Hippolytus, d. 236) that the power
to forgive sins is reserved to the bishops. But as long as the ancient
Church's penitential practice was preserved, the active participation
of the whole community assembled for liturgy also continued. The ecclesiology of the several authors reveals that the process was not regarded as a purely legalistic "Church punishment": exclusion from
the Church's life meant damnation for a human person, and peace with
the Church was relevant for that person's salvation before God. Up
to the year 589 (Third Synod of Toledo) the Latin Church witnesses
indicate that penance was possible only once after baptism. From the
third century onward, however, in conflicts with rigorous ideas of penance (Montanism, Novatianism), a milder view of penance gradually
prevailed. In this view, all serious sins, including the capital sins of

7. See H. Vorgrimler, ibid., based on the extensive works of B. Poschmann and
K. Rahner. For some theologians the investigation of the history of penitential practice and the development of the sacrament of reconciliation has been the key to
understanding the history of dogma.

apostasy, murder, and adultery, could be forgiven; but all sins, even "secret" ones, must be removed through public ecclesial penance. Beginning in the fourth century, penitential practice received greater and greater liturgical development and was provided with regulations for individual cases (which is the reason why the ancient Church's penitential practice is called "canonical penance"). It always began with the establishing of an official separation from the sinner ("penance by excommunication"). The Church's practice was not regarded as a theological problem, since it was anchored in Christology or pneumatology: Jesus Christ forgives sins through the Church, with which he is united, the *totus Christus* in which he alone is the controlling head; the Spirit of God penetrates and rules the Church in such a way that the Church united with the Spirit can be described by the one symbolic word *columba*, dove. Thus it was regarded as a matter of course that in the reconciliation of penitent sinners with the Church, which had been seriously wounded by their sin, peace was also created between sinners and God. In the Latin Church it was the rule that, after the official reconciliation during Holy Week, penitents were subjected for the rest of their lives to gruesome consequences as proof of their genuine repentance (lifelong prohibition of the marriage act, exclusion from certain occupations, etc.). The consequence was that penitential practice, which could only be undergone once, was delayed until late in life or to one's deathbed. Such a postponement was even prescribed by synodal regulations.[8] In the Eastern Churches after 391 we can observe a relaxation of the procedures of this strict public penance. It was increasingly replaced by individual confession to a spiritual guide (often a monk, who need not necessarily be a priest or bishop, if he enjoyed great respect as a spiritual person: "monk's confession"). Then as now, the Eastern Churches attributed the power to forgive sins to liturgical elements apart from the sacrament of reconciliation, e.g., the ascending smoke of incense.

The first notable change took place in a process witnessed from the sixth century onward. The Irish and Anglo-Saxon region, in which influences from the Eastern Church have been demonstrated, consciously changed their previous practice of public penance. Now a repeated absolution by the priest, not only the bishop, following a confession which

8. See, in addition to the literature in n. 7, the works of A. Angenendt (Bibliographies 3, 4, 6 and 7).

might include less serious sins, was possible on any day of the year. At first the severe penances as assurance of repentance were retained, but it became possible very soon to commute them: to contributions of money, repeated prayers, flagellation, etc. This system of commutation necessitated detailed books of penances, and the practice was consequently dubbed "tariff penance." This new form of penitential practice came to the continent with the Irish and Scottish missionaries, and the penitential books of the eighth century show that it had spread everywhere.[9] Church officials tried vainly to resist this new practice, but by the year 1000 it had triumphed. On the whole, however, it does not appear to have made confession a popular practice, since at the time of the Fourth Lateran Council in 1215 it was regarded as necessary to establish official rules for a minimum frequency of confession: every believer who had reached the "age of decision," that is, the age when she or he could understand what sin is, must confess all sins at least once a year (only in Latin, DS 812). The principal motive for this rigorous rule was probably the desire to "net" as many believers as possible through pastoral care.

As Augustinian sacramental theology was transmitted to the Church of the early Middle Ages, ecclesial penitential practice was referred to as the "sacrament of reconciliation" or "sacrament of confession." Since the rise of Scholastic concepts of sacrament and the development of the idea of seven sacraments in the middle of the twelfth century, the *sacramentum paenitentiae* (sacrament of penance) has been counted among the seven sacraments in the narrower sense. The most serious discussion was devoted to the question: whether the priest's absolution acts as a cause of God's removal of sin. Until the middle of the thirteenth century this question was answered in the negative, but then came the second decisive shift in the understanding of this sacrament. From William of Auvergne, Hugh of St. Cher, and William of Middleton onward, we find the theory that the effect of the priest's absolution is God's forgiveness of sins. Bonaventure (d. 1274) and Thomas Aquinas adopted this teaching, and it was subsequently adopted by the Catholic Church. Thomas Aquinas developed a subtle, logically consistent theory to maintain the teaching that God alone forgives sins. According to his idea, the sacrament—the absolution—does not effect

9. On this subject also, see the research of A. Angenendt on pious practices in the early Middle Ages.

the "pouring forth" or production of divine grace; rather, it affects
the internal process in the human person in which he or she opens
himself or herself to God's grace in such a way that it can really remove the guilt that is within.[10] But there always remains the possibility that a person, through a lack of faith or love, may close himself or
herself inwardly against God; thus even in Scholastic theory the sacrament does not work "automatically" or have control over God's grace.

Earlier theological insights into the power of contrition to forgive
sins were combined with this teaching on absolution in this way: true
contrition accomplishes the removal of sins in the same way as does
the sacrament, as just described, since, if it is true repentance, it also
involves an inward longing for the sacrament. If a sinner comes to confession with only "imperfect" contrition, it is transformed by the power
of the sacrament into "perfect" contrition. The Franciscan theologian
John Duns Scotus (d. 1308) simplified this idea in a formula that was
acceptable to the Church: "imperfect" contrition is sufficient, since
sin is forgiven not by contrition but only by the communication of grace
in absolution. According to Thomas, the sacramental sign of the sacrament of reconciliation consists in the "acts of the penitent," that is,
in what the repentant sinner does, and in the priestly absolution. The
penitent's actions (contrition, confession, satisfaction) are the "matter" of the sacrament, and the absolution is its "form." For Duns
Scotus, the acts of the penitent are only an indispensable precondition for the sacramental sign; the sacrament consists only in the judicial words of the priest. In the first millennium, petitionary prayers
dominated the liturgy of the sacrament of reconciliation. Afterward,
they shrank to a brief optative formula combined with an indicative
formula of absolution spoken by the priest: "I absolve you from your
sins." With the shift in the theology of penance in the thirteenth century, the indicative formula of absolution was declared to be the only
"form" of this sacrament. This entailed the loss of any recognition that
the sacrament of reconciliation is a community liturgy, in which the
congregation's prayer for and with the sinner is essential.

10. H. Vorgrimler, *Buße und Krankensalbung*, especially 131–138.

9.5 Ecclesial Decisions

Questioning of the sacrament of reconciliation began with a critique of unworthy ministers; justified demands for reforms often ended in an attempt to challenge the right of a sacrament or an institution to exist.[11] In the midst of the confusion created by the conflicts with the Cathari and the Waldensians, the Fourth Lateran Council in 1215 reaffirmed the possibility of doing penance: "If, after receiving baptism, anyone shall have lapsed into sin, he can always be restored through true penance" (NR 920/DS 802; see the familiar passage NR 926/DS 855).

The Council of Constance in 1415, against John Wycliffe, extended its protection to the confession of sins (NR 626/DS 1157), and in 1418 affirmed the Church's penitential practice and priestly power against Wycliffe and Jan Hus (NR 627-629/DS 1260, 1261, 1265). In the decree of 1439, which, in the context of the Council of Florence's efforts at reunion of the Churches, attempted to impose Roman Catholic teaching on the separated Armenians, the Council followed Thomas Aquinas in writing:

> The fourth sacrament is penance. *Its quasi-matter* consists in the actions of the penitent which are divided into *three parts.* The first of these is *contrition* of the heart, which requires that he be sorry for the sin committed with the resolve not to sin in the future. The second is oral *confession* which requires that the sinner confess to his priest in their integrity all the sins he remembers. The third is *satisfaction* for the sins according to the judgment of the priest, which is mainly achieved by prayer, fasting and almsgiving. The *form* of this sacrament is the words of absolution spoken by the priest when he says: I absolve you. The *minister* of this sacrament is the priest who has authority to absolve, either ordinary or by commission from his superior. The *effect* of this sacrament is absolution from sins (NR 630/DS 1323).

The Reformers' teachings on penance cannot be adequately described in a short space.[12] Martin Luther's concentration on the justification of sinners by faith alone led him to emphasize the internal penitential disposition that should mark the whole life of believers, since God's grace accomplishes nothing for those who do not acknowl-

11. On conflicts concerning penance and Church reactions, see ibid., 154–159.
12. Ibid., 159–166 (bibliography); J. Lell in *NHthG* I (1984) 165–170; K.-H. zur Mühlen in *EKL* I (1986) 602–603.

edge their sins. Closely united with this is believers' mutual forgiveness. Luther found that the Church teachings and practices concerning complete contrition, satisfaction, absolution (and purgatory) conflicted with the gospel's teaching on sinners' being forgiven by God alone; consequently, he rejected them from the start. In Matthew 16:19 and 18:18 he saw the beginnings of external penance and a word of absolution that furnished sufficient grounds for private confession, which he favored, but without an effort to confess all sins individually. After a certain hesitation, however, he denied the dignity of a sacrament to this procedure, since the New Testament gives no evidence of divine institution of a sacramental sign. He regarded baptism as *the* sacrament for forgiveness of sins, and he saw all legitimate Christian efforts to do penance as a return to baptism. Philip Melanchthon shared Luther's doubts about the sacramentality of penitential practice, but, while prescribing only a general confession of sins, he gave this practice a higher value than Luther did. Individual absolution was very important to him as a certification of divine forgiveness. The *Confessio Augustana* included absolution among the sacraments and spoke in favor of retaining private confession (though this is only human law). Although for Melanchthon penance and "mortification" were indispensable, he could not accept the Church's ideas of contrition and the distinctions it drew, since he saw here an emphasis on works of human achievement and not on the effects of the Holy Spirit. Zwingli and Calvin demanded a public ecclesial penitential discipline, but they did not recognize the sacrament. Calvin saw baptism as the only sacrament of reconciliation, but permitted private confession as a form of counseling. Of course, all the Reformers agreed in rejecting an official priesthood with judicial powers; they attributed to every Christian the power to absolve, that is, to strengthen others in faith. They regarded as unjust the practices of the Roman Catholic Church in reserving the absolution of some sins to higher authority and in conveying jurisdictional authority to give absolution.

After Leo X had already condemned some of Luther's theses in 1520, including several relating to penitential practice (NR 631-640/DS 1445-1454), the Council of Trent dealt with the sacrament of reconciliation for the first time at its sixth session in 1547, in connection with the teaching on justification:

> Chapter 14: Those who Sin after Justification and their Restoration to Grace. Those who through sin have forfeited the grace of justification

they had received, can be justified again when, awakened by God, they make the effort to regain through the sacrament of penance and by the merits of Christ the grace they have lost. This manner of justification is the restoration of the sinner which the holy Fathers aptly called "the second plank after the shipwreck of the loss of grace." For Christ Jesus instituted the sacrament of penance for those who fall into sin after baptism, when He said: "Receive the Holy Spirit. If you forgive the sins of any, they are forgiven; if you retain the sins of any, they are retained" (Jn 20:22-23).

Hence it must be taught that the repentance of a Christian after his fall into sin differs vastly from repentance at the time of baptism. It includes not only giving up sins and detesting them, or "a broken and contrite heart" (Ps 51:17), but also their sacramental confession or at least the desire to confess them when a suitable occasion will be found, and the absolution of a priest; it also includes satisfaction by fasts, almsgiving, prayer and other pious exercises of the spiritual life, not indeed for the eternal punishment which, together with the guilt, is remitted by the reception or the desire of the sacrament, but for the temporal punishment which, as sacred Scripture teaches, is not always entirely remitted, as is done in baptism, to those who, ungrateful to the grace of God they have received, have grieved the Holy Spirit (cf. Eph 4:30) and have not feared to violate the temple of God (cf. 1 Cor 3:17). Of this form of repentance it is written: "Remember from what you have fallen, repent and do the works you did at first" (Rev 2:5); and again: "Godly grief produces a repentance that leads to salvation" (2 Cor 7:10); and again: "Repent" (Mt 3:2; 4:17); and: "Bear fruit that befits repentance" (Mt 3:8) (NR 812-813/DS 1542-1543).

This teaching is echoed in canons 29 and 30:

> 29. If anyone says that the one who has fallen after baptism cannot rise again through God's grace; or that he can indeed recover the justice lost, but by faith alone without the sacrament of penance, contrary to what the holy Roman and universal Church, instructed by Christ the Lord and His apostles, has always professed, observed and taught, *anathema sit.*

> 30. If anyone says that after the grace of justification has been received the guilt is so remitted and the debt of eternal punishment so blotted out for any repentant sinner, that no debt of temporal punishment remains to be paid, either in this world or in the other, in purgatory, before access can be opened to the kingdom of heaven, *anathema sit* (NR 847-848/DS 1579-1580).

The whole context is very important, since here the council emphasized the absolute initiative of God's grace in the justification of sinners, but also stressed the opportunity for human beings to act
positively on the basis of the justification received and to struggle actively against sin.

At the fourteenth session in 1551, the council adopted a *Doctrine
on the Sacrament of Penance* in nine chapters (NR 641-659/DS 1667-1693)
and fifteen canons. The teaching defends the existence of the sacrament, instituted "principally" in the words of Jesus in John 20:22-23
(chapter 1). It should be recalled that in the language of Scholastic theology the "institution" can be effected by the exalted Lord acting
through the Holy Spirit. The teaching deals with the difference between
baptism and penance (chapter 2). It describes the sacrament's "form"
and "quasi-matter" (the acts of the penitent), and calls "reconciliation with God" the "reality (*res*) and effect" of the sacrament (chapter 3). It presents the Catholic view of contrition, distinguishing clearly
between "perfect" and "imperfect" types. Whenever contrition is
genuine, according to the council, it is "a gift of God and a prompting
of the Holy Spirit" (chapter 4). Emphasizing the judicial authority of
the priests, the council demands the confession of all mortal sins "of
which penitents after a diligent self-examination are conscious" (chapter 5). It stresses that only priests—but all priests, including bad ones—
can absolve, and this absolution is not a declaration of a pardon that
has already taken place, but is a genuine remission of sins; this is established by the "power of the keys," which in Matthew 18:18 and
John 20:23 is bestowed only on bishops and priests, and not on all the
faithful (chapter 6). Jurisdiction and the reservation of absolution of
particularly serious sins for pedagogical reasons are defended in chapter
7. Chapters 8 and 9 distinguish guilt and punishment and present the
meaning of expiating the punishment due to sin by works of penance.
The canons read:

> 1. If anyone says that in the Catholic Church penance is not truly and
> properly a sacrament, instituted by Christ our Lord to reconcile the faith-
> ful with God Himself as often as they fall into sin after baptism, *anathema
> sit*.
> 2. If anyone confuses the sacraments and says that baptism itself is
> the sacrament of penance, as though these two sacraments were not dis-
> tinct, and that, therefore, penance is not correctly called "the second
> plank after shipwreck," *anathema sit*.

3. If anyone says that these words of the Lord Savior: "Receive the Holy Spirit. If you forgive the sins of any, they are forgiven; if you retain the sins of any, they are retained" (Jn 20:22-23), are not to be understood as referring to the power of forgiving and retaining sins in the sacrament of penance, as the Catholic Church has always understood them from the beginning; but if he distorts them, in contradiction with the institution of this sacrament, to make them refer to the authority of preaching the Gospel, *anathema sit*.

4. If anyone denies that for the full and perfect remission of sins three acts are required of the penitent, constituting as it were the matter of the sacrament of penance, namely, contrition, confession and satisfaction, which are called the three parts of penance; or says that there are only two parts of penance, namely the terrors of a conscience stricken by the realization of sin, and the faith derived from the Gospel or from absolution, by which one believes that his sins are forgiven him through Christ, *anathema sit*.

5. If anyone says that the contrition which is evoked by examination, consideration and hatred of sins, whereby one recounts his years in the bitterness of his soul (cf. Is 38:15), reflecting on the grievousness, the multitude and baseness of his sins, the loss of eternal happiness and the incurring of eternal damnation, along with the resolve of amendment, is not a true and beneficial sorrow and does not prepare for grace, but makes a man a hypocrite and a greater sinner; or finally that this sorrow is forced and not free and voluntary, *anathema sit*.

6. If anyone denies that sacramental confession was instituted, and is necessary for salvation, by divine Law; or says that the manner of confessing secretly to a priest alone, which the Catholic Church has always observed from the beginning and still observes, is at variance with the institution and command of Christ and is a human invention, *anathema sit*.

7. If anyone says that for the remission of sins in the sacrament of penance it is not necessary by divine Law to confess each and all mortal sins which one remembers after a due and diligent examination, also secret ones, and those against the last two precepts of the decalogue, as also the circumstances that change the species of a sin; but says that such a confession is useful only to instruct and console the penitent, and that in olden times it was observed only in order to impose a canonical penance; or says that those who endeavor to confess all sins want to leave nothing to the divine mercy to pardon; or finally that it is not allowed to confess venial sins, *anathema sit*.

8. If anyone says that confession of all sins as it is observed in the Church is impossible and is a human tradition which pious people must abolish; or that it is not binding on each and all of the faithful of Christ

of either sex once a year in accordance with the Constitution of the great Lateran Council, and that for this reason the faithful of Christ are to be persuaded not to confess during Lent, *anathema sit.*

9. If anyone says that the sacramental absolution of the priest is not a judicial act but a mere ministry of pronouncing and declaring to him who confesses that his sins are forgiven, provided only he believes himself absolved, even if the priest does not absolve seriously but in jest; or says that the confession of the penitent is not required in order that the priest be able to absolve him, *anathema sit.*

10. If anyone says that priests who are in mortal sin do not have the power of binding and loosing, or that priests are not the only ministers of absolution, but that to each and all of the faithful it was said: "whatever you bind on earth shall be bound in heaven, and whatever you loose on earth shall be loosed in heaven" (Mt 18:18) and "if you forgive the sins of any, they are forgiven; if you retain the sins of any, they are retained" (Jn 20:23), so that by virtue of these words everyone could absolve from sins, from public ones merely by correction, if the sinner complies, and from secret ones by voluntary confession, *anathema sit.*

11. If anyone says that bishops do not have the right to reserve cases to themselves, except such as pertain to external government, and that therefore, the reservation of cases does not prevent a priest from truly absolving from such reserved sins, *anathema sit.*

12. If anyone says that the whole punishment is always remitted by God together with the guilt and that the satisfaction of penitents is nothing else but the faith by which they realize that Christ has satisfied for them, *anathema sit.*

13. If anyone says, concerning temporal punishments, that no satisfaction is made to God through the merits of Christ by means of the punishments inflicted by Him and patiently borne, or of those imposed by the priest, or finally of those voluntarily undertaken, as fasts, prayers, almsgiving or other works of piety; and that, therefore, the best penance is merely a new life, *anathema sit.*

14. If anyone says that the satisfactions by which penitents atone for their sins through Jesus Christ are not a worship of God but traditions of men which obscure the doctrine of grace, the true worship of God and the benefit of Christ's death itself, *anathema sit.*

15. If anyone says that the keys have been given to the Church only to loose and not also to bind and that, therefore, the priests, when imposing penances on those who confess, act contrary to the purpose of the keys, and to the institution of Christ; and that it is a fiction that, after the eternal punishment has been removed by virtue of the keys, there often remains a temporal punishment to be expiated, *anathema sit* (NR 660–674/DS 1701–1715).

It is a subject for theological discussion to what extent the council here desired to make binding dogmatic definitions, and to what extent the threats of excommunication in the canons are only legal prescriptions that appeared indispensable at the time.[13] This is true particularly of canons 6, 7, and 8. (The historical statement in canon 6, which was outside the council's competence, is not at issue.) The fact that a confession of sins is required by "divine law" follows from the existence of sacramental confession: human beings must acknowledge their sins before God. The demand that they do so by individual confession to a priest is not *equally* necessary to the sacrament of penance. This demand advanced by the Church is not a contradiction to what Jesus Christ revealed and set in motion. But in principle it is compatible with other forms of confession of sins—an important insight for ecumenism. Canon 7 should be interpreted on the basis of this fundamental standpoint in canon 6. Here the Church places special emphasis on obedience. If sacramental absolution is described in Scotist terms as a judicial act (canon 9), this is not meant to compare the sacrament of penance to a secular judicial process. To describe the sacrament as making present the gracious judgment of God does not contradict the Council of Trent.

Trent's teaching on penance determined both thought and practice in the Catholic Church well into the twentieth century. Repeated efforts at restoration of individual confession within Protestantism indicate that ecumenical dialogue on this sacrament is not a hopeless undertaking.[14]

The most fundamental yield of extensive research into the history of penance was the rediscovery of the ecclesial dimension of penitential practice. In the language of Scholastic theology the *res et sacramentum*, the second effect of the sacrament of penance, was recognized to be the reconciliation of the repentant sinner with the Church, while the final effect (in the realm of grace) is reconciliation with God.[15] This opened the possibility of a clearer recognition of the visible sign of this sacrament and of renewing its presence in the liturgy. The absolute

---

13. For more detail, see H. Vorgrimler, *Buße und Krankensalbung*, 177–182.

14. Ibid., 166–168 (bibliography); in addition, see E. Bezzel, *Frei zum Eingeständnis. Geschichte und Praxis der evangelischen Einzelbeichte* (Stuttgart: 1982).

15. This thesis is explained in more detail in K. Rahner, *Schriften* VIII, 469; cf. H. Vorgrimler, *Buße und Krakensalbung*, 195–196.

priority of divine grace that moves sinners to repentance and reconciliation is not thereby diminished.

The Second Vatican Council called for a reform of the sacrament of penance (SC 72), referring in this context to the Church's role in penitential practice (SC 109). The renewed view of the sacrament is expressed in a theological statement: "Those who approach the sacrament of penance obtain pardon from the mercy of God for offenses committed against [God]. They are at the same time reconciled with the Church, which they have wounded by their sins, and which by charity, example, and prayer seeks their conversion" (LG 11). There is also a special reference to the bishops' responsibility for penitential discipline (LG 26; on priests' role in penance LG 28, PO 5).

The crisis of the sacrament of reconciliation in the Catholic Church did not begin with Vatican Council II. Resistance to a morality that has been one-sidedly developed as a morality of guilt and places Christians constantly under indictment is in harmony with the liberating, forward-looking message of Jesus. The statements found in the New Testament and the tradition about sin that leads to eternal death make it doubtful that such deadly sins occur frequently in the life of an average Christian. Christians' value systems and consciousness of guilt have not changed without reason. Rather, attention has shifted from the microstructure of individual faults to the macrostructure, in which we encounter the truly burdensome facts of dehumanization, oppression, seduction, and exploitation, and the destruction of the human and natural world. It is not true that divine revelation refers only to the destructive acts that are produced by (serious) sin in the heart of the individual sinner; it points instead, in many concrete examples, to the evil that is done to fellow human beings and is not eliminated by a merely symbolic reconciliation. The decline of individualistic narrowness does not indicate less willingness to engage in dialogue; rather, what people are looking for is a genuine situation of exchange of views and a real ability to engage in dialogue. Many of those who are in despair or seek counsel have need of persons with therapeutic skills. On the other hand, despite the urgency of rendering help in desperate situations, we must not forget that the sacrament of penance is part of the Church's liturgy.[16] A number of social and therapeutic *desiderata*

16. Is it really too much to ask that canon law recognize the fact that a sacrament is liturgy? In describing the various liturgical forms of the sacrament of pen-

were fulfilled by the penitential services that have developed since 1947. When, in line with the wishes of Vatican Council II, the sacrament of penance received a renewed form, community services of reconciliation were given a fixed place in the Church's penitential practice. At the same time, an effort was made to preserve Trent's prescription of individual confession of serious sins, while doing justice to the request for "general absolution" following a general, communal confession of sins. In the *Pastoral Norms* of the Congregation for the Doctrine of the Faith (1972)[17] and in a new *Ordo Paenitentiae* from the Congregation for Divine Worship (1973)[18] the Church leadership in Rome insisted that, after a general absolution, penitents must make an individual sacramental confession of any mortal sins, if there is opportunity (cf. CIC 1983, canon 961). If there is substantial doubt whether a sin was serious or mortal, of course, the obligation of confession does not exist. The reform of the liturgy expanded the prayer-form of the sacrament even in the case of individual confession: after a confession of God's reconciliation with the world through his Son and the sending of the Holy Spirit for the forgiveness of sins there follows a petition: "Through the Church's assistance may God grant you pardon and peace." Only then does the priest extend his hands and pronounce absolution: "I absolve you from your sins in the name of the Father and of the Son and of the Holy Spirit."

9.6 Summary

The sacrament of reconciliation is the liturgy that, in the form of petition, confession, and absolution, makes present the gracious judgment of God on repentant sinners. Within the Church it is a sensible sign of human conversion from a situation of having gone astray, something that does not simply happen to us, but in which we ourselves

ance, R. Weigand, "Das Bußsakrament," *HKR* 692–707, pursues a thoroughly restrictive, legalistic trend; see 695–698. This reaches its ultimate at the point when it is said that a confession by telephone (with telephone absolution) is to be recognized as valid (698–699). Such an action may make therapeutic sense, in reassuring scrupulous people, but it certainly has nothing to do with the Church's penitential tradition and liturgy.

17. The text is in AAS 64 (1972) 510–514.

18. R. Kaczynski, *Enchiridion Documentorum Instaurationis liturgicae* I (1963-1973) (Turin: 1976) 981–997.

actively cooperate. The individual's desire for sacramental and non-sacramental penance is a share in the penance of the penitential Church, supported by the constant memory of the suffering and death of Jesus and its connection with the sin of humanity. In the sacrament of reconciliation there is still an element of the ancient Church's procedure for setting itself apart, but the Church can really distance itself only from sin, and not from sinners, since their guilt is the guilt of the Church itself. When the Church accepts the confession of sins and speaks God's word of reconciliation, it is not exercising a judicial authority over human actions. The sacrament of reconciliation is the effective memory of God's gracious judgment, in which the love of the Father through the Son and for the Son's sake, in the Holy Spirit, removes all human guilt.

9.7   *Indulgences*

The theological background of the Catholic concept of indulgences[19] is the doctrine of "punishment for sins," or better, the "painful consequences of sin." It is rooted in early Christian penitential practice, in which the Church indicated its conviction that God's removal of the guilt of sin from a human life did not automatically cause the consequences of that sin (both the suffering caused by the sin and the sinner's evil inclinations, etc.) to disappear. These consequences had to be obliterated gradually and with considerable effort, through penitential works, while the Church stood by the penitent in solidarity and prayer.

Historically, indulgences meant the release from works of penance, which were replaced by the promise of the Church's prayer and the imposition of a substitute action. In this sense, it was first in eleventh-century France that bishops and confessors permitted a substitution of the work to be done. At the end of the eleventh and in the course of the twelfth century the popes took up this new practice, giving indulgences to those who took part in or donated money for a crusade. Even in the twelfth century this custom encountered strong theological opposition. Beginning with Hugo of St. Cher (d. 1263), Scholastic

---

19. For basic information see G. A. Benrath in *TRE* I (1977) 347–364; H. Vorgrimler, *Buße und Krankensalbung*, 203–214 (with bibliography); R. Henseler, "Der Ablaß," *HKR* 707–712.

theology developed a teaching on "the treasury of the Church," the store of superfluous graces won by Jesus Christ and the saints, from which the Pope could grant indulgences. Theologians like Albert, Bonaventure, and Thomas adopted this view and provided it with further theological underpinning; Clement VI adopted it in 1343 (NR 677–679/DS 1025–1027). The requirement of confession before gaining the indulgence gives a glimpse of the remnant of the connection with ancient penitential practice. But it soon began to be taught that indulgences could also be applied to the dead. In the late Middle Ages, in the fourteenth and fifteenth centuries, indulgences became a commercial source of funds controlled by popes and bishops, and for the people in general it was the occasion of a richly developed set of superstitions. Sharp theological criticism arose repeatedly.

Popes defended the doctrine of indulgences against John Wycliffe and Jan Hus (NR 680–681/DS 1266–1267) and against Martin Luther's attack on the Church "treasury" and condemnation of indulgences as a "pious fraud" (NR 682–687/DS 1647–1652). The Council of Trent, in an honest effort at reform, warned against abuses and against too many indulgences, but it defended the doctrine and taught that it was "most salutary and . . . to be retained" (NR 688–689/DS 1835). The council did not take a position on Leo X's teaching of 1518 that indulgences are the remission of a temporal punishment in the sight of God for sins whose guilt has already been removed, and that indulgences are granted by the authority of the Church from its treasury of merits, for the living through absolution, and for the dead through prayers of petition (only in Latin, DS 1447–1449).

In light of the research on the origin of indulgences within the history of dogma, Bernhard Poschmann (d. 1955) and Karl Rahner sought to correct the legal and jurisdictional perspective on indulgences and to understand them as a particular type of Church petition on behalf of a penitent sinner in the working off of the unhappy temporal consequences of his or her sins. This approach was also intended to eliminate the idea that indulgences are easier actions substituting for necessary penances. In his reform of indulgences in 1967, Paul VI partially accepted this view of the matter. He dealt with the working off of the consequences of sin and with Christians' mutual aid to one another in overcoming sin. He also referred to the teaching on the "treasury of the Church," but said that "it is Christ the Redeemer Himself in whom the satisfaction and merits of His redemption still exist and retain their efficacy." He preferred not to regard indulgences as prayers of petition, but rather as an authoritative distribution from the Church's treasury (NR 690–692). In this text the Pope also declared that it belongs to the freedom of the children of God to decide whether they wish to gain indulgences or not.

Current canon law views indulgences as "remission before God of the temporal punishment for sin the guilt of which is already forgiven, which a properly disposed member of the Christian faithful obtains under certain and definite conditions with the help of the Church which, as the minister of redemption, dispenses and applies authoritatively the treasury of the satisfactions of Christ and the saints" (CIC 1983, canon 992). Indulgences can be applied to the dead by way of suffrage (canon 994); the Apostolic See alone can give to others the power to grant indulgences (canon 995). The handbook of indulgences was edited and reissued as *Enchiridion indulgentiarum* (Rome 1986).

The worldwide crisis regarding indulgences may signal mistrust in the Church's claim to have at its disposal the "redemptive merits" of Jesus Christ, which in principle are not within our dimension at all. This need not mean, however, that interpersonal compassion and mutual petition have ceased within the Church.

Bibliography 7

Sacrament of Penance

Amato, A. *Il sacramento della penitenza nella teologia greco-ortodossa. Studi storico-dogmatici (sec. XVI-XX).* Saloniki: 1982.

Angenendt, A. "Missa specialis. Zugleich ein Beitrag zur Entstehung der Privatmessen." In K. Hauck, ed. *Frühmittelalterliche Studien* 17 (Berlin: 1983) 153–221 (also on penitential manuals).

_____. "Theologie und Liturgie der mittelalterlichen Toten-Memoria." In K. Schmid and J. Wollasch, eds. *Memoria* (Munich: 1984) 79–199, at 131–156: "Die Buße im Früh-Mittelalter," and at 164–168 "Sterbebuße."

Bäumler, C., and W. Neidhart, eds. "Seelsorge, Schuld und Vergebung." *Theologia Practica* 19 (1984) 267–354.

Bernhard, J. "Le Sacrement de pénitence au Concile de Trente." *Revue de droit canonique* 34 (1984) 249–273.

Calvo Espiga, A. "Algunas orientaciones actuales de la teología de las indulgencias." *Burgense* 21 (1980) 417–450.

Catholicisme X (1985) 1007–1061 (Péché), 1125–1168 (Pénitence).

De Clerck, P. "Célébrer la pénitence, ou la réconciliation?" *Revue de théologie de Louvain* 13 (1982) 387–424.

Delumeau, J. *Le péché et la peur. La culpabilisation en Occident (XIIIe-XVIIe siècles).* Paris: 1983.

De Margerie, B. "La mission sacerdotale de retenir les péchés en liant les pécheurs." *Recherches de science religieuse* 34 (1984) 300–317, with continuation up to Trent.

De Martel, G. "Les textes pénitentiels du ms Lisbonne 232." *Sacris Erudiri* 27 (1984) 443–460.

Der sakramentale Dienst der Versöhnung. Concilium 8:1 (1971).

Dooley, C. *Devotional Confession. An Historical and Theological Study*. Louvain: 1982.

Dooley, K. "From penance to confession." *The Celtic Contribution: Bijdragen* 43 (1982) 390–411.

Fleming, T. L. *The Second Vatican Council's teaching on the sacrament of penance and the communal nature of the sacrament*. Rome: 1981.

Frend, W. H. C. *Saints and sinners in the early church*. London: 1985 (history of penance in the first six centuries).

Gaudemet, J., "Le débat sur la confession dans la Distinction I du de penitentia (Décret de Gratian, c. 33, q. 3)." *Zeitschrift der Savigny-Stiftung für Rechtsgeschichte, Kanonist. Abt.* 102 (1985) 52–75.

Groupe de la Bussière. *Pratiques de la Confession. Des Pères du désert à Vatican II. Quinze études d'histoire*. Paris: 1983.

Guilluy, P. "Pardon et péché dans la nouvelle alliance." *Initiation à la pratique de la théologie* IV. 2d ed. Paris: 1984, 268–294.

Hägele, G. *Das Paenitentiale Vallicellianum I. Ein oberitalienischer Zweig der frühmittelalterlichen Bußbücher*. Sigmaringen: 1984.

Hallonsten, G. *Satisfactio bei Tertullian*. Malmö: 1984, 120–151.

Henseler, R. "Der Ablaß." *HKR* 707–712.

Jorissen, H. "Die Bußtheologie der Confessio Augustana." *Catholica* 35 (1981) 58–59.

Kerff, F. "Das Paenitentiale Pseudo-Gregorii III. Ein Zeugnis karolingischer Reformbestrebungen." *Zeitschrift der Savigny-Stiftung für Rechtsgeschichte. Kanonist. Abt.* 100 (1983) 46–63.

Lendi, R. *Die Wandelbarkeit der Buße*. Frankfurt und Berne: 1983.

Lozano Sebastián, F.-J. *La penitencia canónica en la España Romano-Visigóda*. Burgos: 1980.

Marliangéas, B. M. "Bulletin de théologie sacramentaire. Pénitence et réconciliation." *Revue des sciences philosophiques et théologiques* 66 (1982) 441–461.

Mélia, E. "L'acte ecclésial de la réconciliation dans l'Eglise orthodoxe." *Revue de droit canonique* 34 (1984) 336–348.

Merle, R. *Le pénitence et la peine*. Paris: 1985.

Metzger, M. "La pénitence dans les 'Constitutions Apostoliques.' " *Revue de droit canonique* 34 (1984) 224–234.

Mühlsteiger, J. "Exomologese." *Zeitschrift für katholische Theologie* 103 (1981) 1–32, 129–155, 257–288 (traces the confession of sins through the history of penance).

Munier, C. "La pastorale pénitentielle de St. Césaire d'Arles (503–543)." *Revue de droit canonique* 34 (1984) 235–244.

Nocke, F.-J. *Wort und Geste* (see Bibliography 1) 84–132.

Payer, P. J. "The humanism of the penitentials and the continuity of the penitential tradition." *Mediaeval Studies* 46 (1984) 340–354.

Penance and Reconciliation. International Bibliography 1975–1983. Strasbourg: 1984.

Peters, A. "Buße, Beichte, Schuldvergebung in evangelischer Theologie und Praxis." *Kerygma und Dogma* 28 (1982) 42–72.

Platelle, H. "Pratiques penitentielles et mentalités religieuses au Moyen Age." *Mélanges de science religieuse* 40 (1983) 129–155.

Sancho, J., and others. *Reconciliación y penitencia*. Pamplona: 1983.

Schützeichel, H. *Katholische Calvin-Studien*. Trier: 1980, 29–48 (Calvin's attitude to the sacrament of penance).

Tillard, J.-M. R., and others. "Le sacrement de la reconciliation." *Studie Moralia* 21 (1983) 3–202.

Vergebung in einer universöhnten Welt: Concilium 22:2 (1986).

Vögtle, A. *Offenbarungsgeschehen und Wirkungsgeschichte*. Freiburg: 1985, 109–140: "Das Problem der Herkunft von 'Mt 16,17–19' " (bibliography).

Vorgrimler, H. *Buße und Krankensalbung*. Handbuch der Dogmengeschichte IV/3. Freiburg: 1978 (bibliography).

Vorgrimler, H., and J. Lell. "Buße/Vergebung." *NHthG* I (1984) 150–170 (bibliography).

Weigand, R. "Das Bußsakrament." *HKR* 692–707.

Zalba, M. "La doctrina católica sobre la integridad de la confesión." *Gregorianum* 64 (1983) 95–138.

10

Anointing of the Sick

10.1 *Biblical Foundations*

The biblical texts on which the practice of anointing the sick has rested since the early days of the Church, Mark 6:12-13 and James 5:14-15, should be seen in connection with Jesus' and the early Church communities' attitude toward the sick. Both the Old and New Testaments traced sickness, at least in large part, to the destructive effects of sin, and saw both sickness and sin also as results of the action of evil forces on human beings. A naive, demythologizing theology presumed to be able to set aside biblical statements about evil powers and forces as something that passed away along with the ancient view of the world. But the recognition that spiritual energies beyond the individual level can influence human beings, and that the negative decisions and attitudes that have collected within humanity over time can "poison" people and make them sick, has revived the older view of things—of course, with the elimination of the notion that demons are some sort of ghostly entities. Jesus' activity was totally directed to disrupting the context of evil and making it possible for new attitudes and relationships to enter: that new set of attitudes and relationships is called "the reign of God." In the beginning stage of the reign of

God that means an attack on all the elements in human life that alien-
ate people and make them ill, with the promise that in the perfected
reign of God sickness and death will be destroyed. The designation
of the "reign of God" as the central theme of Jesus' activity means
also that Jesus was primarily concerned to fulfill the will of God, which
certainly included attention to those in need of help and healing of
human relationships, but which also inescapably required the recognition, praise, and glorification of God as the creator and Father. Jesus
did not focus his activity on healing, as did many great figures in antiquity. His work among the sick was always a practical announcement
of the rule of God, and was often expressly connected with the driv-
ing out of evil and the forgiveness of sins. To put it another way: these
were not medical and therapeutic, but more properly real-symbolic,
charismatic actions.[1] In them Jesus made it evident to the senses how
the merciful God accepts human beings—both sinners and the sick—
in their need.

According to Mark 6:7-13, Jesus included the Twelve, as his companions and messengers, in his mission in such a way that they also
preached, healed, and exorcised. In doing so, they anointed with oil,
the healing aid generally recognized in the time of Jesus. Of course,
in antiquity bodily contact in itself was an important part of the healing process. Jesus practiced it in various ways (including the use of
saliva: John 9:6). The tradition gives special notice to his imposition
of hands in healing (Luke 4:40). The attention of the earliest Christian
communities to the sick, not only in a charitable and therapeutic sense,
but also in word and symbolic action, is also very close in time to Jesus
himself. In the instructional work of the late first century circulated
under the name of James, "the brother of the Lord," the author speaks
of the illness of fellow Christians in connection with the subject of
prayer: "Are any among you sick? They should call for the elders of
the church and have them pray over them, anointing them with oil
in the name of the Lord. The prayer of faith will save the sick, and
the Lord will raise them up; and anyone who has committed sins will
be forgiven. Therefore confess your sins to one another, and pray for

---

1. R. Pesch, *Das Markusevangelium* (Freiburg: 1976) I, 127. Cf. also H. Vorgrimler, *Buße und Krankensalbung* (Freiburg: 1978) 216-218 (bibliography); W. Kirchschläger, *Jesu exorzistisches Wirken aus der Sicht des Lukas* (Klosterneuburg: 1981); O.
Betz and others, "Heilung/Heilungen," *TRE* XIV (1985) 763-774; W. Schrage, "Heil
und Heilung im Neuen Testament," *Evangelische Theologie* 46 (1986) 197-214.

one another, so that you may be healed. The prayer of the righteous is powerful and effective" (Jas 5:14-16). The words used for sickness here seem to refer to a serious illness, but are not restricted to the death agony. The elders, given the Jewish-Christian tone of the writing, would be the presiding officers of the community; their primary duty on behalf of the sick is prayer. Prayers offered in faith are promised a response consisting of salvation, raising up and (if necessary) the forgiveness of sins. If anointing with oil is done "in the name of the Lord," i.e., by calling on his name which brings salvation, what is being done is more accurately characterized as a symbolic action than as a medicinal practice. The hoped-for effect touches the health and salvation of the human person in a holistic sense, in which one aspect cannot be elevated above another. Sins, in the meaning of this letter, are not mere ordinary failings, but those that bring death (cf. Jas 1:15; 5:20). The initiative to healing and forgiving activity lies with God alone; the text gives no ground for seeing the actions it recommends as miraculous healings.

10.2 *The History of Anointing of the Sick*

Anointing of the sick was not recorded among liturgical actions in the first centuries of the Church; we find neither canonical regulations for its celebration nor theological reflections on it. The oldest texts in which there is mention of it are prayers for the blessing of the oils with which sick persons were anointed. These are found from the beginning of the third century onward:[2] the oil is to receive a new power in order that it may become a means of healing for soul and body. It could also be taken as a drink. The first non-liturgical text on anointing the sick is a letter from Innocent I in the year 416, in which for the first time the text of the Letter of James is cited in connection with anointing (NR 693-694/DS 216). The Pope here speaks about the correct way of handling the consecrated oil; there is no intention of presenting a comprehensive teaching on anointing of the sick. According to this letter, anointing with blessed oil is permitted for *all* Christians in their affliction and that of their families. But the oil can only be consecrated by the bishop. Bishops have the power to anoint; the text of James speaks of "presbyters" because the bishops, with their

2. H. Vorgrimler, *Buße und Krankensalbung*, 218–220: the oldest witnesses, with notes on sources.

numerous duties, cannot go to all those who are sick. The blessed oil (*chrisma*) is one of the sacraments (*genus est sacramenti*), and therefore penitents may not be anointed with it because (before reconciliation) they are prohibited from receiving the sacraments. This part of the letter was often cited in the Western Church and was included in the most important collections of ecclesial law. However, the very influential *Decretum Gratiani* (first half of the twelfth century) omitted just those passages that referred to the sick as recipients and to the faithful, i.e., the laity, as ministers of the sacrament.

According to sixth-century witnesses, Christians could still anoint themselves and their families with blessed oil in time of sickness (and not merely when in danger of death); magicians seem to have offered a certain degree of competition at the time. The findings up to this time are confirmed by Bede in the eighth century (d. 735). On the basis of James 5:16, Bede saw confession and reconciliation as the completion of anointing.

Beginning in the eighth century, and especially from the ninth century onward, the theology and practice of anointing the sick changed. It became, together with confession and Eucharist, the sacrament of the dying. The reasons for this were, in the first place, the serious life-long obligations that had to be accepted as a consequence of being anointed, comparable to penitential obligations; secondly, anointing was seen as a part of reconciliation. The order of the three sacraments was still in flux. Until the thirteenth century, anointing of the sick was carried out after confession and reconciliation and before the Eucharistic "viaticum." From that point onward until Vatican II it was universally given as the last of the three sacraments of the sick. It was reserved to the priest after the ninth century. The rite was not uniform. In some places the priest blessed the oil immediately before anointing the sick, and in other places the bishop blessed a special oil for the sick. Frequently, the five senses of the sick person were anointed, but there is attestation of more than twenty anointings, each with its own prayer. Sometimes the anointing was supposed to take place on seven successive days, and in some regions, as is still the case in the Byzantine rite today, and as Thomas Aquinas knew the rite, several priests were required for anointing. For various reasons, the practice was frightening, a circumstance that repeatedly put this sacrament in crisis.[3]

3. Ibid., 221–222, with examples and sources.

In Scholastic theology the anointing of the sick, which until the twelfth century was usually called *oleum infirmorum* after the consecrated oil, received the name *extrema unctio*, the last anointing, since it was now the *sacramentum exeuntium*, the sacrament of the dying. Anointing of the sick has been counted among the seven sacraments since that number gained acceptance in the first half of the twelfth century. Important high-Scholastic theologians ascribed its institution to the apostles, while others taught that Jesus Christ had instituted it, although, like confirmation, it had first been officially proclaimed by the apostles. The greatest theological problem regarding anointing of the sick was, for Scholastic theology, how to accurately account for its effect(s). Increasingly, the holistic view, and with it the aspect of bodily healing, receded into the background. Finally, the common view came to be that this sacrament eliminates the (last) obstacles to a person's entry into heavenly glory and perfects the Church's efforts for the salvation of the soul. For some seven hundred years thereafter, the "eschatologizing" and "spiritualizing" of this sacrament held the field.

10.3 *Ecclesial Decisions*

Before the Council of Trent, the anointing of the sick was treated with extreme brevity in official Church statements. In the thirteenth century it was mentioned three times among the other sacraments: in 1208 it was still "anointing of the sick," in 1254 it was called "extreme unction" (only Latin, DS 794, 833, 860). Martin V's catalogue of questions for followers of John Wycliffe and Jan Hus, in 1418, contains the statement that a Christian commits mortal sin if she or he shows contempt for the reception of the sacraments of confirmation, extreme unction, and marriage (only Latin, DS 1259). The sacramental doctrine of the *Decree for the Armenians*, taken from Thomas Aquinas, states:

> The fifth sacrament is extreme unction. Its *matter* is olive oil blessed by the bishop. This sacrament may not be given except to a sick person whose life is feared for. He is to be anointed on these parts: on the eyes on account of sight, on the ears on account of hearing, on the nostrils on account of smelling, on the mouth on account of taste and speech, on the hands on account of touch, on the feet on account of movement, on the loins on account of the lust seated there. The *form* of this sacra-

ment is as follows: through the holy anointing and through his benevolent mercy may the Lord forgive you your sins committed through sight, etc. Similarly with the other members. The *minister* of this sacrament is the priest. The *effect* is the healing of the mind and, as far as it is good for the soul, of the body as well. Of this sacrament blessed James the apostle says: "Is any among you sick? . . ." (Jas 5:14-15) (NR 695/DS 1324-1325).

While the Eastern Churches separated from Rome generally recognize anointing with oil with prayer as one of the seven sacraments instituted by Jesus Christ (though practice and opinion are quite different in the various Churches), the Reformers denied the sacramentality of anointing of the sick. Martin Luther and John Calvin saw the biblical witnesses as accounts of miraculous healing; the corresponding gift was not given to the later Church. They vigorously attacked the practice of anointing the dying. Luther opposed the sacramentality of anointing the sick with the observation that it was not instituted by Jesus Christ and had not been promised grace by him. But he included it among those aids, such as the use of holy water, through which a believer can achieve peace and forgiveness of sins.

The Council of Trent considered the defense of the sacramentality of anointing of the sick an urgent duty. In its fourteenth session in 1551 it adopted a *Doctrine on the Sacrament of Extreme Unction* in three chapters and four canons. The canons, with their special claim to obligation, read:

1. If anyone says that extreme unction is not truly and properly a sacrament instituted by Christ our Lord (cf. Mt 6:13) and promulgated by the blessed apostle James (Jas 5:14), but only a rite received from the Fathers or a human invention, *anathema sit*.

2. If anyone says that the sacred anointing of the sick neither confers grace, nor remits sins, nor comforts the sick; but that it does no longer exist as if it consisted only in the grace of healing of olden days, *anathema sit*.

3. If anyone says that the rite and usage of extreme unction which the holy Roman Church observes is contrary to the doctrine of the blessed apostle James and, therefore, must be changed; and that it can without sin be held in contempt by Christians, *anathema sit*.

4. If anyone says that the presbyters of the Church who, as blessed James exhorts, should be brought to anoint the sick are not priests or-

dained by a bishop but the senior members of each community, and that, for this reason, the proper minister of extreme unction is not only the priest, *anathema sit* (NR 700-703/DS 1716-1719).

Canon 1 contains no new dogma, since the sacramentality of anointing of the sick had already been dogmatically proclaimed in the seventh session of 1547 (NR 506/DS 1601); the biblical attestation is not part of the intent of the statement. Canon 2 rejects the Reformers' opinion, mentioned above, that the biblical witnesses refer to a gift of healing, which is a thing of the past. Canon 3 is consciously formulated with extreme care as regards historical fact; it indicates the manner in which the Church has sought and still seeks to reconcile rites of later origin with the New Testament: what comes later cannot contradict what is found in the Bible. Canon 4 protects the sacramental order. According to this canon, the priest is the proper, ordinary minister of anointing. That does not exclude the possibility that other, "extraordinary" ministers of anointing—for example, deacons—could be called.

The "doctrine" lays great stress on the place of extreme unction at the end of one's life. The sacrament is said to be "alluded to" in Mark 6:13, recommended to the faithful and promulgated by James; James also establishes the matter, form, minister, and effect of the sacrament. On this point, the council remarks that "the anointing very aptly represents the grace of the Holy Spirit with which the soul of the sick is invisibly anointed" (ch. 1: NR 697/DS 1695). This is further explained as removal of sins and their lingering effects, strengthening the soul of the sick person so that she or he may more easily bear the inconveniences and trials of illness and resist the temptations of the evil one, and "at times . . . when it is expedient for the salvation of the soul" the restoration of bodily health (ch. 2: NR 698/DS 1696). In this "doctrine" the bishops are mentioned before the priests as the proper ministers of anointing; the recipients are sick persons, "especially" those who are near death. This "especially" played an important role in the reorientation of the sacrament in the twentieth century, since Trent did not limit it exclusively to the dying (in ch. 3: only Latin, DS 1698). The teaching further states that the sacrament can be received more than once, in case the sick should recover after being anointed, and then again fall into a critical condition. On the historical question, the council's statements are similar to those in canon 3. It calls contempt for this sacrament a great sin and an offense to the Holy Spirit.

The Council of Trent thus succeeded in avoiding a one-sided theology. Its primary intent was to defend the sacramental institutionalization of anointing of the sick beyond the mere status of a charism, to show that Catholic practice was, in fact, not contrary to Scripture, and to teach the salvific importance of this sacrament for the sick. The opinion that anointing of the sick primarily represents a spiritual aid at the end of life was dominant, but the council did not insist dogmatically that this was a "sacrament of the dying." In subsequent centuries there were tendencies to expand the "eschatologizing" of this sacrament so as to make it a "consecration at death," or a "consecration of the resurrection body," but since the middle of the twentieth century there have also been efforts toward a renewal of "anointing of the sick."

These reform efforts[4] affected the Constitution on the Liturgy of the Second Vatican Council to the extent that the name "anointing of the sick" was chosen as more fitting, and the moment at which a Christian begins, because of sickness or the weakness of old age, to be in danger of death is described (SC 73). The order of the sacraments of the sick is said to be confession, anointing, and Eucharist (SC 74), and a revision of the anointings and prayers is proposed (SC 75). The council then taught, as a consequence of this new orientation, that "by the sacred anointing of the sick and the prayer of her priests, the whole Church commends those who are ill to the suffering and glorified Lord, asking that He may lighten their suffering and save them (cf. Jas 5:14-16). She exhorts them, moreover, to contribute to the welfare of the whole People of God by associating themselves freely with the passion and death of Christ (cf. Rom 8:17; Col 1:24; 2 Tim 2:11-12; 1 Pet 4:13)" (LG 11).

The requested revision brought the following result: the new *Order for the Consecration of Chrism, the Oil of Catechumens, and the Oil of the Sick* of 1970 reserves the blessing of oil to the bishop only as a general rule; in case of real need it can also be blessed by a priest. In the prayer of blessing, the effects of anointing are named: it is "a sacred sign of thy mercy that drives out sickness, pain and distress, a protection for body, soul and spirit." The revision of anointing of the sick itself[5] in

4. For an overview of both movements: ibid., 231–232, with source references.
5. R. Kaczynski, *Enchiridion Documentorum Instaurationis liturgicae I (1963-1973)* (Turin: 1976) 905–914.

1972, which is expressly stated to be only for the Latin rite (for that of the Eastern Churches, cf. OE 12, 27) restores to the sacrament its liturgical form. An introductory rite and service of the Word is followed by a silent imposition of hands by the "minister"; then comes a praise of the blessed oil (or, if necessary, the blessing of the oil). The simplified anointing is given on the forehead and hands, with the prayer: "Through this holy anointing may the Lord in the richness of his mercy help you; may he stand by you in the power of the Holy Spirit. May the Lord who frees you from sin save you, and in his grace may he raise you up." The anointing of the sick is to be given when anyone is seriously ill (also before an operation, or in the weakness of old age even when no illness is present). It can be given to a number of people at the same time, in the church or in another appropriate place. It can be repeated for a different illness, or if the original condition grows worse. It is intended not only to strengthen the faith of the sick person, but also to give expression to that faith.

The reform of this sacrament, with the radical changes in the "formula of administration" shows how much freedom the Catholic Church permits itself in the shaping of the sacraments.[6] It expresses in a very fortunate manner the fact that the sacrament is a liturgy, and that the sacramental "formula" is essentially a prayer of petition, an epiclesis of the Holy Spirit.[7]

10.4 Summary

The sacramental locus of anointing of the sick is clearly illness, and not the end of life. But when the Church recognizes sickness as the place for a sacrament, it is taken seriously as a threat to human life. Whenever it is serious, it is a sign of our mortality. It confronts the sick person inescapably with the question of faith in the face of suffer-

6. This recognition was first clearly expressed in the reform of the sacrament of orders by Pius XII in 1947 (see 11.3.2 below). The reforms connected with Vatican II show to what a small extent earlier ideas and regulations must be regarded as untouchable. Thus it was possible to regard the *Decree for the Armenians*, which, as a conciliar statement from 1439 had previously been so influential, as simply describing the factual state of things *at that time*.

7. On this, see E. J. Lengeling, " 'Per istam sanctam unctionem . . . adiuvet te Dominus gratia Spiritus Sancti.' Der Heilige Geist und die Krankensalbung," in G. J. Békes and G. Farnedi, eds., *Lex orandi lex credendi* (Rome: 1980) 235–294.

ing, of that person's relationship with God in a situation in which the presence of God "now already" should be practiced and clung to, as something that at some point is intended for the human person forever without interruption— that is, it always poses the question of the end of life. For fellow Christians, for the Church, it means not only the duty to abandon false consolations in combating suffering wherever it can be confronted. It also calls for mutual sympathy in human (i.e., physical) and religious forms. The symbolic action of anointing the sick can express an endurance of this situation in faith and hope in God, and at the same time, through physical touch, it can indicate the human presence that, if it is not only symbolic, effects healing.[8] It is the confession of the community and of the sick within it that we may hope for decisive salvation from God the Father through the Son in that divine Spirit whose intervention is requested in this symbolic action. But for those for whom the anointing with oil is alienating, and to whom it cannot easily be communicated, it is consoling to consider that the Eucharist is and remains the appropriate sacrament for the dying.[9] This sacrament, like the anointing of the sick, presupposes that the situation is not concealed, but rather is brought to consciousness and thus placed in the presence of the loving and merciful God.

8. This aspect has led to a rediscovery of anointing of the sick, for example in the Anglican communion. Cf. the bibliography in H. Vorgrimler, *Buße und Krankensalbung*, 227, n. 60.

9. On this, see especially R. Kaczynski, "Die Feier der Krankensakramente," *Internationale kath. Zeitschrift* 12 (1983) 423–436. Kaczynski here also rejects G. Greshake's suggestion that the anointing of the sick should be reinterpreted as a "sacrament of renewal of baptism in the face of death." Kaczynski correctly points out (p. 435) that Eucharistic communion already is that sacrament.

Bibliography 8

Alvárez Gutiérrez, C. G. *El sentido teológico de la Unción de los enfermos en la teología contemporánea (1940-1980)*. Rome: 1981.

Jorissen, I., and H. B. Meyer. *Pastorale Hilfen in Krankheit und Alter. Über Krankheit, Alter und das Sakrament der Krankensalbung*. Innsbruck: 1974.

Kaczynski, R. "Die Feier der Krankensalbung." *Internationale katholische Zeitschrift* 12 (1983) 423-436.

Kirchschläger, W. *Jesu exorzistisches Wirken aus der Sicht des Lukas*. Klosterneuburg: 1981.

Lengeling, E. J. " 'Per istam sanctam unctionem . . . adiuvet te Dominus gratia Spiritus Sancti.' Der Hl. Geist und die Krankensalbung." In G. J. Békes and G. Farnedi, eds. *Lex orandi lex credendi*. Rome: 1980, 235-294.

Probst, M., and K. Richter, eds. *Heilssorge für die Kranken*. Freiburg: 1975.

Schützeichel, H. *Katholische Calvin-Studien*. Trier: 1980, 75-98 (Calvin on anointing of the sick).

Stefánski J. "Von der letzten Ölung zur Krankensalbung." In P. Jounel, R. Kaczynski, and G. Pasqualetti, eds. *Liturgia* (FS A. Bugnini). Rome: 1982, 429-452.

Vorgrimler, H. *Buße und Krankensalbung*. Handbuch der Dogmengeschichte IV/3. Freiburg: 1978, 215-234 (with bibliography).

Ziegenaus, A. "Die Krankensalbung." In H. Luthe (see Bibliography 1) 421-480.

236

11

The Sacrament of Orders

11.1 Introduction

The sacrament of orders is very closely connected with office, or more precisely with the offices of service in the Church; it is thus impossible to discuss the one apart from the other. It is just this topic of office in the Church that incorporates the problems that in turn have influenced the understanding of the sacrament of orders. The most important of them should be mentioned in this introduction.

Basic to the whole thematic complex is ecclesiology, the theological understanding of the Church,[1] which needs a solid historical basis. Catholic theology is always in danger of tracing too many details of the historical existence and constitution of the Church to the Jesus of history. It is thought that that is the only way to insure divine legitimation: only what was concretely founded by Jesus himself can be considered to be of divine origin, an institution of divine law (*iuris divini*). Now, there can be no doubt that, as regards the existence of the Church and its essential institutions, we must maintain a connection with Jesus,

1. As soon as it appears, it will be possible to refer for this topic to the ecclesiology of M. M. Garijo Guembe.

but present-day theology is not the first to have tried to think of this connection in a theologically fuller, "broader" form. In its decree on the institution of a sacramental confession of sins by divine law, the Council of Trent designated the concrete form recognized from the early days of the Church as corresponding to Christ's institution and command, and thus not as a purely human invention (NR 665/DS 1706). But even in Scholastic theology "institution" was not necessarily identical with a historical action; it could also be seen as an impulse coming from the exalted Jesus Christ. This indicates two lines or dimensions that must be present in the Church and its essential institutions: historical proximity or correspondence (which is something different from concrete institution or foundation) and an impulse of the divine Spirit. It is not difficult to recognize that the Church and its offices, from this point of view, were not instituted in a purely historical fashion, but also in a Trinitarian and salvation-historical way. It is sufficient for historical purposes if a development corresponds to (i.e., conforms positively and at least does not contradict) the content of the preaching and practice of Jesus.

In determining the historical contexts, it is important to ask how a particular development could have begun such a short time after Jesus' departure, if it could not have had some positive connection with him. The beginning of the earliest Christian community (at that time still within Judaism), and thus the beginning of the Church, presumes a consciousness that it was legitimate to carry on Jesus' mission, to continue witnessing to him and his message, to win over other people, and to live in a new form of human community. In the continuation of the mission and in the identity of the message we find fundamental elements of historical continuity, and thus of "divine law."

As a matter of course, different functions and forms of service arose within the newly-founded community of faith. The connection with Jesus, who did not wish to separate himself and his companions from Israel, can be seen in two factors. In the first place, Jesus himself, in teaching and sending out disciples, apparently made a distinction between those who believed in him as a group and those who were called to serve in a special way. It is the task of exegesis to discover the motives for this distinction. Secondly, the Easter experiences of the resurrected Jesus were not given to all in the same way. On the basis of these distinctions, a core group consisting of eyewitnesses and direct hearers of Jesus' word crystallized; they could and should witness to the identity of the historical Jesus with the Risen One.

On the basis of these factors of mission and witness, the Church has understood itself and continues to understand itself as "apostolic," independently of the precise meaning of the concept of "apostle."[2] "Apostolic succession" (*successio apostolica*) in the broad sense exists when the Church continues in the faith of the first disciples and apostles, particularly the Trinitarian and Christological confession, and carries on its proclamation and its mission in that faith. Obviously, a practical discipleship of Jesus is essential as well.

The concept of "apostolic succession" in the narrower sense is derived from the meaning of witness, which constitutes the Church itself: office in the Church exists to preserve the identity and continuity of the witness of faith. It receives its legitimation not only from the identity of its faith and confession with the faith and confession of the first witnesses, but also through its historical origins in the first witnesses. This view, however, is not shared by all Christian Churches; it is precisely at this point that ecumenical problems regarding office and orders begin (see 11.5 below). The Catholic Church cannot surrender the principle of apostolic succession as an essential element of the Church and a criterion for the true Church of Jesus Christ in the broader *or* in the narrower sense, because its messengers and witnesses must prove themselves not only through their faith and Christian praxis (which could prove fragile), but also through the legitimacy of their discipleship. Only certifiably legitimate missionaries have the right to preach a word that commands belief. The identity and continuity of a human community, as a historical entity, cannot be founded solely on something that in itself demands interpretation, such as a book (e.g., the Bible). It also requires a legitimate succession of witnesses and messengers.

This view of things accounts for a unique, specifically Catholic understanding of the relationship between offices of service and the community. On the one side, all together make up the one Church. All together are hearers, believers, and confessors. All together, with Jesus Christ, make up one body, a community of faith in the Holy Spirit. This fundamental equality and unity has received its sensibly-

2. For initial information, see the articles in TRE III (1978) 430–483; EKL I (1986) 221–223, both with bibliography.

perceptible sacramental expression in baptism. On the other hand, the office of service is something "before" or "over against" the community: the messengers or witnesses present and confront the community with the apostolic word, which contains and interprets the message of Jesus—the Word of God—in order that it may again and again be heard, accepted, and transmitted through the community's confession. By this act, the messengers or witnesses do not take the place of the head, as if they were the head of the body of Christ and ordinary believers were its members. The messengers or witnesses are, rather, signs or pointers to that fundamental, unique "before" and "over against," who is and remains Jesus Christ himself (not least as the real subject of all liturgy).

Having said this, we have already laid the foundations for a theology of the sacrament of orders. The office of service in apostolic discipleship is constitutive for the Church. Therefore the solemn acceptance of a person into this office of service is a sacrament. The duties of the office of service, which in biblical language can also be called a service for the growth of the body of Jesus Christ or a building up of that body, have been sketched in the preceding paragraphs in light of the Church's original situation, as a service of the gospel. In the course of history this service has taken on some very different features in the Church's praxis: from these servants the basic functions of the Church (*martyria, leiturgia, diakonia*) are expected, not exclusively, but in a special way. To *martyria* belongs the special service of preaching; to *leiturgia* the leadership in divine worship, as well as most of the sacraments; and to *diakonia* the witness of Christian praxis. It is obvious that these duties, if they are properly carried out, will make a total demand on any human being. Thus it is understandable that in choosing and preparing such persons the Church looks to quite different dimensions, and must adopt quite different points of view, than does any other association, no matter how humanitarian its work, in choosing its functionaries. It is equally clear from historical experience that human beings fall short of the ideal in one way or another, and that some of them fail. It is just this kind of realistic view of human weakness and incapacity that aids us in seeing the content of this service more sharply: the word is to be proclaimed, the presence that is to be implored and indicated in a sensibly-perceptible way, are not the word and presence of the official person. They are and remain the word and presence of God who alone is sovereign. The fact that the bearers of this office of service must not and cannot personally be that "before" and "over against," of which we spoke before, but instead only point to them by their actions, is expressed in the teaching that the sacrament of orders bestows a "sacramental character."

From what has been said it must have become clear that the essentials of the office of service are what God intends for the building up and life of the Church. They are therefore given by the divine Spirit who is called upon and is present in the sacrament. That means, on the one hand, that these gifts of God are not the Church's property, and thus cannot be bestowed by a community (by means of "delegation," "empowerment," etc.). On the other hand, they are given by God for the building up and life of the greater whole, so that the office-bearers are never in and for themselves "the Church," and what they alone do remains fragmentary (and this applies to all three of the Church's basic functions), so long as it is not cooperatively borne and completed with and by the community.[3]

There are concrete forms of office that obscure this most central meaning of office and obstruct its positive effects. Among these are the factual division of the Church in two classes (clerics and laity), as well as the factual exercise of power on the part of many officeholders. Such obstacles to true service cannot be eliminated by theological insight alone.[4] Among the elements of orders and office that are more negative than positive should be counted the juridical language employed: is it really appropriate to call the gifts necessary for the building up and life of the Church "powers" (*potestates*)? When there is talk of possessing, bestowing and restricting "powers," the dimensions of petition to the Holy Spirit, of faith, and of the effects that arise from and strengthen faith fade into the background or disappear.

The office of service in the Church developed historically with different accents as regards the content of that service, a topic we will ad-

3. On the one hand, this does not imply a "democratizing" of the Church in principle, but on the other hand a much greater cooperation on the part of church communities in the appointment of their ministers is theologically legitimate and practically possible.
4. There are very clear norms in the New Testament that are critical of lordship and power: cf Mark 10:42-45; Matt 23. It is true that the Church may not be regarded from the point of view of a division of power. But it would be dishonest to act as if there were not a massive exercise of power in the Church and everything that occurs were selfless "service."

dress in more detail below. This development is regarded by the Church as a legitimate development on the basis of what Jesus himself did, and therefore abides within the framework of "divine law." But that means that it cannot be reversed or given fundamental revision. If the accent were differently located, the critical points could shift, and some things could be forgotten, even though nothing could be totally eliminated. However, we may say that the development is open to the future, so long as we believe in the presence of the divine Spirit, with the result that new forms may be added to the full-grown shape of ecclesial offices of service as they now exist.

11.2 The Origins of Office in the Church

11.2.1 Biblical Findings

In light of the close connection between office and orders, two questions arise with regard to the New Testament: in what forms the office of service in the Church first existed and what we can know about the induction of a person into office.

The historical question, beginning with Jesus himself, can only refer to his circle of Twelve. During the earthly lifetime of Jesus we cannot speak of apostles, since "apostle" is definitely a post-Easter concept.[5] According to the best-substantiated exegesis, the circle of the Twelve is almost certainly pre-Easter.[6] Since Jesus did not intend to gather a new people of God or found an exclusive community within Israel, the Twelve cannot be regarded from the outset as progenitors of Christianity commissioned as such by Jesus. It is most probable that, at the beginning of his public activity, Jesus called together an open, growing group of people who were to be his personal followers. When doubts arose about the validity of his message even within this group of disciples, he founded the group of Twelve. This action was therefore in the first instance a move to secure the existence of a faithful group of disciples. The fact that even Matthew's Gospel quotes some

---

5. Cf. the literature in n. 2 above.
6. A. Vögtle, "Das Problem der Herkunft von 'Mt 16, 17-19,' " in his *Offenbarungsgeschehen und Wirkungsgeschichte* (Freiburg: 1985) 109–140, at 139–140, n. 109. In what follows I am also relying on A. Vögtle.

logia as directed to the Twelve and repeats the same logia in a different redactional context as addressed to all believers shows that even a long time after Jesus' departure the distinction between the Twelve and the other disciples was not seen as a hierarchical one. (Something similar can be said about the resurrection witnesses and the other disciples in John's Gospel.) It is not impossible to see the founding of the group of Twelve as a symbolic action, that is, an indication of Jesus' continuing desire to gather together all Israel.

We cannot say anything definite about the transition from these pre-Easter Twelve to the post-Easter apostles. In any case, temporally speaking, Paul's self-designation as "apostle of Jesus Christ" lies between those two points, but Paul neither thought of himself as an office-holder nor did he apparently feel any concern about the fate of his communities after his death, since he expected the return of the Lord to take place very soon.[7] His apostleship remained a special case. But Paul belongs within the later concept of an apostle to the extent that, because of his experience of Jesus, he could also claim to be a hearer and eyewitness to him. Thus Paul was also a recipient of the revelation of God embodied in Jesus. But it is precisely this central characteristic of apostleship—direct witness and reception of revelation—that makes it impossible to view apostleship as an office, in which there could be "successors" in any sense of the word. "In their character as unique recipients of revelation within the history of salvation, in such a way that they could constitute a normative tradition, the apostles could not have 'successors,' whether intended or directly named by themselves; only with respect to their responsibility for the preaching and preservation of the gospel and of the life of the community in harmony with the gospel could there be any talk of 'successors.'"[8]

But it was not only "successors of the apostles" who took up this responsibility. It is historically possible to show that the responsibility existed, but it is not possible to restrict its shouldering to successors of the Twelve or other apostles. It would also be completely wrong to try to find evidence in the New Testament for leadership over a universal Church. What we find there is only the structure of offices

---

7. A. Vögtle, "Exegetische Reflexionen zur Apostolizität des Amtes und zur Amtssukzession," ibid., 221–279 (with extensive literature), at 235. About the group and activities of those who might have been called apostles *before* Paul we know next to nothing.

8. Ibid., 221.

in some local communities. But while it is wrong, on the one hand, to posit a direct development of apostolic succession from the Twelve through the apostles to the bishops, it is also false to set the charisms (free gifts of grace) mentioned in the oldest, Pauline, witnesses, in opposition to offices or to distinguish charismatic and non-charismatic roles.

For Paul, all the events in the life of a community, everything that is mentioned in the lists of charisms, and all roles of service that are mentioned apart from those lists are to be traced to the work of the divine Spirit. He offers us neither precise data for reconstructing a community constitution nor a model of what a community ought to be. On the basis of the things that Paul mentions we can understand the later development by which certain spiritual gifts were recognized as indispensable and were institutionalized.[9] In listing the charisms, even Paul emphasizes some functions (which he already found in place) that have a tendency to endure and to be tied to a particular person: teacher, prophet, presider. Paul accepted the fact that a community called those who would exercise certain functions and gave them institutional titles such as *episkopos* and *diakonos* (Phil 1:1). Nowhere is it evident that Paul regarded the episcopal office as particularly important or indispensable; in the two decades after Paul's death the "synagogal presbyterate" dominated as the "regular official structure" in the territories of Paul's missionary activity.[10]

Paul's writings do not reveal any order of rank in the various names given to functions tending toward the status of offices. The responsible and controlling body remains the whole (local) community directly subject to Jesus Christ. Clearly, the measure, norm, and corrective of all charisms and roles were and remained love and the building up of the body of Jesus Christ. Paul appeals to the freedom and independence of the communities; he himself only offers assistance.[11] The whole of community life and its relationship to the apostle are supported by a trust "in the uniting and directing power of the Spirit."[12]

9. Ibid., 232, as well as for what follows.
10. Ibid., 230.
11. Ibid., 238.
12. Ibid., 239. See the important observations on the beginnings of office in the Church in the work of B. Holmberg (see Bibliography 9). Holmberg also concludes

Among the other New Testament evidence that is important for the development of offices in the Church is the pseudepigraphic letter "to the Ephesians," circulated in the name of Paul. Anton Vögtle dates it to about the years 80–90. The preaching of the apostles and prophets remains the norm, while the roles of service that are necessary from time to time are brought forth directly by the exalted Lord.[13] "Office" is a result and function of the gospel that is to be handed on; the functions of preaching and leadership must be regarded as constitutive for the Church. Anton Vögtle firmly agrees with this thesis of Helmut Merklein.[14] Teaching and leadership in the community are firmly connected with one another; people who are gifted in this way and whose talents have been tested are factually acknowledged by the community and can be regarded as "successors of the apostles," without being themselves the recipients of revelation. *Charis* remains the inclusive factor.

The First Letter of Peter, written not long after Ephesians, shows how the charismatic idea of community is reconciled with the necessity for a clear, stable leadership. Here we find an expression of concern for the survival of the community in the post-apostolic period. As in the Acts of the Apostles, which is some years older, and in the later Letter of James, there emerges in 1 Peter (5:1ff.) the group of presbyters (as in the synagogue), who are an already recognized leadership group.[15] The risen Christ himself, however, is the shepherd and bishop of the faithful (2:25); the leaders of the community are not called shepherds, because the Risen One is at work in them:[16] their existence is not traced in 1 Peter to God (as in 1 Cor 12:28) or to the Holy Spirit (as in Acts 20:28) or to the exalted Lord (as in Eph 4:11).

In the Acts of the Apostles, the presbytery appears without further introduction (11:30) and is associated with the episcopal group (20:28). The author of Acts had an interest in the "principle of continuity," as the appointment of community presbyters by Barnabas and Paul

that Paul contributed to the institutionalization of authority in the Church less through his own initiative than through acknowledgment of what was taking place in the communities.

13. A. Vögtle, "Exegetische Reflexionen," 244. In dating other writings I am also following Vögtle.
14. Ibid., 246.
15. Ibid., 249–250.
16. So A. Vögtle, ibid., 252, with Helmut Merklein.

(14:23) shows.[17] It is not the charismatic community, but the Holy Spirit who appoints presbyters (14:28; cf. the discourse at Miletus in 20:17-34); it is to the Spirit that the presbyters must give account for the exercise of their office; they are not only to lead the people of God's own choosing, but also to protect it against dangers, in particular to secure the apostolic tradition against false teachings within and without. Thus particularly on the basis of Acts 20 we can see how care for the tradition of faith/teaching and office/leadership are combined. The Holy Spirit and ecclesial office are, each in its own way, "elements that create Church."[18]

In the last third of the first century we thus find the first evidence to document, on a relatively broad scale, the efforts to emphasize the apostolic tradition (some of which was already written down) as normative and to protect it against alterations. Late witnesses to the development of these efforts are found in the Pastoral Letters and 2 Peter. Concern for "that which has been entrusted to you" led to insistence on following apostolic teaching, but still not to any efforts to demonstrate a succession of office reaching back to the Twelve and to Paul through some series of imposition of hands. In the second and third Christian generations it was still possible for someone to enter into office through an immediate pneumatic experience.[19]

Finally, we should say something very briefly about terminology. For a while it was popular (and some echoes of this are still heard today) to make a polemic contrast between the beginnings of office in the New Testament, with the demonstrated emphases on teaching and leadership (for the preservation of the unity of the community), and the cultic aspect. The postbiblical development of offices was criticized as a retreat to cultic officialdom, as "sacerdotalizing," etc. Special emphasis was placed on the fact that the words *episkopos* (supervisor), *pres-*

17. Ibid., 257. The meaning of the imposition of hands remains unclear. In the literature there is frequent reference to the influence of Numbers 27:18-23. Remarkably enough, the "transferral of the spirit" to the students of the rabbis (Deut 34:9) is not made use of here. The verses discussed include Acts 6:6; 13:3; 14:23; 1 Tim 4:14 and 2 Tim 1:6 (in the last two cases: transmission of a charism by the imposition of hands?); 1 Tim 5:22 (ordination or reconciliation?). Cf. also O. Knoch, "Die Funktion der Handauflegung im Neuen Testament," *Liturgisches Jahrbuck* 33 (1983) 222-235.

18. A. Vögtle, "Exegetische Reflexionen," 256, 262-263.

19. Ibid., 267. See, in Bibliography 9, also the works of H. von Lips, *Glaube—Gemeinde—Amt*, G. Lohfink, "Die Normativität," and W. Trilling, "Zum 'Amt.'"

byteros (elder), *diakonos* (servant) were secular terms, and that other, earlier designations of office like "teacher," "presider," "shepherd" are not cultic-sacral terms either. The polemic literature we are speaking of resorts to a number of simplifications. Of course, there are also genuine theological problems here, the core of which lie in the fact that a cult that must appease its god through divine worship, a form of sacrifice based on the idea that God's pleasure is found in self-denial even to the point of the sacrifice of one's own life, and a priesthood that regards itself as indispensable for communication between God and humanity, are all absolutely incompatible with Jesus' preaching about God. It is undeniable that the New Testament in general rejects sacrificial works in the Temple (but not prayer in the Temple!), and that for this reason, in the early period, everything suggestive of cultic persons was excluded from the designation of Christian offices.

The cultic critique in the New Testament, and particularly that of Jesus himself, exists within the context of Judaism. It should be seen as continuous with the sharp prophetic criticism of the sacrifices (cf., for example, Hos 6:6; Isa 1:10-17; Mic 6:5-8; Jer 7:21-23; Ps 50:7-15). The New Testament adopted the positive alternative within Judaism as its own: sacrifice of praise and thanksgiving for the mighty acts of God (Ps 50:23), the practice of justice toward the poor (Isa 1:17; Mic 6:8), and merciful love (Hos 6:6, cited in Matt 9:13 and 12:7) are to take the place of the sacrificial cult. Nevertheless, this renewed practice of devotion in no way excludes praise, petition, and calling upon God, including liturgical forms. Israel's hope also included a pure sacrifice (Mal 1:11) and a renewed priesthood (Mal 3:3-4; Sir 45:7, 15, 24). New Testament expressions do not go out of their way to avoid liturgical language: for example, we read that the whole life of believers should be an act of worship, that all are the temple and the house of God, and that the faithful are God's own priestly people (1 Pet 2:5, 9; Rev 1:6; 5:9-10; 20:6 with reference to Exod 19:6 and Isa 61:6). Other details could be mentioned (apart from the disputed "priestly service" of Paul in Rom 15:16),[20] especially in connection with Jesus: not only in Hebrews (5-10), but also in Ephesians 5:2, he is called gift and sacrifice (*prosphora* and *thysia*); his blood is interpreted as the blood of the covenant according to Exodus 25:5-8; he gives a liturgical stylization

20. Cf. A. Vanhoye, *Prêtres anciens, prêtre nouveau selon le Nouveau Testament* (Paris: 1980).

to the Last Supper and confers a blessing as he departs (Luke 24:50-51); the faithful share in his priesthood (Heb 10:14-25; 13:16). Thus the New Testament, up to the end of the first century and possibly as late as the first half of the second century, offers a wealth of malleable "material," including the beginnings of institutionalization, from which later specific offices, orders, and the theologies belonging to them could arise. Two methodological errors are to be avoided: the later developments are neither in such sharp contrast to the "center of the gospel" that they can only be regarded as wrong, nor does the development begin with the apostles at Jerusalem who, with one exception, were called by Jesus. Quite apart from the fact that the Twelve were only designated at a late date (Acts 8:1) as the patriarchs of the early Church resident in Jerusalem,[21] there is no direct line even from this group to the "monarchical" bishops of the postbiblical period. As regards movements toward sacramental orders, we find no traces. At a later period, the induction of deacons through prayer and imposition of hands (Acts 6:6) served as a model for a consecration that transmitted, or rather, implored the presence of the Spirit, but scholars do not agree whether the imposition of hands mentioned in the New Testament can be regarded as an "ordination."

11.2.2 *Postbiblical Developments*

The postbiblical evidence from the first and second centuries[22] shows a continued development and fixing of ecclesial offices, but there is no reflection on ordination as an event. The theological focus is on concern for adherence to apostolic tradition, both in faith and teaching and in institutional matters.

The *Letter of Clement* indicates that in the Corinthian community leadership and liturgy ("the offering of sacrifice") were official functions. Besides the office that was both presbyteral and episcopal in

21. So A. Müller, "Amt als Kriterium" (see Bibliography 9) 102.

22. On this subject see, from the works in Bibliography 9, especially J. Martin, *Der priesterliche Dienst* III; G. Kretschmar, "Die Ordination im frühen Christentum"; J. Rhode, "Urchristliche und frühkatholische Ämter"; A. Jilek, "Bischof und Presbyterium"; B. Kleinheyer, "Ordination und Beauftragungen"; from earlier literature, see K. Rahner and H. Vorgrimler, eds., *Diaconia in Christo* (Freiburg: 1961), and P. Fransen, "Weihen, Heilige," *Sacramentum Mundi* IV (Freiburg: 1961) 1249-1293.

structure, there were also deacons. These offices were traced to the will and direction of God and are here for the first time compared to the Jewish hierarchy.

Ignatius of Antioch is often spoken of as the witness in whose writings we see that the development toward a "monarchical episcopate" or "monepiscopate" has been completed. In reality he offers us only one regionally limited view of things. His theological interest is shaped by his habit of thinking in images or types; here emerges a remarkable typology that does not correspond to the later Catholic hierarchy. The bishop is the image of God the Father, the deacons are to be revered like Jesus Christ, and the presbyters are compared to the apostolic college. Church office is, for Ignatius, the preferred place of the Holy Spirit and the Spirit's activity, and he sees the Church as existing nowhere except where this office exists. The bishop presides at the liturgy and is responsible for the unity of the community.

In contrast to these two witnesses, other writings, even from a subsequent period, refer only to presbyters (2 *Clement, Hermas*).

During the great upheavals brought about in the second century by adherents of gnosis and mystery cults and by sectarian divisions in the Church, a strong consciousness of the institutional and historical aspects of the Church arose. The most prominent testimony to that consciousness comes from Irenaeus of Lyons. He strengthened the theological insight that had emerged in the last third of the first century, the recognition that the apostolic element was normative for the Church. He exerted himself to show that the Church is and remains in the truth only when it is in continuity with the Church of the apostles. The Catholic Church's apostolic succession is visible in the succession in office: through the fact that an unbroken official line can be traced from the apostles to the bishops, it is certain that the apostolic tradition of faith and doctrine was preserved and not falsified, since the "successors of the apostles" have received the "reliable charism in truth."

Tertullian was the first to refer to the bishop as "*summus sacerdos*," or high priest, probably under the influence of a Melchisedech theology (Ps 110:4; Heb 5–7). Theologically, the idea that the Old Testament institutions were also fulfilled in the New Testament was gaining popularity. It was also Tertullian who gave a collective Latin technical name to the Church's officeholders: *ordo*. He found this concept, which among the Romans referred to the leadership group, a special body in contrast to the people, in the Latin translation of Psalm 110:4. To this day it is used in the Romance languages to describe the sacrament of consecration or "orders": *sacramentum ordinis*. What had been glimpsed in the *Letter of Clement* was now fully evident: there were no longer any psychological or theological hesitations toward the adoption of non-Christian notions like "high priest," "priest," and "state" or "rank" in Christian language referring to office. In the third century Cyprian went still farther: for him, the *sacerdotium* relates to the Eucharistic altar; he speaks of a *clericus* (from the Greek *kleros*, lot), referring to those who, because of their state, have a special concern for and relationship to God. Origen uses similar language: its biblical roots are in Deuteronomy 4:20; 9:29 and Acts 1:17. The associated concept of *laikos* for the ordinary people appears as early as the *Letter of Clement*. Cyprian called the various offices within the one *ordo* "*gradus*," thus carrying the hierarchizing trend further.

It was certainly owing to the Church's defensive attitude toward threats within and without, especially the struggle with Gnostic teachings, that beginning in the second century charismatic community functions are mentioned less and less frequently outside the *ordo*, although there have been free charismatic impulses within the Church at all times. It is remarkable that even Tertullian knew of women prophets who had the right to speak during public worship.

Meanwhile, at Rome, Hippolytus had brought together elements of the liturgy and theology of orders in his *Apostolic Tradition*. The office of bishop, with its duties of preaching, shepherding, and priestly service, is the complete form of the ecclesial office that is conferred through prayer and the imposition of hands. In this consecration, "the power of the spirit of leadership" is implored for and bestowed upon the candidate; thereby, he is incorporated into the mission of Jesus Christ and the apostles which is the work of the Holy Spirit. The essential tasks of the bishop appear to be the offering of the Eucharistic gifts donated by the community and presented by the deacon (praise and thanksgiving are spoken by the entire community, but the bishop alone utters the *eucharistia* and conducting public penance. In comparison to the bishop, the presbyters remain shadowy figures; the members of the presbyteral college support the bishop in the performance of his duties. The deacons are not subject to the presbyters, but to the bishop; they exercise a mediating service between him, or rather the altar, and the community. The special relationship between bestowing the Spirit through the imposition of hands and Eucharist is made clear through statements that are not related directly to the offices in question: "confessors" can act as priests even without having received the imposition of hands, because their martyrdom has shown that they already possess the Holy Spirit. Widows do not receive an imposition of hands, because their important (charitable) office is not related to the Eucharist.

If Hippolytus' model was not universally adopted within the Church, if we take it together with other evidence it permits the conclusion that the components of office have clearly emerged by the third century, i.e., service over a long period of time, special competences and a rule of succession. What is constitutive for office is apostolicity, and office in turn is constitutive for the Church.[23] It is clear that the conferral of three offices is understood sacramentally and that two of them include a competence related to the Eucharistic liturgy.

The *Apostolic Tradition* became a dominant influence by being taken up in the *Apostolic Constitutions*, a fourth-century Syrian legal and liturgical church order that forms the basis of all ordination liturgies in the Eastern Churches. (There are some variations: an expansion of the epiclesis and a description of the priest as the normal liturgist of the proclamation of the word and the celebration of the Eucharist.)

Thus, the postbiblical development led to formation of a structure of Church offices and, within that structure, to the dominance of the bishop, a position that was theologically justified on the basis of apostolicity. Between the sixth and ninth centuries there occurred an important shift, the reasons for which were manifold.[24] In this brief overview it must suffice to indicate the lines of development that were important for the theology of orders, and to limit ourselves to the Western Church. In Rome in the fifth century the prayers at the imposition of hands quite clearly place the presbyters, as a *secundus ordo*, below the bishop, whom they are to assist in his task of preaching. But under Old Gallican (sixth century) and particularly Frankish influence (eighth century), their service at the Eucharist became central. From then on, a separate image of the priest developed: priests are the sacrificial priests of the new covenant, to whom, through sacramental ordination, the power to consecrate the Eucharist is irrevocably given. The theology of the episcopal office declined at the same time. The bishop's

23. A. Müller, "Amt als Kriterium," 106.
24. For a good summary, see P. Fransen, "Weihen, Heilige," 1262–1265.

role was interpreted theologically less as a shepherd's office in the community, and more as a perfection of "fullness" of the priesthood. But what dominated the picture of the bishop was his juridical status: his models within salvation history are Moses and Aaron.

The rite of ordination was also changed. From the third century onward, the heart of the rite for ordaining bishop, priest, and deacon was prayer with the imposition of hands. "Imposition of hands" in the first three centuries could also describe a simple choice or selection; similarly, *ordinare* could retain the meaning of "designate." Beginning in the fourth century, fixed concepts for the rite of ordination were gradually established, in particular "imposition of hands," "blessing" (*benedictio*) or "consecration" (*consecratio*). In addition to these three offices, there were a series of lesser roles of service, both in the East (first attested by Clement of Alexandria and Origen) and in the West (first attested by Tertullian and Cyprian). One was inducted into these through a simple rite; their number shifted between two and eight. Some of these were also conferred on women.

The bishop (chosen by the people) received the imposition of hands, according to the *Apostolic Tradition*, from another bishop; after the Council of Nicaea in 325 and the Synod of Arles in 314 the consecration of a bishop must be carried out by three bishops. To the imposition of hands was added an imposition of the book of the Gospels. Priests were consecrated by the bishop through imposition of hands; from the time of the *Apostolic Tradition* the other priests present also laid hands on the candidate. Deacons received ordination through the imposition of the bishop's hands alone. (On deaconesses, see 11.4.4 below.) The Council of Chalcedon in 451 forbade, in canon 6 (COD 66), the "absolute ordination" of presbyters, deacons, and other "ecclesial orders," i.e., in East and West every ordained person must be related to a particular community (church or monastery): "relative ordination."

Under Frankish influence, however, from the seventh century onward the consecration of a bishop was expanded to include an anointing of the head with chrism, the presentation of staff and ring, and an enthroning: the bishop's power is regarded as "sovereign." The ordination of priests now included an anointing of the hands, the presentation of bread and wine (or, rather, paten and chalice), and a second imposition of hands to bestow the power to forgive sins: the priest's service is regarded as primarily liturgical. A Roman synod in 1099 permitted "absolute ordination."

A new liturgy of consecration for the "lesser orders" in the Latin Church was prescribed in Gaul in the tenth century: Frankish influence was evident from the prominent place given to the presentation of the "instruments" of the particular service. The "lesser orders" were now understood to include the roles of porter, lector, exorcist, acolyte, and subdeacon. These no longer had any real function in the community: they were stages of ordination on the way to the priesthood, intended to prepare the candidates for the various aspects of priestly service.

11.3 *The Development of Teaching about the Sacrament of Orders*

11.3.1 *From Antiquity to the Scholastics*

In the earlier centuries of the Church, the theology of orders first concentrated on the bishop: in the liturgy of consecration, in which he was accepted into an *ordo episcoporum*, the Church prayed that he might receive the gracious assistance of God to enable him to fulfill his tasks. For the sake of preserving the unity of the Church, certain duties were reserved to the bishop. There is no false systematization involved in dividing the episcopal office according to three central categories of duties: the service of proclamation, liturgy, and leadership of the community—with the observation that the bishop's function in proclamation and liturgy is also one of leadership (i.e., of final responsibility). A proper theological understanding viewed the bishop as being included within the service and mission of Jesus Christ from the Father in the power of the Holy Spirit. This inclusion meant that the bishop had received the grace of God by means of which he, as image (*typos*) of the Father or (especially after the fourth century) of Jesus Christ, could make visible and perceptible the One who is always invisibly present, for the sake of strengthening and faithfully preserving the faith handed on by the apostles. At the beginning of the third century, when this service was theologically interpreted as priestly, the "grace of priesthood" was seen to be primarily realized in the bishop. (To clarify this development it is necessary to repeat here some of what was said in 8.4.7 above.)

In both the Western and Eastern Church from the fourth century onward there was a tendency to focus on the spiritual "ability" of officeholders[25] and to accept a theological equality of bishops and priests. Episcopal witnesses (from the bishops of Rome, the Roman ordination liturgy, etc.), by contrast, deliberately portray the priesthood of priests as subordinate, *secundi meriti munus*. The important witnesses for the presbyteral tendency were taken up by Frankish theologians and thus passed on to Scholastic theology. As soon as the question of "ability" gave way to that of "power," the opinion developed that the most important power of any Church office was related to the sacraments, and since the priest, through his ordination, possessed an unsurpassable power with respect to the Eucharist and the sacrament of reconciliation, it could not be further increased by episcopal ordination. The influential Peter Lombard (d. 1160) therefore taught that episcopal ordination was not a sacrament, whereas the ordination of a priest, since the clarification of the concept of sacrament in the middle of the twelfth century, was regarded as *the* sacrament of orders. The special character of the episcopal office was seen, instead, as relating to jurisdiction ("pastoral power").[26] Thus with regard to priests, one spoke of a "*potestas in corpus eucharisticum,*" and with regard to bishops of a "*potestas in corpus mysticum.*" From this division arose differing "images" of the priest and the bishop, which in turn were subject to historical fluctuations.[27]

The two areas of "power and ordination" and "power of jurisdiction" were, of course, not completely separate.[28] In sacramental theology, the refusal of sacraments is important. Priests could (and can) only give absolution in the sacrament of reconciliation if the "power" granted them at ordination has also been jurisdictionally "conferred on" them. In the Western Church the bishop remained the "minis-

25. The motives for this are not clear. For Jerome, it is associated with attacks on deacons and on the bishop of Jerusalem. It is often coupled with his name, but was also represented by other important ancient witnesses, such as Ambrose and John Chrysostom. Cf. ibid., 1271–1273.

26. Canonists maintained the sacramentality of episcopal consecration. For the progress of the controversy, see ibid., 1272–1273.

27. There is a special literature on this point, which cannot be introduced here, but which is in urgent need of social-historical expansion. For initial information, see ibid., 1264–1267.

28. Very instructive for a preliminary view is K. Mörsdorf, "Heilige Gewalt," *Sacramentum Mundi* II (Freiburg: 1969) 582–597.

ter'' of confirmation in ordinary cases. But in particular, he was and is the ''minister of holy orders.'' Only a bishop may ordain priests and deacons,[29] and in the normal instance several bishops acting together are required for the consecration of a bishop.

11.3.2 Historical Decisions

The first official teachings concern the ''validity'' of orders conferred by heretics, schismatics, or even simonists: they are valid (only Latin, DS 478 in the year 601, DS 705 in the year 1106). The second Council of Lyons in 1274, which spoke of the sacraments as seven in number (NR 928/DS 860) no longer demanded of the separated Eastern Churches, as Rome had still done in 1254, that they accept the minor orders.

In the text produced by the Council of Florence in 1439 as part of the negotiations toward union with the separated Armenian Church, the Scholastic ideas on the sacrament of orders are reproduced in a brief passage borrowed from Thomas Aquinas:

> The sixth sacrament is that of Order. Its *matter* is that by the handing over of which the Order is conferred: thus the presbyterate is conferred by handing over the chalice with wine and the paten with the bread; the diaconate by giving the book of the gospels; the subdiaconate by handing over the empty chalice covered with an empty paten; and similarly the other orders by assigning the things pertaining to their office. The *form* of the presbyterate is this: ''Receive the power of offering the Sacrifice in the Church for the living and the dead, in the name of the Father and of the Son and of the Holy Spirit.'' And similarly for the forms of the other Orders, as is contained in detail in the Roman Pontifical. The ordinary *minister* of this sacrament is the bishop. The effect is an increase of grace so that one may be a suitable minister [at the altar] (NR 705/DS 1326).

This represents (in a form that is not dogmatically binding) the teaching of the Church at that time which, as regards matter and form, is no longer valid. The consecration of a bishop is not even mentioned.

---

29. Certain other consecrations are also normally performed only by the bishop (see ch. 13 below). On historical expectations in which priests were ordained by priests, see P. Fransen, ''Weihen, Heilige,'' 1270–1271 (with sources).

The Reformers decisively restored the idea of the "universal" priesthood (the expression used at that time: something like "common" or
"mutual" priesthood would be better).[30] From that standpoint they
opposed the distinction between clerics and laity; they disputed the
existence of the sacrament of orders and the power of orders conferred
by it. Luther taught expressly that baptism ordains all Christians as
priests and bishops, so that, from that point on, they have no further
need of a special priestly mediation. In light of the New Testament,
it was not denied that there are legitimate offices (*officia*) in the community of the faithful, but only *one* office was regarded as of "divine
law," namely that of preaching, a duty of every believer. From this
also a "distinction" between office and community can be derived.
There are particular officeholders who are called by the Holy Spirit and
"ordained" by those having authority in the community, i.e., inducted
into their office with petitionary prayers, for the sake of public order
in the community. (See 11.5 below for further remarks on this point.)

The Council of Trent, in opposition, defended the existence of a
visible, external priesthood, in such a way that "priestly service" (*sacer-
dotii ministerium*) is the overarching concept for an institution that exists by "divine command" (*Dei ordinatione*, also *divina res*) and is
arranged in hierarchical stages. At the same time, the teaching on the
existence of the sacrament of orders was strengthened. The conciliar
statements are found in four chapters and eight associated canons from
the twenty-third session in 1563. The chapters read:

> Chapter I: The Institution of the Priesthood of the New Law
>
> Sacrifice and priesthood are by the ordinance of God so united that both
> have existed under every law. Since, therefore, in the new covenant the
> Catholic Church has received from the institution of Christ the holy,
> visible sacrifice of the eucharist, it must also be acknowledged that there
> exists in the Church a new, visible and external priesthood into which the
> old one was changed. Moreover, the sacred scriptures make it clear and
> the tradition of the Catholic Church has always taught that this priest-
> hood was instituted by the same Lord our Savior, and that the power
> of consecrating, offering and administering his body and blood, and like-
> wise of remitting and retaining sins, was given to the apostles and to
> their successors in the priesthood.

30. On the Reformers' ideas, see W. Lohff in *LThK* II, 1222–1224, and further
material in the collection edited by H. Vorgrimler, *AMT UND Ordination in
ökumenischer Sicht* (Freiburg: 1973).

Chapter II: The Seven Orders

But since the ministry of so holy a priesthood is something divine, in order that it might be exercised in a more worthy manner and with greater veneration, it was fitting that in the perfectly ordered disposition of the Church there should be *several distinct orders of ministers*, serving in the priesthood by virtue of their office, and that they be so distributed that those already having the clerical tonsure should ascend through the minor to the major orders. For, the sacred scriptures mention unmistakably not only the priests but also the deacons, and teach in the most authoritative words what is chiefly to be observed in their ordination. And from the very beginning of the Church the names of the following orders and the ministries proper to each one, namely, those of subdeacon, acolyte, exorcist, lector and porter, are known to have been in use, though they were not of equal rank. For the subdiaconate is counted among the major orders by the Fathers and the holy councils, in which very frequently we also read about the other, lower orders.

Chapter III: Order is Truly a Sacrament

Since from the testimony of scripture, apostolic tradition and the unanimous agreement of the Fathers it is clear that grace is conferred by sacred ordination, which is performed by words and outward signs, no one ought to doubt that order is truly and properly one of the seven sacraments of Holy Church. For the apostle says: "I remind you to rekindle the gift of God that is within you through the laying on of my hands; for God did not give us a spirit of timidity but a spirit of power and love and self-control" (2 Tim 1:6-7).

Chapter IV: The Ecclesiastical Hierarchy and Ordination

But since in the sacrament of order, as also in baptism and confirmation, a *character* is imprinted which can neither be *erased* nor taken away, the holy council justly condemns the opinion of those who say that the priests of the new covenant have only a temporary power, and that those who have once been rightly ordained can again become laymen if they do not exercise the ministry of the word of God. And if anyone should assert *that all Christians are without distinction priests* of the new covenant, or that all are equally endowed with the same spiritual power, this is nothing else than *upsetting the Church's hierarchy*, which is "like an army with banners" (cf. Song 6:3), as if, contrary to the teaching of St. Paul, all were apostles, all prophets, all evangelists, all pastors, all doctors (cf. 1 Cor 12:29).

Therefore the holy council declares that, besides the other ecclesiastical grades, the *bishops*, who have succeeded the apostles, principally belong to this hierarchical order and have been, as the same apostle says (Acts 20:28), "established by the Holy Spirit to govern the Church of the Lord;" that they are superior to priests, confer the sacrament of confirmation, ordain ministers of the Church, and can perform most of the other functions over which those of a lower order have no power.

The holy council teaches, furthermore, that in the ordination of bishops, of priests and of other grades, the consent, call or mandate, neither of the people nor any *civil power or authority*, is necessary to the extent that without it the ordination would be invalid. Rather it decrees that all those who ascend to the exercise of these ministries, being called and installed only by the people or by the civil power or authority, and those who in their rashness assume them on their own, are not to be regarded as ministers of the Church, but "as thieves and robbers, who have not entered by the door" (cf. Jn 10:1) (NR 706-712/DS 1764-1769).

The canons read as follows:

1. If anyone says that there is in the New Testament no visible and external priesthood, or that there is no power of consecrating and offering the true body and blood of the Lord and of remitting and retaining sins, but only the office and bare ministry of preaching the Gospel; or that those who do not preach are not priests at all, *anathema sit*.

2. If anyone says that besides the priesthood there are in the Catholic Church no other orders, major and minor, by which, as by various steps, one advances towards the priesthood, *anathema sit*.

3. If anyone says that order or sacred ordination is not truly and properly a sacrament instituted by Christ the Lord, or that it is a kind of human invention devised by men inexperienced in ecclesiastical matters, or that it is only a kind of rite by which are chosen the ministers of the word of God and of the sacraments, *anathema sit*.

4. If anyone says that by sacred ordination the Holy Spirit is not given and that, therefore, the bishops say in vain: "Receive the Holy Spirit;" or if anyone says that no character is imprinted by ordination; or that one who has once been a priest can again become a layman, *anathema sit*.

5. If anyone says that the sacred anointing which the church uses at holy ordination not only is not required but is despicable and pernicious, and so are also the other ceremonies, *anathema sit*.

6. If anyone says that in the Catholic Church there is no hierarchy instituted by divine ordinance, which consists of bishops, priests and ministers, *anathema sit*.

7. If anyone says that bishops are not superior to priests; or that they do not have the power to confirm and ordain, or that the power they have is common both to them and to priests; or if anyone says that orders

conferred by them without the consent or call of the people or of the civil power are invalid; or that those who have neither been rightly or- dained by ecclesiastical and canonical authority nor sent by it, but come from some other source, are lawful ministers of the word and of the sacra- ments, *anathema sit.*

8. If anyone says that bishops chosen by the authority of the Roman Pontiff are not true and legitimate bishops but a human invention, *anathema sit* (NR 713-720/DS 1771-1778).

Priesthood was interpreted by Trent in light of the liturgy, and par- ticularly on the basis of the "powers" reserved to priests. The starting- point in the two covenants is problematic, and the teaching on the hier- archy is set independently alongside. According to canon 6, this hier- archy rests not on divine institution, but on divine ordinance. The question whether the consecration of a bishop is a sacrament is deliber- ately left open. The doctrine of an enduring sacramental character im- printed at ordination implies not only an acknowledgment of the faithfulness of God, whose gracious gifts (granted through the Holy Spirit) are given irrevocably and without regret. It also protects the right of the community to services that are independent of the per- sonal quality of the officeholder. In a positive sense, however, this means that the service to which ordained persons are called lays claim to their whole existence and cannot be a mere function. In the hierar- chy, the bishops (with no special mention of the pope) are described as the superior authority. The manner of division and the style of this text show that the intent is only to refute the Reformers' positions and not to present a complete theology of orders; consequently, there is practically no attempt at biblical foundation. One-sided positions are rejected; quite obviously the council did not intend to deny the im- portance of preaching the Word or of the common priesthood of be- lievers, nor did it wish to refuse the people a part in the selection of bishops.[31]

Of special importance for sacramental theology as a whole, and for the sacrament of orders in particular, was and is Pius XII's apostolic constitution, *Sacramentum Ordinis* of 30 November 1947 (NR 724/DS 3857-3861). Here the pope expressed his views on the Church's com-

31. On the Tridentine teaching on orders, from Bibliography 9 see L. Ott, *Das Weihesakrament* and P. de Clerck, "Ordination"; from Bibliography 1, A. Duval, *Les sacrements au Concile de Trente.* For a critique of Trent, see B. Snela's article in *NHthG* III (1985) 433-434.

petence regarding the sacraments; he declared that only the imposition of hands constitutes the "matter" in the ordination of deacons, priests, and bishops, and that the "form" is simply those words "determining the application of the matter" and unequivocally signifying the effects of the sacrament, namely, the *potestas ordinis* and the grace of the Holy Spirit. This declaration was basic to the statements of Vatican II on sacramental theology and the liturgical reforms that followed. The Pope thus decided that the handing over of the liturgical vessels is not (or is no longer) part of the sacramental action of ordination.

11.3.3 *Vatican Council II and the New Code of Canon Law*

The renewal movements of the twentieth century have contributed, particularly through a wealth of biblical and patristic studies and research into the history of liturgy, to a revision of the main emphases in the theology of orders. These efforts were reflected in the documents of the Second Vatican Council, both in the pathbreaking constitution on the liturgy and especially in *Lumen Gentium*. By contrast, ecumenical discussions of the problem of office have not left such prominent traces in the conciliar texts; they made their more significant progress only after the council (see 11.5 below).

In describing ordination and offices in the Church, Vatican II followed its established course: while preserving earlier teaching, it sought to broaden the point of view, to shift the points of emphasis, and thus to renew both theology and praxis. The distinction between clerics and laity was retained as a matter of course, but it was relativized by the emphasis on, and the precedence given to those things that all members of the Church have in common. The first concept that is given prominence is that of the "people of God" (LG II), which, if it is properly employed, should really consider Israel as included, and not merely "related to" it (LG 16).

The second comprehensive factor is the common priesthood. Through baptism, *all* are consecrated priests, called and empowered to offer spiritual sacrifices, to preach and to bear witness. This is considered a sharing in the priesthood of Jesus Christ (LG 10). A distinction is then drawn within this common priesthood:

> Though they differ from one another in essence and not only in degree,
> the common priesthood of the faithful and the ministerial or hierarchi-

cal priesthood are nonetheless interrelated. Each of them in its own special way is a participation in the one priesthood of Christ. The ministerial priest, by the sacred power he enjoys, molds and rules the priestly people. Acting in the person of Christ, he brings about the Eucharistic Sacrifice, and offers it to God in the name of all the people. For their part, the faithful join in the offering of the Eucharist by virtue of their royal priesthood. They likewise exercise that priesthood by receiving the sacraments, by prayer and thanksgiving, by the witness of a holy life, and by self-denial and active charity (LG 10).

According to this council, the way in which the two kinds of priestly activity are complementarily related to one another is similar to the way in which the common sense of faith of all believers is related to the teaching office of the Church: in the latter case, the common basis is a sharing in the prophetic office of Jesus Christ (LG 12).

After thus laying the groundwork, the council next speaks of "The Hierarchical Structure of the Church, with Special Reference to the Episcopate" (LG III). The chapter title indicates where the emphasis will be placed, clearly following the indications from the third century (Hippolytus' church order and the subsequent Eastern liturgies).[32] The council takes as its starting point the officeholders' possession of a "sacred power," without describing that power any more precisely (LG 18). It speaks of the Twelve, of the unity of the apostles with and under Peter who formed a college, i.e., as the council interprets it, a "fixed group" (LG 19) who appointed their successors to carry on their ministry. Thus the bishops are to be regarded as shepherds of the Church who "by divine institution" have succeeded to the place of the apostles (LG 20; cf. 28: the apostles have legitimately handed on to different individuals in the Church various degrees of participation in their ministry). Concerning bishops, the council teaches that Jesus Christ is present and active in them to the extent that they are his servants. He acts "above all," but not exclusively through their service in this sacramental manner, a service that includes preaching the word of God (which is mentioned first by the council, both here and elsewhere). The council then proceeds to the teaching that the consecration of a bishop confers "the fullness of the sacrament of orders." Thus, the traditional theology of orders with its ascending ladder of ordinations

---

32. On what follows, see the commentaries on the council. I am here using my own text from *Kleines Konzilskompendium*, 109–115.

and the concept of episcopal consecration as an unessential addition to priestly ordination has been abandoned; *ordo* means those sacramentally ordained, a complex entity corresponding to the ancient concept of the *sacerdotium*. The "fullness of the priesthood" belongs to the bishop, and the other degrees of ordination confer a limited, though not in every way dependent, share in that fullness.

The council goes on to state that episcopal consecration confers the three offices of sanctifying, teaching, and governing. The two "powers" of orders and jurisdiction are here seen in their internal, that is, their sacramental unity. However, the council says that the exercise of the office of teaching and governing can only be carried out in complete union with the pope and the whole body of bishops (addressing at the same time the ecumenical problem of true bishops who are separated from Rome). At the end, this very important article (LG 21) speaks of the sacrament of orders in its "fullness"; here the council teaches the sacramentality of episcopal consecration:

> For from tradition, which is expressed especially in liturgical rites and in the practice of the Church both of the East and of the West, it is clear that, by means of the imposition of hands and the words of consecration, the grace of the Holy Spirit is so conferred, and the sacred character so impressed, that bishops in an eminent and visible way undertake Christ's own role as Teacher, Shepherd, and High Priest, and that they act in His person. Therefore it devolves on the bishops to admit newly elected members into the episcopal body by means of the sacrament of orders (LG 21).

From that point, the council turns to the theme of the episcopal college existing in the Church by divine will and possessing, with and under the pope, the highest and fullest power: ". . . one is constituted a member of the episcopal body by virtue of sacramental consecration and by hierarchical communion with the head and members of the body" (LG 22).

The bishop of Rome is the perpetual and visible source for "unity in multiplicity"; the "visible" principle because the real and ultimate principle is the Spirit of Jesus Christ. In parallel fashion, the individual bishop is the visible principle of the unity of his particular Church. The conciliar teaching that the universal Church *consists of* and is composed of the individual Churches is an important one (LG 23). After articles on the mission and teaching office of the bishops (LG 24 and

25), the council turns to the local churches: the whole Church is truly present in the local Church, in word, Eucharist, and love; the bishop is the proper priestly presider in each of these individual local Churches and in every community existing around an altar (LG 26).

The council next speaks about the bishops' work of governing (LG 27), and then turns its attention to priests. There is no detailed discussion of particular historical questions; it is simply stated that the apostles themselves "legitimately handed on to different individuals in the Church various degrees of participation" in their ministry. Through a variety of expressions—"in the image of Christ," "partakers of the function of Christ the sole mediator," "acting in the person of Christ"—the council intends to express a special and direct relationship of the priest to Jesus Christ. Parallel to the bishops, the priests by virtue of sacramental ordination share in the three offices and thus are true priests. The primary emphasis given to the duty of preaching also parallels the teaching on bishops. The priests of a local Church, in unity with their bishop, constitute "one priesthood" in analogy to the collegiality of the bishops. In the local Churches they make the bishops "present in a certain sense," take on some of his duties, lead "that part of the Lord's flock entrusted to them, [making] the universal Church visible in their own locality," and share in concern for the diocese and the whole Church. The revival of ecclesiological elements from the patristic period (beginning with Ignatius of Antioch) is evident here (LG 28, supplemented by PO).

Following this section on priests, Vatican II wanted not only to present its teaching on deacons, but also to offer an opportunity for a reintroduction of the diaconate as a permanent office in the Latin Church. The council teaches that the deacons are sacramentally ordained and thus belong to the hierarchy. However, in contrast to bishops and priests they are not ordained to the priesthood (*sacerdotium*), but to a ministry of service (*ministerium*). The fact that *sacerdotium* is here understood in terms of Eucharistic "powers" is also evident when the text says that the deacons are "at a lower level of the hierarchy." The particular office of deacons is only suggested: they are to make tangible the service of the hierarchy to the people of God. The duties listed are those that in the Church's history were more or less often assigned to the deacons (LG 29).

What is new in the vision of Vatican II is primarily its dynamic: beginning with the mission of Jesus Christ in the Holy Spirit and with the idea that human beings are given a share in that mission, the council views Church office as a share in the threefold office of Jesus Christ in service to the people.[33] The sacrament of orders is seen from the point of view of episcopal consecration as the primary and comprehensive case of ordination to office;[34] the theological relationship of the three ordinations to one another is not explained in detail. The council maintains the traditional teaching that ordination (to priesthood and episcopate), with the conferral of its special character, empowers its subject to act "in the person of Christ" (cf. also PO 2), and though priests are considered in their relationship to the bishop, the source of their priesthood is not the episcopal office, but Jesus Christ alone.[35]

The new Code of Canon Law attempts to remain true to this point of view adopted by Vatican II. It says of the sacrament of orders that "by divine institution" it makes human beings to be consecrated servants (*sacri ministri*) by the ineradicable character it imprints. They are ordained and delegated to this service (*consecrantur et deputantur*), in order that, according to the grade of ordination (*pro suo quisque gradu*) and in the person of Christ the head, they may fulfill the duties of teaching, sanctifying, and governing, and pasture the people of God (CIC 1983, canon 1008). The expression *consecrari* indicates that this is an experience that lays claim to the whole of a person's existence, a deeper matter than a mere induction into office which, under certain circumstances, can also be called *ordinari*. "*Ex divina institutione*" was deliberately chosen instead of "*ex Christi institutione*," in order not to say that Jesus Christ had appointed priests and deacons. The sacramental character and the acting in the person of Christ are not necessarily to be understood as applying to deacons.[36] *Ordines* in the Latin Church are "*episcopatus, presbyteratus et diaconatus*" (CIC 1983, canon 1001 § 1): since 1 January 1973 only these three constitute the clerical orders. Minor orders, including the subdiaconate, were abolished in the Latin Church at that time. Lectors and acolytes continue, for the services of reading and of serving at the altar, but they are no longer called *ordines*. Instead, they are *ministeria*, and are not conferred by an *or-*

33. Cf. L. Schick, *Das dreifache Amt Christi und der Kirche* (Frankfurt: 1982).
34. H. Müller in *HKR* 716–717.
35. Ibid.
36. Ibid., 718.

dinatio (ordination or induction into office), but by an *institutio* (installation or commissioning).[37] Those commissioned, like the ministers of communion, are not part of the *clerus*; they exercise their offices as lay persons.

The external sign of each of these three ordinations is the imposition of hands and the appropriate prayer of ordination.[38] These prayers are as follows. For the ordination of bishops: "Send down upon this chosen one the power that comes from you, the Spirit of leadership which you gave to your beloved Son Jesus Christ. He gave the Holy Spirit to the apostles, and they founded your sanctuary, the Church, everywhere on earth, to the everlasting praise and glory of your Name." For the ordination of priests: "Almighty God, we pray you: give to your servants the dignity of priesthood. Renew in them the Spirit of holiness. Grant, O God, that they may hold fast to the office they have received from your hand; let their lives be an incentive and a guideline for all." For the ordination of deacons: "Send down upon them, O Lord, the Holy Spirit. May his sevenfold gifts strengthen them so that they may perform their service with fidelity."[39]

Regarding the "minister" of the sacrament of orders, the new Code of Canon Law gives special attention to the concept of validity and the question: who is allowed to administer the sacrament? Theologically relevant is the determination that every validly consecrated bishop in turn validly ordains to the episcopate, presbyterate, and diaconate (CIC 1983, canon 1012).[40]

Concerning the recipients, the Code says that "according to canon 1024 only a baptized man is capable of validly receiving sacred orders."[41] (On the ordination of women, see 11.4.4 below.) Admission to orders is granted on the basis of a divine call to this ecclesial service which, according to the Church's long experience, can be recog-

---

37. Ibid., 719. On this point, see especially B. Kleinheyer, "Ordinationen und Beauftagungen" (Bibliography 9).

38. Paul VI, apostolic constitution *Pontificalis Romani* (18 June 1968), *AAS* 60 (1968) 369–373, confirming the 1947 decision of Pius XII; motu proprio *Ministeria quaedam* (15 August 1972), *AAS* 64 (1972) 529–534.

39. See H. Müller, *HKR*, 719–720.

40. Ibid., 720–723, with guidelines for what is permitted and remarks on problematic "cases."

41. Ibid., 723.

nized in the aptitude and attitude of the candidate; the local Church sets up a series of criteria for such recognition.[42]

11.4   *The Sacrament of Orders: Systematic Aspects*

11.4.1   *Bishop*

From the historical point of view, "ordained office" in the Church is so broadly conceived that it offers the possibility of placing the emphases differently according to the demands of a particular period. In the course of time the "images" of the priest have shifted, and not everything that theology may have introduced into its "priestly image" could be maintained in light of authentic tradition. According to our present conception, the theological emphasis in sacramental priesthood is clearly on the bishop. It is in looking at the bishop that we can most clearly discern what "ordination" is and what are its effects.

Ordination in Catholic thinking is not merely an induction into office. It is a conferral of the Spirit in the form of an epiclesis, i.e., in the petition of the Church that, in faith, is certain of being heard. This prayer thus refers to the charism, the effectiveness of the gift of the divine Spirit who is believed to be present. It is the Church's faith that God will enable the one ordained to make sensibly present (in the manner of a real image) in the Church, and through it in the world, the work of Jesus Christ: in this person Jesus Christ is and remains the one who is really acting, in his Spirit, to the glory of the Father; the ordained person is taken into this service, but is not, as a person, the representative of the absent Jesus Christ.[43]

It is obvious that the Holy Spirit of God belongs to the Church, the body of Jesus Christ, as a whole: the earthly Jesus made this steadfast promise to the faithful, and the exalted Jesus leads them through his Spirit. In sovereign freedom, he awakens in the Church those gifts that

---

42. More detail (including the impediments to ordination) and bibliography, may be found in ibid., 724–727.

43. This is well described by A. Müller, "Amt als Kriterium," 111, with the additional remark that the Church in antiquity was influenced in this question not by Aristotelian ideas of causality, but by Platonic concepts of relationship. P. J. Cordes also (see Bibliography 9) wishes to understand acting *in persona Christi* as "exclusively relating to the action" (p. 111).

he desires to grant it. The Church firmly maintains that among these effects of the Spirit is the uniting of the Church into an organized society, and therefore its structuring in *ordines* and the bestowal of the charism of governance in the *ordo* as one among many charisms.

The Spirit who is active in the Church effects, according to New Testament witnesses (Rom 8:26), its prayer of petition. The Spirit has also moved the Church to combine its prayer of ordination with the gesture of imposing hands, familiar since ancient times, into a sacramental sign, without any necessity that this had to have been expressly ordered by Jesus Christ or the apostles.[44] In this liturgy, which in this sense confers the Spirit, the ordained person is at the same time incorporated into a community within the Church, made up of bishops, priests, and deacons.

Through episcopal consecration a bishop is inducted into the college that witnesses to the apostolic faith, binds the local Churches within the continuity of faith, represents the unity of the Church, bears responsibility for the liturgy as the glorification of God, and thus guarantees the empirical identity, the recognizability of the Church. The dynamic of this office is both historical and eschatological: it is no contradiction to the providence of the divine Spirit that this office has become historical, shaped by decisions taken in time and space; and it corresponds to the finality of the divine message, which is preserved and transmitted by this means, that such an important development is irreversible and irrevocable.

This being-taken-into-service for Jesus Christ, the one who is really active, a service that lays claim to a human being in totality (''existentiell''), participates in such irrevocability; it can, of course, be transformed from a situation of lively activity to one of rest (e.g., when a bishop goes into retirement), but it can never be reversed as if it had not happened. That is the meaning of the doctrine of the sacramental character or mark, which at the same time implies that an ordination can only be given once and may never be repeated.[45]

44. A. Müller, "Amt als Kriterium, 119.

45. There are some good observations on the sacramental character in the sacrament of orders in P. Fransen, "Weihen, Heilige," 1286–1289. Fransen views the sacramental character primarily as the visible rite of ordination, "through which the ordinand is legitimately incorporated in the college of his Ordo and thereby takes on himself a body of rights and duties" (1288).

That the one thus ordained and accepted into service remains a hearer among hearers, a believer among believers, a sinner among sinners, and is not changed into some kind of "higher being," is perfectly obvious.

The special sacramental grace is to be understood as the assistance of the loving and justifying God for the fulfillment of the specific mission or service intended for the office.[46]

11.4.2   *Priests*

The priest is the bishop's assistant. His duties depend to a certain extent on the particular situation, so that the theological "image" of the priest is not completely settled; some duties, however, have remained constant in the tradition and were undergirded by Vatican II (and developments since): among these, the priestly role in the celebration of the Eucharist was determinative for the priest's "image" and continues to be so. In most areas where priests are active today, we can rightly speak of a "sacramental pole" and an "institutional pole" of their tasks.[47] The priest's capacities in the sacramental area are not given by the bishop and do not come from the assignment of his duties nor from the community: they come through ordination, whose effect is that priests—as was already said of the bishop—are able to be images and instruments of Jesus Christ, who is invisibly present. It is he who proclaims his Word through their ministry and who, in the liturgy, glorifies his Father in the Holy Spirit for the salvation of humanity. In the concrete exercise of their ministry in celebrating the sacraments within the liturgy, including the ministry of the Word, they are dependent on the bishop whom they represent. It is not without some justice that this double dependency and obscuring of the human person "behind" the liturgical symbolic actions and "behind" the Word of another has led some people to speak of a "depersonalization" of the priest.[48] It is true, of course, that the liturgy achieves its

---

46. Ibid., 1289.
47. Ibid., 1284–1285. (Literature on this subject is instructive concerning various recent theologies of priesthood, not all of which, however, were accepted: e.g., Karl Rahner's theology based on the preaching of the Word, with its somewhat dangerous tendency toward an institutionalization of the prophetic role.)
48. Ibid., 1283.

end independently of the qualities of the presider. But that does not mean that the priest's service can be understood as a mere function; the theological concept of the "servants of Christ" is not adequately served by a functional minimum. It must meet the demands of a particular spirituality that, at its core, is a Jesus-mysticism. In the tasks of pastoral care and in catechesis, as well as in the institutional area, there are still sufficient opportunities for the application of one's own personal talents. Regarding the sacramental character and the grace of priestly ordination, what has been said of the bishop also applies here.

The theology of the priestly office of service need not be radically altered in view of what seems to be a critical situation. The structure of offices, with a college of ordained priests serving with and belonging to a single bishop, arose under the impulse of the divine Spirit and has proved itself in the "normal" situation of the Church and in the fulfillment of its tasks. In the present critical shortage of priests, the fundamental meaning of the common priesthood of all believers, the consciousness of their capability for faith, prayer, and liturgy, and hope in the unshaken charismatic activity of the divine Spirit, even apart from the sacraments, for the continuing life of Christian communities can and must suffice. (See also the previous remarks on spiritual communion: 8.4.9). It need not be supposed that in such critical situations the community itself can "empower" people of its own choice to sacramental service. But the crisis can contribute to a correction of lopsided notions of priesthood and serve to incorporate priests more thoroughly and more perceptibly within their communities. This means, among other things, that both in the sacramental area (e.g., baptism, assisting at marriages, anointing the sick, preaching, blessing, and conducting funerals) and in the institutional field (in teaching, organization, etc.) priests will be replaced by other, non-priestly persons. The revival of priestly collegiality can help to build up the image of the priest as a prominent spiritual authority.[49]

49. Against E. Schillebeeckx's attempt to make relative ordination the ideal, we would emphasize the positive value in the fact that a priest is primarily seen in the context of the college of presbyters. This college embodies many opportunities for mutual help and a flexibility that is not present when a priest is completely dependent on—and "handed over to"—a parish or other local community.

11.4.3 *Deacons*

There were two primary reasons for the renewal of the permanent, ordained diaconate in the Latin Church:[50] (1) the hierarchy of the ordained, as a group set apart in the Church, should make it evident that *diakonia*, service in the social-charitable area, is also laid upon them and that this service is exercised in the closest possible connection with the liturgy; (2) in the crisis situation caused by the shortage of priests, assistance should be provided in various areas (although the Church from the beginning reserved the role of presiding at the Eucharist and at the sacrament of reconciliation to those in priestly orders). The duties of the deacon are not tightly circumscribed, nor can they be; none of the tasks that Vatican II mentioned as possible assignments for deacons (LG 29) is exclusively reserved to them. Nonetheless, all that the deacon does is done *as* a member of the hierarchy, of the *clerus*; whether married or not, the deacon is one of the sacramentally ordained. In his person, the deacon makes it clear that the liturgy must have concrete consequences in the world with all its needs, and that work in the world that is done in the spirit of charity has a spiritual dimension. Sacramental ordination asks for and effects in deacons the grace to perform this service.

In addition, the Latin Church also retains a sacramental ordination of deacons as a stage on the way to priesthood. This is intended to make candidates aware of the diaconal dimension of their calling. Ordinarily, these deacons also perform concrete tasks of that nature for a period of time.

11.4.4 *The Ordination of Women*

On this issue, it is not a question of blessings given to and by women (see chapter 13 below), but of women's access to ordained ministry,

50. In addition to the commentaries on LG 29, see K. Rahner and H. Vorgrimler, *Diaconia in Christo* (Freiburg: 1961), with bibliography; J. G. Plöger and H. J. Weber, *Der Diakon. Wiederentdeckung und Erneuerung seines Dienstes* (Freiburg: 1980), with bibliography; H. Schwendenwein, "Der ständige Diakon," *HKR* 229–238; S. Zardoni, *Idiaconi nella chiesa* (Bologna: 1983). Information on the further practical and theological development of the diaconate can be found in the periodical *Diaconia XP* published by the Internationales Diakonats-Zentrum, Freiburg im Breisgau (not to be confused with the *Diakonia* published in Vienna).

the subject of discussion in this chapter in connection with the sacrament of orders. The twentieth century has witnessed an increasing consciousness on the part of women of their oppression and degradation (sometimes in the form of elevation on a pedestal), of their unequal treatment in the socio-economic realm, and of restrictions placed on their equality as citizens. A worldwide emancipation movement has had a sensitizing effect, and has won a place in the Catholic Church as well.[51] Among the requests directed to Vatican II was that for the admission of women to priestly ordination. In an ecumenical context, it was pointed out that women pastors are being ordained in a number of Protestant Churches.

In Catholic sacramental theology before Vatican II the exclusion of women from priestly orders (CIC 1917, canon 986) was regarded as unproblematic. Karl Rahner set off a dogmatic discussion of the question: is this exclusion founded on revelation, i.e., is it "of divine law?"[52] In its declaration, *Inter insigniores*, of 15 October, 1976,[53] the Congregation for the Doctrine of the Faith concluded that, in fidelity to the model of the actions of Jesus Christ and the apostles, the Church does not feel authorized to admit women to priestly orders, since the priest must represent the man Jesus Christ (among other things, as bride-

51. Cf. the historical overviews in *Frauen in der Männerkirche?* (*Concilium* 16/4 [1980]). The feminist theological literature to date is immense; cf. the current bibliographies under a special heading in *Ephemerides Theologicae Lovanienses*. Cf. also M. Kaiser, "Die Stellung der Frau in der Kirche," HKR 179–181, with bibliography.

52. H. van der Meer's dissertation, *Priestertum der Frau* (1962), directed by Karl Rahner and published at Freiburg in 1969, saw no adequate reasons for the exclusion of women from priestly orders. A dissertation by M. Hauke directed by L. Scheffczyk, *Die Problematik zum das Frauenpriestertum vor dem Hintergrund der Schöpfung- und Erlösungsordnung* (Paderborn: 1982) came to the opposite conclusion, that is, that the exclusion of women from ordained priesthood has a divine basis. W. Beinert writes correctly concerning Hauke's work (*Theologie und Glaube* 73 [1983] 203): "Qui nimis probat, nihil probat [who proves too much, proves nothing]. This is an ideological work based on an enormous body of (not very well assimilated) material from all possible fields of knowledge. The opportunity for a detailed and objective discussion of a question to which a well-founded solution must be given, one way or the other, has been wasted in this book. One can well imagine that it will have the opposite effect from that intended: anyone familiar with its argumentation will be tempted to adopt the contrary thesis."

53. *AAS* 69 (1977) 98–116. A German commentary with a tendentious commentary (denying the possibility of priestly ordination for women from the outset) is *Die Sendung der Frau in der Kirche* (Kevelaer: 1978).

groom of the Church). Important counter-arguments, for example that every woman who "administers" a sacrament (baptism, marriage) "represents" Jesus Christ, were not discussed. The declaration admits that it can offer no conclusive proof to justify the practice of the Church, but it declines to treat the question in the context of discussion about equal rights for women, since access to the priesthood should not be regarded as a right. The declaration's style of argumentation has been subjected to sharp criticism.[54] Nevertheless, the new Code of Canon Law retained the precise wording of the old Code, excluding women from the sacrament of orders (CIC 1983, canon 1024).

Thus it is highly probable that for the immediate future women's access to the priesthood is blocked. The reasons for this are clear. The Latin Church makes no decisions, certainly not those that have broad implications, under any sort of deliberate pressure. The question was bound to be decided negatively from the moment it was advanced in the form of an emancipatory demand couched in terms of class struggle, often combined with a coercive threat that, if ordination were not permitted, women would leave the Church. There are no compelling theological reasons for the Latin Church's refusal; not even the new Code of Canon Law claims that its position is "of divine law." However, in the foreground of present theological discussion there are two grounds for denying women's ordination that are worthy of serious consideration, and may even be called plausible: (1) in a development lasting nearly two thousand years, what has emerged is a structure of office that is completely masculine in form. Such a development cannot be abruptly interrupted; it can only be revised forward, in the sense of a new and expanded form; (2) the question must be seen in an ecumenical context in which the separated Eastern Churches regard themselves as the special defenders of the authentic apostolic tradition. An admission of women to the priesthood without the agreement of the Eastern Churches would do damage to ecumenical efforts.

The possibility of ordaining women as deacons is quite another matter. There was such an ordination in the early days of the Church.[55]

54. H. Pissarek-Hudelist, "Die Bedeutung der Sakramententheologie Karl Rahners für die Diskussion um das Priestertum der Frau," in H. Vorgrimler, ed., *Wagnis Theologie* (Freiburg: 1979) 417–434 (with bibliography); H. Müller, *HKR*, 724 (with bibliography).
55. In recent literature, see: H. Frohnhofen, "Weibliche Diakone in der frühen Kirche," *Stimmen der Zeit* 111 (1986) 269–278, with bibliography; C. Oeyen, "Priester-

There are important reasons for thinking that women were part of a group of co-workers, even in New Testament times, from which later arose the ordained ministry of women deacons or deaconesses. We have evidence of women deacons in Asia Minor in the second century and in Syria in the third century; the Western Church partly rejected them, but they existed there also from the fifth century, and there were still women deacons at Rome in the eleventh century, and in the Byzantine Church until the fifteenth century.[56] In the East, and in imperial law, they were counted among the *clerus*.[57] According to the *Didascalia* (a north Syrian church order from the third century), the woman deacon (or deaconess) is to be honored as a type of the Holy Spirit. The question whether their ordination is sacramental could not be asked before the reflections on sacramental theology in high Scholasticism. In the Byzantine liturgy, it has all the characteristics of a major ordination.[58]

In light of the existing common tradition in East and West there is no serious reason to continue excluding women from the flexibly conceived permanent diaconate.[59] Diaconal orders for women would undoubtedly be a sacramental ordination, and the women so ordained would be part of the *clerus*.

amt der Frau?'' *Ökumenische Rundschau* 35 (1986) 254–266. The periodical *Diakonia XP* (see n. 50 above) also lists literature on the ordination of women to the diaconate.

56. A. G. Martimort, *Les diaconesses* (Paris: 1982) interprets the sources with an openly minimalist tendency. In his opinion, all the documents mentioning women deacons in which liturgical ministries are not mentioned do not refer to real deacons (cf. C. Oeyen, ''Priesteramt der Frau?'' 257). Of course, Martimort also pays no attention to the fact that before the Council of Nicaea in 325 *diakonos* could mean both men and women deacons.

57. On this point, see H. Frohnhofen, ''Weibliche Diakone,'' and in more detail O. Barlea, *Dei Weihe der Bischöfe, Presbyter und Diakone in vornicänischer Zeit* (Munich: 1969).

58. C. Oeyen, ''Priesteramt der Frau?'' 256 (with bibliography); E. Theodorou, ''Das Priestertum nach dem Zeugnis der byzantinischen liturgischen Texte,'' *Ökumenische Rundschau* 35 (1986) 267–280, at 271. Fundamental to the discussion are the findings of C. Vagaggini, ''L'ordinazione delle diaconesse nella tradizione greca e bizantina,'' *Orientalia Christiana Periodica* 40 (1974) 145–189.

59. H. Müller, *HKR*, 724, points to a motion of the Würzburg synod of 1975 asking the Pope to consider the question of the diaconate for women, based on positive assessments by Y. Congar, P. Hünermann, O. Semmelroth and H. Vorgrimler. The request had, by 1986, received no answer. Cf. M. Kaiser *HKR*, 181.

11.5   Ecumenical Dialogue

11.5.1   The Perspective of the Eastern Churches

If it is true that the essential differences between the Roman Catholic Church and the separated Eastern Churches concern the Petrine office in particular, there are also theological disagreements regarding other offices. These divergences, however, are not such as to divide the Churches; they appear within a legitimate spectrum of variation in which one point of view can have a critical and corrective function for another.

The Eastern liturgy,[60] which, next to the Bible, is the most important source for the theology of the Eastern Churches, distinguishes the ordination (cheirotonia) of the three upper levels (bishop, priest, and deacons, both male and female) from the blessing (cheirothesia) of the lower grades. The three major ordinations have the same structure: a solemn agreement of those present to the ordination of a candidate; an epiclesis to the Holy Spirit for the grace necessary to exercise the particular office; imposition of hands; clothing.

The Eastern Churches recognize something corresponding to what is called "divine law" in the Latin Church: what comes from God and is constitutive for the Church need not be expressly witnessed in the New Testament; instead, it is understood as coming into existence within history and at the same time as effected by the Holy Spirit. The three canonical grades of ordained ministry are regarded as the constitutive form with the greatest historical and ecumenical dignity. In these, the major emphasis lies on the office of bishops: the Church of Jesus Christ is episcopal in form. The college of bishops is seen as the group of those who are the successors of the apostles; the consecration of a bishop by three other bishops, prescribed since Nicaea in 325, means that the one consecrated is received into the episcopal college and—by means of the "apostolic succession" conferred through the unbroken series of imposition of hands—it signifies the continued building up of the Church on the foundation of the apostles. In the local Churches, where the body of Christ is constituted not by addi-

---

60. On this, see E. Theodorou, "Das Priestertum," and, still unsurpassed, J. D. Zizioulas on ordination in the Eastern Churches in H. Vorgrimler, ed., *Amt und Ordination in ökumenischer Sicht* (Freiburg: 1972) 72–113.

tion, but by a mutual inclusion of one within another, the bishop is considered the representative and delegate of Jesus Christ.[61]

The fundamental service is performed by Jesus Christ, who was sent by the Father; the minister is only his instrument, acting within a Christological and pneumatological perspective. In the view of the Eastern Churches the priest should not be regarded as acting *in persona Christi*; rather, the priest is the *symbolon Christou*, a representative who does not ontologically assume the place of Christ, but works through the grace of the Spirit. In Latin terms, the priest acts *in nomine Christi* and *in persona Ecclesiae*. The Eastern Churches cannot agree that the sacraments can be administered with indicative formulae or that the Eucharistic transubstantiation could (in case of necessity) be accomplished without an epiclesis.[62]

Through the epiclesis, the laity become fellow-liturgists. But there is a qualitative, essential, and not only gradual or functional distinction between spiritual office and the lay state. Clerics and laity are related to one another as communicating bodies: the ordained priesthood is the precondition for the priesthood of all.[63]

Among the sacramentally ordained, the deacon has a middle location between divine worship and charitable work, but none of the deacon's duties extends into the "strictly consecratory" (Eucharistic) realm of the *sacerdotium*.[64]

In summary we may say that the functions of ecclesiastical office effect among the faithful the disposition for the gracious activity of the Holy Spirit; this circumstance is sacramentally embodied in the functions of office. The spiritual office is a representation of the charismatic reality, namely the reality of Jesus Christ, who is present in the Church through his Holy Spirit.[65] This fundamental sacramental-theological view is no different from the Roman Catholic position.

61. E. Theodorou, "Das Priestertum," 274–275.
62. Ibid., 276–277.
63. Ibid., 277–278.
64. Ibid., 278–279. To say that the duties listed for deacons in LG 29 are exclusively reserved to the deacon is a misunderstanding (ibid., 278).
65. Ibid., 280.

11.5.2   *A Minimal Consensus*

The theological concept of office in the Eastern churches and in the Roman Catholic Church encounters objections in the theology that emerged from the Reformation. Nevertheless, ecumenical discussions with the Reformation Churches have made a positive beginning and are not without result. Harald Wagner summarizes the minimal consensus that has been reached so far as follows:[66] The call of all Christians to preach the gospel, accepted in faith by all the Churches, does not exclude offices and ministries assigned to particular persons. The holders of those offices and ministries are dependent on an inner call from the Holy Spirit and on the confirmation of their service by the whole Church. This confirmation and delegation from the Church is done through ordination, which, as a rule, is conferred by officials who are already themselves ordained, and who, with prayer and the imposition of hands, call the ordinands to special office in the Church. The ordinand, relying on the grace of God, accepts the obligation to serve in obedience to God's word and in unity with the confessions (dogmas) of the Church. An apostolic succession is accepted by all the Churches in the sense that the faith of a Church must agree with the witness of the apostles and thus maintain a continuing connection with the apostles' fundamental ministry. Church office has authority only to the extent that it serves the absolute authority of the word of God. It "represents" Jesus Christ and his position within the community only insofar as it gives expression to the gospel.

Within Catholicism, the following arguments, consciously directed in an ecumenical spirit to speak to the Protestant position, have been successfully advanced;[67] office is seen as a sharing in the three "offices of Christ" (as described in Calvinist theology). Here the primacy of the preaching of God's word receives special emphasis. The nature of office, including the office of governance in the community, as service is brought to the fore. The teaching on the "sacramental character" is "softened," if this is interpreted primarily as meaning that ordination is not repeatable. Apostolic succession is considered a suc-

---

66. H. Wagner, "Das Amt vor dem Hintergrund der Diskussion um eine evangelisch—katholische Grunddifferenz," *Catholica* 40 (1986) 39–58. I am following Wagner (48–49) literally. Cf. also Bibliography 2; on the previous status of ecumenical discussion, see S. Regli (Bibliography 2).

67. A. Müller, "Amt als Kriterium," 113.

cession in faith, a succession both of the living word and of persons. The question of the sacramentality of orders appears subject to a solution, if the theology of *all* the Churches, under the influence of exegetical research, can be disengaged from a fixation on the institutional words of the historical Jesus and can conceive the notion of sacramentality in broader terms. When Protestant theology does not deny to office the dimension of the Holy Spirit, it implicitly accepts its sacramentality.[68]

11.5.3 *Questions Still Outstanding*

Apart from the fact that there are individual Christians in all Churches who, from a joy in division for its own sake, indulge in finer and finer hairsplitting in order to emphasize the differences among the Churches,[69] the statements that have separated us heretofore are (1) those regarding apostolic succession in episcopal office and (2) those concerning the sacrament of orders, to the extent that it empowers those ordained to represent Christ (and so, as is said, levels out the essential difference between God and human beings), so that it is essential for the one who presides at a "valid" Eucharistic celebration. Differences of opinion exist within Catholicism, especially with regard to the representation of Christ and, in connection with that, the empowerment of the priest through the sacrament of orders. It is widely accepted that the reservation of leadership in the Eucharistic celebration is necessary for Church order. That an empowerment for that role does not mean that priests act in their own name and by their own power is a basic and common conviction. In that case, however, expressions that state or imply that ordination causes an "ontological assimilation" to Jesus Christ can only create confusion.

68. Ibid., 118. Cf. also the suggestions for unity in H. Fries and K. Rahner, *Einigung der Kirchen—reale Möglichkeit* (Freiburg: 1983; 6th ed., 1985), especially H. Fries' replies to criticisms at 157–189.

69. Thus it is no longer comprehensible that Eilert Herms, in his controversy with the Lima document (*Kerygma und Dogma* 31 [1985] 67–96) says that office exists only to witness to revelation and not, as in the Catholic view, to hand it on. If such a statement means anything at all, it must be based on the idea that revelation is fixed once and for all, even in its linguistic form, so that faith can only refer to that fixed revelation and must abandon all thought and understanding. That kind of Platonic-idealistic construct should, however, no longer bear the name of divine revelation.

Bibliography 9

Office and Ordination

a) Books

Amt und Dienst in den liturgischen Versammlungen (*Concilium* 8/2) 1972.

Barlea, O. *Die Weihe der Bischöfe, Presbyter und Diakone in vornicänischer Zeit.* Munich: 1969.

Becker, K. J. *Der priestliche Dienst* II. Freiburg: 1970.

Betti, U. *La dottrina sull'episcopato del Concilio Vaticano II.* Rome: 1984.

Cordes, P. J. *Sendung zum Dienst. Exegetisch-historische und systematische Studien zum Konzilsdekret "Vom Dienst und Leben der Priester."* Frankfurt: 1972.

Cunningham, A. *The Bishop in the Church.* Wilmington: 1985 (collection of patristic texts).

Das Recht der Gemeinde auf einen Priester (*Concilium* 16/3) 1980.

Deissler, A., and others. *Der priesterliche Dienst* I. Freiburg: 1970.

Delhaye, P., and L. Elders, eds. *Episcopale munus.* Assen: 1982.

Der Bischof und die Einheit der Kirche (*Concilium* 8/1) 1972.

Der Streit um das Amt in der Kirche. Regensburg: 1983.

Faivre, A. *Naissance d'une hiérarchie.* Paris: 1977.

Farnedi, G., and P. Rouillard, eds. *Il ministero ordinato nel dialogo ecumenico.* Rome: 1985.

García Manzanedo, V. *Carisma—ministerio en el Concilio Vaticano Segundo.* Madrid: 1982.

Gaudemet, J. *Les élections dans l'Eglise latine des origines au XVIe siècle*. Paris: 1979.

Gegenseitige Anerkennung der Ämter (Concilium 8/4) 1972.

Gemeinsame röm-kath./ev.-luth. Kommission [Lutheran-Roman Catholic Common Commission]. *Das geistliche Amt*. Paderborn and Frankfurt: 1981.

Genn, F. *Trinität und Amt nach Augustinus*. Einsiedeln: 1986 (only Jesus Christ has *potestas*, according to Augustine; representation is not an Augustinian teaching).

Ghirlanda, G. *"Hierarchica Communio."* Rome: 1980 (the bishop according to *Lumen Gentium*).

Greshake, G. *Priester sein. Zur Theologie und Spiritualität des priesterlichen Amtes*. Freiburg: 1982 and further editions.

Hainz, J., ed. *Kirche im Werden. Studium zum Thema Amt und Gemeinde im NT*. Paderborn: 1976.

Holmberg, B. *Paul and Power. The Structure of Authority in the Primitive Church as Reflected in the Pauline Epistles*. Lund: 1978.

Hopko, T., ed. *Women and the Priesthood*. Crestwood, N.Y.: 1983.

Jilek, A. *Initiationsfeier und Amt. Ein Beitrag zur Struktur und Theologie der Ämter und des Taufgottesdienstes in der frühen Kirche*. Frankfurt and Berne: 1979.

Kertelge, K. *Gemeinde und Amt im Neuen Testament*. Munich: 1972.

König, D. *Amt und Askese. Priesteramt und Mönchtum bei den lateinischen Kirchenvätern in vorbenediktinischer Zeit*. St. Ottilien: 1986.

Laurence, J. D. *'Priest' as Type of Christ. The Leader of the Eucharist in Salvation History according to Cyprian of Carthage*. New York, Frankfurt, and Berne: 1984.

Lecuyer, J. *Le Sacrement de l'ordination. Recherche historique et théologique*. Paris: 1983.

Macquarrie, J. *Theology, Church and Ministry*. London: 1986.

Marliangéas, B.-M. *Clés pour une théologie du ministère. In persona Christi. In persona Ecclesia*. Paris: 1978.

Martelet, G. *Théologie du sacerdoce I*. Paris: 1984.

Martimort, A. G. *Les diaconesses*. Rome: 1982.

Martin, J. *Der priesterliche Dienst III*. Freiburg: 1972.

Mumm, R., ed. *Ordination und kirchliches Amt*. Paderborn and Bielefeld: 1976 (results of ecumenical discussion).

Ott, L. *Das Weihesakrament*. Handbuch der Dogmengeschichte IV/5. Freiburg: 1969.

Rahner, K. *Vorfragen zu einem ökumenischen Amtsverständnis*. Freiburg: 1974.

————. *Reform und Anerkennung kirchlicher Ämter*. Mainz: 1973.

Rhode, J. *Urchristliche und frühkatholische Ämter*. Berlin: 1976.

Richter, K. *Die Ordination des Bischofs von Rom. Eine Untersuchung der Weihe liturgie*. Münster: 1976.

Schick, L. *Das dreifache Amt Christi und der Kirche*. Frankfurt and Berne: 1982.

Schillebeeckx, E. *Christliche Identität und kirchliches Amt.* Düsseldorf: 1985.

Schröer, H., and G. Müller. *Vom Amt des Laien in Kirche und Theologie.* Berlin and New York: 1982.

Tillard, J.-M. R. *L'évêque de Rome.* Paris: 1984.

Université d'Angers, ed. *L'évêque dans l'histoire de l'Eglise.* Angers: 1984.

Vanhoye, A. *Prêtres anciens, prêtre nouveau selon le Nouveau Testament.* Paris: 1980.

Vogel, C. *Ordinations inconsistantes et caractère inamissible.* Turin: 1978.

Von Lips, H. *Glaube—Gemeinde—Amt. Zum Verständnis der Ordination in den Pastoralbriefen.* Göttingen: 1975.

Vorgrimler, H., ed. *Amt und Ordination in ökumenischer Sicht.* Freiburg: 1973.

Weß, P. *Ihr alle seid Geschwister. Gemeinde und Priester.* Mainz: 1983; see articles by L. Lies in *Zeitschrift für katholische Theologie* 108 (1986) 176–179 and P. Weß, ibid., 179–185.

Zardoni, S. *I diaconi nella chiesa.* Bologna: 1983 (history and theology).

Zemp, P. *Das Sakrament der Weihe.* Fribourg (Switzerland): 1977.

Zollitsch, R. *Amt und Funktion des Priesters. Eine Untersuchung zum Ursprung und zur Gestalt des Presbyterats in den ersten zwei Jahrhunderten.* Freiburg: 1974.

b) Articles

Angenendt, A. *Kaiserherrschaft und Königstaufe.* Berlin: 1984, 135–136: absolute and relative ordination of priests in historical perspective.

Blank, J., and B. Snela. "Priester/Bischof." *NHthG* III (1985) 411–441 (with bibliography).

Congar, Y. "Note sur ene valeur des termes 'ordinare, ordinatio.' " *Recherches de science religieuse* 68 (1984) 7–14.

Dassmann, E. "Zur Entstehung des Monepiskopats." *Jahrbuch für Antike und Christentum* 17 (1974) 74–90.

DeClerck, P. "Ordination, Ordre." *Catholicisme* X (1983) 162–206.

Döring, H. "Das Amt im ökumenischen Kontext." *Theologische Revue* 78 (1982) 185–192 (with bibliography).

Dupuy, B. D. "Theologie der kirchenlichen Ämter." *MySal* IV/2 (1973) 488–594.

Faivre, A., and others. "Le devenir des ministères." *Lumière et vie* 33 (1984) 1–106.

Fischer, B. "Das Gebet der Kirche als Wesenselement des Weihesakramentes." *Liturgisches Jahrbuch* 20 (1970) 166–177.

Frohnhofen, H. "Weibliche Diakone in der frühen Kirche." *Stimmen der Zeit* 111 (1986) 269–278 (with bibliography).

Hein, M., and H.-G. Jung. "Bischof, Bischofsamt." *EKL* I (1986) 518–522.

Hilberath, B. J. "Das Verhältnis vom gemeinsamen und amtlichen Priestertum in der Perspektive von Lumen gentium 10." *Trierer theologische Zeitschrift* 94 (1985) 311-326.

Hödl, L. "Das priesterliche Amt in der Kirche." *Münchener Theologische Zeitschrift* 34 (1983) 22-36.

Hoffmann, J. "L'Eglise et son origine." *Initiation à la pratique de la théologie* II (Paris: 1983) 55-141 (with bibliography).

Jilek, A. "Bischof und Presbyterium." *Zeitschrift für katholische Theologie* 106 (1984) 376-401 (on Hippolytus).

Kaczynski, R. "Das Vorsteheramt im Gottesdienst nach den Zeugnissen der Ordinationsliturgie des Ostens und des Westens." *Liturgisches Jahrbuch* 35 (1985) 69-84.

Karrer, M. "Apostel, Apostolat." *EKL* I (1986) 221-223.

Klauck, H.-J. "Gemeinde ohn Amt? Erfahrungen mit der Kirche in den johanneischen Schriften." *Biblische Zeitschrift* 29 (1985) 193-220.

Kleinheyer, B. "Handauflegung zur Geistmitteilung." *Liturgisches Jahrbuch* 30 (1980) 154-173.

————. "Ordinationen und Beauftragungen." In B. Kleinheyer, E. von Severus, and R. Kaczynski, *Sakramentliche Feiern* II (Regensburg: 1984) 7-65.

————. "Apg 1,24 im Kontext der Weiheliturgie." *Zeitschrift für katholische Theologie* 107 (1985) 31-38.

Knoch, O. "Die Funktion der Handauflegung im Neuen Testament." *Liturgisches Jahrbuch* 39 (1983) 222-235.

Kretschmar, G. "Die Ordination im frühen Christentum." *Freiburger Zeitschrift für Philosophie und Theologie* 22 (1975) 35-69.

Legrand, H. "Les ministères de l'Eglise locale." *Initiation à la pratique de la théologie* II (Paris: 1983) 181-273.

Lengeling, E. J. "Die Theologie des Weihesakramentes nach dem Zeugnis des neuen Ritus." *Liturgisches Jahrbuch* 19 (1969) 142-166.

Lohfink, G. "Die Normativität der Amtsvorstellungen in den Pastoralbriefen." *Theologische Quartalschrift* 157 (1977) 93-106.

Müller, A. "Amt als Kriterium der Kirchlichkeit? Kirchlichkeit als Kriterium des Amtes?" *Theologische Berichte* (Zürich) 9 (1980) 97-128.

Müller, H. "Die Ordination." *HKR* 715-727.

Neumann, J., and others. "Bischof." *TRE* VI (1980) 653-697 (with bibliography).

Oeyen, C. "Priesteramt der Frau?" *Ökumenische Rundschau* 35 (1986) 254-266.

Rohls, J. "Das geistliche Amt in der reformatorischen Theologie." *Kerygma und Dogma* 31 (1985) 135-161.

Roloff, J., and others. "Apostel/Apostolat/Apostolizität." *TRE* III (1978) 430-483.

Schwendenwein, H. "Der ständige Diakon." *HKR* 229-238.

Stein, A. "Diakon." *EKL* I (1986) 848–850.

Stockmeier, P. "Das Amt in der Alten Kirche." In H. Althaus, ed. *Kirche: Ursprung und Gegenwart* (Freiburg: 1984) 39–61.

Theodorou, E. "Das Priestertum nach dem Zeugnis der byzantinischen liturgischen Texte." *Ökumenische Rundschau* 35 (1986) 267–280.

Tortras, A. M. "El ministerio a la luz de las liturgias de ordenación." *Estudios eclesiásticos* 60 (1985) 411–441.

Trilling, W. "Zum 'Amt' im Neuen Testament." In U. Luz and H. Weder, eds. *Die Mitte des Neuen Testaments* (Göttingen: 1983) 316–344.

Vanhoye, A., and H. Crouzel. "Le ministère dans l'Eglise." *Nouvelle Revue Théologique* 104 (1982) 722–748 (New Testament and early Church).

Vodopivec, G. "Lo Spirito Santo e il ministerio ordinato." *Euntes Docete* 36 (1983) 329–360.

Vogt, H. J. "Zum Bischofsamt in der frühen Kirche." *Theologische Quartalschrift* 162 (1982) 329–360.

Wagner, H. "Das Amt vor dem Hintergrund der Diskussion um eine evangelisch-katholische Grunddifferenz." *Catholica* 40 (1986) 39–58.

Zizioulas, J. D. "Episkopé et Episkopos dans l'Eglise primitive." *Irénikon* 56 (1983) 484–502.

12

The Sacrament of Marriage

12.1 Introduction

Marriage is a "legally recognized relationship between two human persons of different sex for a full community of life."[1] According to the belief of the Catholic Church, the marriage of two baptized persons is a sacrament. Thus marriage focuses a variety of dimensions into one. Since we can only speak of the sacramental aspect here, very important questions must remain outside the discussion: in sacramental theology we cannot deal with sexuality and its human forms, or with the emancipation of women, or with the problems in the life of couples or in communities of persons living together, or with celibacy and its values.

In the view of classic Scholastic theology, God created marriage in Eden. When a distinction is made between the orders of creation and redemption, we must therefore say that marriage originates in the order of creation. The Book of Genesis does indeed speak very eloquently about woman and man (1:27; 2:21-24), and if even an individual human

1. A. Stein in *TRE* IX (1982) 355.

being can be a real symbol of God (see 1.3 above), the relationship of man and woman is all the more appropriate for this type of symbolism. A consideration of marriage as a sacrament can begin with the consideration that puberty, marriage, sexuality, and giving birth have been connected with religious symbolism in nearly every culture.

On the other hand, some more urgent and differentiated questions need to be posed to the religious view of marriage. A more profound notion of God's action within history and of divine revelation can at least frame the question whether God creates human institutions at all, or whether, instead, such matters of organization are left to human initiative, although God gives impulses of divine will to indicate what direction institutions and organizations ought to take. In addition, it can and must be asked whether the relationship of two persons spoken of in Genesis can be called "marriage," given the meaning of the word as we use it today.

In fact, marriage as an institution has undergone so many historical changes that we may ask whether, over many centuries, a stable core that could be called the "essence of marriage" has survived. As a legal institution, marriage has its historical and social basis primarily in the guaranteeing of property relations.[2] It first appears in history as an economic community of production. Patriarchalism dominates the common life: the wife is regarded as a piece of acquired property; the purpose of marriage is the begetting of male heirs; polygamy is legitimate, but in practice is reduced to polygyny; the man's right to sexual activity outside marriage is connected with his interest in acquiring sons through concubines, slave women, etc. This notion of marriage, very widely evidenced in the Old Testament, is, if the institution of marriage is from God, to be traced to the order of creation, since it was not practiced by deviants and immoral people, but by our ancestors in faith.[3]

An idea of marriage that was completely material in orientation dominated in Christendom as late as the period of the Enlightenment (Kant) and its ideas of natural law. The essence of marriage was seen in a contract whose purposes were clearly defined: begetting and education of progeny, mutual support for the partners, and an orderly

2. H. Ringeling, ibid., 351.
3. Theological excuses offered in earlier periods (e.g., that God gave a dispensation for the patriarchs' polygamy) need not be discussed here.

satisfaction of the sex drive. This also represents the official view of marriage in the Catholic Church until Vatican II. The concept of marriage as a legal institution alone left room for different forms; at any rate, it offered no obstacle to the assertion of patriarchal power. The idea of a loving relationship formed by equal partnership, freedom, and tenderness was extremely important both in Judaism and in Christianity, but it was mentioned in connection with marriage only in passing, and certainly not as something essential. A change in the concept of marriage in favor of love was initiated by nineteenth-century Romanticism ("revolution of emotions"), but it made no headway in the Church or in society.[4] Some individual theologians and anthropologists did the preliminary work within the Christian Churches in the first half of the twentieth century toward a renewed concept of marriage, a concept that in itself was pressed by emancipatory movements outside the Churches.[5] Among those scholars were, on the Protestant side, Karl Barth, and, among Catholics (though at first saddled with the Church's ban on publication), Herbert Doms and Ernst Michel, who based their work on the concept of Christian personalism. Their key terms were unity of body and soul, equality of persons, and mutual responsibility. More recent theologians of marriage, as well as the documents of Vatican II, drew ideal images of marriage.

The present era is, in contrast, characterized by serious crises, two of which should be mentioned: the increasing inability of couples to maintain successful relationships, and the rapid decline of the authority of the Catholic Church. The devaluation of marriage as a legal institution and the disconnection of sexual activity from marriage have demonstrated that some types of liberation do not guarantee the success of love.[6] The Roman Catholic magisterium has offered bitter re-

4. For the history, see I. Weber-Kellermann, *Die deutsche Familie. Versuch einer Sozialgeschichte* 5th ed. (Frankfurt: 1979); G. Duby, *Ritter, Frau und Priester. Die Ehe im feudalen Frankreich* (Frankfurt: 1985); M. Schröter, *"Wo zwei zusammenkommen in rechter Ehe . . ." Sozio- und psychogenetische Studien über Eheschließungsvorgänge vom 12. bis 15. Jahrhundert* (Frankfurt: 1985); J. Goody, *Die Entwicklung von Ehe und Familie in Europa* (Berlin: 1986).

5. These also led, in the course of about eighty years (for example: from the civil code in Germany to the reform of marriage law in the Federal Republic in 1977) to a gradual, but drastic, retreat of law from the field of moral judgments.

6. For an analysis of this crisis threatening not only marriage, but every kind of loving relationship, see among others J. Willi, *Die Zweierbeziehung* (Reinbek: 1975); D. Claessens and others, *Familiensoziologie* (Königstein: 1980); N. Luhmann, *Liebe*

sistance and continues to do so (especially under John Paul II),[7] but at a cost: its attitudes toward divorced persons who have entered a civil marriage (*Familiaris consortio*, 1981) and toward birth control (*Humanae vitae*, 1968) have been rejected and ignored by a great many Catholics as expressions of unfeeling harshness. Where human abilities fall short, consideration of the sacrament becomes all the more important, and it need not be ecumenically divisive. "In contrast to traditional definitions of the purposes of marriage and the biologistic teleology of late scholastic natural-law doctrines, personal values, the model of partnership in marriage, and the mutual love of the partners are emphasized as the norm and the formative element; and when these are mediated by the christological idea of covenant, it would appear that an ecumenical agreement on the concept of the sacrament of marriage may also be possible."[8]

12.2 Biblical Foundations

12.2.1 Old Testament

The content of the passages concerning marriage in the first two chapters of Genesis is astonishingly dense and at a very high level, even in the older passages written by the Yahwist (2:21-24): woman and man are intended by God to live in an equal partnership and to be mutually complementary. According to the priestly writer (1:26-27) man and woman were created "in the image and likeness of God."[9] Here it is said of all human beings (without distinction of gender) that, because they are human, they are the image of God. No theology of sexuality and marriage can be derived from this; what is meant is that all human beings have the duty "of protecting and preserving the order of life that is given in creation," that they "are to be a manifestation

als Passion. Zur Codierung von Intimität (Frankfurt: 1982); R. Sennett, *Verfall und Ende des öffentlichen Lebens. Die Tyrannei der Intimität* (Frankfurt: 1983); R. A. Johnson, *Traumvorstellung Liebe. Der Irrtum des Abendlandes* (Olten and Freiburg: 1985); J. Willi, *Koevolution. Die Kunst gemeinsamen Wachsens* (Reinbek: 1985).

7. On the different position of Protestants: H. Ringeling in *TRE* IX, 353.

8. Ibid, 353-354.

9. For an analysis of the idea of the human as image of God, see E. Zenger, *Gottes Bogen in den Wolken* (Stuttgart: 1983) 84-96.

and a medium of revelation of divine power and activity on earth." They are "to govern and lovingly shape the world as their home, the paternal house that has been bestowed upon them."[10] Thus the partnership of woman and man does not consist in their revolving around one another and seeking "fulfillment" in their relationship, but in devoting themselves with one accord to their mutual tasks.

The Old Testament texts that are of great importance for a theology of marriage are those in which marriage or betrothal are used as images and comparisons for the relationship between God and God's people, Israel (e.g., Hos 1-3; Jer 2:2; 3:1; Ezek 16; 23; Mal 2:14-16). These images are not lacking in that tenderness, intimacy, and tempestuous emotion that are part of a deeper understanding of marriage. Nor is it an overinterpretation of the texts to say that here the marriage or bridal relationship is regarded as a covenant of enduring fidelity in the eyes of YHWH. Although the Old Testament mentions no special religious rites of marriage, it does give evidence of the importance of the blessing given by the parents to the bride or to the couple (Gen 24:60; Tobit 11:17).

The ceremonies of marriage in Judaism in the time of Jesus[11] had both a legal and a festive aspect. Betrothal or promise of marriage came first, before the bridegroom (on the average, eighteen years old) "took possession of" the bride (usually about twelve years of age), whereby he symbolically represented the people Israel's being taken up by its God. The process, whose central feature was a huge family feast with a bridal meal lasting several days, was concluded as the bride was conducted to her new home. From a purely legal standpoint, the marriage was undoubtedly a contract based on the intentions of the fathers of the couple. A variety of grounds were given for which a husband could publicly dismiss (i.e., divorce) his wife; however, he could not retain possession of her dowry. In order to improve the lot of wives who had been cruelly dismissed by making it possible for them to marry again, the Torah provided for the giving of a letter of divorce (Deut 24:1-4).

10. Ibid., 90.

11. H.-F. Richter, *Geschlechtlichkeit, Ehe und Familie im Alten Testament und seiner Umwelt* (Berne and Frankfurt: 1978); B. Reicke in *TRE* IX, 319-320; A. Tostato, "Il trasferimento dei beni nel matrimonio israelitico," *Bibbia e Oriente* 27 (1985) 129-148 (with bibliography)—an important article for avoiding a negative cliché! Also M. Hutter, "Das Ehebruch-Verbot," *Bibel und Liturgie* 59 (1986) 96-104 (with bibliography).

12.2.2 *Jesus and the Jesus Traditions*

Jesus never doubted that the will of God is to be found in the Mo-
saic Torah, but where the Torah contains legal language, he sought
the deeper and more radical sense of what was written there.[12] In the
Jesus logion at Mark 10:9 *par.*, Genesis 1:27 is combined with Genesis
2:24: the origin and indissolubility of marriage are attributed to God.
Jesus did not intend thereby to appear as a new lawgiver, especially
since, in view of the chance that the reign of God would be realized
in the near future, the question of marriage would be relativized in
any case (Mark 12:25 *par.*).

In a scene composed by the Christian community (Mark 10:1-9) in
which the authentic Jesus logion Mark 10:9 was embedded, Jesus is
asked whether a separation is permitted under any circumstances. He
declines to get involved in legal interpretation. When Deuteronomy
24:1-4 is depicted here as a concession to hardhearted human beings,
we may be dealing with some anti-Jewish polemic from the early Christian community. But Jesus' intention fits in here: since God intends
the enduring unity of the partners, any separation is against the divine will; therefore there should be no legal provisions for it. This stance
would have to have a positive effect on the position of women.

The teaching given the disciples in Mark 10:10-12 is also a compo-
sition of the early community. It envisions a case in which a man
divorces his wife and marries again, or a woman divorces her husband
and marries again: both cases constitute adultery. Here, apparently,
Jesus' saying about the impossibility of separation (Mark 10:9) has been
translated into a Gentile Christian context, and given an even stricter
form.

In the Sermon on the Mount we find Jesus' logion about the impossibility of separation (Matt 5:31-32) with the additional statement
that a man who gives his wife a letter of divorce is guilty of her remarriage and thereby of adultery: again this is a position that not only
favors fidelity in marriage but also gives an advantage to women, since
the appeal is to the special responsibility of the husbands. Nonetheless, v. 32 adds the "*porneia* clause": Matthew's community evidently
considered itself "empowered" in particular cases—"*porneia*" often
meant idolatry in the New Testament—to make an exception to the

12. Still important for the interpretation is V. Eid and P. Hoffmann, *Jesus von
Nazareth und eine christliche Moral* 3d ed. (Freiburg: 1979) 109–146.

indissolubility of marriage; they did not interpret the Jesus logion as a law.

In Matt 19:1-2 the controversy scene from Mark 10:1-9 is reproduced in such a way that Jesus is shown as if he should take a position on the rabbinic discussion between the schools of Hillel (emphasis on male authority: divorce of the wife allowed for any cause) and Shammai (restriction of male authority: divorce only in cases of adultery and suspicious behavior).[13] Jesus declines to do so; here again he interprets the will of God according to Genesis 1:27 and 2:24, but the "*porneia* clause" is repeated.

The saying in Luke 16:18, which may go back to Jesus, reiterates that there can be no separation and remarriage without adultery.

The tendencies to see marriage as an enduring partnership of equals could then, and can now, appeal to Jesus' own intention. But in the concrete interaction with Jesus' message, we can discern a stricter and a milder line of interpretation.

12.2.3 Paul and the Letter to the Ephesians

In 1 Corinthians 7, Paul took a position on marriage in reaction to enthusiastic-ascetic groups in Gentile Christian Corinth, who had a religiously-based fear of sexuality and marriage (cf. vv. 1-9 and 36-38). He sought justifications for both and found them in human weakness (cf. also vv. 26-28). In vv. 10-11 he refers to the Jesus saying about the impossibility of separation, applied to both partners and, in the case of the wife, combined with a prohibition on remarriage.

As a response to the fear of Christian married people that they could become unholy through marital relations with a Gentile partner, Paul declares that the Christian partner "sanctifies" the unbeliever and also their children (v. 14). The Christian partner may not separate from the unbelieving partner, because of Jesus' prohibition, but the unbeliever may separate, and in such a way that the Christian partner has a right to remarry (vv. 12-16 *passim*, the source of the so-called Pauline privilege). Thus Paul also sees a possibility of holding to Jesus' instruction in principle and yet of making certain exceptions.

In vv. 25-28, Paul speaks of those who are not married. Here he represents marriage as of only temporary value (in light of the "es-

13. More detail can be found in Z. W. Falk's article in *TRE* IX, 315-317.

chatological reservation''). Two motives may be distinguished for his
preference for celibacy: in the anxious expectation of the immediate
end, there was really no purpose in beginning something long-lasting
like marriage, and—something important for Paul himself—the missionary task made it impossible to concern oneself with the things of
this world. Nevertheless, Paul says that marriage is also a good thing.

In the so-called ''household codes'' in the New Testament there
are a number of paraenetic passages on the correct behavior of husband and wife toward one another. Among these, Ephesians 5:22-33,
a text that does not come from Paul, has been especially important in
the Church's theology of marriage. Here again, in the context of the
times, we read of a natural superordination of the husband over the
wife, but husbands are challenged to love their wives ''just as Christ
loved the Church and gave himself up for her'' (v. 25). In vv. 28-31,
this love is further explicated and founded on Genesis 2:23-24, and
the union in love of husband and wife is compared with the unity of
the members in the body of Christ. The author says that ''this is a great
mystery [*mysterion*, translated in the Old Latin as *sacramentum*], and
I am applying it to Christ and the Church'' (v. 32). The more probable
interpretation of this difficult saying is that the union of the partners
in marriage is and (paraenetically!) must be an image of the union of
Jesus Christ with his Church. In other words: Paul's breathless expectation of the end has faded, marriages have become the usual thing
among Christians also, and not merely as something permissible, but
with a positive imaging function in the divine plan of salvation realized in Jesus Christ; or: even now, within the context of marriage, it
is possible to live the new relationships that, according to Jesus' preaching, characterize the reign of God.

12.2.4 Additional Statements

The beginnings of a theology of marriage in the New Testament
show that marriage is relevant not only for the theology of creation,
but also for Christology, ecclesiology, and the theology of grace. The
comparison of a marriage with the relationship between God and God's
people, Israel, is continued in the comparison with the relationship
between Jesus and his Church, in the images that depict Jesus as bridegroom and salvation as a marriage feast. It is possible, and even com-

manded, to marry "in the Lord" (1 Cor 7:39) and to live one's married life "in the Lord," so that it becomes a way of salvation with positive effects on partner and children (1 Cor 7:12-16).

Ideas shaped by their cultural and temporal context appear everywhere and create the impression that the correct behavior of a husband within marriage is that of active care and provision, while the wife is to be passively adaptable. But the theological and religious viewpoint overcomes these notions in principle, for statements of equality are also to be found (Gal 3:28; 1 Pet 3:7).

In this context, adultery is *the* sin that destroys not only order (in propertied relationships) but the transparent character of marriage as a religious image. Jesus radicalizes the matter when he says that adultery does not begin only with actions that are legally determinable, but with desire itself (Matt 5:28). However, people who are concretely guilty of this sin are to be treated with compassion (John 8:2-11).

The celibacy of Jesus (as well as John the Baptizer and Paul) was not, at first, considered a model or an obligation for those in ecclesiastical office (1 Tim 3:2-12; Titus 1:6). However, in certain Christian groups there seems to have been a question about how often in the life of individual Christians (after the death of a spouse) marriage was permitted (see the texts just cited, as well as 1 Tim 5:9). There was probably a widespread conviction that marriage is not perpetuated in the heavenly life with God (Matt 22:23-29 *par.*; 1 Cor 7:29-31).

12.3 Historical Decisions

12.3.1 The Development of a Theology, Liturgy, and Law of Marriage

In the same way as Jesus and Paul found marriage already in place and took their positions on it as an existing reality, later missionaries preached the gospel in societies that had marriages, marriage law, and (among the Romans and Greeks) marriage crises. Roman ideas were especially important for later developments in the Latin Church. There were two aspects to marrying. The first was legal in nature, a part of family law. From this point of view the marriage (*sponsalia*) was a contract, regarded as a public announcement of an agreement in intention (*pactio coniugalis*). The second aspect was the beginning of common life (*nuptiae*), which was already subject to religious interpretation

among the Romans: the familial hearth was always understood as having religious significance. Thus when Christians married, this was the
place for a special blessing. We have a paucity of evidence from the
first two centuries: according to Ignatius of Antioch, Christians should
only marry with the assent of the bishop; in Tertullian's work the
Church appears as an agent and conciliator in marriages and there is
mention of a *benedictio* of the married couple at the Eucharist. Still, it
is probable that the Jewish prayer of blessing was adopted since Christians used blessing prayers on all other important occasions.[14]

There is an abundance of evidence from the fourth and fifth centuries. The Church Fathers' idea of marriage appears especially in their
exegesis of biblical texts. Marriage concluded according to civil law is
considered to be affirmed by God; however, the monogamy that was
customary in Roman law is, by contrast to the Roman notion, regarded
as indissoluble since the "bond," as spoken of in Genesis 2:23-24 (a
text very often cited) was "instituted" by God. The theological dimension of marriage as image of the union of Jesus Christ and his Church
is often addressed. Thus marriage is seen to be a positive value leading to salvation, even though in general celibacy is more highly es-
teemed. Stoic ideas about the purposes of marriage are taken over:
in the first place, it serves for the begetting of offspring; love is mentioned also, and is viewed as an overcoming of egoism and, in its Christian aspect, an imitation of the love of Jesus.

The practice of sexuality in marriage offered the Church Fathers
some difficulties. Here we must mention the important contribution
of Augustine.[15] He saw in marriage, which he called *sacramentum* (with
reference to Eph 5:32), both the legal bond (*vinculum*) and the religious
real symbol (*signum*) that, in every marriage, indicates the marital union
of Jesus Christ with the Church and is perfected in baptism, which
accomplishes our incorporation in the body of Christ. Thus the order
of the goods of marriage (*bona*) is to be regarded in this way: first, offspring (*bonum prolis*: Gen 1:28, but only perfected in baptism!); second, an exclusive sexual fidelity (*bonum fidei*: Gen 2:23-24 in Jesus'

---

14. On this, see K. Stevenson, *Nuptial Blessing* (London: 1982); D. Dacquino,
Storia del matrimonio cristiano alla luce della Bibbia (Turin: 1984).

15. Cf. the more precise and just interpretation of E. Schmitt, *Le mariage chrétien
dans l'oeuvre de saint Augustin* (Paris: 1983); P. Langa, *San Agustín y el progreso de
la teología matrimonial* (Toledo: 1984).

interpretation); third, the fulfillment of natural love in sanctification (*bonum sacramenti*: Eph 5:32). Contrary to a long tradition stretching from Philo to Jerome, Augustine presumed that the first parents in Eden were already sexually active before the Fall, so that marital acts are in themselves good. However, original sin had introduced an evil into this good thing, concupiscence or disorderly lust, which strongly disorders reason. It was only because of these circumstances that Augustine considered it necessary that there be a justifying reason for marital acts, and he saw that justification in the orientation of these acts to the begetting of offspring.

Weddings remained, as before, a matter of secular law, but the witnesses attest that the rite of veiling (*velatio*), prayer of petition, and prayer of blessing (*benedictio*) had become customary; according to the *Liber Praedestinatus III* (mid-fifth century) they were also combined with a celebration of the Eucharist. The bride's white veil (taken over from the consecration of virgins and well evidenced in the fourth century) symbolized the union of Jesus Christ with his bride, the Church. Other originally pagan rituals as well, such as crowning with the bridal crown or crowns (*coronatio*) and the joining of the right hands (*dextrarum coniunctio*) were introduced into the liturgy here and there. Around 400 we also have evidence of a *missa pro sponsis*.

In collections of canons of ecclesiastical law we find that, from the fourth century onward, the Church established a number of impediments to marriage, especially difference of religion and blood relationships. The Church Fathers are reticent on the question whether, after the death of a spouse, a second or perhaps even a third marriage is permitted for the surviving Christian partner, or else they answer in the negative. There is frequent evidence of separation due to difference of religion (*privilegium Paulinum*), as is separation because of adultery. Fairly often, remarriage was overlooked or even expressly permitted,[16] sometimes after completion of a penance imposed by the Church.

---

16. Evidence assembled by H. Crouzel in *TRE* IX, 329. On the Eastern Churches' views on marriage see also R. Hotz, *Sakramente*, 249–250. It is wrong to say that the Eastern Churches permit divorce and remarriage. The Eastern Churches maintain the indissolubility of marriage, but in dealing with people whose marriages have been broken, they follow the principle of compassion, which, in the divine *oikonomia*, takes precedence over the principle of dogma.

In the Eastern Church a different view arose, beginning in the early tenth century. At that time a priest's blessing became necessary for a valid Christian marriage. Church weddings were made up of two rituals, the "pledge" and the "crowning." To the present time, and in express reference to Ephesians 5:32, a marriage blessed by a priest is regarded in the Eastern Churches separated from Rome as a sacrament.

In the Western Church a tendency began in the Frankish period to place the wedding itself under Church auspices. Since the priest was generally regarded as a reliable person, Charlemagne, for example, desired that a priest would undertake the "marriage examination," i.e., inquire about possible impediments to marriage and then officiate at the wedding uniting the couple. The influential *Decretum Gratiani* in the mid-twelfth century demanded both conditions, but still regarded a marriage before a secular official as valid. By 1200 only Church marriage survived, in a rite performed at the church door, in which the priest no longer prays in the optative form, "may God join you" (*deus vos coniungat*), but declares in the indicative: "I join you" (*ego vos coniungo*); this rite is followed by a wedding Eucharist in the church. Beginning about 1300, the marriage itself took place in the church.

In the "Germanic" world the dominant notion was that a valid marriage took place with the first marital intercourse, and that alone made it indissoluble (copula theory). This idea first appeared in a theological context in the work of Hincmar of Rheims (d. 882): the union of a man and a woman, if they are baptized, becomes a sacramental and indissoluble marriage through this consummation, even if it only takes place in secret. The copula theory was later defended by the important canonical school of Bologna.

Against the copula theory, the consent theory of Roman law was still maintained by some theologians: the expression of willingness, the marriage vow itself (*sponsalia de praesenti*), is the efficient cause (*causa efficiens*) of marriage and makes it indissoluble. Consummation has only a complementary character. In order to be a sign of the union of Jesus Christ with the Church (and provided that the married couple are members of Jesus Christ through faith), the marriage must be consummated. This was the teaching of, for example, Ivo of Chartres (d. 1116), Hugh of St. Victor (d. 1141), and, with them, the important school of Paris.

Pope Alexander III (d. 1181), who himself was a canonist, promoted a compromise that is still valid in Catholic canon law: the consent of the partners founds a true and valid marriage, but only the consummation of the marriage makes it absolutely indissoluble.

In the meantime, theological reflection on the sacraments had arrived at a certain clarity; by the middle of the twelfth century the classical concept of a sacrament had been established. In the eleventh century, Peter Damian (d. 1072) had listed marriage as one of twelve sacraments, but most important for the fixing of the number of seven sacraments was the work of Peter Lombard (d. 1160).[17] He counted marriage among the seven and called it a sacred sign of a sacred thing. The contest between the copula theory and the consent theory also influenced the discussion of the question regarding the moment when the sacrament comes to be. Alexander III's decision was that the marriage of baptized persons that comes about with their consent is a genuine sacrament, even before its consummation. (Before consummation it is called *matrimonium ratum et non consummatum*).

There were difficulties in Scholastic theology in applying the concepts of "matter" and "form" to marriage.[18] Important theologians denied that the sacrament of marriage had a material element. Even for Thomas Aquinas, the words have primary importance: consent through words spoken directly to one another (*verba de praesenti*) constitute the efficient cause and *forma* of the sacrament of marriage. Thereby the bond of marriage comes into being and a disposition is created that enables the partners to receive divine grace, thanks to the divine institution of the sacrament. The effect (*res*) of the sacrament is seen as being, on the one hand, at the level of symbolism (union of Jesus Christ with the Church), and on the other hand at the level of obligation (to married life and indissolubility). Thomas regarded the priestly blessing at marriage as only a sacramental (see chapter 13 below). Thus it was possible to think of the couple themselves as "ministers" of the sacrament of marriage. This conclusion, and still more the fixation on marriage as a legal action, did not take into account the fact that marriage, as a sacrament, is the Church's liturgy. This was still acknowledged, however, in the Eastern Churches.

17. J. Finkenzeller I, 123.
18. Ibid., 140, 142.

12.3.2 *Statements of Earlier Church Teaching*

Adherents of the lay and reform movements of the twelfth century rejected various sacraments and rites of the Church. In opposition to them, the Second Lateran Council of 1139 defended Church marriages (only Latin, DS 718), as did the Council of Verona in 1184. It was at that council that marriage was called a "sacrament" for the first time in a doctrinal statement (only Latin, DS 761).

In the confession of faith presented to the Eastern Roman emperor in 1267 for the purpose of reuniting the Churches of East and West, we read: "On *marriage* she [the Church] teaches that a man may not have more than one wife at the same time, and a woman may not have more than one husband at the same time. But if a proper marriage is dissolved by the death of one of the partners, she says that then a second and third marriage are permitted, if no other canonical impediment of another sort exists" (NR 928/DS 860). In the same text, marriage is numbered among the seven sacraments of the Church.

In the decree intended to advance the reunion of the separated Armenians with Rome, the Council of Florence in 1439 taught, following Thomas Aquinas:

> The seventh is the sacrament of matrimony which is the sign of the union of Christ and the Church according to the saying of the apostle: "This is a great mystery, and I mean in reference to Christ and the Church" (Eph 5:32). The efficient cause of matrimony is the mutual consent duly expressed in words relating to the present. A triple good is found in matrimony. The first is the begetting of children and their education to the worship of God. The second is the faithfulness which each spouse owes to the other. Third is the indissolubility of marriage, inasmuch as it represents the indissoluble union of Christ and the Church. But, although it is permitted to separate on account of adultery, nevertheless it is not permitted to contract another marriage since the bond of a marriage legitimately contracted is perpetual (NR 730/DS 1327).

The Reformers[19] challenged the Church's teaching on marriage from two points of departure: the higher value placed by the Church on celibacy in contrast to marriage, and the dominant role played by canon law. Luther's formulation, that marriage is a "worldly thing," is often

---

19. For initial information, see M. E. Schild's article in *TRE* IX, 336–346, on Luther and the other Reformers.

misunderstood by Catholics. He saw marriage as founded in the divine order of creation; sexual desire and the longing for marital union existed even before the Fall and were good; since the Fall, marriage is a condition of love, faith, and the cross. Marriage is not a sacrament, since the New Testament contains no word of Christ promising a sacrament of marriage, but on the basis of the order of creation it is a sign (parable) of God's gracious action, and now it is a sign of the union of Christ with his members. In his distinction of God's spiritual and worldly "regimes" or "kingdoms," Luther included marriage within the worldly regime. He praised celibacy as the charism of a few who are able to give themselves undividedly to prayer and the preaching of the gospel. Luther combined this view with sharp attacks on the Church's practice of subjecting marriage to canon law, of recognizing marriages made in secret, of witnessing vows of celibacy, etc. He required that marriages be made in public, i.e., that consent, as the act that brings about the marriage, be given before witnesses. In cases of adultery and the malicious abandonment of one partner, he permitted the dissolution of marriage (which in itself is indissoluble); so did Melancthon, who spoke of actions that can destroy a marriage that of its own nature is indissoluble.

The Council of Trent, in its seventh session in 1547, established the Roman Catholic Church's number of seven sacraments and listed marriage among them (NR 506/DS 1601). At the same time, it taught that grace is conveyed by the sacraments (NR 511-513/DS 1606-1608). At the twenty-fourth session in 1563 it presented its *Doctrine on the Sacrament of Matrimony* and twelve attached canons. The essentials of the doctrine are as follows:

> *The first father of the human race*, inspired by the divine Spirit, proclaimed the perpetual and indissoluble bond of matrimony when he exclaimed: "This at last is bone of my bones and flesh of my flesh. . . . Therefore a man leaves his father and his mother and cleaves to his wife, and they become one flesh" (Gen 2:23-24).
>
> But that only two are united and joined together by this bond, *Christ the Lord* taught more clearly when, referring to these words as having been uttered by God, he said: "So they are no longer two but one" (Mt 19:6), and immediately confirmed the stability of the bond which was proclaimed long ago by Adam in these words: "What therefore God has joined together, let no man put asunder" (Mt 19:6; Mk 10:9).
>
> Christ himself, who instituted the holy sacraments and brought them to perfection, merited for us by his passion the *grace* which perfects that

natural love, confirms the indissoluble union and sanctifies the spouses. St. Paul suggests this when he says: "Husbands, love your wives, as Christ loved the Church and gave himself up for her" (Eph 5:25), adding immediately: "This is a great mystery and I mean in reference to Christ and the Church" (Eph 5.32).

Since, because of the grace of Christ, matrimony under the law of the gospel is superior to the marriage unions of the old law, the holy Fathers, the Councils and the tradition of the universal Church have with good reason always taught that it is to be numbered among the *sacraments of the new law*. Contrary to this teaching, ungodly and foolish men of this age, not only have entertained false ideas concerning this holy sacrament but, in their usual way, under the pretext of the gospel they have given freedom to the flesh, and, by word and writing, they have asserted—not without great harm to Christ's faithful—many things alien to the understanding of the Catholic Church and to customs approved since the apostolic times (NR 731-734/DS 1797-1800).

The council chose to say nothing about the matter, form, and minister of this sacrament, things that the Scholastics otherwise thought were discernible for all the sacraments.

The canons read:

1. If anyone says that matrimony is not truly and properly one of the seven sacraments of the law of this gospel, instituted by Christ the Lord, but that it was devised in the Church by human beings and does not confer grace, *anathema sit*.

2. If anyone says that it is lawful for Christians to have several wives at the same time and that this is not forbidden by any divine law, *anathema sit*.

3. If anyone says that only those degrees of consanguinity and affinity which are mentioned in Leviticus (18:6ff) can impede contracting marriage and invalidate the contract; and that the Church cannot dispense from some of them or declare other degrees impedient and diriment, *anathema sit*.

4. If anyone says that the Church did not have the power to establish diriment impediments for marriage or that she has erred in establishing them, *anathema sit*.

5. If anyone says that the marriage bond can be dissolved because of heresy, or irksome cohabitation, or because of the wilful desertion of one of the spouses, *anathema sit*.

6. If anyone says that marriage contracted but not consummated is not dissolved by the solemn religious profession of one of the spouses, *anathema sit*.

7. If anyone says that the Church is in error for having taught and for still teaching that in accordance with the evangelical and apostolic doctrine (cf. Mk 10; 1 Cor 7), the marriage bond cannot be dissolved because of adultery on the part of one of the spouses, and that neither of the two, not even the innocent one who has given no cause for infidelity, can contract another marriage during the lifetime of the other; and that the husband who dismisses an adulterous wife and marries again and the wife who dismisses an adulterous husband and marries again are both guilty of adultery, *anathema sit*.

8. If anyone says that the Church errs when she declares that for many reasons separation may take place between husband and wife with regard to bed and board or cohabitation for a definite period or even indefinitely, *anathema sit*.

9. If anyone says that clerics in sacred orders or regulars who have made solemn profession of chastity can contract marriage, and that one so contracted is valid despite the ecclesiastical law or the vow; and that the contrary opinion is nothing but a condemnation of marriage; and that all those who feel that they do not have the gift of chastity, even though they have vowed it, can contract marriage, *anathema sit*. For God does not refuse that gift to those who ask for it rightly, and "He will not let you be tempted beyond your strength" (1 Cor 10:13).

10. If anyone says that the married state surpasses that of virginity or celibacy, and that it is not better and happier to remain in virginity or celibacy than to be united in matrimony, *anathema sit*.

11. If anyone says that the prohibition of the solemnization of marriages at certain times of the year is a tyrannical superstition derived from pagan superstition; or condemns the blessings and other ceremonies which the Church uses in solemn nuptials, *anathema sit*.

12. If anyone says that matrimonial cases do not belong to ecclesiastical judges, *anathema sit* (NR 735-746/DS 1801-1812).

The council defended not only the sacramentality and grace-giving power of marriage, but also the Church's competence to make canonical rules regulating matters relating to marriage.[20] The teaching on the indissoluble bond of marriage is clearly stated. Canon 7 was the ob-

---

20. Cf. R. Lettmann, *Die Diskussion über die klandestinen Ehen und die Einführung einer zur Gültigkeit verpflichtenden Eheschließungsreform auf dem Konzil von Trient* (Münster: 1966); G. Baldanza, "La grazia sacramentale matrimoniale al Concilio di Trento," *Ephemerides Liturgicae* 97 (1983) 89-140; A. Duval, *Des sacrements* (see Bibliography 1).

ject of a thorough discussion on the history of dogma:[21] the council deliberately chose formulations protective of Roman Catholic practice against the charge of error; at the same time, it did not wish to condemn the milder practice of the Eastern Churches and its basis in the teaching of the universally accepted Church Fathers.

At the same twenty-fourth session in 1563, the council passed its decree *Tametsi* for the reform of the marriage ceremony (excerpts, only in Latin, in DS 1813-1816). Up to the Council of Trent, the Church had never issued an obligatory form for marriage, such that, if it were not used, the marriage would not be recognized as valid by the Church. But because of the great number of secret marriages, in which an existing bond of marriage or other impediments were simply ignored, the council now issued a disciplinary decree requiring that the marriage must take place before the pastor (or a priest with appropriate faculties) and two or three witnesses. Any Catholic who did not adhere to this obligatory form could not make a valid marriage.[22]

Thus in the course of a millennium and a half, a solid Catholic notion of marriage had developed. While in the first millennium civil marriage and the Church's liturgical blessing of the spouses had existed independently of one another, now it was the case that, for Catholics, the identity of valid marriage and Church wedding was obligatory. Since consent (interpreted as a contract) was still considered the essence of marriage, from that point onward doctrine and canon law maintained the inseparability of the contract and the sacrament. In the course of modern development, with its mixed confessional situation and the increasing alienation of many people from the Church, the Catholic concept of marriage came into conflict with the claims of state and society, as seen, for example, in the attack of Josephinism on the Church's whole jurisdiction in matters of marriage, culminating in the introduction of compulsory civil marriage in many countries.[23] Among

---

21. P. Fransen, "Das Thema 'Ehescheidung nach Ehebruch' auf dem Konzil von Trient," *Concilium* 5 (1970) 343-348 (with bibliography). Fransen here summarizes earlier, more extended investigations.

22. More detail may be found in R. Lettmann, *Diskussion*.

23. On this development, see W. Molinski, *Theologie der Ehe in der Geschichte* (Aschaffenburg: 1976) 196-213.

the public statements that sharpened the Church's teaching on marriage, we should mention the encyclical *Arcanum Divinae Sapientiae* of Leo XIII in 1880 (NR 747–750/DS 3142–3146), the 1917 CIC and Pius XI's encyclical *Casti connubii* in 1930 (NR 751–760/DS 3700–3714). Even though theological discussion, especially in the twentieth century, under the influence of personalistic thought and biblical renewal, has strongly criticized the Church's contractual view of marriage as reducing it to an object, a just view of the question should not overlook the considerable contributions of the Church's contractual thinking to the emancipation of women and the liberation of both spouses from the powerful socio-economic ties of tribe and clan. This resulted directly from the fact that the Church always insisted on the *free* consent of the wills of both partners and regarded a consent given under duress as invalid.

12.3.3 Vatican Council II and the New Code of Canon Law

The documents of Vatican II were the product of a great variety of efforts toward a renewed and deepened religious-theological view of marriage. The Constitution on the Liturgy called for a revision and enrichment of the rite of marriage (SC 77 and 78), and the dogmatic Constitution on the Church spoke of the sacrament as follows:

> Finally, Christian spouses, in virtue of the sacrament of matrimony, signify and partake of the mystery of that unity and fruitful love which exists between Christ and His Church (cf. Eph 5:32). The spouses thereby help each other to attain to holiness in their married life and by the rearing and education of their children. And so, in their state and order of life, they have their own special gift among the People of God (cf. 1 Cor 7:7).
>
> For from the wedlock of Christians there comes the family, in which new citizens of human society are born. By the grace of the Holy Spirit received in baptism these are made children of God, thus perpetuating the People of God through the centuries. The family is, so to speak, the domestic Church. In it parents should, by their word and example, be the first preachers of the faith to their children. They should encourage them in the vocation which is proper to each of them, fostering with special care any religious vocation (LG 11).

The council also spoke of marriage and the family in other places.[24] Most important are six articles (47–52) in the pastoral constitution *Gaudium et spes*.

Article 47 offers a foundation for active concern to establish the dignity of marriage and family even outside Christianity and points to present-day dangers to both. Article 48 selects the word "covenant" as a description of marriage, as a way of escaping the legal and objective view that had improperly taken over the most prominent place in Catholic teaching and was evident in the technical term "marriage contract." Pleas for the word "contract" were determinedly rejected (and the description in canon law of the "object of the contract" as a mutual donation of "rights over the body" most certainly had to be renounced as an unbearable example of objectivizing). The article does say that marriage is ordered to the procreation and education of children, but it carefully avoids setting up any hierarchy of the "goods of marriage." As a balance to earlier, biologistic ideas, it emphasizes instead the central importance of love (in the second paragraph) and describes the sacramentality of Christian marriage on that basis. The rest of the article deals primarily with the duties of children (adding a brief appreciation of widowhood) and sees marriage and family as manifesting "the Savior's living presence in the world." Article 49 speaks of the "true love between husband and wife in marriage." It describes what this love is and what are its effects, and states that it is uniquely expressed and perfected in the marital act. Therefore the council ascribes moral value to these acts of union; the only, and quite sensible, cautionary clause speaks of marital actions as being "expressed in a manner which is truly human" (something which may differ according to the couples involved). These conciliar statements will seem all too commonplace to today's Christians. But many groups of Catholic believers were brought up within a mentality that saw marriage as a kind of legalized immorality and demanded an external motive to lend a moral color to every marital act. The council did away with that notion. The conclusion of the article points out that public opinion on marriage can be influenced by the witness of spouses within the society; it also indicates the need for a correct and timely sex edu-

---

24. E.g., LG 35 and 41, AA 10 and 29, GE 3, 6 and 8, and GS 12, 61, 67 and 87. The summary presented here follows my introduction in *Kleines Konzilskompendium* 434–436.

cation for children. Article 50 then deals with the procreation and education of offspring, a topic that for centuries held a one-sided grip on Catholic morality. But this article neither expressly states nor hints that every individual marital act, taken for itself, is or should be aimed at procreation. All it says is that marriage as a whole, by its nature, is ordained to the procreation and education of children. In this matter the spouses are, as the second paragraph says, cooperators with the love of God the creator "and . . . so to speak, the interpreters of that love." The expressions here chosen show that the spouses are not subjected to blind, purely biological laws of nature and should not submit themselves to fate in a kind of trust in God falsely understood. The article mentions the factors that responsible parents must take into account, and comes to the conclusion that the spouses themselves must (and may!) make the final decision about conceiving a child (including the timing and number of their children). The final paragraph in this article recalls once again that marriage is an institution not only for the procreation of children, and thereby—with a reference to the love of God—establishes the right of childless couples to the fullness of marriage. Article 51 discusses the obstacles that often exist to an increase in the number of children. In clear and unmistakable words it points to the dangers of complete abstinence from intercourse in marriage. It draws clear boundaries against abortion and infanticide; it emphatically recalls the special dignity of human sexuality, and again concludes that marital actions performed in accordance with human dignity "must be honored with great reverence." It further states that, for a responsible regulation of births, the moral aspect of any behavior is determined not only by good intentions and motives, but by objective criteria. This indicates the reason why in this area the Church has a fundamental right to speak, even though the exercise of that right must decidedly take other forms than those of detailed analyses of the marital act, the prescription of individual norms for couples by their confessors, etc. The article skirts the question of birth control methods. It is well known that Church norms for birth control—to the extent that the methods chosen do not offend human dignity or damage a life already conceived—are not matters of dogma, but of authentic instructions that must be received by believers with respect and internal, but not irrevocable, acceptance. Article 52 treats the nature of the family, the tasks of its members, and the duties of the state toward it. The last three paragraphs request that the secular sciences continue to research methods of birth control, that pastors support and sustain spouses (note the discreet and tactful formulation!), and finally, that married couples should be true witnesses to the mystery of Christ's love.

The conciliar texts, together with John Paul II's apostolic letter *Familiaris consortio* of 1981, summarizing the Church's tradition regarding marriage, were the bases for the new Catholic law of marriage.[25] Here we would like to point out some essential elements with theological relevance. Marriage is still understood as a contract (exchange of vows) and the legal relationship resulting from it (married life): the contract comes about through the mutual expression of will. To express the fact that marriage is not only a legal relationship, but also a personal and religious reality, canon law takes up the council's word "covenant":[26] in this irrevocable covenant the partners mutually give themselves to one another and accept one another (CIC 1983, canon 1057 §2). Together they thereby found a common destiny for the whole of life (ibid., §1). The paraphrasing of this "covenant" with ideally romantic phrases like "personal self-donation of the partners" in canon law shows that the Code has still not dealt with justified "personal" demands: marriage cannot mean that a human being "gives" himself or herself to another; rather, she or he must live with the partner in a relationship that permits each to remain his or her own person and to fulfill his or her own self. Otherwise the legal institution of marriage will not be freed of its twisted character as a legalized deprivation of human freedom.

The "aims of marriage" appear in a changed order and partly in new terms: marriage is directed to the good of the spouses and to the procreation and education of offspring (canon 1055 §1).

As a matter of course, the new Code maintains the singleness and indissolubility of marriage as essential characteristics (canon 1056), as well as the concept that in every valid marriage, by its nature, an enduring and exclusive bond is created (canon 1134). In a kind of relativizing of the teaching on the essential characteristics of marriage,[27] the

---

25. On this, see the authors in *HKR* as well as K. Lüdicke, *Eherecht* (see Bibliography X).
26. M. Kaiser in *HKR*, 731ff. For the sake of precision, I have followed him word for word in writing about the new provisions of canon law.
27. Ibid., 736.

ecclesial authority still claims the right to dissolve unconsummated and non-sacramental marriages (canons 1142-1150).

Canon law regards marriage not only as contract and covenant, but also as sacrament (canon 1055), a sign of the covenant of God with humanity, the covenant of Jesus Christ with the Church, giving the spouses both a special strengthening and a consecration in order that they may fulfill the dignity and obligations of their state (canon 1134). There can be no valid bond of marriage between baptized persons that is not also a sacrament (canon 1055 §2).

In the well-founded opinion of canonists, the new Code of Canon Law says nothing about the "minister" of the sacrament of marriage: some type of official participation by the Church is involved in setting forth this symbol of the covenant and bringing this fulfillment of the Church's life into being.[28]

Marriage before the Church's minister is the regular form for Catholics and therefore is generally obligatory (canon 1117). In the Eastern Churches it has long consisted in the liturgical blessing of the bridal pair. In the Western Church it consists of the legal act of requesting and receiving the consent of the couple (canon 1108 §2). The Church's official participation may not be regarded in a minimalistic fashion, in the mere fact that the exchange of vows is public.[29]

The new Church law for marriage gives a great deal of attention to the concept of validity, something that is more appropriately applied to a legal action and a legal institution than to a sacrament, since it is only from a valid legal action that legal effects result, while God alone knows whether a sacrament has been effective in bestowing grace. The preconditions for a valid marriage are a full competence for marriage, a faultless will to marry on the part of both partners, and a rite of marriage that is without defects.[30]

The supreme ecclesiastical authority maintains its claim to be able to declare authentically what are the things that, by divine law, impede the contract of marriage (canon 1075 §1), and also to establish other impediments (not of divine law) for the baptized (canon 1075 §2). As regards secular and material legal consequences of marriage, the Church recognizes the competence of the state, but regarding the

28. Ibid., 739.
29. Ibid., 739-740.
30. Details may be found in the CIC.

personal aspects, Church authority claims competence only for marriages in which a Catholic Christian participates, since the Church of Jesus Christ is not composed solely of the Roman Catholic Church.[31] No claim to ecclesiastical authority is posed in cases of marriage between unbaptized persons.

A marriage between persons, at least one of whom is obligated to observe the Church's form of marriage (i.e., is Catholic), is in principle only valid if the consent is given before the ordinary of the diocese or the pastor of the parish, or by another priest, deacon, or even a lay person (canon 1112 gives details of this instance) delegated by them. There must also be two witnesses to the consent (canon 1108 §1). In addition, there is provision for emergency marriage before two witnesses only (canon 1116 §1). Those who have left the Church are not obligated to observe the Church's form of marriage (canon 1117). The marriage of a Catholic to a non-Catholic partner who is a member of one of the Eastern Churches, blessed by a non-Catholic priest, is valid (canon 1127). If a Catholic can show that there are serious difficulties in adhering to the Church's form of marriage, she or he can be dispensed from the obligation (canon 1127). If this occurs in a mixed (interconfessional) marriage, the non-Catholic partner must be told that a dispensation has been requested; he or she must know that, in that case, even through a non-Catholic Church wedding or a merely civil ceremony—the spouses can choose the form, although a Church wedding is to be preferred—a valid, sacramental marriage exists. This logically applies also to marriages between persons of different religion (canon 1129).[32]

An interconfessional marriage can be contracted with the permission of the ordinary of the diocese (canons 1124-1125), if the Catholic partner's faith is not endangered thereby, and if the Catholic spouse solemnly promises to do all in his or her power to see that all children of the marriage are baptized and educated as Catholics (canon 1125 §1); a further condition is that the non-Catholic partner be informed promptly of this promise (canon 1125 §2). Both partners must be instructed concerning the purposes and essential characteristics of marriage, none of which may be excluded by either partner (canon 1125

31. M. Kaiser, *HKR*, 746, with reference to LG 8.
32. On this complex of laws, which are very important in practice, see B. Primetshofer's article in *HKR*, 788-793, as well as H. Heinemann, *HKR*, 807.

§3). A "double marriage" is not permitted, but an ecumenical "common" or "cooperative" marriage may be allowed.[33]

In Catholic canon law a marriage is absolutely indissoluble if, in the eyes of the Catholic Church, it has been validly contracted and consummated, and if both partners are baptized. In Catholic teaching, only the marriage of baptized persons is sacramental. "Only its sacramentality lends to marriage that solidity that permits no subsequent dissolution."[34] There are canonists who think that the sacrament comes to be only because the partners are baptized, apart from any faith on their part.[35] The problem touches a very painful situation within the Church, namely the fact that after the failure of many marriages, often begun without any serious religious commitment, and following divorce and remarriage, many people come to religious maturity and request that the Church admit them to the sacraments. Here are two standpoints in irreconcilable opposition within the Church: one lenient, the other inexorable.[36]

33. In a "double marriage" the rites of both Churches are performed, each by the official of that confession, either separately or in one ceremony. In an "ecumenical marriage" one officiant performs the rite of his or her Church and the other participates in the service of the Word. H. Heinemann, HKR, 803–804; M. Kaiser, HKR, 645.

34. H. Flatten, HKR, 815. Cf. his article in its entirety.

35. Ibid., 816–817. On the contrary, T. Schneider, Zeichen (see Bibliography 1) 290–291, says that a minimal intention to marry as Christians is necessary for the existence of the sacrament.

36. In the stricter Catholic opinion, represented, for example, by H. Flatten, HKR, 817–819 (and which can also refer to John Paul II for support), Catholics who are civilly divorced and remarried are not excluded from the Church, but they are denied the sacraments of reconciliation and Eucharist. They can only be admitted to these sacraments when they promise, as a sign of their repentance, to live in their new marriage "as brother and sister." The basis for this attitude lies in the fear of "breaking the dam": if the Church begins in practice to retreat from its rigid position, the idea will get around that the Catholic Church accepts divorce, and the consequence will be that more and more people will enter into "trial marriages." The lenient view, in which the failure of a marriage and the values of a new union should be conscientiously examined in each individual case, and according to which the Church must find ways to enable the persons concerned to make a new beginning also with God and in the Church's sacramental life, is represented by, for example, T. Schneider, Zeichen, 298–300, referring to W. Kasper and K. Lehmann. Cf. n. 16 above: the Eastern Churches, basing their thinking on the primacy of the principle of mercy (which is of divine origin) accord themselves the corresponding "permission" to act with leniency.

What at first glance looks like a Church divorce is, in reality, in most cases the Church's decision that a marriage did not exist from the beginning.[37] But there really are Church dissolutions of marriages: in the case of nonconsummation, through a papal decree of dissolution;[38] in marriages of two unbaptized persons, one of whom is later baptized, in which case, by the Pauline privilege as interpreted by the Church (see 12.2.3 above), the old marriage is dissolved when the baptized partner enters a new, valid marriage;[39] in nonsacramental marriages, through a papal decree of dissolution.[40] Of special importance in the so-called Third World is the new canonical regulation applying to polygamy (canon 1148 has polygyny in mind, but logically it would also apply to polyandry): if a man becomes a Christian, he may continue to be married to only one wife; if it is difficult for him to retain his first wife, he may choose another among his wives as his permanent wife.[41]

In view of these possibilities for dissolution and the statements in canon law concerning the "papal decree of dissolution," it is hard to make clear why the canon law and the theology of marriage rest on the idea of a permanent "bond of marriage," even in the most extreme cases of marital breakdown. We must maintain, together with the Eastern Churches separated from Rome and with the Churches of the Reformation, that marriage is indissoluble and that divorce cannot become a legal possibility among Christians. But is it impossible to recognize signs that show that the bases of a marriage have been destroyed and that the bond of marriage can perish with them?

12.4   Theology of Marriage: Summary

The literature on the sacrament of marriage shows that, on the one side, the legal obligations (unity and indissolubility) dominate, while on the other side the most prominent question concerning the sacrament itself is: what does it do for the spouses; what is the grace that it effects? In all this, little attention is paid to the fact that the sacra-

37. On this, and on the legal process, see H. Flatten, *HKR*, 819–821.
38. Ibid., 821–822.
39. Ibid., 822–824 (according to canons 1143–1150).
40. Ibid., 824–826.
41. On the problems connected with this, see N. Bitoto Abeng in *EKL* I (1986) 971–974.

ment of marriage is the Church's liturgy. If we adopt that point of view, the question of the "minister" of the sacrament must be approached differently from the way it appears in the literature. The one who truly acts in the sacrament is Jesus Christ, who is at work in the Church, through his Spirit, for the glory of God the Father. Looked at from the human side, the liturgy of marriage is a matter of the conscious consent of the partners and those celebrating with them to this glorification of God, which in this case occurs through marriage as an "enduring sacrament," i.e., the sacrament of married life that begins with the marriage ceremony. For it to succeed, the blessing of God in the Holy Spirit is necessary: therefore the marriage ceremony must be epicletic in form.

In the twentieth century, because of the division of the Church into clerics and laity, and thereby of those celebrating the liturgy into "minister" and "recipient," it was important for many lay people to hear from theologians that they did not receive the sacrament of marriage "conferred" by a priest, but that they themselves "conferred" it (although canonists objected that no one could "confer" what he or she did not already possess). The priest assisting at a marriage was then called the "official witness." To consider the ceremony of marriage as liturgy does not mean a new clericalizing of the theology of marriage, as if now the priest should be elevated to the status of "minister" of the sacrament. All I am saying is that the spouses celebrate this liturgy (whose true support lies in Jesus Christ) together; it is a liturgy of the Church in which therefore (except in an emergency) other members of the Church should also participate, and which must essentially consist not only in the declaration of consent, but also in the prayer of blessing.

In this liturgy of marriage, the love of God for humanity, which in turn has found its "sacramental" expression in the love of Jesus Christ for the Church, is made present in a perceptible manner, and it is just in this way that the Church recreates itself in its smallest form as a "house church." Marriage, as an "enduring sacrament," implies this continuing symbolic value and the ongoing state of being Church and building Church. From this fact alone results the indissolubility of the marriage of believing Christians and the unity (monogamy) of this marriage, things that cannot be made conclusive with purely rational arguments based on nature. The result of this theological reflection is that marriage—at least a marriage that is deliberately sacramental—cannot be built on a love that is primarily thought of as feeling, emotion, sympathy, or attraction. In line with classic Christian philosophy, love is instead to be understood as an act of the will illuminated by reason. In this view, love expresses itself not only in the decision made at the beginning, but above all in fidelity.

The effective grace of the sacrament of marriage thus is directed (1) to its deliberate religious symbolism and its being-Church; depending on the individual abilities of the partners, this aspect embraces fruitfulness, which is a gift of God's grace, since children are to continue the building up of the Church; and (2) to the lifelong will to fidelity. When human strength appears too weak for both of these, the memory of the sacrament recalls that God's grace is able to empower human freedom to self-transcendence,[42] in which human persons, even in restricted situations, can grow beyond themselves. Still further, faith trusts that its epiclesis will be heard, so that God's protection will rest on the spouses throughout their lives.

42. So F. Böckle in *Handbuch der christlichen Ethik* II, 117–135.

Bibliography 10

The Sacrament of Marriage

Aymans, W. "Die Sakramentalität christlicher Ehe in ekklesiologisch-kanonistischer Sicht." *Trierer theologische Zeitschrift* 83 (1974) 321–338.

Baldanza, G. "La grazia sacramentale matrimoniale al Concilio di Trento." *Ephemerides Liturgicae* 97 (1983) 89–140.

Baltensweiler, H. *Die Ehe im Neuen Testament.* Zürich: 1967.

Bernhard, J. "Le décret 'Tametsi' du Concile de Trente." *Revue de droit canonique* 30 (1980) 209–234.

Böckle, F. "Ehe und Ehescheidung." *Handbuch der christlichen Ethik* II 2d ed. (Freiburg: 1979) 117–135.

Corecco, E. "Die Lehre der Untrennbarkeit des Ehevertrages vom Sakrament im Lichte des scholastischen Prinzips 'Gratia perficit, non destruit naturam.'" *Archiv für katholisches Kirchenrecht* 143 (1974) 374–442.

Cottiaux, J. *La sacralisation du mariag de la Genèse aux incises Matthéennes.* Paris: 1982.

Christen, E. "Ehe als Sakrament." *Theologische Berichte* (Zürich) 1, 11–68 (with bibliography).

Dacquino, D. *Storia del matrimonio cristiano alla luce della Bibbia.* Turin: 1984.

Desserprit, A. *Le mariage, un sacrement.* Paris: 1981.

Die Zukunft der Ehe in der Kirche (Concilium 9/8-9) 1973.

Duss-von Werdt, J. "Theologie der Ehe—Der sakramentale Charakter der Ehe." *MySal* IV/2 (1973) 422–449.

311

Eid, V., and L. Vaskovics, eds. *Wandel der Familie—Zukunft der Familie.* Mainz: 1982.

Engelhardt, H., ed. *Die Kirchen und die Ehe.* Frankfurt: 1984 (with the Church regulations—Roman Catholic, Protestant, Orthodox, Anglican—and the civil laws).

Evdokimov, P. *The Sacrament of Love. The nuptial mystery in the light of the orthodox tradition.* New York: 1985 (Original: *Sacrement de l'Amour.* Paris: 1980).

Fransen, P. "Das Thema 'Ehescheidung nach Ehebruch' auf dem Konzil von Trient." *Concilium* 5 (1970) 343–348 (bibliography and a summary of previous research).

_____. *Hermeneutics of the Councils.* Louvin: 1985, 126–197 (researches on the teaching on marriage before Trent).

Gregg, R. C. "Die Ehe: Patristische und reformatorische Fragen." *Zeitschrift für Kirchengeschichte* 96 (1985) 1–12.

Grimm, R. *L'institution du mariage.* Paris: 1984.

Guzetti, G. B. "Il nesso contratto-sacramento nel matrimonio dei battezzati in un ricente dibattito." *Scuola Cattolica* 110 (1982) 211–253.

Handbuch des katholischen Kirchenrechts. Regensburg: 1983: Kaiser, M. "Grundfragen des kirchlichen Eherechts," 730–746; Zapp, H., "Die Vorbereitung der Eheschließung," 746–754; idem, "Die rechtliche Ehefähigkeit und die Ehehindernisse," 755–756; Primetshofer, B., "Der Ehekonsens," 765–782; idem, "Die Eheschließung," 782–795; Heinemann, H., "Die konfessionsverschiedene Ehe," 796–808; Geringer, K.-T., "Die Konvalidation der Ehe," 808–815; Flatten, H., "Nichtigkeitserklärung, Auflösung und Trennung der Ehe," 815–826.

Kasper, W. *Zur Theologie der christlichen Ehe.* Mainz: 1977.

Kleindienst, E. *Partnerschaft als Prinzip der Ehepastoral.* Würzburg: 1982 (also on sacramentality).

Kleinheyer, B., E. Von Severus, and R. Kaczynski. *Sakramentliche Feiern II.* Regensburg: 1984: Kleinheyer, B., "Riten um Ehe und Familie," 67–156.

Koch, G., and W. Breuning. *Die Ehe des Christen. Lebensform und Sakrament.* Freiburg: 1981.

Kramer, H. *Ehe war und wird anders.* Düsseldorf: 1982.

Kruse, H. "Eheverzicht im Neuen Testament und in der Frühkirche." *Forum Katholischer Theologie* 1 (1984) 94–116.

Langa, P. *San Agustin y el progreso de la teología matrimonial.* Toledo: 1984.

Lettmann, R. *Die Diskussion über die klandestinen Ehen und die Einführung einer zur Gültigkeit verpflichtenden Eheschließungsform auf dem Konzil von Trient.* Münster: 1966.

Lüdicke, K. *Eherecht.* Essen: 1983.

Malone, R., and J. R. Connery, eds. *Contemporary Perspectives on Christian Marriage.* Chicago: 1984.

Mieth, D. *Ehe als Entwurf*. Mainz: 1984 (also on communal living without marriage).

Molinski, W. *Theologie der Ehe in der Geschichte*. Aschaffenburg: 1976.

Nautin, P. "Le rituel de mariage et la formation des Sacramentaires 'Léonien' et 'Gélasien,' " *Ephemerides Liturgicae* 98 (1984) 425–457.

Ott, D. *Christliche Ehe heute*. Frankfurt: 1983.

Pannenberg, W. *Anthropologie*. Göttingen: 1983, 415–431 (with bibliography).

Pesch, R. *Freie Treue. Die Christen und die Ehescheidung*. Freiburg: 1971.

Rahner, K. "Die Ehe als Sakrament." *Schriften* VIII (1967) 519–540.

Ratschow, C. H., and others. "Ehe/Eherecht/Ehescheidung." *TRE* IX (1982) 308–362 (with bibliography).

Reinhardt, K., and H. Jedin, eds. *Ehe—Sakrament in der Kirche des Herrn*. Berlin: 1971.

Richter, K., H. Plock, and M. Probst. *Die kirchliche Trauung*. Freiburg: 1979.

Ritschl, D., and others. "Ehe, Ehescheidung." *EKL* I (1986) 956–985 (with bibliography).

Ritzer, K. *Formen, Riten und religiöses Brauchtum der Eheschließung in den christlichen Kirchen des ersten Jahrtausends*. 2d ed. Münster: 1981.

Schillebeeckx, E. *Le mariage*. Paris: 1966 (fundamental).

Schmälzle, U. F. *Ehe und Familie im Blickpunkt der Kirche*. Freiburg: 1978.

Schmitt, E. *Le mariage chrétien dans l'oeuvre de saint Augustin. Une théologie baptismale de la vie conjugale*. Paris: 1983.

Sequeira, J. B. *Tout mariage entre baptisés est-il nécessairement sacramentel?* Paris: 1985.

Stevenson, K. *Nuptial Blessing. A Study of Christian Marriage Rites*. London: 1982.

Van Gansewinkel, A. "Ehescheidung und Wiederheirat in neutestamentlicher und moraltheologischer Sicht." *Theologie und Glaube* 76 (1986) 193–211 (with bibliography).

Verspieren, P. "Le mariage, un sacrement?" *Initiation à la pratique de la théologie* IV. 2d ed. Paris: 1984, 421–442.

Vogel, C. "Le rôle du liturge dans la formation du lien conjugal." *Revue de droit canonique* 30 (1980) 7–27.

Weber, L. M. *Mysterium Magnum*. Freiburg: 1964.

13

The Sacramentals

The idea of "sacramentals" goes back to the clarification of the concept of sacraments in the twelfth century. When the number of sacraments was established at seven, liturgical actions that were somehow associated with the sacraments (e.g., the blessing of water for baptism, of the various oils for anointings, and of the altar for the Eucharist) and were highly respected, but did not achieve the status of sacraments, were given the name "sacramentals."[1] This indicated that they had a certain similarity to the sacraments. Vatican Council II explained the meaning of sacramentals in the Constitution on the Liturgy, as follows:

> 60. Holy Mother Church has, moreover, instituted sacramentals. These are sacred signs which bear a resemblance to the sacraments: they signify effects, particularly of a spiritual kind, which are obtained through the Church's intercession. By them [people] are disposed to receive the chief effect of the sacraments, and various occasions in life are rendered holy.

1. M. Löhrer, "Sakramentalien," *Sacramentum Mundi* IV (1969) 341–347 (344–345 on the history of the term).

61. Thus, for well-disposed members of the faithful, the liturgy of the sacraments and sacramentals sanctifies almost every event in their lives; they are given access to the stream of divine grace which flows from the paschal mystery of the passion, death, and resurrection of Christ, the fountain from which all sacraments and sacramentals draw their power. There is hardly any proper use of material things which cannot thus be directed toward the sanctification of [human beings] and the praise of God.

The sacramentals have their origin in Judaism,[2] in the praise of God that culminates in a plea for God's blessing. The Old Testament represents not only God as the one who blesses: it also recognizes people who bless, i.e., people who, after giving thanks for the signs of God's power present among the people, recognize that they are dependent on God's blessing and implore God for further concrete, saving actions. Even in Old Testament times, such blessings had taken on a stylized form. Formulas of blessing were devised not only for human persons, but also for objects such as food and drink, or fields and harvests. Ultimately all requests for blessing were directed toward a rich, overflowing life, which for believers is nothing else than a sharing in God's own life.

The New Testament from Paul onwards, as an inheritor of Jewish tradition, contains stylized requests for blessing in full measure. The Jewish prayer for the blessing of "peace" is augmented by the Christian plea for "grace." It is clear that the theological background in both Old and New Testaments is the conviction that the word is effective. The New Testament also retains the deepest of all desires: for the blessing of a share in God's life—for "grace" is nothing else than that.

On this biblical basis there developed, in the history of Christianity, a wealth of consecrations and blessings.[3] These were always subject

2. R. Schmid, "Segnen und Weihen in der Bibel," in J. Baumgartner, ed., *Gläubiger Umgang mit der Welt* (Zürich and Freiburg: 1976) 13–29; P. Schäfer in *TRE* V (1980) 560–562; I. Nowell, "Der narrative Kontext von 'Segen' im Alten Testament," *Concilium* 21 (1985) 81–88.

3. R. Kaczynski in B. Kleinheyer and others, *Sakramentliche Feiern* II (Regensburg: 1984) 233–274. Kaczynski rightly treats exorcism (which, despite its formulae couched in a tone of command, is nothing but the Church's petition for one who is sick) separately from the sacramentals; see ibid., 275–291. For a brief historical description, see D. Power, "Die Segnung von Gegenständen," *Concilium* 2 (1985) 96–106.

to three dangers: (1) the temptation to divide God's creation dual-istically into a sacred and a secular realm and to sacralize as much as possible; (2) the false belief that evil powers had released from people who freely surrendered themselves to them a dangerous, independent power that had to be ritually expelled; (3) the superstition that a bless-ing introduced a positive, magical power into blessed persons and objects.

Although the Reformers raised powerful objections against super-stition and abuses, reformed Christianity retained a good many bless-ings of persons and things. The combination of word with gesture was not rejected.[4] Thus we find liturgical blessings of persons with the pre-ferred formulae of Numbers 6:24-26 and 2 Corinthians 13:13, as well as the blessing of churches.[5] The Eastern Churches separated from Rome surpass the Roman Church in their use of signs of the cross, blessed oil, incense, and holy water.

The new Catholic Code of Canon Law[6] uses a formula that was first used in an official document by Pius XII in his encyclical, *Mediator Dei*, in 1947 (only in Latin, DS 3844), to describe the difference between sacraments and sacramentals. The distinction consists in the fact that sacramentals do not bring about their effects through the power of the saving work of Jesus Christ made present (*ex opere operato*), but by the power of the Church's prayer of petition (*ex opere operantis Ecclesiae*) (CIC 1983, canon 1166). We must, of course, add that the Church's petition can only be made in the power of the Holy Spirit who calls the Church to prayer.

Canon law places great emphasis on the authority of the Roman Church's hierarchy and on the administration of the sacramentals in an orderly manner (canon 1167).

The Church's use of language in this area is complicated. Tradi-tionally, sacramentals are divided into consecrations/dedications and blessings. Consecration meant that persons, things, or places were re-moved from purely secular purposes and symbolically dedicated to God alone. Blessing meant the Church's petition for God's saving action in the person or thing being blessed. To take several examples: con-

4. J. G. Davies in *TRE* V (1980) 565.
5. Cf. ibid., 568–569, for informative discussion of the blessing of churches since the eighth century.
6. What follows is indebted to H. J. F. Reinhardt's article in *HKR*, 836–839.

secrated places included churches and cemeteries; consecrated things could be altars or bells; consecrated persons were abbots and abbesses, etc. Places to be blessed might include houses or fields, blessings were given to various persons including the sick, the old, bridal couples, and things that could be blessed include automobiles, herbs, fruits of the harvest, and so on.

The 1983 Code of Canon Law uses the following concepts: the consecration of persons, combined with an anointing, is called *consecratio*; the dedication of places and things, with anointing, is *dedicatio*; the consecration (alteration of the purely secular purpose) of persons, places and things without an anointing is called *benedictio (constitutiva)*. Only bishops, or priests who have received special permission, may perform such consecrations (canon 1169, canons 1206–1207). The reason for this is apparently that the Church leadership ought to be apparent on such occasions. A bishop can also remove a particular consecration (for example, if a church is to be sold).

The other blessings are *benedictiones (invocativae)*; they should be performed by a bishop or pastor, another priest or a deacon if they are accompanied by proclamation of the Word or celebrated in a sacramental manner. However, the new Code of Canon Law leaves no doubt that lay people can also bless.

Obviously, the request for a blessing from God does not accomplish "more" if it is done by a priest. It would be a magical notion to suppose that a papal blessing has more power than, for example, parents' blessing of their children.

The Roman book of blessings (1984) contains some remarkable theological and practical statements.[7] It sees the blessings as a confession that all things are filled by the saving presence of God. It strives to make clear that the blessings are the Church's liturgy by suggesting that they should at the least be combined with a service of the Word and common prayer. A mere sign of the cross is never adequate: even the slightest appearance of a transfer of power should be avoided. Only objects that can be used for good purposes and are not ambiguous may be blessed. The Church forbids the blessing of weapons (as, since 1947, it has forbidden the blessing of political emblems). Blessings given by lay persons can no longer be considered private in contrast to those given by the Church.

7. On this, see the commentary by J. Lligadas in *Concilium* 21 (1985) 149–156.

Thus, from a theological perspective, the sacramentals are not mere signs. They are liturgical actions with a basically epicletic structure[8] (or a structure made up of anamnesis and epiclesis). The inclusion of objects or places within this dialogical event between God and humanity expresses a concern for the goods of creation, as well as the faith that all the good things of creation, together with humanity, glorify the God who is present in their midst.

8. J.-M. R. Tillard, "Segen, Sakramentalität und Epiklese," *Concilium* 21 (1985) 140–149. A blessing is like a seal embossed on a prayer to the Holy Spirit: ibid., 147.

Bibliography 11

The Sacramentals

Baumgartner, J., ed. *Gläubiger Umgang mit der Welt. Die Segnungen der Kirche.* Zürich and Freiburg: 1976.

Bommes, K. In H. Luthe (see Bibliography 1) 597–671.

Jorissen, I., and H. B. Meyer. *Zeichen und Symbole im Gottesdienst.* Innsbruck: 1977 (especially on the topic of blessings).

Jounel, P. In A. G. Martimort, ed. *L'Eglise en prière* III. New ed. Paris: 1984, 282–305.

Kaczynski, R. "Die Benediktionen." In B. Kleinheyer, E. von Severus, and R. Kaczynski. *Sakramentliche Feiern* II. Regensburg: 1984, 233–274.

Kleinheyer, B. *Heil erfahren in Zeichen.* Munich: 1980.

Macht der Segnung—Segnung der Macht (Concilium 21/2) 1985.

Reinhardt, H. J. F. "Die Sakramentalien." *HKR,* 836–839.

Schäfer, P., R. Deichgräber, and J. G. Daves. "Benediktionen." *TRE* V (1980) 560–573.

Westermann, C. *Der Segen in der Bibel und im Handeln der Kirche.* Gütersloh: 1981.

Additional Bibliography

Sacraments in General

Becker, G. *Die Ursymbole in den Religionen.* Graz: 1987.

Bucher, A. *Symbol–Symbolbildung–Symbolerziehung.* St. Ottilien: 1990.

Chauvet, L.-M. *Symbole et sacrement.* Paris: 1987.

Fink, P. (Hrsg.). *The New Dictionary of Sacramental Worship.* Collegeville: 1990.

Koch, G. *Texte zur Theologie: Sakramententheologie.* 2 Bde, Graz: 1991.

Kohlschein, F. (Hrsg.). *Aufklärungskatholizismus und Liturgie. Reformentwürfe für die Feier von Taufe. Firmung, Buße, Trauung und Krankensalbung.* St. Ottilien: 1989.

Lies, L. *Sakramententheologie. Eine personale Sicht.* Graz: 1990.

Meding, W. von. *Natur, Kultur und Sakrament* (zu. P. Tillich), in: *ThZ 43.* (1987) 353–370.

Merz, M. B. *Liturgisches Gebet als Geschehen.* Münster: 1988.

Müller, W. W. *Das Symbol in der dogmatischen Theologie.* Frankfurt: 1990. (K. Rahner, P. Tillich, P. Ricocur, J. Lacan).

Pannenberg, W. (Hrsg.). *Lehrverurteilungen—kirchentrennend?* III. Bd. Freiburg–Göttingen: 1990.

Rocohetta, C. *Sacramentaria fondamentale. Dal ''mysterion'' al ''sacramentum.''* Bologna: 1989.

Ruffini, E./Lodi, E., ''Mysterion'' e ''sacramentum.'' *La sacramentalità negli scritti dei Padrie nei testi liturgici primitivi.* Bologna: 1987.

Taborda, F. *Sakramente: Praxis und Fest.* Düsseldorf: 1988.

Wenz, G. *Einführung in die evangelische Sakramentcalchre.* Darmstadt: 1988.

Zizioulas, J. D. *Being as Communion. Studies in Personhood and the Church.* Crestwood-New York: 1985.

Sacraments of Initiation

Hölzt, F. *Die Sakramente der Eingliederung in ihrer rechtlichen Gestalt und ihren rechtlichen Wirkungen* vom 2. Vatikanischen Konzil bis zum CIC von 1983. Regensburg: 1988.

Kleinheyer, B. *Sakramentliche Feiern I: Die Feiern der Eingliederung in die Kirche (Gottesdienst der Kirche. Handbuch der Liturgiewissenschaft 7/1).* Regensburg: 1989.

Martins, J. S. *I sacramenti del'iniziazione cristiana. Battesima, cresima ed eucaristia.* Rome: 1988.

Ökumenischer Rat der Kirchen. *Kommission für Glauben und Kirchenverfassung. Die Diskussion über Taufe, Euchariste und Amt 1982–1990.* Frankfurt-Paderborn: 1990.

Steffen, U. *Taufe. Ursprung und Sinn des christlichen Einweihungsritus.* Stuttgart: 1988.

Walsh, L. G. *The Sacraments of Initiation: Baptism, Confirmation, Eucharist.* London: 1988.

Eucharist

Ahlers, R. *Communio eucharistica. Eine kirchenrechtliche Untersuchung zur Eucharistielehre im CIC.* Regensburg: 1990.

Fischer, D. *L'Eucharistie chez Calvin, en rapport avec la doctrine du Ministère,* in: FZPhTh 34 (1987) 415–436.

Giraudo, C. *Eucaristia per la Chiesa.* Brescia: 1989.

Hannerland, W. *Die Eucharistie und ihre Wirkungen im Spiegel der Euchologie des Missale Romanum.* Münster: 1990.

Hoenig, E. *Die Eucharistie als Opfer nach den neueren ökumenischen Erklärungen.* Paderborn: 1989.

Ibebuike, P. Ch. *The Eucharist. The Discussion on the Eucharist by the Faith and Order Commission of the World Council of Churches.* Lausanne: 1927; Lima: 1982; Frankfurt: 1989.

Keefe, D. J. *The Eucharist Order of History.* 2 Bde. University Press of America: 1991.

Keller, E. *Eucharistie und Parusie.* Fribourg: 1989.

Klauck, H.-J. *Herrenmahl und hellenistischer Kult, 2. durchgesehene Aufl. mit einem Nachtag.* Münster: 1986.

Macina, M. *Fonction liturgique et eschatologique d l'anamnèse eucharistique.* Lc 22,19; 1 Co 11,2425; in: ELit 102 (1988) 3–25.

Meyer, H. B. *Eucharistie. Geschichte, Theologie, Pastoral (Gottesdienst der Kirche. Handbuch der Liturgiewissenschaft 4).* Regensburg: 1989.

Navarro Girón, M. A. *La came de Cristo.* Madrid: 1989 (*Abendmahlsstreit Paschasius Radbertus bis Gottschalk*). Ökumenischer Rat: s. *Literatur III.*

Rubin, M. *Corpus Christi. The Eucharist in Late Medieval Culture.* Oxford: 1991.

Schaefer, G. K. *Eucharistic im ökumenischen Kontext (von Lausanne 1927 bis Lima 1982).* Göttingen: 1988.

Thaler, A. *Gemeinde und Eucharistie.* Fribourg: 1988.

Vagaggini, C. *La dimension sacrificielle de la communion eucharistique,* in: *Communautés et liturgies* 69 (1987) 215–244.

Verheul, A., u.a. *Eucharistie,* in: *Questions liturgiques* 69 (1988 125–206.

Wehr, L. *Arznei der Unsterblichkeit. Die Eucharistie bei Ignatius v. Antiochien und im Johannesevangelium.* Münster: 1987.

Reconciliation

Borobio, D. *Eclesialidad y ministerialidad en el sacramento de la penitencia,* in: *Salm* 34 (1987) 299–325.

Ders., *Reconciliación penitencial.* Bilbao: 1988.

Goldhahn-Müller, I. *Die Grenze der Gemeinde. Studien zum Problem der Zweiten Buße im NT unter Berücksichtigung der Entwicklung im 2. Jh. bis Tertullian.* Göttingen: 1989.

Handbuch der Ablässe (deutsche Übersetzung des "Enchiridion indulgentiarum," herausgegeben von der Deutschen Bischofskonferenz, mit beigefügter theologischer Erklärung von H. Vorgrimler). Bonn: 1989.

Hasitschka, M. *Befreiung von Sünde nach dem Johannesevangelium.* Innsbruck: 1989.

Korting, G. *Binden oder Lösen. Zur Verstockungs- und Befreiungstheologie in Mt 16, 19; 18, 18.21–35 und Joh 15, 1–17; 20, 23,* in: *STNU/A* 14 (1989) 39–91.

Osborne, K. B. *Reconciliation and Justification. The Sacrament and its Theology.* New York: 1990.

Varo, F. *El léxico del pecado en la Epístola de San Pablo a los Romanos,* in: *Scripta Theol.* 21. (1989) 99–116.

Anointing

Kranemann, B. *Die Krankensalbung in der Zeit der Aufklärung.* Münster: 1990.

Varghese, B. *Les onctions baptismales dans la tradition syrienne.* Löwen: 1989.

Orders

Field-Bibb, J. *Women Towards Priesthood.* Cambridge: 1991.

Gössmann, E./D. Bader (Hrsg.). *Warum keine Ordination der Frau? Unterschiedliche Einstellungen in den christlichen Kirchen.* Zürich: 1987.

Internationales Diakonatszentrum. *Wirkungsgeschichte des Diakonates.* Freiburg: 1989.

Klauck, H.-J. *Gemeinde—Amt—Sakrament.* Würzburg: 1989.

Martelet, G. *Théologie du sacerdoce, Bd II und III.* Paris: 1990.

Ökumenischer Rat: s. Literatur III.

Osborne, K. B. *Priesthood. A History of Ordained Ministry in the Roman Catholic Church.* New York: 1989.

Marriage

Baldanza, G. *La grazie matrimoniale nella riflessione teologica tra l'Enciclica "Casti connubii" e il Vaticano II, in: ELit 103.* (1989) 113–160.

Ders. *La grazia matrimoniale nella fase preparatoria del Concilio Vaticano II, ebd.* 281–308.

Ders. *La grazia matrimoniale nella fase conciliare, ebd.* 104. (1990) 368–414.

Ders., *Die Gnade des Ehesakramentes in der Pastoralkonstitution "Gaudium et Spes,"* in: *In Unum Congregati* (FS Kard. A. Mayer), hrsg. v. St. Haering. Metten: 1991, 219–238.

Baudot, D. *L'inséparabilité entre le contrat et le sacrement de mariage.* Rome: 1987.

Baumann, U. *Die Ehe—ein Sakrament?* Zürich: 1988.

Brooke, Ch. N. L. *The Medieval Idea of Marriage.* Oxford: 1989.

Gies, F. u J. *Marriage and the Family in the Middle Ages.* New York: 1989.

Hartmann, P. H. *Warum dauern Ehen nicht ewig?* Opladen: 1989.

Lüdecke, N. *Eheschließung als Bund. Genese und Exegese der Ehelehre der Konzilskonstitution "Gaudium et spes" in kanonistischer Auswertung.* Würzburg: 1989.

Mackin, T. *The Marital Sacrament. Marriage in the Catholic Church.* New York: 1989.

Muller, E. C. *Trinity and Marriage in Paul.* New York: 1990.

Richter, K. (Hrsg.). *Eheschließung—mehr als ein rechtlich Ding?* Freiburg: 1989.

Index

Acts of the Apostles, on presbytery, 245–46
Adult baptism, as normative, 110, 111
Adultery, 291
Alexandrian theologians, on Eucharist, 155
Anamnetic part of Eucharistic prayer, 149, 151
Anointing of sick, history of, 228–30
Antiochene theologians, on Eucharist, 155
Apostolic succession, 239
Apostolic Constitutions of Eastern Churches, 251
Apostolic Tradition of Hippolytus, on theology of orders, 250–52
Aquinas, Thomas, on Old Testament sacraments, 15, 31, 32, 46, 53, 54, 65, 85, 110; on reconciliation, 209–10; on sacrament of marriage, 295

Augustine, 31, 35, 45, 49, 52, 84, 114, 156, 189, 209, on marriage, 292–93

Baptism, 76, 102–18; as primary sacrament for forgiveness of sins, 204
Baptism of Jesus, 103
Barth, Karl, on marriage, 295
Berengar of Tours, and denial of real presence, 158–59
Betz, Johannes, on Eucharist, 192–93
Bishop, office of in early Church, 181–82, 252–53; sovereign power of, 252; function in early Church, 253; theology of, 266–68
Bishops, Vatican II on, 261
Buber, Martin, 14

Calvin, John, 56; on Eucharist, 165; on penance, 212

Canon Law, new Code, on indulgences, 222; on sacrament of orders, 264–65; on ordination of women, 272; on marriage, 304–08; on sacramentals, 317
Casel, Odo, on eucharist, 192
Chalcedon, Christological dogma of, 31–32
Children, baptism of, 110, 113–16
Christological presuppositions for understanding sacramental theology, 16–17
Church, fundamental tasks of, 20–21
Church, local, 33; theological components of, 33–34; and sacraments, 90–93; reconciliation through the, 204
Church's right to restrict access to Eucharist, 136–37
Communication with God, 5–6, 82
Communio, 187–190
Community as secondary subject of liturgy, 24
Concomitance, dogma of, 160, 164, 167, 168
Confirmation, 122–30; history of, 125–28; as intensification of baptism, 125–26; as non-sacramental in Protestant Churches, 127–28
Congar, Yves, 36
Consecration, words used in, 138–39
Consent theory of Roman law on marriage, 294
Constance, Council of, on penance, 211
Consubstantiation, 164
Contrition, 202
Copula theory of marriage, 294
Council of Trent (*see* Trent, Council of)
Covenant, 21
Cyprian, 35; on priesthood, 250

Damian, Peter, 51, 295
de Lubac, Henri, 36
Deacons, office of, 263
Decree on the Sacraments (1547), 59–60
Diaconate, permanent, 270
Diakonia, 240
Didache, 35
Divine grace and sacraments, 86–89
Doms, Herbert, on marriage, 285
Duns Scotus, John, 210

Eastern Churches, on Church as sacrament, 38, 57, 79, 80; on confirmation, 126; on penitential practices, 208–09; on anointing of the sick, 231; on ordination, 274–75; on marriage, 293note, 294
Ecumenical dialogue on ordination, 276–77
Ecumenical perspectives of baptism, 116–17
Epicletic part of Eucharistic prayer, 149, 151
Eucharist, 76, 132–195; as *the* liturgy, 132; and faith, 134–45; concept of, 152–53
Eucharistic celebration, meaning of, 150
Eucharistic theology, development of, 153–56
Exodus, 14

Faith, 3, 7–8, 11, 29, 82–86, 180, 188; and baptism, 105; as prerequisite for Eucharist, 134–45
Fathers of the Church, on sacraments, 49–50
Feckes, Carl, on Jesus as primordial sacrament, 32
Florence, Council of, on Eucharist, 161–62, 188; on

penance, 211; on orders, 255;
on marriage, 296
Forgiveness, forms of, 203–05

Gaudium et spes, on marriage and
the family, 302–04
General absolution, 219
Giraudo, Cesare, 149
God's self revelation to humans,
6–7
Greek theologians on real
presence of Jesus, 154–55

Hellenistic memorial meals, 141
Herms, Eilert, 277note
High Scholastic theology, 53–54
Hincmar of Rheims, on marriage,
294
Hippolytus, on rite of initiation,
107–08, 181–82; on priesthood,
250–52
Hugh of St. Victor, on definition
of sacrament, 45
Human beings as image of God,
12; as word of God, 13
Hylomorphic doctrine as applied
to sacraments, 52–53

Icons, 9
Ignatius of Antioch, on office of
priesthood, 181, 249
Imposition of hands in baptism,
108–09, in confirmation, 125; in
orders, 252
Indulgences, 220–22
Initiation, rite of, 107–09
Innocent I, Pope, on baptism, 109
Institutio, 74
Irenaeus of Lyons, on orders, 249

James, Letter of, on anointing
with oil, 228–29
Jesus as revealer of God's will, 17
Jesus Christ as primary subject of
liturgy, 23

Jesus' understanding of his own
death, 147
John the Baptizer, 103

Kasper, Walter, 36–37, 134
Kühn, Ulrich, 41, 179

Language, 69–70
Last Supper accounts in New
Testament, 138–44
Lateran Council, Fourth, on
Eucharist, 161; on
reconciliation, 211
Latin theologians on Eucharist,
155
Leiturgia, 240
Lengeling, Emil Joseph, 21
Leo X, Pope, on indulgences, 221
Léon-Dufour, Xavier, on Luke's
account of Last Supper, 142,
145–46
Lévinas, Emmanuel, 14
Life as fundamental sacrament, 11
Liturgy defined, 21–22; aspects of,
22
Lombard, Peter, 46, 52, 53; on
priesthood, 254; on marriage as
sacrament, 295
Luther, Martin, 31, 42, 55; on
Eucharist, 164; on penance,
211–12; on marriage, 297

Mark's Gospel, on anointing of
sick, 227
Marriage, sacrament of, 283–310;
as a legal institution, 284–85;
purposes, 284–85; in Old
Testament, 286–87; in New
Testament, 288–91; conditions
for validity of, 306–07;
dissolution of, 308; as liturgy,
309
Martyria, 240
Matter and form in sacramental
theology, 160

Matthew's Gospel on forgiveness of sin, 206-07, 212
Melanchthon, Philip, 212
Merklein, Helmut, on death of Jesus, 147; on office in the Church, 245
Metz, Johann Baptist, 40, 81
Michel, Ernst, on marriage, 295
Middle Ages and sacramental theology, 50-55
Mystery theology, 62, 63
Myterion, 31, 35, 44, 49
Myth, 70

Natural sacraments, 16, 29
Neo-Scholasticism, 36
New Testament, and sacraments, 47-48; baptism in, 102-07; foundations for confirmation, 122-24

O'Neill, Colman E., 63
Office of service in the Church, 239-42
Oikonomia, 28, 31, 33
Oil, anointing with, 228-29
Old Testament sacraments, 15, 29
Opus operatum, 52, 55
Orders, biblical foundations for, 242-48
Orders, sacrament of, 237-77
Ordination as conferral of the Spirit, 266-67

Paschal lamb as Old Testament sacrament, 15
Paul, St., on baptism, 104-05; on Last Supper, 139-40; on reconciliation, 206; on charisms, 244
Paul VI, Pope, on transubstantiation, 172, on indulgences, 221-22
Penitential practices, history of, 207-09

Peukert, Helmut, 64
Place of sacraments in theology, 20-26
Pneumatological presuppositions for understanding sacramental theology, 18-19; preconditions for Eucharist, 135-36
Preconditions for sacramental theology, 17-18
Presence of God, mediated, 25; in Eucharist, 134-35
Priesthood, of believers, 24; office of, 180-84; common, 260-61; Vatican II on, 262-63
Priestly office, theology of, 268-69

Radbertus, Paschasius, 157-58
Rahner, Hugo, on sacramentality of Church, 34-35
Rahner, Karl, on symbols, 10, 13, 24note, 25, 73; on Christology, 32; on Church as sacrament, 36, 38-40, 41; on sacraments in general, 65, 67; on sacramental theology, 74, 77, 81; on indulgences, 221; on theology of priesthood, 268note; on ordination of women, 271
Ratramnus, on real presence, 158
Real presence of Jesus in the Eucharist, 154-55, 156-59, 166, 172
Reconciliation, as precondition for liturgy, 133-34, 169, 200-222
Reformers, on sacraments, 55-57, 61, 71; on the Eucharist, 164-66; on sacrifice of the Mass, 175; on penance, 211-19; on anointing of the sick, 231; on priesthood, 256; on marriage, 296-97; on sacramentals, 316
Reign of God as central theme in Jesus' life, 226-27

Res et sacramentum, 54, 92, 163, 217
Rite of Initiation, 107–09

Sacerdotium, 262, 263
Sacraments, concept of, 43–44; number of, 51, 52, 55, 56, 65, 75–76, 295, 298; as symbolic actions, 71–72; and salvation, 88; as Church's liturgy, 90–93
Sacramenta signs, 50
Sacramental principle, 13–14
Sacramentals, 314–18; origin of, 315
Sacramentum, sacrare, sacrum, 44–45, 54
Sacrifice of the Mass, doctrine of, 172–80
Schillebeeckx, Edward, 32, 40; on ordination, 269note
Schmied, Augustin, 30
Scholastic theology, of confirmation, 126; of the Eucharist, 160–63; of priesthood, 182–83; of indulgences, 221; of anointing of the sick, 230; of sacrament of orders, 238; of marriage, 283–95
Scholasticism, 46, 51, 57, 59, 73, 88, 90
Schütz, Christian, 64
Semmelroth, Otto, 36
Shekinah, 25
Signs, sacraments as, 49–50, 56, 68, 89, 90
Sin, 200–202
Spirit, divine, 18–19; received in confirmation, 122–23; role of in ordination, 266–67
Spirit baptism, 103, 104, 106
Symbolic action of baptism, 103, 106, 115
Symbolic expression, defined, 10–11

Symbols, 2, 9–11, 68–69, 90
Synoptic Gospels, on Last Supper, 137–43

Tariff penance, 157, 209
Tertullian, on sacrament of orders, 249–50
Thurian, Max, 191
Tillich, Paul, 72
Transubstantiation, doctrine of, 159, 164, 167
Trent, Council of, 58–61, 74, 84, 85, 86, 111, 112, 115, 127; and Reformers on Eucharist, 165–66; on the real presence, 166–72; on doctrine of sacrifice of the Mass, 172–80, 188; on reconciliation, 212–219; on indulgences, 221; on anointing of the sick, 230–33; on sacrament of orders, 238, 256–60; on marriage, 297–301
Trinitarian presuppositions for understanding sacramental theology, 18–19
Twelve, circle of in early Church, 242–43

Validity, of sacrament, 84, 87; of baptism outside Catholic Church, 109–10
van der Leeuw, Gerard, 70
Vatican Council II, on sacrament, 32, 36–37, 40, 61–62; on confirmation, 128; on the Eucharist, 184–87; on theology of bishop's office, 186; on penance, 218–19; on anointing of the sick, 233; on priesthood, 260–66; on bishops, 261; on marriage, 301–08; on sacramentals, 314–15
Vögtle, Anton, on Jesus' death, 147; on offices in the Church, 245
von Balthasar, Hans Urs, 13, 179

Wagner, Harald, 276
Women, ordination of, 270-73
Word of God, 76-79; as prayer in
  administration of sacraments,
  79-81

Zenger, Eric, 12
Zwingli, Huldreich, 56
Zwingli, Ulrich, on the Eucharist,
  165; on penance, 212